THE BIBLE
AND ITS INFLUENCE

Cullen Schippe ♦ **Chuck Stetson**

General Editors

BLP Publishing

New York and Fairfax, Virginia

About the Cover

All three paintings on the cover show modern artistic interpretations of biblical accounts. The three pictures are used within the textbook itself. All the characters depicted are found in the Hebrew Scriptures and are specifically mentioned in the New Testament as well.

Top Left: *Elijah and the Ravens* by He Qi, an artist from the People's Republic of China known for his Asian interpretations of biblical themes, page 104

Top Right: *Jacob's Song* by Marc Chagall, a Russian-born artist noted for his dreamlike, fanciful imagery and brilliantly colored canvases, page 55

Bottom: *Abraham and Isaac* by John August Swanson, a popular American folk artist known for his colorful storyscapes, page 52

Content Contributors
Joanne McPortland
Marjorie Haney Schafer, Ph.D.
Marc Stern, J.D.
Eve Tushnet

Editorial, Design, and Production
Editorial, design, and production services were provided by Monotype, LLC of Baltimore, Maryland.

Bible Translations
Three translations of the bible are used in this work:
1. The King James Version in the public domain.
2. New Revised Standard Version Bible, copyright © 1989, Division of Christian Education of the National Council of the Churches of Christ in the United States of America. Used by permission. All rights reserved.
3. The Jewish Bible, The Tanakh, copyright © 1985 by The Jewish Publication Society. Used by permission. All rights reserved.

BLP Publishing
An imprint of the Bible Literacy Project
10332 Main Street, #353
Fairfax, Virginia 22030

Printed in the United States of America.

ISBN 0-9770302-0-2 Student Text
ISBN 0-9770302-1-0 Teacher's Edition

1 2 3 4 5 6 7 8 9 CDMS 11 10 09 08 07 06 05

contributors

Textbook Reviewers and Consultants*

The following participated in the preparation of this textbook as reviewers and/or consultants:

Robert Alter, Ph.D., professor of Hebrew and comparative literature, *University of California at Berkeley*

Roger Baker, Ed.D, associate professor of English, *Brigham Young University*

Pamela Blair, dean of faculty at *The Winchendon School, Massachusetts*

Harold Bloom, Ph.D., Sterling Professor of the Humanities and English, *Yale University*

Paul Borgman, Ph.D., professor of English, *Gordon College*

Daniel Coleman, Ph.D., assistant professor, *Portland State University, Oregon*

Jack S. Coleman, former director of secondary education, *Shelby County Schools, Tennessee*

John Collins, Ph.D., Holmes Professor of Old Testament Criticism and Interpretation, *Yale Divinity School*

Katherine Conover, M.A., public high school teacher of English, *Janesville, Wisconsin*

Thomas Dozeman, Ph.D., professor of Old Testament, *United Theological Seminary, Dayton, Ohio*

Jean Bethke Elshtain, Ph.D., Laura Spellman Rockefeller Professor of Social and Political Ethics, *University of Chicago Divinity School*

Ellen Frankel, Ph.D., chief executive officer and editor-in-chief, *The Jewish Publication Society*

David Freitag, public high school teacher of English, *Grant High School, Portland, Oregon*

George Gallup, Jr., founding chairman, *George H. Gallup International Institute*

Mary Ann Glendon, J.D., M. Comp. L., Learned Hand Professor of Law, *Harvard University*

Michael Groves, public high school teacher of English, *Portland, Oregon*

Charles C. Haynes, Ph.D., senior scholar, *First Amendment Center, Washington, D.C.*

Stephen Haynes, Ph.D., associate professor of religious studies, *Rhodes College, Tennessee*

Linda Hodges, public school teacher of English, *Jefferson County High School, Tennessee*

Patricia Hoertdoerfer, M.A., M.Div., director of children, family, and intergenerational programs, *Unitarian Universalist Association of America*

Walt Holmes, teacher of history, *Houston High School, Tennessee*

Eric J. Jenislawski, M.A.R., adjunct professor of theology at *Christendom College*

Kenneth D. Johnson, senior fellow for social policy and civil society, *Seymour Institute for Advanced Christian Studies*

Mark C. Johnson, Ph.D., director of national executive initiatives, *YMCA of the USA*

Amy A. Kass, Ph.D., senior fellow, *Hudson Institute;* senior lecturer in the humanities, *University of Chicago*

Herb Levine, Ph.D., executive director, *Fellowship Farm*

Peter Lillback, Ph.D., president, *Westminster Theological Seminary;* senior pastor, *Proclamation Presbyterian Church, Philadelphia*

Tremper Longman, Ph.D., Robert H. Gundry Professor of Biblical Studies, *Westmont College*

Elizabeth Macklin, poet, writer, editor, and translator

Frederica Mathewes-Green, M.A., author and commentator

Barbara Murray, assistant principal, *West Linn High School, Oregon*

Anthony R. Picarello, Jr., J.D., M.A., president and general counsel, *The Becket Fund for Religious Liberty*

Stuart Rowe, teacher of English, *Prairie High School, Washington*

Dan Russ, Ph.D., director, Center for Christian Studies, *Gordon College*

Leland Ryken, Ph.D., Clyde S. Kilby Professor of English, *Wheaton College*

Richard Sklba, S.S.L., S.T.D., auxiliary bishop of the *Roman Catholic Archdiocese of Milwaukee* and Chair of the Board of Trustees for the *Catholic Biblical Association*

Joan Spence, public school teacher, *Battle Ground, Washington*

Charles Talbert, Ph.D., Distinguished Professor of Religion, *Baylor University*

Michael Verde, M.A., teacher of English at *Lake Forest Academy, Lake Forest, Illinois*

Marie Wachlin, Ph.D., professor, *Concordia University, Portland, Oregon*

Emil Wcela, D.D., auxiliary bishop, *Roman Catholic Diocese of Rockville Centre;* former Chair of the Board of Trustees of the *Catholic Biblical Association*

*The names of institutions are for identification purposes.

Bible Literacy Project Board of Advisors

Don S. Browning, Ph.D., Alexander Campbell Professor of Religious Ethics and the Social Sciences, *University of Chicago Divinity School*

Jean Bethke Elshtain, Ph.D., Laura Spellman Rockefeller Professor of Social and Political Ethics, *University of Chicago*

Ellen Frankel, Ph.D., chief executive officer and editor-in-chief, *The Jewish Publication Society*

George Gallup, Jr., founding chairman, *George H. Gallup International Institute*

Marc A. Gellman, Ph.D., rabbi of Temple Beth Torah, Melville, *New York;* member of television's *"God Squad"*

Mary Ann Glendon, J.D., M. Comp. L., Learned Hand Professor of Law, *Harvard University*

Os Guinness, D.Phil., senior fellow, *Trinity Forum*

William J. Moloney, Ph.D., Colorado Commissioner of Education; *Secretary of the Colorado State Board of Education*

Barbara Murray, M.A., assistant principal, *West Linn High School, Oregon*

John M. Perkins, founder, *John M. Perkins Foundation for Reconciliation & Development*

Bible Literacy Project Board of Directors

David Blankenhorn, president, *Institute for American Values, New York*

Kevin Seamus Hasson, founder and chairman, *The Becket Fund for Religious Liberty in Washington, D.C.*

Brewster Kopp, former senior vice president of finance and administration, *Digital Equipment Corporation, Greenwich, Connecticut*

Pamela Scurry, chief executive officer, *Wicker Gardens' Children, Inc., New York*

Chuck Stetson, Chairman of the Board and Managing Director of *Private Equity Investors, Inc., New York*

Monotype, LLC

Jill Goodman	Karen Lange	Margaret Pinette
Bill Heckman	Suzanne Montazer	Jacquie Rosenborough
Bob Heggenstaller	Tony Moore	Hans Roxas
Sarah Jersild	Barbara Pike	Susanne Viscarra

preface

Dear Student,

The Bible has been and still is one of the most influential books ever published. Its influence is seen in literature, art, music, culture, public policy, and public debate. The first English translations of the Bible helped to fashion the English language itself—so much so that, had the Bible not been translated into English when it was, Shakespeare's plays might never have been written.

Biblical allusions are found in great literature and in the daily newspaper as well. Rock musicians, screenwriters, television producers, and advertisers use the Bible as a source. Politicians use the words and accounts of the Bible to frame their debates.

The Bible is a sacred text to Jews and Christians, and it has the respect of Muslims and the members of other world religions. The very fact that it is a sacred text contributes to the Bible's influence. Still, the Bible has literary merit all its own. It is filled with adventure, with poetry and song, with narratives and letters, with visions and comfort, with warning and advice.

The first part of the Bible—the Hebrew Scriptures—both shaped and was shaped by the identity of the Jewish people. Christians kept those Hebrew Scriptures as part of their own Scriptures and saw in them a foreshadowing of Jesus, whom they believed to be the messiah. The gospels and other writings of the New Testament have at their center Jesus of Nazareth and the development of the Christian churches. The actions, words, and teachings of Jesus and his followers also influenced art, culture, and public discourse.

This textbook is an opportunity for you to become informed about the Bible. In this course you will get a tour of the whole Bible to see how it was written and when. You will learn about the different kinds of writing and the various books that make up the Bible. You will also see the expansive influence of the Bible. Your knowledge of the Bible can be a key to unlocking other subjects for you—especially literature, art, music, and the social sciences. You will learn why every well-educated person needs to have a basic knowledge of the Bible.

CONTENTS

PART ONE: THE HEBREW SCRIPTURES

CONTENTS

PART TWO: THE NEW TESTAMENT

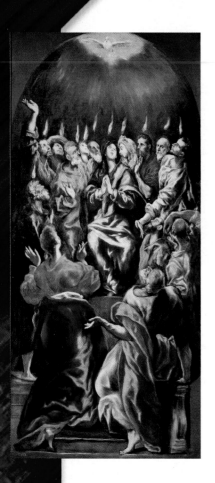

PART ONE
THE HEBREW SCRIPTURES

UNIT ONE

Introductions

Academic study of the Bible in a public secondary school may appropriately take place in literature courses. Students might study the Bible as literature. They would examine the Bible as they would other literature in terms of aesthetic categories, as an anthology of narratives and poetry, exploring its language, symbolism, and motifs. Students might also study the Bible *in* literature, the ways in which later writers have used Bible literature, language, and symbols. Much drama, poetry, and fiction contains material from the Bible.

The Bible & Public Schools:
A First Amendment Guide,
First Amendment Center, 10

In this unit you will discover

- Why it is important and valuable for a high school student to become literate in the Bible—its language, content, plots, and characters

- The basic structure of the Hebrew Scriptures, or Old Testament, how it was formed, and how it is shared by two major traditions

DISCOVER

- The Bible is viewed by many as a sacred text that has influenced all of Western culture.
- The Bible is a collection of books that contain great literature.
- Translations of the Bible helped develop the English language.

GET TO KNOW

- William Tyndale
- John Wycliffe

CONSIDER

- How much do you know about the Bible already?

Why Study the Bible?

For millions of people the Bible is seen as sacred scripture. It is believed by many Jews and Christians to contain God's revelation—an inspired communication from the divine to the human. This scripture has been influencing people for thousands of years. That influence extends not only to the synagogue or to the church. It is felt in the language people speak. It is experienced, too, in much of the art, music, and literature of Western culture. The Bible has influenced law and politics as well. And in the United States, the Bible—its characters, narratives, teachings, and the like—have played an important role in American history and culture.

If your name is Joshua or David or Michael, Mary or Elizabeth or Sarah, Zeke or Deb or Sam or Sue, your name has its source in the Bible. If you have read William Golding's *Lord of the Flies,* John Steinbeck's *East of Eden,* or John Milton's *Paradise Lost,* you have read works inspired in part or as a whole by the Bible. If you have watched Francis Ford Coppola's movie *Apocalypse Now,* or the film *Chariots of Fire,* you have experienced works whose titles come right from the Bible.

Look at the headlines on this page. Each of them contains an allusion or metaphor that is taken from the Bible. Presidential speeches, Supreme Court decisions, editorials in the newspaper, television programs, even video games and cartoons all contain references to the plots, characters, and teachings of the Bible. The Bible is like a source code for much of life and language in the land where you live. If you are unaware of that source code, your education is incomplete.

This course is going to give you an overview of the Bible. But the course is not going to be teaching you about the Bible as a sacred text. You are going to learn about the language, literary forms, plot lines, characters, and contents of the Bible so that you can have a better understanding of literature, art, and culture.

What Is in the Bible?

First of all, the Bible is not so much a book as it is a collection of books. In fact, the Bible is a whole library. The word Bible comes from the Greek *ta biblia,* "the books." The books of the Bible have been written, edited, compiled, and sorted over centuries. The books are used and interpreted quite differently in various faith traditions, as well.

The books of the Bible contain love stories, war stories, dreams, first-person accounts, allegories, chronicles, prayers, jokes and puns, stories and parables, and even erotic poetry. What kind of books will you find in the Bible? You will find just about every kind of book. In the Hebrew Scriptures, or Old Testament, for example, you will find:

- Narratives, such as how God rescued Jonah from drowning in the sea by providing a large fish that swallowed Jonah
- Novellas, or short-story forms, such as that of Joseph's colorful coat, and of his later eventful life

- A songbook, such as the Book of Psalms
- Legal codes, such as almost the whole Book of Leviticus
- National epics and historical narratives like the account of King David—one of the longest biographies in ancient literature
- Visions and prophecies that speak to the conscience of a nation

The New Testament adds Gospels (literally "Good News" accounts) of the life and teaching of Jesus of Nazareth, letters that helped shape the lives and characters of Christians residing in some of the cities of the ancient Roman world, and more visions and warnings about the present and the future.

The Bible in Public Education

■ "Are we allowed to learn about the Bible in public school? Isn't that against the separation of church and state?"

If the Bible were presented as faith, teaching the Bible in school would be contrary to the spirit of the Constitution. But you don't have to look far to see that the contents of the Bible are part of everyday life. Some of that can be seen on the map of the United States. From Maine to California, you see the influence of the Bible in place names, such as New Canaan, Lebanon, Bethlehem, Salem, Corpus Christi (Latin for "Body of Christ"). The Bible also influenced life, work, and culture. For decades, the Bible was used as a textbook—sometimes the only textbook—in public school classrooms. It was and is a book shared by a majority of the people in the country.

As the country became more religiously and culturally diverse, different translations and versions of the Bible were readily available. There soon developed a concern that the use of the Bible in reading class or as the source of daily devotion could lead to sectarian teaching. Over time, the Bible in public education was limited to a daily devotional reading without comment. In 1963, the Supreme Court struck down all state-sponsored religious exercises, including devotional reading of the Bible. Yet in that very court decision, Justice Thomas Clark wrote:

> Nothing we have said here indicates that such study of the Bible or of religion, when presented objectively as part of a secular program of education, may not be effected consistently with the First Amendment.
>
> *Abington v. Schempp*

Still, it seemed a safer course for public education to pull back from granting the Bible a role in the school or classroom. Nonetheless, over the years, educators have seen that not to grant the Bible any place in public education is, in many ways, to offer an incomplete education in literature, language, and culture. It is important, however, to understand that teaching about the Bible can be done legally if such instruction follows the letter and the spirit of the First Amendment. It is the design and purpose of this textbook to do just that. The course you are studying has some very important characteristics built in, so that it follows that First Amendment. Here is the approach you will be following:

1. You are going to study the Bible academically, not devotionally. In other words, you are learning about the Bible and its role in life, language, and culture.
2. You will be given an awareness of religious content of the Bible, but you will not be pressed into accepting religion.
3. You will study about religion as presented in the Bible, but you will not be engaged in the practice of religion.

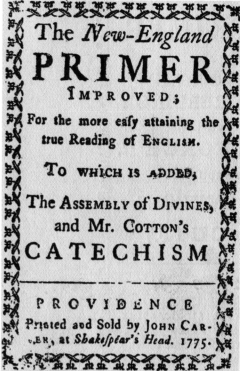

The *New-England* PRIMER IMPROVED; For the more eafy attaining the true Reading of ENGLISH. To WHICH IS ADDED, The ASSEMBLY of DIVINES, and Mr. COTTON's CATECHISM

PROVIDENCE

Printed and Sold by JOHN CAR-vER, at *Shakefpear's Head.* 1775.

Until the turn of the twentieth century, there were two major readers used in American classrooms: *The New England Primer* and the *The McGuffey Reader*. The *New England Primer* was by far the most commonly used textbook for almost 200 years. It was filled with Bible references. Both the McGuffey Readers and *The New England Primer* presented a white, Protestant America with a strong Biblical faith.

4. During this course, you will encounter differing religious views, but the views will neither be encouraged nor discouraged.

5. You will never be asked to conform to any of the beliefs you encounter in this course.

The Bible in American Life

From the very beginning, the Bible has been part of the fabric of the United States. Biblical thought can be found in the writings and speeches of the leaders and heroes who formed the Republic and guided its development. It is used in public debate and political campaigning even today. It is important to note, however, that the Bible was not the only or principal source for the aspirations of the Founders. Thomas Jefferson, James Madison, and others found inspiration in the philosophies of the day, such as the Enlightenment. They acknowledged God as the Creator, but they often looked to writers like John Locke and David Hume to form their beliefs in "unalienable rights" and other principles of democracy.

Nevertheless, the Bible was very much a part of early American life. Various Christian denominations and some Jews arrived on America's shores in the early days of its history. Most of them looked to the Bible as a source of revelation and authority. But what they sought in the new land was the freedom to practice their faith based on their own interpretation of the Bible. In the founding period of the country, the words and sentiments of the Bible were often on the lips and flowed from the pens of the founders.

Such being the impressions under which I have, in obedience to the public summons, repaired to the present station, it would be peculiarly improper to omit in this first official act my fervent supplications to that Almighty Being who rules over the universe, who presides in the councils of nations, and whose providential aids can supply every human defect, that His benediction may consecrate to the liberties and happiness of the people of the United States a Government instituted by themselves for these essential purposes, and may enable every instrument employed in its administration to execute with success the functions allotted to his charge. In tendering this homage to the Great Author of every public and private good, I assure myself that it expresses your sentiments not less than my own, nor those of my fellow-citizens at large less than either. No people can be bound to acknowledge and adore the Invisible Hand which conducts the affairs of men more than those of the United States.

George Washington, First Inaugural Address, 1789

Leaders steeped in biblical language and rhetorical style drove the Civil Rights movement of the twentieth century. Here, the Rev. Dr. Martin Luther King, Jr., a Southern Baptist minister, delivers his ringing "I have a dream" speech at the 1963 March on Washington. His speech drew heavily on biblical themes, as did the speeches of Abraham Lincoln, before whose monument King is shown speaking.

Bible Literacy and Citizenship

On the eve of his assassination, Dr. Martin Luther King gave a great speech. In that speech he spoke not just to the people struggling for civil rights, but also to every person of good will.

We've got some difficult days ahead. But it doesn't matter with me now, because I've been to the mountaintop. . . . And I've looked over. And I've seen the Promised Land. I may not get there with you. But I want you to know tonight, that we, as a people, will get to the Promised Land.

To grasp the full impact of this historic moment, one has to know the biblical references. One needs to know what the "mountaintop" is all about. What does "I may not get there with you" mean? What is this reference to the "Promised Land"?

A century earlier, Abraham Lincoln, the Great Emancipator, gave many speeches that were peppered with biblical references, actual citations, and allusions. On June 16, 1858, in Springfield, Illinois, Lincoln gave a speech against the policy of dividing the United States into free states and slave states. He built the entire speech on a phrase from Luke 11:17, "Every kingdom divided against itself becomes a desert, and house falls on house" *(NRSV)*. The speech is known as Lincoln's "House Divided Speech." And one key to understanding that speech is an understanding of the context of the phrase that generated it.

Lincoln's Second Inaugural Address contained several strong biblical images. The first was a reference to Genesis 3:19. Lincoln said, "It may seem strange that any men should dare to ask a just God's assistance in wringing their bread from the sweat of other men's faces." Here he is condemning slavery and echoing the Bible's words, "In the sweat of thy face shalt thou eat bread" *(KJV)*. In that same sentence, he echoed Matthew 7:1 in the words, "but let us judge not that we be not judged."

A third biblical reference in Lincoln's address is a direct quote of Matthew 18:7, "Woe unto the world because of offenses! For it must needs be that offenses come, but woe to that man by whom the offense cometh!" Lincoln follows the citation with a rhetorical question:

> If we shall suppose that American slavery is one of those offenses which, in the providence of God, must needs come, but which, having continued through His appointed time, He now wills to remove, and that He gives to both North and South this terrible war as the woe due to those by whom the offense came, shall we discern therein any departure from those divine attributes which the believers in a Living God always ascribe to Him?

Words from the Bible are inscribed on public buildings. Political campaigns are laced with references to the Bible. Government officials often choose to be sworn into office with their hands resting on a Bible. Little of America's historic public speeches or its great reform movements or the pilgrim wanderings that led to America's founding is completely intelligible without at least a working knowledge of the Bible.

An important reason for the academic study of the Bible is the help it provides for understanding America's great intellectual, moral, and civic discussion. Knowledge of the Bible can help young people graduate from public schools with a clearer understanding of the American democratic tradition and be better equipped to participate thoughtfully in it.

Literature and Language

Biblical literacy—a working knowledge of the Bible as literature—is a key to a good liberal arts education. That means, quite simply, that the language, narratives, and teachings in the Bible are literature in themselves and therefore worthy of study. It also means that the literature of the Bible has also influenced the development of much other literature, art, music, sculpture, and even filmmaking.

In addition, much of the English language comes from the Bible. When it was first translated into English (in its entirety about 1380 by John Wycliffe), many words were coined to express Biblical concepts. The boxed list on page 12 shows a sampling of words and phrases in use in everyday speech that appeared first in English translations of the Bible.

IN YOUR
journal

Start a journal for this course. Record in the journal the biblical allusions and references you read in the newspaper, see on television, or discover in other courses. You can also record your own reactions to what you are learning. From time to time during the course, there will be some suggestions for your journal work.

A Matthew Brady photo of Abraham Lincoln taken before his historic anti-slavery speech at Cooper Union in New York City on February 27, 1860.

The Independence Missouri Messiah Choir and the Messiah Festival Orchestra are shown at their eighty-fifth anniversary performance. Handel's beloved oratorio is made up entirely of biblical texts and paraphrases.

It is difficult to learn and appreciate Western literature without the ability to recognize Bible references. For example, in Ernest Hemingway's *Old Man and the Sea,* the old man stretches himself on the mast as Jesus was stretched on a cross. In Charles Dickens's *A Tale of Two Cities,* Sidney Carton walks through the garden before he chooses to take another man's place at the guillotine. His walk is a reference to Jesus in the Garden of Gethsemane. The impact of these moments is lost without some knowledge of the Bible.

Few people would dispute the central role William Shakespeare enjoys in the development of modern English, and yet Shakespeare himself was influenced by one of the great translators of the Bible, William Tyndale. As Professor David Daniell stated, "without Tyndale, no Shakespeare" (*The Bible in English,* Yale University Press, 2003).

Tyndale's influence on the English language was solidified in the publication in 1611 of the King James Bible. That version retained about 94 percent of Tyndale's work. In turn, the King James Version has impacted English ever since. Alistair McGrath, a renowned scholar on the literature of the Bible, notes, "Without the King James Bible, there would have been no *Paradise Lost,* no *Pilgrim's Progress,* no Handel's *Messiah,* no Negro spirituals, and no Gettysburg Address."

■ Make a list of other literary, musical, or artistic works influenced by the Bible.

The Bible in Translation

The books of the Bible were originally written in Hebrew, Aramaic, or Greek. Most of the Jewish Bible, or Christian Old Testament, was written in Hebrew. The New Testament was originally written in Greek. Although the content of the Bible has certainly influenced language and culture, what you will experience in this course are English translations of the Bible. The journey the Bible made from its original languages to English was a very difficult trip.

The earliest known copies of parts of the Bible are in the form of individual texts written on scrolls made of leather. The scrolls were wound on wooden spools. Other copies were written on papyrus, a form of paper made from reeds. By the fourth century books were being produced on separate parchment pages held together with hinged wooden covers. Such a book was called a *codex,* from the Latin word for "wood block."

During the fourth century, Saint Jerome translated the Bible into Latin. His translation was known as the Vulgate, which means "common" or "of the people." The edition was translated into the common spoken Latin of ordinary people. (By the way, the word "vulgar" comes from the same root.)

Originally, Bibles (all books, for that matter) were copied by hand in ancient monasteries and rabbinic academies by skilled artisans who often illustrated their handiwork with elaborate detail.

WORDS AND PHRASES APPEARING FIRST IN ENGLISH TRANSLATIONS OF THE BIBLE		
adoption	cucumber	puberty
ambitious	eat, drink, & be merry	scapegoat
bald head	holier than thou	sex
beautiful	house divided	two-edged sword
blab	left wing	under the sun
brother's keeper	liberty	wordy
busybody	network	wrinkle
castaway		

Stanley Malless and Jeffrey McQuain, *Coined by God* (W.W. Norton & Co., 2003)

Johannes Gutenberg invented a system of movable type around 1450. His invention made it possible for the first time to mass-produce books. The very first book printed on Gutenberg's press was two hundred copies of Saint Jerome's Vulgate. Twenty-one of those copies are still in existence today.

In England, the Bible arrived in Latin in the fourth century. By the seventh century, a monk named Caedmus, who was a popular singer, took accounts from the Bible and put them into song in early English. In the tenth century, some bits of the New Testament were translated into English.

In the fourteenth century, the priest John Wycliffe was the first to translate the entire Bible into English from the Vulgate. A group of Wycliffe's fellow priests began copying and distributing this translation. They drew their authority for doing this from the Bible itself and not the church, and as a result became a clear threat to church authority.

Wycliffe and his priests were soon under attack, and Wycliffe was charged with heresy. He lost his teaching position and was called to Rome to answer charges. He died before he could do this. Nonetheless, the church's Council of Constance (1414–1418) condemned his work. The winds of the Reformation were blowing strong in the Church.

The hostility toward the English Bible was severe. English translations were outlawed. It is difficult to imagine, but there was a time when to possess a scrap of paper with a verse of a psalm or the Lord's Prayer in English was a capital offense. The severity of the approach came from a zeal for the church's interpretation of the Bible and from a fear that translators might not respect that interpretation.

Onto the scene came William Tyndale. Tyndale had to travel to Europe to fulfill what he felt was his calling to translate the Bible into English from original languages. He could not do so in England, so he traveled to Germany

William Tyndale:
The Giant of Translators

William Tyndale (1494–1536), more than any other man, shaped the Bible in English. His translation of the New Testament and approximately half of the Hebrew Scriptures was the first English translation from the original texts. As he said himself, he relied only on his own insights. His translation became the basis for all subsequent translations, including the King James Bible.

Tyndale enrolled at Oxford in 1505 and grew up at the university. In 1515, he received his Master's degree at the age of twenty-one. Tyndale was a gifted linguist and had become skilled in eight languages—Hebrew, Greek, Latin, Spanish, French, Italian, English, and German. His insights into Hebrew and Greek were extraordinary—particularly noteworthy since there was a lack of both Hebrew and Greek scholarship in England at the time.

Tyndale was anxious to translate the Bible so even "the boy that drives the plow" could know the Bible. Because of the hostility in England, Tyndale went to the European continent where he translated the Bible into English, finishing the New Testament in 1525–1526, the first five books of Hebrew Scriptures in 1530, and The Book of Jonah in 1531.

Tyndale's words and phrases have all become very familiar in the English language without our even knowing it. Tyndale was a master of memorable phrases that were very near to conversational English, yet distinct enough to be poetic. Tyndale coined such phrases as:

Let there be light	*(Genesis 1:3)*
The powers that be	*(Romans 13:1)*
My brother's keeper	*(Genesis 4:9)*
The salt of the earth	*(Matthew 5:13)*
A law unto themselves	*(Romans 2:14)*
Filthy lucre	*(1 Timothy 3:3)*
Fight the good fight	*(1 Timothy 6:12)*

Tyndale brought a wonderful sense of rhythm to his sentences:

Ask and it shall be given you; seek and ye shall find; knock and it shall be opened unto you. *(Matthew 7:7)*

In him we live and move and have our being. *(Acts 17:28)*

The spirit is willing, but the flesh is weak. *(Matthew 26:41)*

An illustration of Wycliffe's trial.

where he very likely met and received support from Martin Luther, who was then translating the Bible into German. There are few details of Tyndale's life in Europe. He first translated the New Testament, and copies were smuggled into England. Next, he translated the first five books of the Hebrew Scriptures.

Tyndale tried to work in secret, but he was betrayed, brought to trial, and condemned to death. He was led to the stake on October 6, 1536. There he was strangled and his body burned. His last words were "Lord, open the King of England's eyes." Within a year, Henry VIII allowed English Bibles to be distributed, and in 1539, he authorized the Great Bible, which included Tyndale's translation. Within seventy-five years of Tyndale's death, there were over two million English Bibles distributed throughout a country of just over six million people.

Dealing with Translations

There have been more than three thousand new translations of the Bible into English since 1525 when Tyndale printed his first complete New Testament. As you go through this course, remember that you are always dealing with translations—not the original words. Each translation differs slightly because the translators are always making judgments about how words and phrases are best rendered in English. As a result, many translations have been done by committees who struggle to maintain as much of the authentic meaning of the original text as is possible.

For the purposes of this course, it is not necessary for you to do more than realize that there are differences in translation. This course uses the King James Version *(KJV)* and the New Revised Standard Version *(NRSV)*. In the first section on the Hebrew Scriptures, the course adds translations from the Jewish Publication Society *(NJPS)*. These three translations will give you some of the flavor of different English translations.

Bible Dates and History

Biblical dates and time frames can be a bit confusing. How much time did the creation account cover? How long did Methuselah live? When and for how long was David king of Israel? At the outset of this course, it is important to note

Martin Luther, an Augustinian monk, was a church reformer who sympathized with Tyndale and provided translations of the Bible in German.

ENGLISH BIBLE TIMELINE

Here is a bird's-eye view of some highlights on the journey of the Bible into English.

1382	Wycliffe's handwritten manuscript of the complete English translation of the Bible, translated from Saint Jerome's Vulgate
1522	Martin Luther's German New Testament
1525	William Tyndale's New Testament—the first printed English New Testament (Worms edition)
1530	Tyndale's translation of the Pentateuch (the first five books of the Old Testament)
1531	Tyndale's translation of the Book of Jonah
1534	Tyndale's revised New Testament
1535	Myles Coverdale's Bible—the first complete printed English-language Bible (80 books: Old Testament, New Testament, and Apocrypha)
1537	Matthews Bible—the second complete English Bible—by John "Thomas Matthew" Rogers
1539	The Great Bible—the first English-language Bible authorized for public use
1560	The Geneva Bible—the first English-language Bible to add numbered verses to each chapter
1568	The Bishops' Bible—the Bible of which the King James was a revision
1582	The Rheims New Testament—the first Catholic English New Testament translated from the Latin Vulgate
1609/1610	The Douay Old Testament added to the Rheims New Testament, making the first complete English Catholic Bible, also translated from the Latin Vulgate
1611	The King James Bible (originally with 80 books; the Apocrypha officially removed in 1885, leaving 66 books)
1764	Bishop Richard Challoner revised the Douay–Rhiems English translation for Roman Catholics
1782	Robert Aitken's Bible—the first English-language Bible (a King James Version without Apocrypha) printed in America
1791	Isaac Collins and Isaiah Thomas respectively produced the first family Bible and first illustrated Bible printed in America, both King James Versions.
1808	Jane Aitken's Bible—the first Bible printed by a woman (the daughter of Robert Aitken).
1833	Noah Webster's Bible—after producing his dictionary, he revised the King James Bible.
1841	English Hexapla New Testament—an early textual comparison showing the Greek and six famous English translations in parallel columns
1846	The Illuminated Bible—the most lavishly illustrated Bible printed in America (a King James Version)
1854	The first Jewish Bible in English, translated by Isaac Leeser.
1885	The Revised Version Bible—the first major English revision of the King James Bible
1901	The American Standard Version—the first major American revision of the King James Bible
1946/1952	The Revised Standard Version—purported to be a revision of the American Standard Version, but little remains of that translation
1970/1982	The New American Bible—a Roman Catholic translation from the original languages
1970	The New American Standard Bible (NASB), published as a "Modern and Accurate Word-for-Word English Translation"
1971	The Living Bible Paraphrased—Kenneth Taylor's acclaimed, yet greatly criticized, paraphrase to give young people access to the Bible
1978	The New International Version (NIV) published as a "Modern and Accurate Phrase-for-Phrase English Translation"
1982	The New King James Version (NKJV) published as a "Modern English Version Maintaining the Original Style of the King James"
1985	The Jewish Publication Society's new translation (NJPS) of the Hebrew Bible, the Tanakh
1989	The New Revised Standard Version (NRSV)
1996	The New Living Translation, designed to improve the accuracy of Kenneth Taylor's paraphrase

Translations Matter

Take a quick look at one verse from the Book of Genesis (1:4) as it appears in several different translations. Notice the subtle but very real differences in the way a verse is rendered. First, look at the phonetic Hebrew and a literal translation of that Hebrew.

wayar	*elohim*	*et-ha'or*	*ki-tob*
and-he-saw	God	the light	that-good

1. The King James Version: "And God saw the light, that it was good."
2. The New Revised Standard Version: "And God saw that the light was good."
3. The New American Bible: "God saw how good the light was."
4. The New Jerusalem Bible: "God saw that light was good."
5. The New English Bible: "And God saw that the light was good."

Discuss the differences you see and how the meaning of the verse is altered a bit by the way it was translated.

---

that people in ancient times had a very different dating system for indicating when an event occurred. In the time that the Hebrew Scriptures were written down, a common way of dating an event was by relating it to who was ruling the country. The Book of Jeremiah, for example, begins with the words: "The words of Jeremiah, son of Hilkiah . . . to whom the word of the Lord came in the days of King Josiah, son of Amon of Judah, in the thirteenth year of his reign" *(Jeremiah 1:1–2)*. You might say, "I got an A in geometry in the second year Mrs. Hendricks was principal, and she came to Roosevelt High right after Mrs. Walsh and just before Mr. Elder."

The writers, editors, and compilers of the Bible had quite a different view of dates and of history. They were concerned with the meaning of events, of the dynamics of people and their conflicts with others, and of relationships from generation to generation. In this overview of the Bible, it is enough for you to recognize the differences and to be careful not to apply contemporary standards of history, dating, or the sequencing of events to what you read.

What's in This for Me?

Many DVD programs and video games have hidden surprises for the viewers and players. These surprises are sometimes referred to as "Easter eggs" after the children's springtime hunt for colored eggs. People who are into these technologies will scour instruction manuals and the programs to look for hints about these hidden wonders. Computers, too, have layers and layers of programming. Users spend hours on help lines and comparing notes with others to find out the best way to get the most out of both hardware and software.

Study of the Bible offers some of the same satisfaction. The Bible contains keys to culture, to art, to music, and to language. By studying the Bible, you will be able to find hidden surprises in the world around you. This first chapter has teased you a bit with some intriguing information on how the Bible influences your daily life. But here are a few more possibilities for you to consider:

- You can get more out of just about everything you see, hear, or read. The Bible is a code key to the symbols, figures of speech, and plot lines of art, literature, and popular culture.
- You may just do better academically. Studies have shown that increased cultural literacy (a by-product of familiarity with the Bible) often results in higher scores on standardized tests and on college entrance exams.

A NOTE ON DATES

The conventional way of dating in the West has been to use B.C. ("before Christ") and A.D. ("in the year of Our Lord"). Some journalists and certain scholars have begun to use alternative indications, namely B.C.E. ("before the Common Era") to replace B.C. and C.E. ("Common Era") to replace A.D. In this text, we will use such indications only when the context is not obvious.

- You might be better able to participate in society. Many of today's hottest political and social issues involve arguments made from the Bible. The more background you have, the better able you are to understand these debates.
- You could be better able to express yourself. Learning about the Bible can give you images, metaphors, and literary styles that can help you with your own writing and self-expression.

A tenth grader wrote the following:

> Non-devotional teaching about the Bible is important because the Bible is in every aspect of society. In literature, authors such as William Shakespeare, John Milton, and William Faulkner all use biblical references in their writing. *Uncle Tom's Cabin* by Harriet Beecher Stowe is a very influential book in American history. It is so rich with biblical characters and symbols that it cannot be understood or appreciated without some knowledge of Bible narratives. In art, the Bible is not only reflected in masterpieces by Leonardo da Vinci, by Michelangelo, by Raphael, and by Caravaggio, but there are biblical references in such modern films as *The Matrix*. The fact that the Bible is a best seller a few thousand years after the books were collected shows its value for people's lives. I don't think my education would be complete if I didn't learn about the Bible.

An ad for *Uncle Tom's Cabin* by Harriet Beecher Stowe. The book is filled with biblical references and symbols.

Finally, a course that ranges widely over so many aspects of life might just be really interesting. Whether you grew up reading the Bible or have never cracked its binding, you are guaranteed to learn a lot in this course. You will be learning not only about the Bible, but also about yourself and your world.

projects

Choose at least one of these three to get you started on learning about the Bible. The projects will be more interesting if you work with a partner or as a team.

1. Start a course-long research project. The project should show some aspect of how the Bible has influenced art, culture, literature, or society. You can use creative and nontraditional ways of sharing the results of your research.

2. Make a display showing the development of bookmaking from scrolls to printed books. Use models, photographs, or samples to illustrate your display.

3. Select a character or an event in the development of the Bible in English and write a biographical sketch.

Introduction to the Hebrew Bible

The Hebrew Bible is the source of many treasured narratives and memorable images: the garden of Eden, Noah's Ark, the Tower of Babel, Joseph's coat of many colors, the crossing of the Red Sea, the ark of the covenant, the tumbling walls of Jericho, David the shepherd king, Solomon and the queen of Sheba, Elijah's fiery chariot, Daniel in the lions' den. Even if you are familiar with many of these, you may never have had the chance to examine them closely, to understand them in context, to see how they are interrelated, and to trace their influence on Western and American culture. Units two through seven of this course focus on the Hebrew Scriptures.

The Jewish organization of the individual books differs from the ordering used in the Christian Old Testament. The books of the Jewish Bible are grouped into three main divisions:

1. *Torah* is the Hebrew word for "Teaching," often mistakenly translated into English as "law." This first section of the Hebrew Scriptures comprises the Bible's first five books (sometimes called the Pentateuch, from the Greek for "five parts," or *humash,* Hebrew for "five").

The Torah does indeed contain the central teachings and laws of Judaism. There is much more here: it also contains humanity's beginnings, the religious history of biblical Israel from the days of Abraham through the death of Moses, and instructions for conducting worship and celebrating the festivals of the Jewish calendar. And there are the genealogies—lists of humanity's and Israel's family trees, sometimes humorously referred to as "the begats" (from the King James Version's archaic English term for "was the ancestor of," as in Genesis 6:10, "And Noah begat three sons, Shem, Ham, and Japheth").

2. *Nevi'im* is the Hebrew word for "Prophets." This section includes both historical narratives and prophetic messages. The narratives continue the religious history of biblical Israel from the arrival in the Promised Land, through the rise and fall of the kingdom of David and his descendants. Destructive conquests by the Assyrian empire drove most of Israel's twelve tribes into exile. Then, conquests by the Babylonians led to exile for the people of Judah and Jerusalem. The poetic messages are addressed to the people of Israel from their God, alternately reprimanding them for their misdeeds, comforting them in their afflictions, and predicting their future redemption. Linking these two very different literary forms is the presence of the prophets, individuals—often quite unexpected choices—sent by God to guide the people.

3. *Ketuvim* is Hebrew for "Writings," which contains books displaying a wide assortment of themes and literary forms, including prayers, poetry, wise sayings, short narratives, and the continuation of Israel's religious history during and after the Babylonian Exile.

Michelangelo's sculpture of Moses is perhaps the best-known image of this greatest of biblical leaders.

Many Jews refer to the whole of the Hebrew Scriptures as the Bible. Another common title for the Hebrew Scriptures is the acronym **Tanakh,** made up of the initial sounds of the Hebrew words *Torah, Nevi'im,* and *Ketuvim.* Many passages in the Hebrew Scriptures section of this course are quoted from the English edition of the Tanakh published by the Jewish Publication Society.

No matter how the books of the Hebrew Scriptures are grouped, or how diverse they may be in style or genre, they share one consistent theme: the relationship between God and humans, especially the people of biblical Israel. According to the Bible, God has a unique relationship with these "chosen people," who are set apart to be an example to all the world of God's justice and God's mercy. The narrative thread of the Hebrew Scriptures begins at the beginning of time, and follows the people of Israel through their triumphs and tragedies.

How Jews Read the Hebrew Scriptures

In the United States, Judaism is usually practiced according to one of four general traditions. Orthodox Judaism is the most rigorous in its adherence to the Mosaic Law, and the least assimilated into non-Jewish society. Reform Judaism is a more liberal practice, emphasizing innovation as well as tradition. Conservative Judaism follows the Mosaic Law but often acknowledges more than one acceptable interpretation of that law; and Reconstructionist Judaism, a relatively new movement, emphasizes community life over particular traditions. Many American Jews do not follow any of these religious traditions entirely, considering themselves secular, cultural, or ethical Jews who claim various aspects of Jewish identity. Judaism has traditionally fostered a "multiple-lens" approach to reading the Bible. Jews of any background may draw on any or all of these ways of understanding the Bible at any given time:

- A **plain sense** reading (in Hebrew, *peshat*) looks to the surface, though not necessarily literal, meaning of the text, drawing on knowledge of word meanings, grammar, syntax, and context.
- An **inquiring** reading (in Hebrew, *derash*) looks for further layers of meaning. This kind of interpretive reading is what a rabbi or minister does when giving a sermon or homily on a biblical text, using story and example to add understanding. *Midrash,* the Jewish tradition of interpreting the Scriptures through creative storytelling, derives from this way of reading.
- An **allegorical** reading (in Hebrew, *remez*) looks for parallels between the scriptural text and more abstract concepts. This kind of reading sees biblical characters, events, and literary compositions as standing for other truths.
- A **mystical** reading (in Hebrew, *sod*) looks at the biblical text as a symbolic code, which with piety and effort will yield hidden wisdom and personal connection with the divine. The Jewish mystical tradition known as *Kabbalah* relies on complex symbolic interpretation of each individual letter of the biblical text.

These ways of reading the Bible for Jews are meant to be complementary, not mutually exclusive. Jewish reading of Scripture is not overly concerned with establishing one "correct" reading, and many of the greatest scholars of the tradition have been content to entertain several seemingly opposed interpretations of a single passage. The English translation of the Tanakh from the Jewish Publication Society honors this tradition by footnoting alternate readings or translations of particular passages.

The books of Proverbs, Ecclesiastes, and the Song of Songs, included among the *Ketuvim* or Writings in the Hebrew Scriptures, are traditionally attributed to the Israelite King Solomon, who was gifted by God with great wisdom. This illustration from a fourteenth century British manuscript shows Solomon dictating the Book of Proverbs to his court scribes.

Christians and the Hebrew Scriptures

Judaism and Christianity share much of the same narrative in the Hebrew Scriptures. However, the ordering of the books is different. In addition, Christians use quite a different lens when they read the Hebrew Scriptures. In that lens, Christians see the Hebrew Scriptures as pointing toward Jesus Christ and a new covenant established and recorded in the New Testament. Western art and literature draw on the common narrative, although frequently from the Christian perspective.

Christians commonly refer to the Hebrew Scriptures as the Old Testament, which further reflects the Christian perspective. Nonetheless, there is a growing trend in Christianity to refer to these books as the Hebrew Scriptures in order to respect and recognize the common heritage of the two traditions. The second part of this book will have more to say about the Christian perspective of the Hebrew Scriptures.

Characteristics of Hebrew Literature

To read and understand the Hebrew Scriptures, you will need to know a few things about Hebrew language and literature.

- **The importance of the word.** The Hebrew alphabet is one of the oldest in the world, and its early development reflects the importance that ancient Hebrew-speaking peoples gave to spoken and written language. In the Hebrew account of creation, for example, the entire universe comes into being at God's spoken command.
- **Symbolic word choices.** In many biblical passages, personal and place names have symbolic meanings drawn from Hebrew etymologies.
- **Parallelism and repetition.** Most of the Hebrew Scriptures originated in oral tradition, and they bear the marks of narratives told and retold, poetry chanted to musical rhythms, and laws memorized and recited by heart. Both parallelism (setting two accounts or ideas side by side for comparison or contrast) and repetition make it easier to commit oral material to memory and transmit it to new generations. These devices remain important even when the texts are set down in writing. Hebrew poetry, for example, relies almost entirely on parallelism for its structure, as it does not use rhyme or standardized meters.
  - **Figures of speech.** The Hebrew respect for language allows dazzling displays of creative wordplay. Pay particular attention to simile, metaphor, exaggeration, irony, and personification, all of which assist in capturing the ineffable experience of the divine within the limitations of human language.

The Name of God

In Hebrew tradition, names carry enormous power. The personal name of God, as revealed to Moses in the Book of Exodus 3:15, is the most powerful and sacred word of all. This name (which Christian translators have vocalized *Yahweh*) consists of four Hebrew letters, known in Greek as the **Tetragrammaton.** Because the name of God could only be spoken within the holy of holies, the inner sanctuary of the temple, a substitution is made when reading the Hebrew Scriptures aloud. Readers say *Adonai* (usually translated in English as Lord) instead. The name *Jehovah,* given by some Christian traditions as God's name, is based on a non-Hebrew-speaker's error, using the vowel sounds for *Adonai* with the consonants for *Yahweh.*

In everyday practice, many Jews avoid even *Adonai,* preferring other euphemisms such as *Ha-Shem* ("the Name"). Documents containing the name of God are treated with the utmost respect. English-speaking

During the Middle Ages, Hebrew Bibles were illuminated. But in contrast to Christian illuminators, Jewish artists like Joseph Asarfati, who decorated this page, avoided realistic depictions of people in deference to their interpretation of the biblical commandment that prohibits "graven images." This artist pushes the envelope by including figures that are human from the waist up, but have the bodies of fish below.

THE ORGANIZATION OF THE HEBREW SCRIPTURES

This chart will give you an overview of how the Hebrew Scriptures have been assembled for the two major traditions using these books. Notice that there is a difference in contents not only between Jews and Christians, but also among the major divisions of Christianity.

The Tanakh

Torah (The Five Books of Moses)
Genesis (*Breshit*)
Exodus (*Shemot*)
Leviticus (*Wayikra*)
Numbers (*Bamidbar*)
Deuteronomy (*Devarim*)

Nevi'im **(The Prophets)**
Joshua (*Yehoshua*)
Judges (*Shof'tim*)
1 Samuel (*Shmuel Aleph*)
2 Samuel (*Shmuel Beth*)
1 Kings (*Melakhim Aleph*)
2 Kings (*Melakhim Beth*)

The Major Prophets
Isaiah (*Yishayahu*)
Jeremiah (*Yirmiyhu*)
Ezekiel (*Yekezkel*)

The Twelve Minor Prophets
Hosea (*Hoshea*)
Joel (*Yoel*)
Amos (*Amos*)
Obadiah (*Ovadyah*)
Jonah (*Yonah*)
Micah (*Mikah*)
Nahum (*Nakhum*)
Habakkuk (*Habakuk*)
Zephaniah (*Zefanyah*)
Haggai (*Haggai*)
Zechariah (*Zekharyah*)
Malachi (*Malachi*)

Ketuvim **(The Writings)**
Psalms (*Tehillim*)
Proverbs (*Mishlei*)
Job (*Iyov*)
The Song of Songs* (*Shir ha-Shirim*)
Ruth* (*Rut*)
Lamentations* (*Eikhah*)
Ecclesiastes* (*Kohelet*)
Esther* (*Ester*)
Daniel (*Danyel*)
Ezra (*Ezra*)
Nehemiah (*Nehemyah*)
1 Chronicles (*Divrei Hayamim Aleph*)
2 Chronicles (*Divrei Hayamim Beth*)
     *The Five *Megillot* (Scrolls)

The Christian Old Testament

Protestant, Roman Catholic, and Greek Orthodox

Pentateuch (The Books of Moses)
Genesis
Exodus
Leviticus
Numbers
Deuteronomy

The Historical Books
Joshua
Judges
Ruth
1 Samuel (1 Kingdoms in Greek)
2 Samuel (2 Kingdoms in Greek)
1 Kings (3 Kingdoms in Greek)
2 Kings (4 Kingdoms in Greek)
1 Chronicles (1 Paralipomenon in Greek)
2 Chronicles (2 Paralipomenon in Greek)
Ezra
Nehemiah (Ezra and Nehemiah are called 2 Esdras in Greek)
Esther

Wisdom Literature
Job
Psalms
Proverbs
Ecclesiastes
Song of Solomon

The Prophets
Isaiah
Jeremiah
Lamentations
Ezekiel
Daniel
Hosea
Joel
Amos
Obadiah
Jonah
Micah
Nahum
Habakkuk
Zephaniah
Haggai
Zechariah
Malachi

The Apocrypha or Deuterocanonical Books

Books and additions found in the Roman Catholic (RC) and/or the Orthodox (O) Bibles

In both RC and O
Tobit
Judith
The Wisdom of Solomon
Ecclesiasticus (or the Wisdom of Jesus Son of Sirach)
Baruch
The Letter of Jeremiah
1 Macabees
2 Macabees

Only in O
1 Esdras
3 Macabees
4 Macabees (an appendix in the Greek Bible)

Abraham Messer's painting *Talmudists* captures the communal process of discussion and debate through which Jewish commentaries on the Bible were produced and continue to be studied.

Orthodox and Conservative Jews often use the formation *G-d* when writing, so as not to spell out—and possibly subject to desecration— the holy name.

Both Jewish and Christian printed Bibles often observe the custom of separating God's name from ordinary text by setting the words *God* or *Lord* in capitals, when the words refer to the one God of Israel.

The Talmud and *Midrash*

In addition to individual reading and interpretation, Jews since the time of the Second Temple have been able to rely on a communal tradition of scholarly commentary on the Scriptures. Most Jewish traditions hold that along with the written law of the Torah, the Jews have also passed down through the centuries oral teachings that explicate the Torah and help Jews apply it to their daily lives. This "oral Torah" was eventually itself committed to writing around the year 200 and is known as the *Mishnah.*

For three centuries after the compilation of the *Mishnah,* rabbis in Jerusalem and Babylon (the major Jewish communities of the day) analyzed and discussed its teachings. Their interpretations were collected under the name *Gemara.* The *Gemara* also includes Biblical expositions, ethical reflections, and stories elaborating on and illustrating various interpretations of biblical narratives. The Talmud comprises both the *Mishnah* and the *Gemara,* both oral law and later elaborations and commentaries.

To those unfamiliar with the tradition, engaging with the Talmud can be a baffling experience. Sections are organized according to subject matter, not according to biblical sequence, and include many different viewpoints, all of which are meant to be resolved through ongoing study and discussion. There are two general types of commentary: *halakhah,* or "rulings on points of law" and Talmudic literature, and *aggadah,* or "narrative." *Midrash,* "creative interpretation and extrapolation," also weaves its way through the Talmud and other ancient rabbinic works. But since the fall of the Temple, the dual tradition of *Torah* and creative interpretation has given Judaism its central identity and preserved it as a living faith through centuries of persecution.

Hebrew Scriptures in Jewish and Christian Life

> Hear, O Israel! The Lord is our God, the Lord alone. You shall
> love the Lord your God with all your heart and with all your soul
> and with all your might. Take to heart these instructions with
> which I charge you this day. Impress them upon your children.
> Recite them when you stay at home and when you are away,
> when you lie down and when you get up. Bind them as a sign on
> your hand and let them serve as a symbol on your forehead;
> inscribe them on the doorposts of your house and on your gates.
> *Deuteronomy 6:4–9 (NJPS)*

These words, from Moses' farewell address to the Israelites, sum up the centrality of the Hebrew Scriptures in Jewish identity, faith, and daily life. The Tanakh both

The importance of the priestly tradition of temple worship in the formation of the Hebrew Bible is reflected in *Aaron with the Scroll of the Law* by Abraham Solomon, which depicts a rabbi carrying a Torah scroll; the rabbi is robed as Aaron, the brother of Moses and Israel's first High Priest. Aaron's service predated the use of scrolls and the ritual life of the temple, but this image weaves together the priestly, scribal, and rabbinic traditions of Judaism.

THE BIBLE
IN **Literature**

The Jewish tradition of *Midrash*, free and creative commentary on the Scriptures, uses storytelling to illustrate a point of teaching. Learned rabbis would suggest possible interpretations of biblical texts by inventing their own narratives, describing what might have happened, often drawing on clues they perceived hidden in the biblical texts' wording. Below is an example of *midrash* describing the creation of the trees.

The main creation of the third day was the realm of plants, the terrestrial plants as well as the plants of Paradise. First of all the cedars of Lebanon and the other great trees were made. In their pride at having been put first, they shot up high in the air. They considered themselves the favored among plants. Then God spake, "I hate arrogance and pride, for I alone am exalted, and none beside," and He created iron on the same day, the substance with which trees are felled. The trees began to weep, and when God asked the reason of their tears, they said:

"We cry because Thou hast created the iron to uproot us therewith. All the while we had thought ourselves the highest of the earth, and now the iron, our destroyer, has been called into existence." God replied: "You yourselves will furnish the axe with a handle. Without your assistance the iron will not be able to do aught against you."

From *The Legends of the Jews,* Louis Ginzberg
(The Jewish Publication Society of America, 1909)

grew out of and helped shape Jewish religious celebrations, ethical practices, and cultural expressions. For Jews, the Torah contains hundreds of commandments, or *mitzvot* (which can be loosely translated as "blessed obligations"), which touch on every aspect of human experience. The complete Torah and substantial portions of the prophetic books are proclaimed in an annual cycle of weekly readings in the synagogue. Feasts and festivals are celebrated according to biblical instructions and include more readings from the Scriptures.

The Hebrew Scriptures play a similarly important role in the lives of Christians. Jesus was a Jew, as were his first followers. The Hebrew Scriptures were the Bible of the early Christian community. Traditional Jewish respect for the word carried over into Christian religious practice, which followed the structure of the synagogue service. Most Christian **liturgies,** or structured public worship, include readings from the Hebrew Scriptures and often a sung portion of a psalm. Christians honor the Ten Commandments and some of the Mosaic laws. Like Jews, Christians read the Bible as their own spiritual history.

projects

Choose one of these research projects to learn more about the Jewish traditions of reading and studying the Hebrew Scriptures.

1. Write a biographical sketch of one of the Jewish scholars listed below. Be sure to include how the Hebrew Scriptures affected his life and work.
   a. Rashi (1040–1105)
   b. Maimonides (1135–1204)
   c. Moses Mendelssohn (1729–1786)

2. Write a description of one major Jewish festival. Include the following in your description.
   a. The origin of the festival
   b. How the Hebrew Scriptures are used
   c. When it is celebrated
   d. What family traditions are associated with it

Unit Feature
Biblical Allusions

Everybody uses allusions. Allusions, simply stated, are bits of shorthand that aid communications. In your daily conversation, you no doubt refer to the music you are listening to, the celebrities from movies or television, the computer games you play as points of reference in your conversation. If you hear the question, "Who does she think she is, Oprah Winfrey?" You factor everything that you know about Oprah into your understanding of what was asked. "The next time he does that, we are voting him off the island." That sentence reminds you of a popular reality program that pitted people against one another in a contrived survival game.

Down through the centuries, the Bible has proven a very important source of allusions. These allusions are sprinkled liberally throughout literature, art, music, and even the daily news. If you were reading Robert Penn Warren's book *All the King's Men,* you would find a reference to Saul on the road to Damascus. If you didn't know that account, you would miss the author's meaning. (A Jewish student might be wondering what the first King of the Jewish people was doing on that road.) You might recognize the question, "Am I my brother's keeper?" But do you know that Adam and Eve's son Cain was the one who asked the question?

A RICHER UNDERSTANDING OF LITERATURE

Biblical allusions can signal an interpretive framework for either an entire work or a specific aspect of it. In composing *Macbeth,* William Shakespeare developed his plot by constantly reminding us of parallel actions in the Bible, including Jezebel's urging, planning, and helping to execute a crime to gain something for her husband, of Pilate's futilely washing his hands in false innocence, of King Herod's slaughter of the innocents, of King Saul, a doomed king near death consulting a witch. Shakespeare sets the play in a world reminiscent of the narratives of Hebrew Scriptures where evil could taint the whole nation and of pictures of moral and natural collapse in the Book of Revelation. Macbeth's famous "Tomorrow, and tomorrow and tomorrow" soliloquy is a mosaic of biblical allusions.

When William Faulkner wrote a novel about the death of a person's dreams set in the culture of the Deep South, he entitled the book *Absalom, Absalom!* By alluding to King David's fatherly lament over the loss of his son in a saga of death, violence, and tragic betrayal, Faulkner draws attention to the nature of his own narrative. The scholar Robert Alter called the novel "a story of primal sin, the tainting of an inheritance, the loss of a promised land, the violent twisting of the fraternal bone."

Allusions can be either straightforward and simple or hidden and more complex. In the more straightforward form, we see the seventeenth-century English poet John Donne began a sonnet "At the round earth's imagined corners, blow / Your trumpets, angels." What trumpets and angels are in view? The statement remains a mystery until we link it with the apocalyptic visions in the Book of Revelation where we read about "four angels standing at the four corners of the earth" *(Revelation 7.1 [NRSV])* and about seven angels with trumpets who announce events in the end times *(Revelation 8).*

A more complex allusion goes beyond making a connection between the passage and its biblical text. In one of his sonnets, the seventeenth-century English poet John Milton spoke of his blindness as "one talent which is death to hide." Milton's talent was his poetic ability. He linked himself to the unprofitable servant with only one talent in Jesus' parable of the talents

If you come from a non-Western country or have a non-Western faith and you speak English, you still need to know the Bible. Look at Caravaggio's painting *David and Goliath* for example. If you hear "It was a contest as between David and Goliath," and you don't know who David and Goliath were, then you won't get the impact of what was said.

William Faulkner, the Nobel Prize–winning American writer (1897–1962), based the title of his 1936 novel *Absalom, Absalom!* on 2 Samuel 13–18, in which King David's eldest son, Amnon, has incestual relations with his sister Tamar. In retribution, their brother Absalom kills Amnon. The title alludes specifically to 2 Samuel 18, in which David learns of Absalom's death at the hand of Joab. A basic understanding of the plots in Second Samuel gives a reader a deeper understanding of Faulkner's work.

(Matthew 25:14–30). By doing so, Milton expressed the depth of his despair and fear over the inactivity forced on him by his blindness. Yet, Milton did not make a simple equation between himself and the slothful servant of the parable, a story that is used to illustrate a spiritual truth. Milton was only partly like the wicked servant. The servant chose to be unprofitable, while Milton's blindness forced him to be inactive. Milton bent the allusion in the very next lines of his poem: "though *my* soul more bent / To serve therewith my Maker."

You will stumble across biblical allusions everywhere. William Butler Yeats began one of his poems "I will arise and go now," echoing the moment of the Prodigal Son's resolve to go home in what is perhaps Jesus' most widely known parable *(Luke 15:18)*. When T. S. Eliot's unfortunate J. Alfred Prufrock mused to himself what it might have been like to break out of his world of phony social trivialities, he imagined that it would have been like saying "I am Lazarus, come from the dead, / Come back to tell you all." This is a double allusion—to the narrative of Lazarus coming back from the dead *(John 11:38–44)* and to the parable of another Lazarus in which a rich man who is suffering after death begged Abraham to send Lazarus back to warn his brothers about the consequences of an uncaring life *(Luke 16:19–31)*. You will also find these biblical allusions in movies such as *Apocalypse Now* and *The Matrix*, which drew heavily on biblical imagery.

Adapted from Leland Ryken,
"The Literary Influence of the Bible,"
in **A Complete Literary Guide to the Bible**

BIBLICAL ALLUSIONS IN THE ENGLISH AP EXAM

A book designed to prepare students for the Advanced Placement Literature and Composition Exam lists "a profusion of allusions" that students should know. Sixty percent of the allusions listed are biblical and each is defined in the book's glossary.

Abraham and Isaac	Eye for an eye	Joseph in Egypt	Noah and the flood
Absalom	Four Horsemen of the	Judas Iscariot	Pharisees
Armageddon	Apocalypse	Know them by their fruits	Philistines
Blind leading the blind	Garden of Gethsemane	Lamb to the slaughter	Pontius Pilate
Burning bush	Good Samaritan	Last Supper	Prodigal Son
By bread alone	Grail or Holy Grail	Lazarus	Rachel and Leah
Cain and Abel	Heap coals of fire	Lilies of the field	Ruth
Camel through a needle's	Herod	Lion lies down with the lamb	Salome
eye	House has many mansions	Loaves and fishes	Sermon on the Mount
Cast the first stone	Isaac	Lot	Sodom and Gomorrah
Cast bread upon the waters	Jacob	Lot's wife	Solomon
Conversion of Saul	Jacob and Esau	Magi	Swords into ploughshares
Crucifixion	Jacob's ladder	Mammon	Thirty pieces of silver
Daniel	Jephthah's daughter	Mary Magdalene	Through a glass darkly
David and Bathsheba	John the Baptist	Mary the Virgin	Tower of Babel
David and Goliath	Jonah	Massacre of the innocents	
Divide the sheep from the	Joseph and his brothers	Moses	
goats	Joseph and Potiphar's wife	Nebuchadnezzar's dream	

M. Bevilacqua and R. Timoney
AP Literature and Composition: Preparing for the Advanced Placement Examination

UNIT TWO

Genesis— Origins

In the beginning when God created the heavens and the earth, the earth was a formless void and darkness covered the face of the deep.

Genesis 1:1–2 (NRSV)

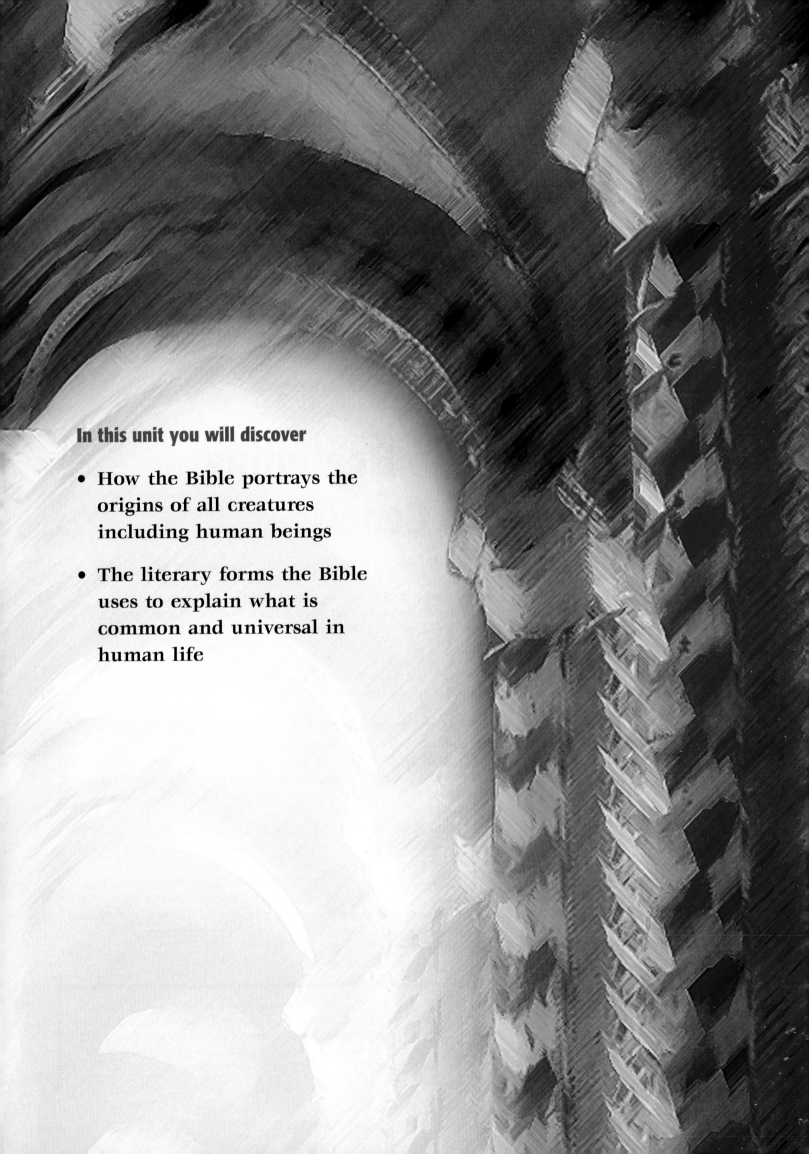

In this unit you will discover

- How the Bible portrays the origins of all creatures including human beings

- The literary forms the Bible uses to explain what is common and universal in human life

KEY BIBLE TEXTS

■ Genesis 1:1–2:25

GET TO KNOW

■ The Creator, Adam, Eve

DISCOVER

■ How the Book of Genesis describes the origins of the world
■ How the Bible distinguishes humans from the rest of creation
■ The way the account of creation influences how people view their relationship with the rest of creation

CONSIDER

■ Why do people want to know how the world began?

In the Beginning
Genesis

The Bible's first book, **Genesis** (meaning "origin"), starts with a stirring narrative of creation:

> When God began to create heaven and earth—the earth being unformed and void, with darkness over the surface of the deep and a wind from God sweeping over the water—God said, "Let there be light"; and there was light.
>
> *Genesis 1:1–3 (NJPS)*

People are curious about origins. How did the world come to be? What is the nature of humanity? How are humans the same as or different from the rest of creation? The Book of Genesis addresses that curiosity.

Scholars and faithful readers differ on the date and authorship of Genesis. Even within the first two chapters, some see two distinct creation narratives (Genesis 1:1–2:4a for the first and 2:4b–25 for the second). Some read Genesis as a literal account of the mechanics of creation. Still others read it as a poem about God's relationship with humans. Many read the book as both. And yet, the main elements of the creation narrative remain the same. Genesis portrays a single God who exists before the creation of the universe. That God creates an abundantly fertile world out of nothing and blesses it as good. In the Genesis account, God is separate from the world He created, and yet that physical world is real—not an illusion or a deception. Genesis offers an account of the origins of the world and the human race that both directly and indirectly has influenced world civilization and continues to influence it.

On Christmas Eve, 1968, during the flight of Apollo 8, the first manned orbit of the moon, astronauts Frank Borman, William Anders, and James Lovell beamed photographs of the earth from space to an audience of millions, while taking turns reading aloud the creation narrative from the Book of Genesis.

Genesis is, in fact, an argument for a civilized world with laws and principles. It demonstrates the value of order drawn out of chaos, of respect for the rights of others, and of the need for people to relate together in harmony.

God the Creator

The Book of Genesis is peopled with fascinating figures, but no portrayal is more striking or memorable than that of God. Whether the reader sees the Bible as divinely inspired or as the work of human ingenuity (or both), the power of this text is undeniable. The God of Genesis is deeply etched into the culture and history of Europe and the Americas.

Where many creation stories from other cultures show the forces of order and chaos, or good and evil, locked in equal combat, Genesis 1 describes a God whose goodness alone is the source of all life and all form. The **abyss**—the primal chaos that is "formless and void"—before creation is not depicted as an evil force that must be overcome. Rather, the abyss needs to be ordered to reach its full potential.

Other origin stories tell of many different gods who themselves are created, and who work together or fight against one another, to create out of the remains of previous creations. In contrast, the first part of Genesis describes one God who is self-sufficient, powerful, and benevolent. The God of Genesis, who needs nothing, chooses to create anyway. God creates not from leftovers but out of that chaos, or as the contemporary scholar Robert Alter translates it, "out of welter and waste."

The description of God continues to expand throughout the Book of Genesis, gradually revealing a God who loves zealously, who chooses favorites, who inflicts terrible punishments, and shows mercy beyond measure—but who is never distant or detached. Genesis is the account of this very personal God's powerful relationship with humanity.

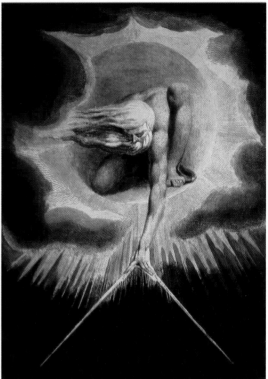

The Ancient of Days, an engraving by visionary artist and poet William Blake (1757–1827). The Creator wields the compass of a master architect to bring order out of chaos.

CULTURAL
CONNECTIONS

Music

Franz Joseph Haydn (1732–1809) composed the choral piece *The Creation* between 1796 and 1798. The libretto (text) is based on Genesis, the Psalms, and John Milton's reworking of the biblical creation account in his epic poem *Paradise Lost*. Haydn's oratorio features choral writing on a grand scale that went beyond what he had written before. Haydn, always a deeply religious man, later reflected, "I was never so devout as during that time when I was working on *The Creation*."

The oratorio begins with a "Representation of Chaos," in which muted instruments create a sense of shifting, formless turmoil. At the words "Let there be light" *(Genesis 1:3)*, the instruments are unmuted and a dramatic, *fortissimo* (very loud) C major chord rings out, followed by three sections detailing the creation narrative. Each section is itself divided into three parts: biblical narrative, description, and praise. Part three is devoted to Adam and Eve, signaling their place at the pinnacle of creation and hinting at their eventual sin.

The first public performance of the entire piece sold out. It was also performed at Haydn's last public appearance, a concert in 1808. Ludwig van Beethoven, who was in attendance, sought out the older composer and knelt to kiss his hand.

The fresco *The Creation of the Animals* by the Renaissance master Raphael (1483–1520) shows the animals emerging fully formed from the mud at God's command. The artist included animals (such as the baboon at left and the elephant and rhino at right), newly introduced to Europeans through traders' voyages to Asia and Africa, as well as creatures of legend (the unicorns that appear at God's right hand).

Seven Days

This first part of the Genesis creation narrative shows God's creative power. While some Christians read Genesis as a literal account of how God created the world, most Christians and Jews read Genesis for a different sort of revelation: for the what and why of creation rather than the how. And of course, it is possible to read the text both ways.

The description of each day of creation follows a general pattern. Each separate act of creation begins with the words "And God said, Let there be . . .," then the text tells us that what God said. This is followed by a naming or description of the particular creation and God's judgment of its goodness, along with a numbering of the day, as in:

> And God said, Let there be light: and there was light.
> And God saw the light, that *it was* good: and God divided the light from the darkness.
> And God called the light Day, and the darkness he called Night. And the evening and the morning were the first day.
> *Genesis 1:3–5 (KJV)*

Many read another pattern in the numbering of day: a balanced pairing of days and works as shown in the chart below.

IN YOUR
journal

Write down your personal reactions to the description of the creation of human beings. What are the underlying attitudes toward people portrayed in this description?

PAIRING OF DAYS AND WORKS		
Day One		**Day Four**
Light	&	Sun, moon, and stars
Day Two		**Day Five**
Separation of the waters and sky	&	Water creatures, birds of the air
Day Three		**Day Six**
Dry land, plants	&	Animals and human beings

The order of the Genesis account is not lifeless or rigid. The exuberance of life bursts through every line. Trees and plants and waters yield abundantly; herds of living creatures leap and gallop, creep and soar. And God finds it all "good."

On the sixth day, after God created the animals, God singled out humanity for a special honor: human beings alone were made in God's own image, both male and female. God gave the care of other living things to these new human beings. And God found the work of this day "very good." In the original Hebrew, this carries a powerful suggestion that the sum of creation together surpasses the goodness of each of its parts. Whereas each part is good, together creation is very good indeed.

On the seventh day, God rested. For Jews and Christians, this is the foundation of the **Sabbath,** a day of rest and prayer. Jews see the Sabbath as stretching from sundown on Friday to sundown on Saturday, while most Christians celebrate Sunday as a Sabbath.

■ What message does God's repeated evaluation of creation as "good" convey?

Stewardship of Creation

Many people read both Genesis 1 and Genesis 2 as God's sharing with humanity the responsibility for maintaining and protecting the natural world.

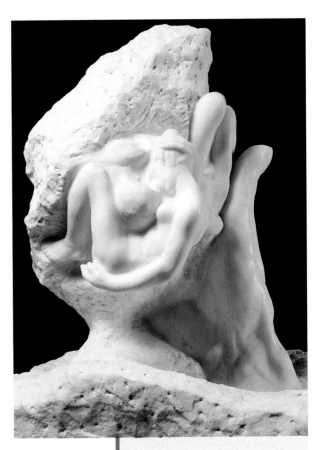

The French sculptor Auguste Rodin (1840–1917) first modeled this marble image, *The Hand of God,* in clay. The sculpture alludes to the process of creation as an infinite circle: A man, the sculptor, creates an image of God, the Creator, sculpting from clay a man in his own image.

> And God said, Let us make man in our image, after our likeness: and let them have dominion over the fish of the sea, and over the fowl of the air, and over the cattle, and over all the earth, and over every creeping thing that creepeth upon the earth.
>
> So God created man in his own image, in the image of God created he him; male and female created he them.
>
> And God blessed them, and God said unto them, Be fruitful, and multiply, and replenish the earth, and subdue it: and have dominion over the fish of the sea, and over the fowl of the air, and over every living thing that moveth upon the earth.
> *Genesis 1:26–28 (KJV)*

> The Lord God formed man from the dust of the earth. He blew into his nostrils the breath of life, and man became a living being. . . . The Lord God took the man and placed him in the garden of Eden, to till it and tend it.
> *Genesis 2:7, 15 (NJPS)*

Note: The English term **dominion,** used in Genesis 1:28, has a more gentle and familial ring in the Hebrew. It gives the sense that the relationship of all creatures is familial and friendly.

■ How might Genesis 1:28 be used to justify either or both sides of environmental debates or animal rights legislation?

Adam and Eve

The second part of the Genesis creation account (Genesis 2:4b–25) shifts focus from cosmic grandeur to a closer, more personal look at humanity's beginnings. In this narrative, God created not only with words, but also with hands. God surveyed land, planted a garden named **Eden,** formed a man and a host of animals from clay as a potter or sculptor would, put the man to sleep as gently as an anesthesiologist, served as a kind of midwife to the birth of the first woman, and presided at what many consider the first wedding.

If the first part of the creation account is a stirring hymn, this chapter is an enchanting love story. God made a person—a man into whom God's own life was breathed. And then God swiftly made a companion for this person, so he would not be alone.

> The Lord God said, "It is not good for man to be alone; I will make a fitting helper for him." And the Lord God formed out of the earth all the wild beasts and all the birds of the sky, and brought them to the man to see what he would call them; and whatever the man called each living creature, that would be its name. And the man gave names to all the cattle and to the birds of the sky and to all the wild beasts; but for Adam no fitting helper was found. So the Lord God cast a deep sleep upon the man; and, while he slept, He took one of his ribs and closed up the flesh at that spot. And the Lord God fashioned the rib that He had taken from the man into a woman; and He brought her to the man. Then the man said,
> "This one at last
> Is bone of my bones
> And flesh of my flesh."
>
> *Genesis 2:18–23 (NJPS)*

These words echo the beauty of Genesis 1:26–27, confirming the biblical theme that humans—both men and women—are created to share God's

CULTURAL
CONNECTIONS

Marriage Ceremonies

In the Genesis account, God created human beings male and female, and intended them for relationship with each other. The text portrays marriage as part of God's original intention for humans, a sexual union for companionship and the rearing of children. Marriage creates a tie so close it transforms the married couple into "one flesh" *(Genesis 2:24)*, each other's closest human bond. The influence of Genesis on Jewish and Christian traditions of marriage is apparent in the wedding ceremonies of many Jews and Christians.

Blessed are you, Unnamable God, source of the universe, who purify us with your commandments and give us marriage as a path to you.

Blessed are you, Unnamable God, source of the universe, who created man and woman in your image and placed eternity in their hearts.

Give joy to these two loving friends, as you gave joy to the first man and woman in the Garden of Eden.
Traditional Jewish wedding blessing, adapted by Stephen Mitchell

In the beginning you created the universe and made mankind in your own likeness. You gave man the constant help of woman so that man and woman should no longer be two, but one flesh, and you teach us that what we have united may never be divided.
From the Roman Catholic Rite of Marriage

The bond and covenant of marriage was established by God in creation. The union of husband and wife in heart, mind, and body is intended by God for their mutual joy; for the help and comfort given each other in prosperity and adversity; and, when it is God's will, for the procreation of children. Those whom God has joined together let no one put asunder.
From the "Anglican Marriage Ceremony," The Book of Common Prayer

Into the Garden: A Wedding Anthology, edited by Robert Haas and Stephen Mitchell

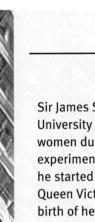

THE BIBLE
AND Science

Sir James Simpson (1811–1870), who taught obstetric medicine at the University of Edinburgh, experimented with using ether to anesthetize women during childbirth, but he wanted something better. He tried many experiments until he finally learned of a new anesthetic, chloroform, which he started using. The practice did not gain widespread acceptance until Queen Victoria was successfully anesthetized with chloroform during the birth of her son, Prince Leopold. While local clergy objected, Simpson reminded his opponents that God made Adam fall into a deep sleep before taking the rib from him. In other words, Simpson's point was that God had anesthetized Adam.

blessings equally. Whatever happens later, however far humans stray from this idyllic beginning, the Bible holds out the message that the human story begins in goodness, joy, community, abundance, and love.

■ According to the text of Genesis, why does Eve's creation make her uniquely suited to be Adam's partner?

A Note on Names

In Hebrew tradition, names have special significance. The term *adam* is a Hebrew word that can mean "humankind" or "earth" or "red." In Genesis 1 and 2, the name Adam also means "human" or "the man." In Genesis 2:23 the man, who has been given the responsibility of naming all living creatures, gives to his counterpart the name "woman" (Hebrew: *isha*), meaning "closely related to man" (Hebrew: *ish*). Later, after God pronounces his judgment on the erring partners, Adam gives his partner a personal name "Eve," which means "mother of all living" *(Genesis 3:20 [NRSV]).*

One World

Although most of the Hebrew Scriptures provide an account of one nation (the Jewish people, or the people of biblical Israel), the first chapters of Genesis are about all of humanity. These chapters describe a worldview that has shaped the way Jews and Christians understand themselves and the universe around them. Through the global influence of American and Western culture, which draws heavily on Jewish and Christian tradition, the worldview of Genesis has had an effect on many peoples and cultures.

What is this worldview? Genesis 1 and 2 contain the seeds of ideas that are integral to American and Western philosophy, literature, and art. These ideas continue to influence the ideas, politics, and economy of the United States and many other nations.

Order

The Genesis account shows an established order and purpose to creation. Although clashes between the religious and scientific worldviews have always been part of history, some scholars argue that faith in the fundamental goodness and order of creation may actually explain why the scientific method emerged first in Western countries.

Sir Francis Bacon (1561–1626), one of the pioneers of scientific methodology, wrote, "There are two books laid before us to study, to prevent our falling into error; first the volume of the Scriptures, which reveal the will of God; then the volume of the Creatures, which express his power." The idea that creation has purpose and order may also help spur progress and reform, and may encourage optimistic approaches to social problems.

When people are struck by an incredible array of natural beauty, the language of paradise and Eden and of the goodness of the world come to mind. The Genesis account both touches and gives voice to people longing for that "perfect place."

Human Dignity

According to Genesis, human beings are a separate creation. Humans are the only creatures made in the image of God. By contrast, some traditions and philosophies see humans as no more or less sacred than other living creatures.

In 1843, Daniel Webster (1782–1852), then a United States senator, described the influence of Genesis and the entire Bible: "The Bible is a book of faith, and a book of doctrine, and a book of morals, and a book of religion, of special revelation from God; but it is also a book which teaches man his own individual responsibility, his own dignity, and his equality with his fellow-man."

Many societies influenced by the Bible have often failed to live up to the principles of Genesis. In fact, when Webster described the influence of Genesis, African Americans were still held as slaves. Nonetheless, the idea of special dignity granted by God, which no human power has the right or ability to strip away, continues to form the Western views of personal ethics, social justice, and law.

One Family

All human beings are ultimately members of the same family. They are related beyond the superficial boundaries of culture, appearance, class, and language. Genesis portrays Adam and Eve as parents of the whole human race. Despite perceived differences of race, tribe, creed, or nationality, everyone has a common origin—a common destiny. This premise has often been either challenged or disregarded. But it is built into the notion of human rights in Western and American thought. In the words of Thomas Paine (1737–1809), one of the more articulate figures of the American Revolution:

The Mosaic account of the creation, whether taken as divine authority or merely historical, is full to this point, the unity or equality of man. The expression admits of no controversy. . . . the equality of man, so far from being a modern doctrine, is the oldest upon record.

The Rights of Man

THE BIBLE
IN Literature

The American poet Robert Frost (1874–1963) is forever identified with the New England landscape he loved. In the sonnet "Never Again Would Birds' Song Be the Same," Frost hears the world through Adam's ears, paying tribute to the power of the beloved to transform the lover's world.

> He would declare and could himself believe
> That the birds there in all the garden round
> From having heard the daylong voice of Eve
> Had added to their own an oversound,
> Her tone of meaning but without the words.
> Admittedly an eloquence so soft
> Could only have had an influence on birds
> When call or laughter carried it aloft.
> Be that as may be, she was in their song.
> Moreover her voice upon their voices crossed
> Had now persisted in the woods so long
> That probably it never would be lost.
> Never again would birds' song be the same.
> And to do that to birds was why she came.

The Complete Poems of Robert Frost
(Holt, Rinehart, and Winston, 1964)

projects

Choose one of the research projects listed below to help you discover more about the influence of the Genesis account on society.

1. Read accounts of the current debate about the use of natural resources and the protection of the environment. How do the accounts reflect both the notion of subjugation and the notion of stewardship?

2. Look up some examples of other ancient literature and mythology of the origins of the world (such as *Enuma Elish, Gilgamesh,* or *Praise of the Pickax*). Compare what you read there with the first two chapters of Genesis. Share your comparisons.

3. Fyodor Dostoyevsky (1821–1881) stated in his novel *The Brothers Karamazov,* "If there is no God, then all things are permitted." Find this passage and read it in context. Then, write a short story about a world in which all things are permitted.

CHAPTER 4

KEY BIBLE TEXTS

- Genesis 3:1–24; 4:1–26; 6:1–9:29; 11:1–9

GET TO KNOW

- Cain, Abel, Noah and his family

DISCOVER

- How Genesis explains human suffering and evil in a world created by a good God
- How the story of Cain and Abel speaks to a contemporary world
- The biblical consequences of human sinfulness and false pride

CONSIDER

- Why is it important for humans to look for meaning in such experiences as suffering and death?

From the Garden to the Tower

The first two chapters of Genesis show a world in harmony, blessing, and goodness. Humanity and the natural world coexist in peaceful abundance and delight. But the universe as we know it is very different from the idyllic garden of Eden. Chapters 3 to 11 of the Book of Genesis offer an interpretation of "What happened?"

These nine chapters offer answers to some of the most enduring and troubling human questions: Where do evil, death, division, strife, and suffering come from? And, what is freedom?

According to Genesis, the original harmony of creation was disturbed by the one creature capable, through freedom, of undoing the order God had created out of chaos. In the garden, God gave the first man and woman free reign, with one modest limit:

And the Lord God commanded the man, "You may freely eat of every tree of the garden; but of the tree of the knowledge of good and evil you shall not eat, for in the day that you eat of it you shall die."

Genesis 2:16–17 (NRSV)

Barely a paragraph goes by before the first humans shatter this one rule. Immediately they deceive themselves and also try to deceive God, making excuses and pointing the finger of blame at one another. In one stroke, the man and the woman are at odds with each other, with the natural world, and with God. And, having tasted of the tree of knowledge of good and evil, they know what they have done. They are suddenly painfully conscious of their nakedness, which now fills them with shame.

Adam and Eve is a witty view of the temptation from the German painter Lucas Cranach the Elder (1472–1553). Adam is clearly bewildered while Eve is confident and knowing. At this moment when creation's innocence is compromised, the lion begins to eye the deer hungrily.

Forbidden Fruit

The account of the first humans' disobedience *(Genesis 3)* has provided Western art, literature, and philosophy with enduring images and themes. The serpent, which the Hebrew Scriptures describe as a "subtle" or clever beast, has over the centuries often become associated with the personification of evil known as the Devil or Satan, and is frequently pictured as a dragon or a hideous demon with a human face. There is a dialogue between the crafty serpent and "the woman in the garden":

SERPENT: "Did God say, 'You shall not eat from any tree in the garden'?"

WOMAN: "We may eat of the fruit of the trees in the garden; but God said, 'You shall not eat of the fruit of the tree that is in the middle of the garden, nor shall you touch it, or you shall die.'"

SERPENT: "You will not die; for God knows that when you eat of it your eyes will be opened, and you will be like God, knowing good and evil."
                              Genesis 3:1–5 (NRSV)

■ According to Genesis 3:6–7, why did the woman decide to eat the forbidden fruit?

What kind of fruit grew on the forbidden tree? If you said "apple," read again: actually, the text does not say. In Jewish tradition, the forbidden fruit is often pictured as a date or a spray of wheat. But in the broad stream of Western culture, which has entered into the popular culture of America today, the forbidden fruit is usually portrayed as an apple. Possibly this reflects the broad influence of St. Jerome's Vulgate (Latin) translation. In Latin the word *malum* can mean both "apple" and "evil." The idea of forbidden fruit has had a long association with illicit sexual desire, perhaps because the Bible makes the connection between tasting the fruit, awareness of nakedness, and shame.

"She took of its fruit and ate; and she also gave some to her husband, who was with her, and he ate. Then the eyes of both were opened, and they knew that they were naked; and they sewed fig leaves together and made loincloths for themselves" *(Genesis 3:6–7 [NRSV])*. They try to hide from God because, as the man tells God, "I heard the sound of you in the garden, and I was afraid, because I was naked; and I hid myself" *(Genesis 3:10 [NRSV])*.

Consequences

According to the text the first human act of disobedience had powerful consequences. All the ills from which the earthly Paradise had been exempt—toil, pain, aging, conflict, corruption, and loss—were now realities. Childbirth became a difficult endeavor; and death entered the world. God laid out for the first human beings the factual, painful results of their act of disorder:

"By the sweat of your face you shall eat bread until you return to the ground, for out of it you were taken; you are dust, and to dust you shall return."
                              Genesis 3:19 (NRSV)

Remorse, shame, and grief are starkly evident in the facial expressions and postures of Adam and Eve in this fresco, *Expulsion from Eden,* by the Renaissance master known as Masaccio (1401–1428?).

God drove Adam and Eve from the easy life of the garden lest they eat of the tree of life. "He placed at the east of the garden of Eden Cherubims and a flaming sword" *(Genesis 3:24 [KJV]).*

■ Do you think Adam and Eve received a fair deal, as described in Genesis? Use evidence from Genesis 3 to support your position.

Perspectives

There are differences in the way Genesis 3 is interpreted by most Jews and Christians. Most Jewish readings of this chapter reject the idea of a permanent, inherited spiritual disability stemming from the actions of Adam and Eve. Instead, many Jewish readings focus on other questions, such as: Is knowledge of good and evil preferable to innocence? Some Jewish interpretations see moral choice for humans as a step down from a state of innocence, where nobody is tempted to do evil. Others see in this narrative an affirmation of the importance of free will, of the capacity to choose between good and evil. Humans today are capable of choosing between good and evil, just as the first humans were. Many ask: If Adam and Eve did not know good from evil, how could God blame them for disobeying?

Christian tradition reads Genesis 3 as the story of "the fall": human beings' fall from God's presence and favor (or grace) into suffering and sin. Adam and Eve's disobedience is often called **original sin.** Many Christians believe this sin has been passed down to all. "For as by one man's disobedience many were made sinners, so by the obedience of one [that is, Jesus] shall many be made righteous" *(Romans 5:19 [KJV]).* Adam and Eve's disobedience brought physical and emotional suffering, moral evil, and death into the world. As John Milton (1608–1674) put it in his famous poem *Paradise Lost:*

> Of Man's first disobedience, and the fruit
> Of that forbidden tree whose mortal taste
> Brought death into the world, and all our woe.

THE BIBLE
IN Literature

Humanity's expulsion from Eden and the lasting consequences of what Christians call "the fall" have haunted poets throughout the centuries. Emily Dickinson (1830–1886), one of America's greatest poets, employed vivid, sometimes startling imagery to make abstract ideas suddenly familiar.

> EDEN is that old-fashioned House
> We dwell in every day,
> Without suspecting our abode
> Until we drive away.
> How fair, on looking back, the Day
> We sauntered from the Door,
> Unconscious our returning
> But discover it no more.

Complete Poems. V. "The Single Hound," p. 108, Harvard University Press, (1924)

The First Murder

The fourth chapter of the Book of Genesis, after the expulsion from Eden, dramatizes the newly disrupted relationships between human beings in a most memorable way: with the account of the first murder. It is fratricide—the murder of a brother by a brother.

> The Lord said to Cain, "Why are you angry, and why has your countenance fallen? If you do well, will you not be accepted; and if you do not do well, sin is lurking at the door; its desire is for you, but you must master it."
>
> *Genesis 4:6–7 (NRSV)*

The narrative of Cain and Abel echoes through Western literature. The American writer John Steinbeck (1902–1968), who used Genesis 3–4 as inspiration for his 1952 novel *East of Eden,* explained the power of the text:

> I believe that there is one story in the world, and only one, . . . Humans are caught—in their lives, in their thoughts, in their hungers and ambitions, in their avarice and cruelty, and in their kindness and generosity, too—in a net of good and evil. . . . this one story [Cain and Abel] is the basis of all human neurosis—and if you take the fall along with it, you have the total of psychic troubles that can happen to a human.
>
> *Journal of a Novel:*
> *The* East of Eden *Letters*

The Flemish artist Peter Paul Rubens (1577–1640) caught the horror of fratricide in his painting *Cain Slaying Abel.*

Cain, the slayer of the innocent Abel, responds to God's offer to explain his actions with an ironic question that has echoed throughout human history.

> The Lord said to Cain, "Where is your brother Abel?" And he said, "I do not know. Am I my brother's keeper?"
>
> *Genesis 4:9 (NJPS)*

Joseph Telushkin, a contemporary Jewish scholar, wrote, "It is no exaggeration to say that much of the rest of the Bible reads as an affirmative response to Cain's heartless question" *(Biblical Literacy [1997]).* Notice that Cain's response is an effort to evade or deceive God. Biblical tradition directly connects sin with falsehood, an inability to face who we are and what we have done. God, however, is not fooled:

> Then He said, "What have you done? Hark, your brother's blood cries out to Me from the ground!"
>
> *Genesis 4:10 (NJPS)*

THE BIBLE
IN Literature

Dante Alighieri (1265–1321), in one of the great epics of Western literature, *The Divine Comedy,* described his view of the afterlife. In this fictional account, Dante saw the murder of family members as one of the worst offenses possible. Dante consigned those who have murdered their kindred to the ninth circle of "lower hell." Dante called this level "Caina," drawing from the Genesis 4 narrative of Cain and Abel. In Dante's description, those who kill their own family members are placed in ice up to their necks with their heads bent forward.

IN YOUR journal

How would you answer the question Cain asked of God? What makes you responsible for another human being?

According to Genesis, humans are responsible for one another—are their brothers' keepers. They are also liable for the consequences of abdicating that responsibility. Cain is judged by God and (like his parents Adam and Eve) receives both punishment (exile) and mercy. The **"mark of Cain,"** though popularly misinterpreted as a brand of shame, is actually a sign of God's protection, so that Cain will not suffer the fate of his brother. Though Abel's blood cries out from the ground, God grants mercy even to the first murderer who pleads for mercy. Cain's punishment, though heavy, will not be more than he can bear.

From Bad to Worse

After Cain was banished, according to Genesis, Cain settled in a part of the world so distant that its very name means "wandering"—the land of Nod. Cain married, had a son named Enoch, and built the first city. Among the descendants of Cain were both artisans and murderers, the inventors of metalwork and music and animal husbandry, and the perpetuators of feuding and vengeance. Genesis portrays virtue as in short supply among early humans, even as their level of civilization and sophistication grew.
God, growing weary and frustrated, decided to undo creation, to wipe the slate clean and start again. Finding just one righteous family on the face of the earth, God decided to preserve this one family from destruction, so their descendants can repopulate the world in goodness. God made arrangements to preserve animal life, too, with the help of his human steward, Noah *(Genesis 6)*.

A Restart

The account of Noah in Chapters 6–9 of Genesis has become a children's favorite. But originally it begins like a nightmare. Noah received a sudden call from God to build an ark in which he and his family were to shelter during the terrible flood to come. In children's books, this ark is shown as a big boat with a kind of barn on top. But this ark is literally a big box or chest. The dimensions God gave Noah in Genesis 6:15 bear this description out. God did not make Noah the captain of a ship. Instead, Noah and his family were asked to make a great act of faith—to surrender their lives, and the lives of all those pairs of living creatures, to God's care while they floated without control in a three-story box on the stormy, chaotic waves.

In *The Animals Entering the Ark*, by the Italian painter Jacopo Bassano (1510–1592), members of Noah's family attempt to herd a world of animals "two by two" into the safety of the ark. Here, the ark resembles a cross between a barn and a wine barrel–appropriate for Noah, whom the Bible credits with making the first wine *(Genesis 9:20–21)*.

The flood continued forty days on the earth; and the waters increased, and bore up the ark, and it rose high above the earth. The waters swelled and increased greatly on the earth; and the ark floated on the face of the waters. . . . everything on dry land in whose nostrils was the breath of life died. He blotted out every living thing that was on the face of the ground, human beings and animals and creeping things and birds of the air; they were blotted out from the earth. Only Noah was left, and those that were with him in the ark. And the waters swelled on the earth for one hundred fifty days.
Genesis 7:17–18, 22–24 (NRSV)

THE BIBLE
IN Literature

Plots

Scholars of ancient literature have long recognized that many narratives reenact common patterns. More recently, it has become clear that all literature is made up of repeated images and motifs known as archetypes. An archetype is a symbol, character type, or plot pattern that ocurrs throughout literature. An example of an archetypal symbol is the season of spring to suggest rebirth. An archetypal character is the hero or heroine. One archetypal plot pattern is the chase and rescue.

Some of the most important archetypal plot motifs appear in the Bible in Chapters 3 and 4 of Genesis:
1. Sibling rivalry
2. Crime and punishment
3. Murder
4. Detective story
5. The rejected one
6. The guilty child
7. Innocent victim(s)
8. Expulsion
9. The wanderer

In comparing Genesis 3 and 4, there are many similar elements to the plots—birth, work, a challenge from God, a failure to live up to the challenge, God arriving and asking what is going on, and consequences, including exile. The themes of Genesis 3 and 4 are the same: In Chapter 3, the man and the woman reject God. In Chapter 4, their son Cain rejects God. At each level there is suspense as to what will take place next. In each plot there is human choice, a call to moral responsibility, sin, consequences, divine patience and judgment, and protection of rights afterwards. These plot archetypes are repeated in various ways throughout the Bible.

Adapted from a lecture of Professor Leland Ryken

The Rainbow Sign

Genesis 8 begins: "But God remembered Noah and all the wild animals and all the domestic animals that were with him in the ark" *(Genesis 8:1 [NRSV])*. And with the words "God remembered," everything changed. In place of the fury of the flood unleashed on sinful mankind, the themes in the account of Noah change to redemption and rebuilding.

The rains eventually ceased and the waters began to recede. Feeling the ark come to rest, Noah opened the small window cut high in the top of the great box and sent out a raven and a dove. The soaring raven didn't return, but the dove—a perching bird—could find no dry spot and returned to the ark. Later, sent out a second time, the dove returned with an olive branch in its beak, letting Noah know that the treetops had begun to emerge. To this day, the image of the dove bearing an olive branch remains a symbol of peace—the peace that was restored to the planet by the flood's end. Finally, on a third try, the dove did not return, signaling that the world was again ready to receive and shelter living things.

Calling forth Noah and his family, God blessed Noah and his sons, repeating the original command, "Be fruitful and multiply, and fill the earth" *(Genesis 9:1; see 1:28 [NRSV])*. God once again

The natural beauty of the rainbow coupled with the Bible's use of it as a sign of promise combine to make the rainbow a popular cultural image.

gave human beings dominion over animals and green plants. God entered into a covenant, a sacred and binding relationship, with Noah and all living things. God stayed his own hand and tempered his anger. The Lord laid down his weapons and set a rainbow in the clouds.

> The Lord said in his heart, "I will never again curse the ground because of humankind, for the inclination of the human heart is evil from youth; nor will I ever again destroy every living creature as I have done.
>
> As long as the earth endures, seedtime and harvest,
>   cold and heat,
> summer and winter, day and night, shall not cease."
>
> God blessed Noah and his sons, and said to them, "Be fruitful and multiply, and fill the earth."
>
> God said, "This is the sign of the covenant that I make between me and you and every living creature that is with you, for all future generations: I have set my bow in the clouds, and it shall be a sign of the covenant between me and the earth. . . . and the waters shall never again become a flood to destroy all flesh."
>
> *Genesis 8:21–9:1, 12–13, 15 [NRSV]*

Even though evil entered the world through human actions, God promised his continuing protection to his beloved creation. Mercy, as well as justice, will abide.

The Children of Noah

According to Jewish tradition (incorporated into Christian thought), the descendants of Noah populated the world. In some traditions, Shem and his children were considered the ancestors of Middle Eastern and Asian peoples, Japheth and his children the ancestors of Europeans, and Ham and his children the ancestors of Africans. Noah cursed Ham's sons with perpetual servitude for having seen his father's drunken nakedness without trying to cover him, as his two brothers did *(Genesis 9:20–27).* These verses were sometimes used by nineteenth-century Christians to argue that Scripture condoned African slavery, even though association of Ham and his descendants with black skin color is nowhere to be found in the text. The Bible has been used to justify both sides in many public controversies in America and elsewhere. As William Shakespeare remarked in the play *The Merchant of Venice,* "The devil can cite Scripture for his own purpose."

People Scattered

The first ten chapters of Genesis account for many of humankind's basic questions—people's origins, why they die, why they fight, and how they survive. One last explanation has been added: how people who sprang from one original family got split into so many separate communities that often misunderstand one another.

The **Tower of Babel** incident takes up only nine verses of Chapter 11. Yet, it has had a great cultural impact. It strikes a chord—even today.

> Then they said, "Come, let us build ourselves a city, and a tower with its top in the heavens, and let us make a name for ourselves; otherwise we shall be scattered abroad upon the face of the whole earth."
>
> *Genesis 11:4 (NRSV)*

But God punished the people's pride by confusing their language. They abandoned their attempt to reach the heavens and were scattered over the face of the earth.

The account of the Tower of Babel closes the part of Genesis that deals with the whole of humanity. The brief tale is a reversal of Genesis 1. Instead of the use of language to create and unify, God uses language to divide and scatter. God brought chaos out of order. This kind of inverted symmetry (a literary device known as **chiasm**) is a feature of many Biblical narratives. Genesis 11:1–9 sets the stage for a major change in the focus of the Hebrew Scriptures. The narrative now leaves behind the scattered nations and takes up the story of one family, one nation, one chosen people.

A vision of the Tower of Babel by the Flemish painter Pieter Bruegel the Elder (1525–1569).

THE BIBLE

IN **Literature**

The short account of the building and destruction of the Tower of Babel uses parallelism. The first four verses deal with the people and their ambitions. The last four verses describe God's frustrating those ambitions. The turning point is in the middle verse, the fifth, when God saw what they were doing.

The form of the verses also creates a parallel structure. The first two verses are strictly narrative, describing humans' actions. Verses 8 and 9 are also limited to narration, describing God's response to those actions. Movement into and out of Shinar further links the beginning and the end of the account. Verses 3 and 4, like 6 and 7, use dialogue to portray human ambitions and God's response to those ambitions. The symmetry highlights the relationship between the form of the people's transgression and the form of the penalty they faced. The people had wanted to "make us a name, lest we be scattered abroad upon the face of the whole earth" *(Genesis 11:4 [KJV])*. God confused their language and scattered them; without land and a language, they could not be a people.

projects

From the list below, choose one of the treatments of temptation and loss of innocence. With a partner discuss what you discover and prepare a brief report on how what you read expressed or challenged the biblical account.

1. The short story "Young Goodman Brown" by Nathaniel Hawthorne (1804–1864)

2. The novel *A Separate Peace* by John Knowles (1926–2001)

3. The novella *The Bear* by William Faulkner (1897–1962)

Unit Feature
Milton and the Bible

The Bible has influenced countless poets and writers throughout the history of Western civilization. The early Anglo-Saxon poets, Chaucer, Dante, William Shakespeare, John Donne, Nathaniel Hawthorne, Herman Melville, Fyodor Dostoyevsky, William Blake, T. S. Eliot, and William Faulkner are just a few of the dozens of names of great literary figures of the Western literary tradition whose works bear the imprint of the Bible.

The Bible can influence authors in various ways. Poets and writers may take a scene from Scripture as the subject of a poem or story. The language of a piece of writing may echo a passage of Scripture. An author may incorporate a theme from a scriptural book or story in his or her work.

Perhaps more than any other writer in the English language, John Milton, the great seventeenth-century writer and poet, showed the direct influence of the Bible in his works. More than citing a few simple allusions to the Hebrew Scriptures and the New Testament, Milton's works are permeated with scriptural images, echoes, stories, and themes.

John Milton

THE LIFE OF MILTON (1608–1674)

Born and raised in London, Milton was given an education quite typical for the late Renaissance age in which he lived. At St. Paul's School, he studied Latin, Greek, and Hebrew and was tutored in modern languages at home. He received Bachelor's and Master's degrees from the University of Cambridge, then moved back to his father's home for a time to continue his education on his own. When he lost his sight in later life, he blamed his blindness on the many hours he had spent reading by candlelight during his youth. After traveling to Italy, he settled in London, married, and began working as a tutor. But the work he was known for, then as now, was his writing.

MILTON THE WRITER

Milton began writing in early childhood. Two paraphrases of Psalms 144 and 136 were written when he was 15. During his university years, he wrote poetry in Latin (the language of scholarship in those days), as well as Italian and English. His first great English poem was "On the Morning of Christ's Nativity." Based on the birth of Christ, Milton wrote it when he was 21.

Even in this very early poem, we see how Milton used the Bible as the basis of his poetic vision. While using the Scripture as the basis of his work, Milton combined details from the Hebrew Scriptures, the New Testament, and the classical mythology of Greece and Rome. This poem was followed by writings in several genres: poetry, drama, and prose.

PARADISE LOST

As the English language grew and developed in the seventeenth century, it needed an epic. In *Paradise Lost,* Milton set out to write an epic poem in English that would rival Greek epics such as Homer's *Iliad* and *Odyssey.* The poem's purpose and theme are indicated in its opening verses:

> Of Man's First Disobedience, and the Fruit
> Of that Forbidden Tree, whose mortal taste
> Brought Death into the World, and all our woe,
> With loss of Eden, till one greater Man
> Restore us, and regain the blissful Seat,
> Sing, Heav'nly Muse, . . .
> And chiefly Thou O Spirit, . . .
> What in me is dark
> Illumine, what is low raise and support;
> That to the highth of this great Argument
> I may assert the Eternal Providence,
> And justify the wayes of God to men.
> *Paradise Lost I.1–6, 17, 22, 23–26*

■ According to these lines, what is Milton's purpose in writing *Paradise Lost*?

Though the poem is based on the Genesis story, Milton draws on material from other parts of the Hebrew Scriptures and from the New Testament in telling his story. He deals with the story of the fall of the Angels, the creation of the world, the creation of Adam and Eve,

Satan's temptation of Eve and Adam, the sin of Eve and Adam, and the casting of the couple out of Paradise. At the end of the work, Milton's Adam wonders if it was a good thing that he sinned:

> . . . full of doubt I stand,
> Whether I should repent me now of sin
> By mee done and occasiond, or rejoyce
> Much more, that much more good thereof
>   shall spring,
> To God more glory, more good will to Men
> From God, and over wrauth grace shall
>   abound.
>
> *Paradise Lost XII.473–78*

■ According to this summary, how does *Paradise Lost* compare to the Genesis story? What has Milton added? Why do you think he made additions such as these?

MILTON'S SATAN

Many critics think the central character of *Paradise Lost* is not God or Adam, but Satan. Milton devoted a great deal of time and space to developing the character of this fallen angel. One of the first glimpses of Satan is provided in Book I, where he ponders on his position in hell:

> The mind is its own place, and in it self
> Can make a Heav'n of Hell, a Hell of Heav'n.
> What matter where, if I be still the same,
> And what I should be, all but less than hee
> Whom Thunder hath made greater? Here at
>   least
> We shall be free; th' Almighty hath not built
> Here for his envy, will not drive us hence:
> Here we may reign secure, and in my choyce
> To reign is worth ambition though in Hell:
> Better to reign in Hell, than serve in Heav'n.
>
> *Paradise Lost I.254–63*

This painting by Hungarian artist Mihály Munkácsy (1844–1900) shows the blind Milton dictating *Paradise Lost* to his daughters.

This is an engraving of Satan by Gustave Doré (1832–1883), from his edition of *Paradise Lost.*

■ How does this image of Satan differ from the depiction of the clever serpent in Genesis?

■ In these verses what does Milton seem to consider as Satan's chief flaw?

Remarking on Milton's Satan and its influence on readers, one scholar noted:

> More than one Protestant, into whose
> youthful conception this character came like
> a new planet—in those otherwise dreary hours
> of "Sabbath-reading"—still believes in his heart
> that the Satan of Milton is the "true" Satan,
> and turns back to Scripture to feel a loss. To
> a greater extent than any other English poet
> the Bible influenced John Milton. More than
> any other English poet, he has influenced
> the Bible.
>
> Margaret Crook, *The Bible and Its Literary
> Associations,* p. 307

This comment could apply, indeed, to the whole creation account. Milton's vivid images in *Paradise Lost,* as well as his other works, not only have been profoundly influenced by the Bible, but also have influenced how many in the Western world look at the Bible.

Genesis— Call and Promise

Go from your country and your kindred and your father's house to the land that I will show you. I will make of you a great nation, and I will bless you, and make your name great, so that you will be a blessing.

Genesis 12:1–2 [NRSV]

In this unit you will discover

- The role of Abraham and Sarah in the Hebrew Bible and the narratives that surround the development of a people

- The ancestor accounts of Isaac and Jacob and Joseph, of Rebekah and Rachel and Leah

Abraham and Sarah

Family narratives serve a number of purposes. They keep alive a family's journeys through time and space, often preserving information about original languages and customs long after the family has become part of a new land and culture. Family narratives highlight the personal characteristics the family prizes—heroism in the face of danger, the ingenuity to overcome obstacles, love and familial loyalty that outlast time. Sharing stories of those who have gone before helps family members reaffirm their own sense of connectedness and belonging.

A major theme from Genesis Chapter 12 to the end of Genesis is relationships. God calls one person—Abram (later called Abraham)—and begins to teach him and his descendants how to get along and live together. Abram and his descendants, like people throughout time, have problems and don't always do the right thing. Abraham's sons, the half brothers Isaac and Ishmael, never really see each other after childhood except to bury their father when he dies. Isaac's sons, Esau and Jacob, don't get along very well with each other; Jacob leaves home to avoid harm from Esau. Jacob's sons don't get along, particularly because Jacob dotes on Joseph, the second youngest son. Joseph's brothers almost kill him and in the end sell him off as a slave to a caravan going to Egypt.

Joseph survives and brings great blessings to his father and brothers. By the end of Genesis, the sons of Jacob (whose other name is Israel) have formed a family that is the source of the twelve tribes of Israel.

This part of Genesis begins with Abram and Sarai (whom God will rename Abraham and Sarah). They were citizens of Ur, a great center of ancient Mesopotamian civilization. In a theme that will recur throughout the Bible, this family narrative begins with a call, a mission from God:

The Lord said to Abram, "Go forth from your native land and from your father's house to the land that I will show you. I will make of you a great nation,

The Departure of Abraham by Jacopo Bassano shows Abram, a nomadic herdsman, as a wealthy European merchant leaving a comfortable home.

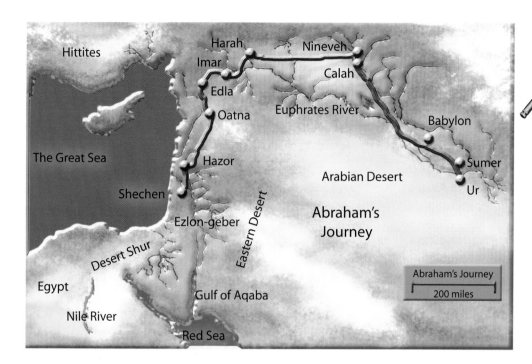

Harah
Imar
Edla
Oatna
Hittites
Nineveh
Calah
Euphrates River
Babylon
Sumer
Ur
The Great Sea
Hazor
Shechen
Ezlon-geber
Arabian Desert
Eastern Desert
Abraham's Journey
Desert Shur
Egypt
Nile River
Gulf of Aqaba
Red Sea

Abraham's Journey
200 miles

Look It Up

Choose at least one of the questions below. Find the answers in the actual biblical text.

1. What ritual does God use to make known the covenant with Abram? What does God say will happen to Abram's descendants? (Read Genesis 15:2–21.)
2. What signs did God ask of Abram and Sarai's descendants to show that they accepted God's covenant? (Read Genesis 17:9–14.)
3. What were the circumstances of the birth of Isaac? How was his birth a sign of God's part of the covenant? (Read Genesis 18:1–15 and 21:1–7.)

And I will bless you;
I will make your name great,
And you shall be a blessing.
I will bless those who bless you
And curse him that curses you;
And all the families of the earth
Shall bless themselves by you."

Genesis 12:1–3 [NJPS]

Abram is unusual in his response to this call from God. Later the Hebrew Scriptures show various prophets demurring, showing doubts, or arguing with God about their mission. Seventy-five-year-old Abram simply obeys: "So Abram went, as the Lord had told him; and Lot went with him" *(Genesis 12:4 [NRSV])*.

And so the saga of Abram begins. It is a journey of faith. This little family of nomads will range over thousands of miles, stopping at places that will carry significance for future members of the "great nation" of their descendants: Canaan, Egypt, and the site that will become Jerusalem.

Abram and Sarai are portrayed as flesh-and-blood humans with personalities. The text does not always show Abram's, Sarai's, or other people's emotional reactions; but, when it does, those reactions are vivid. They question God, plead or bargain with him, and even burst into laughter at God's seemingly impossible promises.

Surprising Candor

In Genesis 12:10–20, Abram, driven to Egypt by his own hunger, worried that his wife's beauty might endanger his life, so he passed off his wife as his sister. According to the text, when Pharaoh took Sarai into his harem, he was prevented from committing unwitting adultery only by the arrival of **plagues** (diseases and other natural misfortunes) that conveyed God's displeasure.

The dismissal of Hagar and Ishmael was a popular subject of Renaissance paintings. Here the Dutch painter Herri met de Bles has surrounded the two figures with the vastness of a European landscape, not the Middle Eastern desert.

CULTURAL
CONNECTIONS

*A*merican History

The language of covenant is an integral part of American legal and governmental tradition, partly because English Pilgrims and Puritans identified themselves with Abraham, who was called to set out on a long journey searching for a land of promise.

The Mayflower Compact, an agreement among the members of the Plymouth Colony, set the tone for future governmental charters in the British colonies and, eventually, in the new country of the United States. They wrote upon landing at Plymouth Rock in 1620,

> We whose names are underwritten . . . Having undertaken a voyage to plant the first colony . . . do by these presents solemnly and mutually in the presence of God, and of one another, Covenant and Combine our selves together into a civil body politic . . .

The Massachusetts Bay Company, a Puritan institution formed by John Winthrop in 1629 to encourage both settlement and trade, also maintained the symbolic connection to Abraham's call and the theme of covenant. In a 1630 speech aboard the ship *Arabella* bound for New England, Winthrop reminded his fellow company members, "We are entered into covenant with [God] for this work. Now if the Lord shall please to hear us, and bring us in peace to the place we desire, then hath He ratified this covenant and sealed our commission."
Norton Anthology of American Literature, Volume I

Later, Sarai, longing for a child, persuaded her husband to take a concubine, or mistress, named Hagar. But when Hagar actually got pregnant, Sarai had a fit of jealousy. "I have given my maid into thy bosom; and when she saw that she had conceived, I was despised in her eyes," Sarai complained to her husband. "Behold, thy maid is in thy hand; do to her as it pleaseth thee," Abram replied. Genesis records that it pleased Sarai to behave "harshly," driving Hagar to flee into the wilderness until an angel persuaded her to return, promising that her son Ishmael would also found a great nation. (Read Genesis 16:5–11.)

The heroes in Genesis are not cardboard figures of perfect virtue. Great faithfulness to God is shown side by side with very human feelings and failings: fear, doubt, anger, jealousy, deceit, and cruelty. Modern readers of these accounts are often struck by what they see as unethical behavior. It is always good to remember not to try to apply current standards to the biblical accounts. Recognize that the flawed humanity of its characters is one reason Genesis continues to intrigue readers and inspire artists.

Signs of Promise

In addition to the themes of calling and of journey, the account of Abram's life is marked by an emphasis on God's promises. The biblical term for the ongoing relationship between God and humans, generally brought into being by God's promise and the response of human beings, is a **covenant**, a formal, solemn, and binding agreement. The account of Abram and Sarai is the first example of God's making a covenant with one particular family, whom both Jewish and Christian traditions see as the founders of the Jewish people. In choosing and calling Abram, God set in motion the process by which the descendants of Abraham and Sarah (according to Genesis) became a chosen people, with special responsibilities to God.

When Abram was 99 years old, God gave him a new name and a new covenant:

IN YOUR
journal

Ask an older family member to share one or two favorite family stories with you. Retell one of these stories in your journal, noting any similarities of theme, tone, or events you find between your family's story and the Genesis account of Abraham and Sarah.

Phillip Ratner's *Abraham* honors Abraham, showing his name in Hebrew letters at the top.

"I am God Almighty, walk before me, and be blameless. And I will make my covenant between me and you, and will make you exceedingly numerous."

Genesis 17:1–2 [NRSV]

Abram fell on his face, and God gave him a new name—no longer "Abram," which means "exalted ancestor," but "Abraham," which means "ancestor of a multitude."

"I will make you exceedingly fruitful; and I will make nations of you, and kings shall come from you. I will establish my covenant between me and you, and your offspring after you throughout their generations, for an everlasting covenant, to be God to you and to your offspring after you."

Genesis 17:6–7 [NRSV]

Sodom and Gomorrah

The biblical account of Abraham and Sarah contains a subplot that follows Abraham's nephew, Lot. Within this subplot is one of the most memorable events of Genesis, offering a surprising insight into the deeply personal relationship between Abraham and God.

Because the servants of Abraham and Lot had quarreled, Abraham proposed an amicable parting of the ways, dividing up the land that God had promised. Lot chose the fertile southern plain, also the site of two Canaanite cities of Sodom and Gomorrah. Lot and his family settled in Sodom. Sodom and Gomorrah had an evil reputation, according to the text: "Now the people of Sodom were wicked, great sinners against the Lord" *(Genesis 13:13 [NRSV])*. Once again (as in the account of the great flood), God lost patience with the wickedness of humans and determined to destroy the cities of the plain and start fresh.

In a startling move, however, Abraham stepped in as a kind of public defender and pleaded with God to act justly: "Will you indeed sweep away the righteous with the wicked? Shall not the Judge of all the earth do what is just?" *(Genesis 18:23, 25 [NRSV])*. Would God really destroy fifty good men along with the wicked people? Abraham bargained with God. Forty-five? Forty? Thirty? Twenty? What about ten good men? And God relents: "For the sake of ten I will not destroy it" *(Genesis 18:31 [NRSV])*. This is not the last time the Bible depicts God as being open to petition from human beings.

But the righteous were few in Sodom, as the terrible incident described in Genesis 19:1–11 confirms. Warned by the angelic visitors, Lot and his wife and two daughters fled the city. Told not to look back, Lot's wife could not resist one last backward glance, and she was transformed:

Then the Lord rained upon Sodom and Gomorrah brimstone and fire from the Lord out of heaven; And he overthrew those cities, and all the plain, and all the inhabitants of the cities, and that which grew on the ground. But his wife looked back from behind him, and she became a pillar of salt.

Genesis 19:24–26 [KJV]

INTO EVERYDAY *language*

Fire and brimstone (a word for sulfur, from "burning stone") have become traditional symbols of God's wrath. In common speech, the term can mean "hell" or simply "some dire consequence" meted out by an authority. For example: "When the disorderly students finally saw the principal, she was breathing fire and brimstone."

The Test

One of the more disturbing narratives in Genesis begins innocently enough. "Some time later, God put Abraham to the test" *(Genesis 22:1).* God asked Abraham to take his son Isaac to the land of Moriah and to sacrifice him to God. (That meant killing the boy.) With a very heavy heart, Abraham packed for the trip, took Isaac, and set out to obey God's command. In the end, a messenger stayed Abraham's hand, but the account is a chilling one indeed. (Read Genesis 22:1–19.)

■ What is your initial reaction to this story? What questions does the reading of the account provoke?

Two Views

Jews and Christians have traditionally framed this account differently in terms of its meaning and significance. While both views highlight Abraham's unquestioning faithfulness to God, the Jewish tradition stresses the test of Abraham's faith and the affirmation of God's mercy in releasing Abraham from the horror of human sacrifice. The Christian tradition sees in the willingness of Abraham to sacrifice his beloved son a foreshadowing of the sacrifice of Jesus by God, his Father. Where Christians refer to the "sacrifice of Isaac," Jews see this event as the "binding *(akedah,* in Hebrew) of Isaac." The account of the binding of Isaac is repeated in synagogues all around the world during Rosh Hashanah, the Jewish New Year, as a sign of the special covenant between God and the Jewish people. In the binding of Isaac, as elsewhere, the text of the Bible shows God asking hard things of people, who then do things they would not consider otherwise, trusting to God's commands and God's care.

American primitive artist John August Swanson drew on the bright colors of Bulgarian icons and the intricate decorative elements of Islamic art as influences for his panel *Abraham and Isaac,* depicting the binding of Isaac.

Father Abraham

The account of Abraham as the model of faith and the father of the chosen people is important to Jews and Christians alike. But Abraham is also venerated as a patriarch, or founding father, of another of the great world religions, Islam. The **Qur'an**, the scripture of Islam, refers many times to Abraham, repeating, enlarging upon, and even contradicting some of the details in Genesis. Muslims honor Abraham as the first **monotheist,** worshipper of the one true God they call Allah. Muslims consider themselves the descendants of Ishmael, the son Abraham had with Sarah's slave, Hagar. They prize the covenant God made with Hagar when she was abandoned in the wilderness:

> Come, lift up the boy and hold him by the hand, for I will make a great nation of him.
> *Genesis 21:18 [NJPS]*

This shared respect for Abraham makes the long-standing conflicts among Jews, Christians, and Muslims—from the medieval crusades to today's Middle Eastern clashes—surprising on one hand and understandable on the other. When Abraham's children dispute, the repercussions can be global.

A center of pilgrimage for Jews, Christians, and Muslims, the traditional burial site of Abraham and Sarah in Hebron has also been the site of violent clashes between modern-day Israelis and Palestinians.

projects

Choose one or more of the suggestions below and report on your findings:

1. In the library or on the Internet find examples of art, literature, or music inspired by the various incidents in the lives of Abraham and Sarah. Share your favorites.

2. Do more research on the binding of Isaac. Look for information on ancient sacrifices. Discuss what you discover.

3. Pore through the newspaper or a news magazine to find some story about human conflict. Then, draft a resolution in covenant language that you think would resolve the conflict. Share your draft.

KEY BIBLE TEXTS

■ Genesis 24; 25:19–34; 27–33; 35; 37; 39–50

DISCOVER

■ The rivalry between Esau and Jacob

■ The meaning of Jacob's dream and his wrestling match

■ How Joseph's dream affected Jacob and his other sons

GET TO KNOW

■ Isaac, Rebekah, Esau, Jacob (Israel), Laban, Leah, Rachel, Joseph and his siblings, Potiphar, Potiphar's wife

CONSIDER

■ Why are dreams (both waking and sleeping ones) important avenues for self-understanding?

Ancestors

The Genesis account of Abraham's family is filled with dramatic plot twists and surprise endings. A hero of faith dares to plead for God to be merciful. A good wife laughs at angels and reacts with all-too-human jealousy toward the concubine she herself has provided for her husband. The miraculous birth of a long-awaited son is followed by an apparent command to sacrifice that son.

As the focus of the narrative moves from Abraham and Sarah to their child and grandchildren, the twists and turns increase. The Genesis account of the lives of Isaac and Rebekah, Jacob and his wives, and Joseph and his brothers offer a gripping family saga full of love and envy, anger and reconciliation, deceit and integrity. Even if you recognize yourself nowhere else in the Bible, you will surely find some part of your life here.

In the midst of this dramatic whirlwind, the character of Isaac stands as a still point, a calm center. As in the account of the *akedah,* or binding, where he remained silent, Isaac's adult life was marked by submission to the will of God. Isaac missed his mother after her death, and he found in his wife, Rebekah, a love that helped him forget his grief. Isaac and Ishmael, separated as children, met briefly as adults to bury their father. But the focus of the Genesis narrative moves quickly to the twin sons of Isaac and Rebekah, whose sibling rivalry begins even before birth. Rebekah is told:

> Two nations are in your womb,
> Two separate peoples shall issue from your body;
> One people shall be mightier than the other,
> And the older shall serve the younger.

Genesis 25:23 [NJPS]

In José de Ribera's painting *Isaac Blesses Jacob*, Rebekah seems to be staring defiantly at the viewer, daring anyone to challenge her actions on her younger son's behalf.

■ How does Genesis describe the contrasts between Esau and Jacob, the twin sons of Isaac? (Read Genesis 25:27–28.)

Blessing and Deception

There is a hint of the contrast between the twins in the description of how Esau traded his **birthright** for a bowl of lentil stew *(Genesis 25:27–34)*. Esau, the outdoorsman, was active, physical, and impetuous. He was his father's favorite. Jacob, the shepherd, stayed closer to home and was his mother's favorite. Esau, the text of Genesis implies, got what he deserved for weighing momentary hunger pangs more heavily than his status as an elder son. Esau "despised his birthright." When an aged, dim-sighted Isaac decided to carry out the ceremonial blessing that would transfer the inheritance to Esau, Rebekah moved quickly to claim the blessing for Jacob through outright deception. Despite the deception, however, it was once again the younger man whom God marked for special destiny, foreshadowing the bitter family feud to come.

Both Esau and Isaac reacted to the deception in very human ways. Despite Isaac's deep sadness and Esau's heartfelt pleas, Isaac had given his blessing. He had to abide by his decision and bestow his blessing on Jacob. Esau plotted deadly revenge against Jacob. He hesitated only out of respect for his father. Rebekah sent Jacob to safety with her brother Laban, on the pretext of finding Jacob a wife from their own people—unlike Esau, who had grieved his parents by taking two wives from the local tribe, "daughters of Hittites."

The Dream

Genesis clearly affirms that Jacob's inheritance and blessing were part of God's plan. If this were an ancient Greek drama, for instance, the Furies, the personification of divine retribution, would have pursued Jacob for violating the family order. Instead of the horrific Furies, however, Jacob was visited by a dream of angels:

> And he dreamed, and behold a ladder set up on the earth, and the top of it reached to the heaven: and behold, the angels of God ascending and descending on it.
>
> *Genesis 28:12 [KJV]*

Waking from the dream, Jacob knew that he had been granted an unprecedented sign of divine favor. In an impulse common to people in all cultures, Jacob marked the occasion by setting up a memorial, a pillar fashioned from the stone that had served as his pillow. He anointed the altar with oil and gave the place a new name: *Bethel,* or "house of God."

This dream was the first of many that would play a significant role in the lives of Abraham's descendants. With a few great exceptions, the biblical narratives that follow rarely describe God speaking in the divine voice. Instead, the text more commonly shows God speaking through intermediaries: dreams, visions, angelic messengers, and selected human representatives.

INTO EVERYDAY *language*

An old English translation calls the red lentil stew for which Esau trades his birthright a *mess of pottage.* The phrase has come to mean anything of trivial or temporary value for which one trades away a lasting treasure—in short, "a bad deal."

Jacob's Song by Marc Chagall, a Russian-born artist noted for his dreamlike, fanciful imagery and brilliantly colored canvases.

In Paul Gauguin's *The Vision after the Sermon (Jacob Wrestling the Angel)*, a young woman of nineteenth-century Brittany envisions Jacob and the angel after hearing a particularly inspiring Sunday sermon on Genesis 32:23–32.

Marriage and Reunion

In the narrative of Jacob's marriages, the pattern of family trickery and deceit continues. Jacob was smitten when he saw his cousin Rachel bringing her flocks of sheep to the well. But even in the Bible, the course of true love seldom runs smooth. Perhaps it was poetic justice that Jacob, who impersonated his brother's appearance in order to win Isaac's blessing, was now tricked into marrying Rachel's older sister, Leah, even though it was Rachel he desired. The deceiver was deceived, and physical appearance was trumped by familial obligation.

The Wrestling Match

The account of Jacob is marked by family separation and family reunion. These turning points are paired with supernatural encounters, indicating that the narrative is dealing with something larger than one family's story. Jacob left home to avoid his brother's murderous revenge; on his way, he had a dream of heavenly messengers. When he dared to return home again, following God's command, Jacob had a more mysterious experience of the divine presence.

Jacob had sent his brother Esau a peace offering. He heard that Esau was coming, accompanied by 400 followers. Though Jacob had taken the precaution of sending gifts and soothing words to Esau, he was "greatly frightened." Had God led Jacob into a trap, calling him back to Hebron only to be destroyed by his own brother?

On the eve of his meeting with Esau, Jacob was attacked by a stranger and drawn into a fierce wrestling match, one that lasted the whole night and ended in a draw. The stranger dislocated Jacob's hip. But even in his pain and fear, Jacob would not loosen his hold on the stranger without receiving in return a blessing. Once again, Jacob turned adversity to his benefit. The stranger, who would not reveal his own name, gave Jacob the blessing in the form of a new name:

> **Your name shall no longer be Jacob, but Israel, for you have striven with beings divine and human, and have prevailed.**
> *Genesis 32:29 [NJPS]*

There are many ways to read the incident of Jacob's wrestling match with the stranger. Genesis is clear in presenting the encounter as a physical battle, not a dream or a vision. Jacob was physically injured. From the stranger's refusal to speak his name and his words about wrestling with the divine, tradition has understood Jacob's opponent to be an angel, a messenger of God. The blessing and the new name of **Israel** given to Jacob were signs of the renewal of God's covenant with the descendants of Abraham. Jacob's ability to hold his own that night foreshadowed that his meeting with Esau would not destroy him. On the purely human level, Jacob probably wrestled that night

Egypt looks more like Renaissance Italy in Bacchiacca's *Joseph Receives His Brothers on Their Second Visit to Egypt.*

with his own fear, guilt, and pride. And out of this experience came, on the human level, a moving scene of family reconciliation.

■ When Jacob and Esau met, what gesture of reconciliation did Jacob make? How did Esau respond? What words of Jacob showed how much this meeting meant to him? (Read Genesis 33:1–17.)

Joseph the Dreamer

The promise that Abraham and Sarah's descendants would outnumber the stars in the sky started to come true in their grandson Jacob, who fathered twelve sons and a daughter. Of all the family stories with which the Book of Genesis abounds, perhaps the most popular is the sprawling narrative of Jacob's son Joseph. It takes up more than a quarter of Genesis. The text features individuals with sharply defined personalities. The setting shifts between Joseph's homeland in Canaan and the unfamiliar land of Egypt. The plot includes family rivalry, deception, slavery, sexual seduction or rape, imprisonment, famine, the power of dreams, the miracle of forgiveness—and one particularly memorable article of clothing. It all began, like so many of the family stories in Genesis, with parental preference and sibling rivalry:

Velasquez's *Joseph's Bloody Coat Brought to Jacob* shows the deception of Jacob by his sons and echoes Jacob's deception of his own father, Isaac.

> Now Israel loved Joseph more than any other of his children, because he was the son of his old age; and he had made him a long robe with sleeves. But when his brothers saw that their father loved him more than all his brothers, they hated him, and could not speak peaceably to him.
>
> *Genesis 37:3-4 [NRSV]*

Joseph himself was a remarkable individual. His first voluntary action in the narrative, however, was not admirable. Joseph acted as an informer, a teenage tattletale. And to make matters worse, he received a great symbol of his father's favoritism—a fine garment. The gift is variously translated as "a coat with sleeves," "an ornamented tunic," or "a coat of many colors." Joseph also had an annoying tendency to share his dreams of personal grandeur. As a result, his brothers' anger and resentment seem natural enough. They did, however, take their reaction a bit far.

Once again, the youngest child has been marked to rule the elders. But by the midpoint of the story, Joseph has grown from an immature braggart to a fully rounded, sympathetic young man. By the end he will have become a compassionate savior full of mercy.

Other individuals also showed depth of character. There is the regret of Reuben and the grief of Jacob. There is the passion of Potiphar's wife. And finally there is the anxiety of the condemned prisoners. The account displays emotions that ring true even in today's world.

Structure and Meaning

Structure plays as important a role as characterization in the account of Joseph. The plot hinges on a series of repeating patterns. Three sets of dreams, each consisting of two dreams on the same theme, are key to this structure. Woven through the dream pattern are the alternating rise and fall and rise of Joseph. Learning to recognize this kind of structural pattern, which recurs throughout the Bible in various forms, will add to your understanding and appreciation of Biblical narratives.

IN YOUR *journal*

Joseph grew up in Canaan speaking one language and had to learn to live in a strange land with a different language and many different customs. What would it be like (or is it like) to be a person living in a country other than the one you knew as a child?

Unit Feature

Literary Views of Abraham and Isaac

The Abraham narrative has influenced modern Western thought through the works of two philosophers, one Christian and the other Jewish: Søren Kierkegaard and Martin Buber.

KIERKEGAARD

In his book *Fear and Trembling,* Kierkegaard (1813–1855), a Danish religious philosopher known as the father of existentialist philosophy, studies the nature of faith by interpreting Abraham's near sacrifice of Isaac. Kierkegaard was born in Copenhagen, Denmark, to Michael Pedersen Kierkegaard and his wife, Ane Sørendatter Lund.

Kierkegaard began a career as a writer; his works criticized the philosophy of Georg Wilhelm Friedrich Hegel (which was very influential in his day) and also the Danish Church (which Kierkegaard felt was not living or presenting an authentically Christian way of life). Kierkegaard's works incited much controversy, and a journal called *The Corsair* criticized him and poked fun at him so that he became a figure of ridicule. He died in 1855 at the age of 42.

Like many of Kierkegaard's other works, *Fear and Trembling* was written under a pseudonym. The name he used was Johannes de Silentio (John the Silent), and the basis of the discussion is the story of Abraham and Isaac from the Book of Genesis:

This undated drawing of Kierkegaard was done by his brother, Christopher.

> There was once a man; he had learned as a
> child that beautiful tale of how God tried
> Abraham, how he withstood the test, kept his
> faith and for the second time received a son
> against every expectation. What he yearned
> for was to accompany them on the three-day
> journey, when Abraham rode with grief before
> him and Isaac by his side. He wanted to be
> there at that moment when Abraham raised
> his eyes and saw in the distance the mountain
> of Moriah, the moment he left the asses
> behind and went on up the mountain alone
> with Isaac. For what occupied him was not the
> finely wrought fabric of imagination, but the
> shudder of thought.
>
> *Fear and Trembling*

This painting by Michelangelo Caravaggio is called *The Sacrifice of Isaac.* How does Caravaggio's depiction of Abraham correspond with Kierkegaard's description of him as a "knight of faith"?

Kierkegaard calls Abraham a "knight of faith." He is called upon to sacrifice his son, but not for a higher ethical purpose (the good of the people). Indeed, Isaac is the hope of the future, the seed of the people. Abraham's action can't be justified to others and appears absurd. Abraham had to make a "leap of faith" to something that was uncertain, hoping all the while that somehow he would receive Isaac back. "He who walks the narrow path of faith no one can advise, no one understand. Faith is a marvel, and yet no human being is excluded from it; for that in which all human life is united is passion, and faith is a passion" *(Fear and Trembling)*.

Martin Buber

MARTIN BUBER

Martin (whose Jewish name was Mordecai) Buber (1878–1965) was a German Jewish religious philosopher and a biblical translator and interpreter. His philosophy was centered on the encounter, or dialog, that people have with one another, and ultimately it pointed to a relationship with the divine. His most important work is the book *I and Thou.* He was born in Vienna, but when he was 3 years old, his mother left his father, and Martin went to live with his grandfather in what is now Lviv, Ukraine. His grandfather was a wealthy philanthropist who was a Hebrew scholar. Although Martin drifted from Judaism for a time, he returned to his roots. He fled the Nazi regime and went to live in Israel. His writings are intensely personal, and he teaches that it is by treating others as subjects—not objects—that people are truly human.

In his book *Images of Good and Evil,* Buber looks at the *akedah,* or binding of Isaac, in quite a different light than did Kierkegaard. He sees the journey up Mount Moriah as part of Abraham's overall journey to the land of promise. Abraham had, in Buber's view, made an idol of his long-awaited son. In binding Isaac he is beginning to get his priorities straight. Abraham's response to God's strange request was not so much a leap of faith as a step toward a true relationship with his son and with God. He could then be free to be himself and could be rid of the "dimness" that kept him from recognizing the goal of his journey. Once he related as a person, he could then become the parent of a great nation.

A POETIC VIEW

Wilfred Owen, a young poet, enlisted in the British army at the outbreak of World War I. The horrors of trench warfare moved Owen to write some of the most scathing condemnations of war ever composed. Owen saw war as a cruel tragedy in which the actions of elderly diplomats, generals, and government leaders result in the deaths of young soldiers. His poem "The Parable of the Old Man

This statue, entitled *Abraham and Isaac,* by George Segal, was commissioned as a memorial of the May 4, 1970, National Guard shooting of student demonstrators at Kent State University during a Vietnam War protest. Segal chose to deal with the topic metaphorically, using the biblical story of Abraham and Isaac. In preparation, Segal had read the works of Kierkegaard and Buber as well as the poem by Wilfred Owen. Kent State requested a more literal interpretation—a young woman placing a flower in the barrel of a militiaman's rifle. Segal refused. The statue is now on the campus of Princeton University.

and the Young" gives a darker, more cynical ending to the Genesis account of the binding of Isaac:

> So Abram rose, and clave the wood, and went,
> And took the fire with him, and a knife.
> And as they sojourned both of them together,
> Isaac the first-born spake and said, My Father,
> Behold the preparations, fire and iron,
> But where the lamb for this burnt offering?
> Then Abram bound the youth with belts and
>   straps,
> And builded parapets and trenches there,
> And stretched forth the knife to slay his son.
> When lo! an angel called him out of heaven,
> Saying, Lay not thy hand upon the lad,
> Neither do anything to him. Behold,
> A ram, caught in a thicket by its horns;
> Offer the Ram of Pride instead of him.
> But the old man would not so, but slew his
>   son,
> And half the seed of Europe, one by one.
> *The Collected Poems (1963)*

The narrative of Abraham and the sacrifice of Isaac is a powerful one, and it has been the source for poetry, drama, painting, and sculpture. It is a story that teaches much about the human journey no matter which interpretation you might favor.

UNIT FOUR

Exodus and the Land of Promise

Go and tell Pharaoh king of Egypt to let the Israelites go out of his land.

Exodus 6:11 [NRSV]

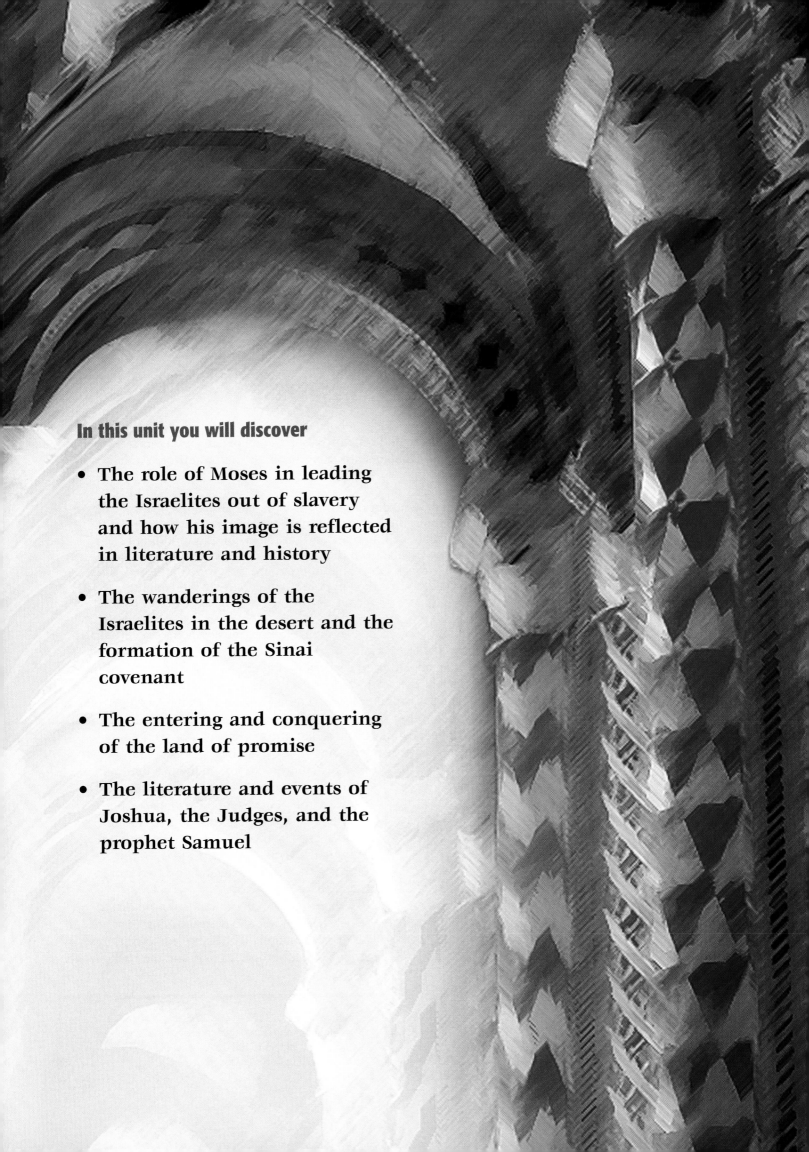

In this unit you will discover

- The role of Moses in leading
  the Israelites out of slavery
  and how his image is reflected
  in literature and history

- The wanderings of the
  Israelites in the desert and the
  formation of the Sinai
  covenant

- The entering and conquering
  of the land of promise

- The literature and events of
  Joshua, the Judges, and the
  prophet Samuel

KEY BIBLICAL TEXTS

■ Exodus 1:1—15:27

DISCOVER

■ The fate of Jacob's descendants in Egypt

■ The call of Moses to lead the Israelites out of Egypt

■ The events of the Book of Exodus commemorated in the Jewish festival of Passover

GET TO KNOW

■ Moses, Miriam, Aaron, Pharaoh, Jethro

CONSIDER

■ Why do accounts of a journey from bondage to freedom have such a strong appeal?

Out of Slavery

The Book of **Exodus** begins where Genesis left off, describing the changed conditions faced by Jacob's descendants in Egypt. These descendants are now known as the **Israelites.** Trouble is on the horizon:

> Now a new king arose over Egypt, who did not know Joseph. He said to his people, "Look, the Israelite people are more numerous and more powerful than we. Come, let us deal shrewdly with them, or they will increase and, in the event of war, join our enemies and fight against us and escape from the land." Therefore they set taskmasters over them to oppress them with forced labor. . . . But the more they were oppressed, the more they multiplied and spread, so that the Egyptians came to dread the Israelites.
>
> *Exodus 1:8–12 [NRSV]*

The great themes of Exodus—oppression, exile, liberation, and the journey home—reverberate among people throughout the world. Scholar Michael Walzer called Exodus a "classic narrative, with a beginning, a middle, and an end: problem, struggle, resolution—Egypt, the wilderness, the Promised Land." In contrast to many other ancient epics, which are mostly odysseys of adventure and return home, Exodus is a "march toward a goal, a moral progress, a transformation." In the Israelites' march, many have read a message of hope. As Walzer phrased it, "What is promised is radically different from what is: the end is nothing like the beginning. In the literature of the ancient world only the Aeneid resembles the Exodus in its narrative structure, describing a divinely guided and world-historical journey to something like the Promised Land." The journey from Egypt to Canaan is the journey from bondage to the Promised Land.

Moses and the Israelites' delivery from bondage has been retold and remembered not only by the Israelites' descendants in the Jewish faith but by people struggling for freedom in many times and places.

American revolutionaries saw America as "God's new Israel" and attacked King George III as a "British Pharaoh." The slaves and abolitionists of America before the Civil War and the millions who

Nicolas Poussin (1594–1665), perhaps the most influential French painter of the seventeenth century, gave great drama to the event in his *Pharaoh's Daughter Finds Baby Moses.*

suffered imprisonment, torture, and death under the rule of twentieth-century Nazi and Soviet regimes described their conditions in Exodus terms. The Mormons' trek across the country in search of religious freedom in Utah was couched in Exodus language. In more than one case, both sides of a conflict have seen themselves in the role of the Israelites. American writer and reporter Lincoln Steffens's 1926 defense of Leninist (Communist) politics was called "Moses in Red." In South Africa, for example, the Boer nationalists who fought British rule took inspiration from Exodus, which also inspired black nationalists fighting the apartheid regime of the Boers' successors.

Moses

Moses emerged as one of the Isrealites' greatest leaders and prophets. But he first appeared as a helpless baby under a ruler's death sentence to all male children. Pharaoh gave orders to the Egyptians: "Every boy that is born to the Hebrews you shall throw into the Nile."

To save him, Moses's mother placed the 3-month-old baby in a basket among the reeds of the river. His sister stood watch to see what would happen: Would Moses live or die? A daughter of the great Pharaoh drew Moses up from the river and took pity on him. Moses's alert sister, Miriam, immediately volunteered to get a Hebrew woman—Moses's own mother—to nurse the child. And so Moses, who would lead his people out of 400 years of slavery, began with the best of both worlds: his mother's loving care and a royal home. (Read Exodus 2:2–10.)

As a young man, although he had been raised as an Egyptian, Moses went out among his own people. He saw an Egyptian (perhaps an overseer) beating a Hebrew slave. Moses carefully looked around. Was he trying to be sure no one was watching, or was he hoping that some other Israelite would be brave enough to interfere? Seeing no one, he killed the Egyptian and hid the body. But the next day, when Moses tried to break up a fight between two Israelites, he was shocked to discover they already knew about the dead Egyptian. Who else would find out? Would he be punished?

In Domenico Fetti's *Moses and the Burning Bush*, the prophet is shown removing his sandals at God's command.

Fearing Pharaoh's wrath, Moses fled Egypt for the surrounding wilderness. Sitting by a well, Moses noticed that seven young women who turned out to be daughters of the priest of Midian (a man named Jethro) were being bullied by shepherds as the priest's daughters attempted to water their father's flock. Moses not only drove the bullies off, but (as the daughters reported to their father) he "even drew water for us and watered the flock." Jethro gave Moses a hero's reception and welcomed him into his family. He even offered him his daughter Zipporah in marriage. (Read Exodus 2:11–21.)

Moses went from being a prince of Egypt to herding the sheep of Midian. But according to Exodus, God had more strange turns in store for Moses.

The Burning Bush

Like Abraham before him, Moses received a call from God. Near Horeb, the "mountain of God," an angel appeared to him in a flame of fire: "the bush was blazing, yet it was not consumed." Amazed, Moses turned aside to investigate. And then it happened; God called to him by name: "Moses, Moses!" Moses responded, "Here I am." God instructed him to remove his sandals, out of respect for holy ground. And then God identified himself: "I am the God of your father, the God of Abraham, the God of Isaac, and the God of Jacob."

INTO EVERYDAY *language*

The word *exodus* is from the Greek and means literally "the road out." It is now used to describe any mass departure or emigration—from former slave Frederick Douglass's 1880 essay "The Negro Exodus from the Gulf States" to the latest news story about a "mass exodus" of refugees.

The land that was to be the destination for Moses and the Israelites was referred to as a *land of milk and honey*. That phrase is now a common term for any vision of Utopia or for any situation in which the living is easy. For example, "When Betty got the new job, she thought she was in the land of milk and honey."

THE BIBLE
IN **Literature**

One Jewish commentary on Exodus says that God chose to appear to Moses as a flame in a scrubby desert thorn bush "to teach you that no place on earth, even a thorn bush, is devoid of God's presence." Both the Jewish and the Christian traditions teach that while the world is not itself divine, it can be a vehicle for divine revelation. Literature in English, especially the poetry of the Romantic period, often explores the theme of encountering God in nature, as in these memorable lines from Elizabeth Barrett Browning's poem "Aurora Leigh":

> Earth's crammed with heaven,
> And every common bush afire with God,
> And only he who sees, takes off his shoes—
> The rest sit round it and pluck blackberries.

God said to Moses: "I have observed the misery of my people who are in Egypt. . . . Indeed, I know their sufferings, and have come to deliver them from the Egyptians, and to bring them up out of that land to a good and broad land, **a land flowing with milk and honey**" *(Exodus 3:1–8 [NRSV])*.

God then told Moses to speak God's truth to Pharaoh's power. This call made Moses one of the great **prophets** of the Hebrew Scriptures. The word *prophet* means "one who speaks for God." When Moses complained that he was such a poor speaker that he would be unable to persuade Pharaoh, God reassured him that "I have made you like God to Pharaoh, and your brother Aaron shall be your prophet" *(Exodus 7:1 [NRSV])*.

But why should the Israelites have accepted Moses as their leader? Moses asked for God's own name as proof to the Israelites that his mission had divine authority.

God's answer is still a deep mystery. The Jewish translation into English preserves the Hebrew wording for the name of God:

> Moses said to God, "When I come to the Israelites and say to them 'The God of your fathers has sent me to you,' and they ask me, 'What is His name?' what shall I say to them?" And God said to Moses, *"Ehyeh-Asher-Ehyeh."* He continued, "Thus shall you say to the Israelites, 'Ehyeh sent me to you.'" And God said further to Moses, "Thus shall you speak to the Israelites: The Lord, the God of your fathers, the God of Abraham, the God of Isaac, and the God of Jacob, has sent me to you:
> This shall be My name forever,
> This My appellation for all eternity.
> *Exodus 3:13–15 [NJPS]*

God's name is not a noun but a verb *(ehyeh)*: "I am that I am" or "I will be what I will be." What does that mean? One common interpretation is that humans cannot know the essence of God. Men and women understand God only by actions and attributes. Remember, Jewish tradition forbids speaking God's divine name, which is denoted in the Bible as YHVH.

Like Abraham, Moses tried to negotiate with God. He offered many reasons why he might not have been the best choice to approach Pharaoh on behalf of the oppressed Israelites.

CULTURAL
CONNECTIONS
American History

Songs known as Negro spirituals grew out of the experience of slaves in the American South. Meeting in small groups, often secretly, slaves set the Bible to music with such rhythms and emotional power that it has influenced every subsequent trend in American popular music, from folk to jazz to rock, from blues to country to hip-hop.

No biblical account had more impact on the development of African American Christianity than the Book of Exodus. The call-and-response song "Go Down, Moses" is one of the best-known Negro spirituals. Call-and-response is still a characteristic of African American worship. The refrain "Let My people go!" has moved generations of human rights activists.

When Israel was in Egypt's land
    ("Let My people go!")
Oppressed so hard they could not stand
    ("Let My people go!")
[Chorus] Go down, Moses, way down in Egypt's land
      Tell ol' Pharaoh to let my people go!

Thus saith the Lord, bold Moses said
    ("Let My people go!")
If not I'll smite your firstborn dead
    ("Let My people go!")
No more shall they in bondage toil
    ("Let My people go!")
Let them come out with Egypt's spoil
    ("Let My people go!")
We need not always weep and mourn
    ("Let My people go!")
And wear these slavery chains forlorn
    ("Let My people go!")
Your foes shall not forever stand
    ("Let My people go!")
You shall possess your own good land
    ("Let My people go!")
O let us all from bondage flee
    ("Let My people go!")
And soon may all the earth be free
    ("Let My people go!")

From Rise Up Singing: The Group Singing Songbook

Pharaoh's Hardened Heart

As the narrative progresses, God gave Moses various miraculous signs to persuade Pharaoh. But God warned Moses, "I will harden his heart, so that he will not let the people go." A hard-hearted man is one who does not allow his softer, warmer emotions to affect his actions; he is not open to compassion, love, or wonder.

Moses and Aaron obediently went to Pharaoh and gave him the Lord's message: "Let my people go." Pharaoh was dismissive: "Who is the Lord, that I should heed him and let Israel go? I do not know the Lord, and I will not let Israel go." (Read Exodus 4:21, 5:1–2.)

And so began the **ten plagues of Egypt:** rivers ran with blood, frogs infested the land, gnats swarmed over Egypt. At first the magicians of Pharaoh's court were able to match plague for plague. But according to Exodus, when all the dust of the earth was turned to gnats in the third plague, the magicians threw in the towel and told Pharaoh, "This is the finger of God!" *(Exodus 8:19 [NRSV]).* And the plagues continued; after the gnats, flies swarmed, a deadly disease struck the Egyptians' livestock, festering boils tortured people and animals alike, huge clumps of hail killed beasts and people, locusts devoured the crops the hail

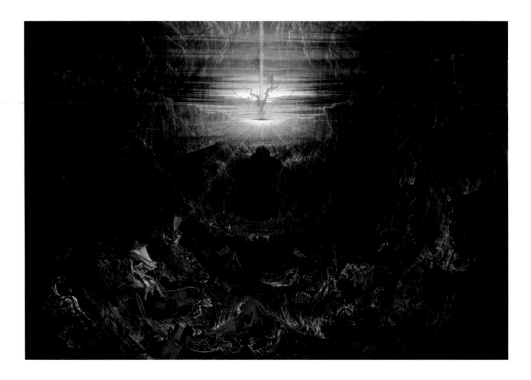

The Israelites, led by the pillar of fire, are safe in the distance from the looming waters in painter Samuel Colman's "The Delivery of Israel Out of Egypt."

Safe on the other side, the Israelites watched as the water returned and devoured Pharaoh's pursuing army. Then Moses and the Israelite men burst forth in a song of praise and thanksgiving:

> I will sing unto the Lord, for he hath triumphed gloriously: the horse and his rider hath he thrown into the sea. The Lord is my strength and song, and he is become my salvation.
>
> *Exodus 15:1 [KJV]*

Moses' sister, the prophet Miriam, picked up a tambourine and led all the women of Israel in a victory dance, also singing the refrain from what has come to be known as the "Song of the Sea." They celebrated God's defeat of the Egyptian military just when the people of Israel faced seemingly insurmountable odds.

The Israelites' unabashed joy that God destroyed Israel's enemies may sit uneasily on modern ears. But the God portrayed in the Hebrew Scriptures does not hesitate to take sides, condemning those who refuse to cooperate with God's plan. In the Jewish tradition, the Hebrew experience as slaves in Egypt forms the basis of a sense of justice that calls for special and merciful treatment of strangers, the poor, and the oppressed.

American artist Ben Shahn designed this **Haggadah** in memory of his father. The frontispiece, shown here, features a ceremonial lampstand, or *menorah*, the traditional symbol of Israel's role as a light to the nations. At the bottom of the page, in Hebrew, is the beginning of the traditional Passover prayer: "Blessed art thou, O Lord our God, who has created us, sustained us, and brought us to this day."

The Prophet Miriam

Moses' sister Miriam plays a very important part in the life of Moses and in the Exodus account. She is one of the very few women who are accorded the title *prophet*. She was with Moses from the beginning and, along with their older brother Aaron, she provided the complete description of just who Moses was and is. An enjoyable literary exercise is to read through the Exodus account, trying to see the events through Miriam's eyes.

Here are some statistics that reinforce the importance of Miriam:

- People mentioned by name in the
  Hebrew Bible   1,426
- The number of women named   111
- Women in Hebrew Bible who have the
  title prophet   5
- Women in the Christian Scriptures with
  the title prophet   1
- The female prophets by name and where
  they are given the title
  —Miriam (Exodus 15:20)
  —Deborah (Judges 4:4)
  —Huldah (2 Kings 22:13; 2 Chronicles 34:22)
  —Isaiah's wife (Isaiah 8:3)
  —Noadiah (Nehemiah 6:14)
  —Anna (Luke 2:36)

In this stained glass window by Sir Edward Burne-Jones, Miriam, the sister of Aaron and Moses, leads the Israelite women in a dance of victory after the escape from Egypt.

projects

Choose one of these projects:

1. Research, prepare, and present a report on the significance of Moses both as a biblical figure and as a symbol. Include information on historical figures who have been compared to Moses.

2. Develop a creative presentation of the themes of liberation and deliverance expressed in the Exodus narrative. Feel free to choose poetry, song, painting, dance, or a play as your medium. Make your creation as contemporary as you can.

3. Read the Song of Moses in Exodus 32:1–43. Write a report on what you read. Remember that this Moses who shows himself to be both a poet and a musician was self-described as slow of speech.

KEY BIBLE TEXTS

- Exodus 15:22–27; 16–20; 31:18; 32–34, 40; Leviticus 4, 11, 16, 19, 25; Numbers 11–14, 20:1–13; 22–24; 27:12–23; Deuteronomy 24, 28–34

DISCOVER

- How the Israelites experienced God's presence in the wilderness
- The Ten Commandments

- Why Moses did not enter the Promised Land
- The challenge Moses left the Israelites before his death

GET TO KNOW

- Moses, Aaron, Miriam

CONSIDER

- What would life be like without laws?

The Wilderness and the Law

Tradition makes Moses the author of the Torah, the Jewish term for the first five books of the Bible. These books, from Genesis through Deuteronomy, contain the narrative of the Israelites' origins and growth as a people, a narrative in which the law given on Mount Sinai plays a most significant role. To this day, the laws of the Sinai covenant are commonly referred to as **Mosaic Law,** after the great leader who communicated, interpreted, and disseminated them.

When the Book of Exodus picks up the account, the Israelites have every reason to celebrate. They have gained freedom from slavery in Egypt. They have left with the spoils of Egypt. They have God's promise of a land flowing with milk and honey. But how will this community manage itself without a common enemy?

Barely had the Israelites' wild chorus of triumph died away before the people began to grumble. Just three days into the wilderness they encountered the bitter waters of Mara and "the people murmured against Moses, saying, 'What shall we drink?'" According to Exodus, God told Moses to cast a tree into the water, which miraculously sweetened it. And then God "made for them a statute and an ordinance":

If you will listen carefully to the voice of the Lord your God, and do what is right in his sight, and give heed to his commandments and keep all his statutes, I will not bring upon you any of the diseases that I brought upon the Egyptians, for I am the Lord who heals you.

Exodus 15:26 [NRSV]

There is a pattern in this account that repeats itself time and again during the Israelites' wanderings. The people complain and rebel. Moses intercedes with God. God provides for the people's needs. God's help comes with strings

The heavenly bread falls like snowflakes in this illumination by an anonymous fifteenth-century painter known as the Master of Manna.

attached—commandments or laws that the Israelites must obey in order to keep faith. Then, the people promise to be faithful—until the next time!

Exodus 16 describes one of the most memorable examples of this pattern. Once again the people murmur against Moses and Aaron: "If only we had died by the hand of the Lord in the land of Egypt, when we sat by the fleshpots and ate our fill of bread; for you have brought us out into this wilderness to kill this whole assembly with hunger" *(Exodus 16:3 [NRSV]).*

Despite this rank ingratitude, God promises the Israelites to "rain bread from heaven for you." When the morning dew lifts, the people of Israel discover the ground is covered with a "fine flaky substance, as fine as frost on the ground" *(Exodus 16:4–15 [NRSV]).* Israelites call it **manna** (loosely, in Hebrew, "whatchamacallit"), and this bread from heaven will sustain them for the forty years in the wilderness necessary to shape these former slaves into God's people. But more than bread will be provided to the people of Israel. For, as the text of Deuteronomy later declares, "one does not live by bread alone, but by every word that comes from the mouth of the Lord" *(Deuteronomy 8:3 [NRSV]).*

African American artist Charles Rogers painted this striking portrait of a black Moses with the Law. The civil rights movement in the United States identified with Moses and the Exodus. The language and imagery of the movement was often couched in biblical terms.

Moses the Lawgiver

The portrait of Moses given in Exodus changes and deepens: from heroic liberator to political leader, wise judge, lawgiver, and prophet with the privilege of speaking with God "face to face," as no figure in the Hebrew Scriptures will ever again claim to have done.

The greatest event of the Israelites' wilderness journey is the encounter with God at **Mount Sinai** *(Exodus 19–34).* The idea of a covenant between God and people runs throughout the text of the Hebrew Scriptures. Recall that through Noah, God made a covenant with all humanity never again to destroy the whole Earth. God's covenant with Abraham included a promise to make a great nation out of his descendants. But a covenant as the organizing law of a society is, as scholar Michael Walzer puts it, "the political invention of the book of Exodus." Walzer notes, "There is no precedent for a treaty between God and an entire people or for a treaty whose conditions are literally the laws of morality."

In Exodus 19, God makes another covenant with the Israelites: "You have seen what I did to the Egyptians, and how I bore you on eagles' wings and brought you to myself. Now therefore, if you obey my voice and keep my covenant, you will be my treasured possession out of all the peoples. Indeed, the whole earth is mine, but you shall be for me a priestly kingdom and a holy nation." And the people of Israel replied, "Everything the Lord has spoken we will do" *(Exodus 19:4–8 [NRSV]).*

Amid trumpet blasts and violent quakes, God summoned Moses to the top of Mount Sinai to receive a new set of commandments. When he came down from the mountain, Moses was forever changed; the skin of his face glowed with rays of light so stunning that he thereafter had to wear a veil when speaking with humans.

The Ten Commandments

How could these wandering multitudes be brought together as a people? The people would need to know, clearly, what was expected of them as parties to the covenant. So, according to Exodus, God gave them the law, a code of

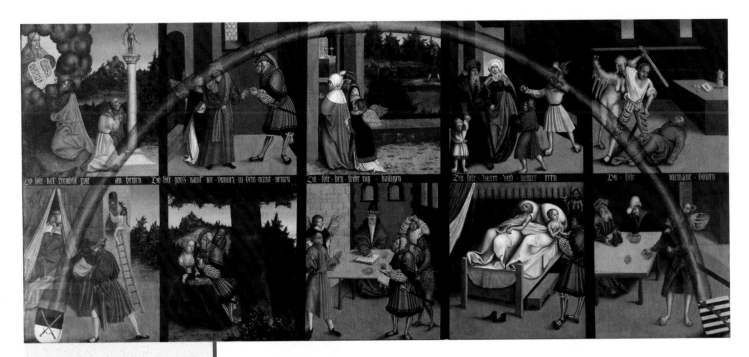

Lucas Cranach the Elder (1472–1553), a great German painter and a friend of Martin Luther, depicted the Lutheran numbering of the Ten Commandments in this panel entitled *The Ten Commandments*, painted for the City Hall in Wittenberg, Germany.

conduct that marked the Israelites as God's chosen people. (Jewish tradition asserts that on Sinai the people of Israel received not only the written law but also the equally authoritative oral law.)

Many of the hundreds of individual laws that were revealed at Mount Sinai and recorded in the Torah strengthened the Israelites' religious and national identity, setting them apart from the other peoples of their time. But the core expression of the law—which, according to Exodus, was brought down by Moses on stone tablets written by the finger of God—is the **Decalogue** (Greek for "ten words"), or the **Ten Commandments.**

The Ten Commandments are among the oldest codes established to regulate ethical behavior. They deal with the fundamental quandaries of human life. Although the commandments appear straightforward, their demands are often hard to fulfill:

> I am the Lord thy God, which have brought thee out of the land of Egypt, out of the house of bondage.
> Thou shalt have no other gods before me.
> Thou shalt not make unto thee any graven image, or any likeness of any thing that is in heaven above, or that is in the earth beneath, or that is in the water under the earth.
> Thou shalt not take the name of the Lord thy God in vain.
> Remember the sabbath day, to keep it holy. Six days shalt thou labour, and do thy work: But the seventh day is the sabbath of the Lord thy God: in it thou shalt not do any work.
> Honour thy father and thy mother.
> Thou shalt not kill.
> Thou shalt not commit adultery.
> Thou shalt not steal.
> Thou shalt not bear false witness against thy neighbour.
> Thou shalt not covet thy neighbor's house, thou shalt not covet thy neighbor's wife, nor his manservant, nor his maidservant, nor his ox, nor his ass, nor any thing that is thy neighbor's.
> *Exodus 20:2–17 [KJV]*

IN YOUR
journal

Moses is portrayed in Exodus as both a liberator and a lawgiver. Is there a contradiction between these two roles? How do laws such as the Ten Commandments restrict and how might they enhance liberty, especially when people live in groups? Use examples from Exodus to illustrate your argument.

There are differences in the way the commandments are numbered. In listings of the commandments, the Jews combine the first four items into three commandments, and divide the tenth item into two. The common numbering of the Roman Catholics follows the Jewish tradition. You will find it interesting to compare the version of the Ten Commandments as they appear in the Book of Exodus with the version found in the Book of Deuteronomy 5:6–21. What are the differences? Read also Deuteronomy 6:4–9. These words show an amazing attitude toward the law. They are also the words found in the little ornamental scroll called a *mezuzah* that Jewish people mount on their entryways even today.

The Ten Commandments are not the first law code in recorded history. They are, however, significantly different from other well-known ancient codes like the Babylonian Code of Hammurabi. The Ten Commandments are universal laws, not the case-by-case law of other codes. Unlike other codes, which issue from priestly or royal authority, the Decalogue is portrayed in Exodus as coming directly from God.

The Ten Commandments transcend the usual formula for judicial codes. They carry no degrees of seriousness of offense and no mitigating excuses. The Ten Commandments are also unusual among ancient codes in prohibiting the making of idols and "graven images," requiring a day of rest, and regulating attitudes (respect for parents, lack of covetousness) as well as actions. In laying out the responsibilities individuals have toward God and toward one another, the Ten Commandments offered a basis upon which ethical behavior would be judged in many nations for millennia to come. For Jews, they are considered the core of the much larger body of commands in the Torah. Christian tradition not only views the Ten Commandments as endorsed by Jesus *(Matthew 5:19, 19:18)* but as an expression of **natural law,** the basic moral truths that people of good will can recognize through reason and conscience.

American folk artist Erastus Salisbury Field captured the joy with which the Israelites carried the ark of the covenant with them in his painting *The Ark of the Covenant.*

Sacred Space: The Tabernacle

At God's command, according to Exodus, the stone tablets of the law were eventually placed in a richly decorated chest that has become famous in Western imagination as the **ark of the covenant.** The instructions for building the ark are given in some detail in Exodus 25:10–22. The ark was carried in procession while the people traveled, and when they rested it held the place of honor in the sacred space known as the **tabernacle,** another word for "tent," organized according to a hierarchy of holiness. In the innermost part of the tent, concealed by a veil or curtain, was the **holy of holies,** the resting place of the ark.

The Golden Calf

Moses lingered on the heights of Mount Sinai, and the people of Israel went to Aaron with a request: "Come, make gods for us, who shall go before us; as for this Moses, the man who brought us up out of the land of Egypt, we do not know what has become of him" *(Exodus 32:1 [NRSV]).* Aaron obligingly made "an image of a calf" out of golden jewelry. The people of Israel feasted and made sacrifices before the golden calf.

The incident with the golden calf is one more example of the pattern that runs throughout the Hebrew Scriptures:

Adoration of the Golden Calf by Nicolas Poussin

- God initiates a relationship with the people.
- The people vow faithfulness to the law and covenant.
- The people violate the terms of the covenant and the law, often giving excuses to justify themselves.
- God punishes or threatens to punish the people, usually by allowing them to suffer the consequences of their actions.
- A leader or representative intercedes for the people with God and calls the people to show signs of repentance.
- God relents, either withholding or tempering the punishment or delivering the people from their distress, often through miraculous means.
- God invites the people to renew the covenant and obey his commands.

Laws for Living

The rest of the Book of Exodus and the remaining three books of the Torah are devoted to further defining the full body of the law given on Sinai and recounting the events that occurred during the Israelites' forty years of wandering. The laws provided principles and practices that are a part of Judaism today. For example, five festivals established in Leviticus are still celebrated by Jews: **Rosh Hashanah,** the Jewish New Year *(Leviticus 23:23–25);* **Yom Kippur** or Day of Atonement *(Leviticus 16:17–30);* Passover *(Leviticus 23:5–8);* **Shavuot,** also known as the Feast of Weeks *(Leviticus 23:15–21);* and **Sukkoth,** a harvest festival also known as the Feast of Booths *(Leviticus 23:33–34).*

In the Jewish tradition, there are 613 commandments. The commandments cover all aspects of human life, including personal injury and warfare. They cover murder and its consequences as well as obligations toward vulnerable members of society. There are also ritual laws, dietary laws, and laws concerning sexual behavior, property, and the management of a household.

There are also laws offering protection to slaves, a legal practice unheard of in the ancient world. For example, every fifty years, slaves must be offered freedom: "And you shall hallow the fiftieth year and you shall proclaim liberty throughout

CULTURAL CONNECTIONS

usic

Arnold Schoenberg (1874–1951) wrote the words and the music for an opera based on Exodus. While the plot of *Moses und Aron* generally follows the biblical account, beginning with God's call to Moses in the burning bush, the opera ends with Moses left alone and dispirited after the episode of the golden calf. Schoenberg uses Moses and Aaron to symbolize differing views of God: In Schoenberg's depiction, Moses views God as an ineffable deity, almost an abstraction, while Aaron believes God is more tangible and more amenable to being swayed by human prayers and offerings. Aaron attempts to explain Moses' statements to the Israelites, but Moses often disputes Aaron's interpretation of his words. The two parts are even cast differently: Moses is a speaking role, whereas the role of Aaron is sung by a tenor.

the land to all its inhabitants" *(Leviticus 25:10)*. The idea of a **jubilee year** was imported into Christian tradition in the Middle Ages as a time of pilgrimage to Rome every fifty years for the remission of sins. The concept is often invoked today in calls for debt relief for poor nations. "Come the jubilee" became a rallying cry for slaves in the American South. The words of Leviticus 25:10 are inscribed as the motto on the Liberty Bell that was rung to celebrate the American Declaration of Independence in 1776.

Ancient Sacrifice

The notion of ritual sacrifice can seem very foreign. Many ancient cultures had a tradition of such sacrifice. Some of these sacrifices demanded the killing and burning of animals or of grain. Recall the ram Abraham sacrificed in place of Isaac or the lamb's blood that spared the Israelites from the tenth plague. The first intention of all sacrifice for the Israelites comes from the Hebrew word *korban,* meaning to "draw near." The purpose of sacrifice was to draw near to God. Animals or grain would be placed on an altar as an offering of praise, thanksgiving, or atonement. God deserved the best, and so the person making the sacrifice had to be willing to offer the first fruits of the land or a perfect animal from the flock. The portions set aside for God were often consumed by fire in a burnt offering. At times the community could share and eat the sacrifice.

Keeping Kosher

Leviticus lays out the rules of *kashrut,* or what modern Jews call "keeping kosher." The word *kosher* means "ritually acceptable." Ancient Hebrews divided the world into the holy, the ordinary, and the ritually impure. The dietary laws, like the other laws, help create an identity for the Israelites and move them nearer to holiness— nearer to God. Jews who keep kosher, for example, are forbidden to mix meat and dairy products. (There's no

This drawing of Moses by calligrapher Hillel Braverman is actually a micrograph—a picture composed of thousands of tiny words. The artist used every word of the Book of Deuteronomy, in Hebrew, to draw the image, which can be seen today in the Library of Congress.

INTO EVERYDAY *language*

The phrase *the fleshpots of Egypt* described the full stomachs the Israelites had while in Egypt. In today's language the phrase usually describes a longing for forbidden pleasures or luxuries that are long gone.

The *golden calf* that the Israelites cast as an idol has come down to everyday usage as the epitome of avarice or materialism.

A *scapegoat* is a person who is unjustly blamed for the sins or misfortunes of others. The phrase comes from the Torah. In Leviticus 16, Aaron is commanded to take two goats and throw dice to see which one will be sacrificed. The unlucky goat is to be slaughtered, but the other goat is to be set free to "bear on itself all their iniquities to a barren region, and the goat shall be set free in the wilderness" (*Leviticus 16:20–22*).

such thing as a kosher cheeseburger.) Many contemporary observant Jews use two different sets of plates and utensils—one for meat and the other for dairy. Some animals, such as shellfish, birds of prey, and pork, are forbidden as intrinsically impure. Other animals can be eaten if they are slaughtered correctly.

Doing Justice

In Jewish tradition, the 613 commandments, or *mitzvot,* include commands to protect the poor and the weak. Property owners were forbidden to reap every last bit of food from their lands. The wheat on the edge of the field or the grapes fallen in the vineyard were left "for the poor and the alien" *(Leviticus 19:10)*. Wages were to be paid promptly, and justice was to be delivered impartially: "you shall not be partial to the poor or defer to the great" *(Leviticus 19:15)*. Israelites were commanded not to punish children for the sins of parents, or vice versa *(Deuteronomy 24:16)*. This has become a bulwark principle of justice: only the individual who commits the crime can be punished by law, not (as in many ancient societies) his or her kin or tribe. And it is in Leviticus that the rule later singled out by Jesus of Nazareth as one of the two great commandments was first enunciated: "you shall love your neighbor as yourself" *(Leviticus 19:17)*.

There is a phrase in Exodus 21:24 that has often been misunderstood—"an eye for an eye, a tooth for a tooth." Rather than a declaration of retaliation and revenge, this measure originally meant quite the opposite. It is a call for justice and a command to limit retribution. Since at least Rabbinic times, Jews have interpreted this not literally but as a call for just financial compensation to victims for any wrong done, as some of the examples that follow this command suggest. For example, "If someone leaves a pit open . . . and an ox or donkey falls into it, the owner of the pit shall make restitution, giving money to its owner, but keeping the dead animal" *(Exodus 21:33)*. The law represents a humane restraint on the powers of the state, and it has contributed to the concept of *proportionality* that underlies most Western theories of justice.

Moses' Farewell Challenge

The Book of Deuteronomy, which closes the Pentateuch, is structured as a series of farewell sermons given by Moses to the people as they are about to enter the Promised Land. He put before them abundance on one hand and suffering and death on the other. Herein lies the heart of reaching the Promised Land. Moses knew that he must remind the Israelites, one last time, that their only hope would always lie in faithfulness to the God who made the promise:

> See, I set before you this day life and prosperity, death and adversity. For I command you today to love the Lord your God, to walk in His ways, and to keep His commandments, His laws, and His rules, that you may thrive and increase, and that the Lord your God may bless you in the land that you are about to enter and possess. But if your heart turns away and you give no heed, and are lured into the worship and service of other gods, I declare to you this day that you shall certainly perish; you shall not long endure on the soil that you are crossing the Jordan to enter and possess. I call heaven and earth to witness against you this day: I have put before you life and death, blessing and curse. Choose life.
>
> *Deuteronomy 30:15–19 [NJPS]*

In 1659, Rembrandt painted *Moses Smashing the Tables of the Law*. In the painting the artist captured the moment when Moses, disgusted by the Israelites' slide into idolatry, cast the tablets to the ground in a righteous rage.

Of the generation that left Egypt, only Joshua and Caleb, who were completely faithful to God, would cross the Jordan. Moses himself would not cross over into the Promised Land; he had disobeyed God by striking the rock to obtain water. (Read Numbers 20:7–12.)

The English novelist George Eliot, in her poem "The Death of Moses," put words in God's mouth. She summed up the profound significance of Moses's life not only for the Israelites, but also for the ages:

> He has no tomb.
> He dwells not with you dead, but lives
>   in Law.

projects

Choose one or more of the projects listed below. You might want to work in teams to complete the work.

1. Moses as lawgiver has had a profound influence down through history. Find at least three historical figures who have been influenced by Moses or who have been compared to Moses and write brief biographical sketches for each. In the sketch, stress the likeness to or the influence of Moses the lawgiver.

2. Investigate the concept of "natural law." How has this notion influenced civil disobedience or religious liberty?

3. In 2002, Chris Hedges of the *New York Times* wrote a series of ten articles acknowledging the significance and continuing impact of the Ten Commandments in contemporary American life. Research and find the series. Do a summary and a critique of his work.

KEY BIBLICAL TEXTS

- Joshua 1:1–6:27; Judges 2:8–19; 4:1–5:31; 6:1–8:35; 13:1–16:31; 1 Samuel 1:1–3:21; 4:1–22

DISCOVER

- The challenges of the Promised Land
- The leadership of Joshua

- Life among the Israelites during the time of the Judges
- The heroic qualities found in the leaders during the early years in Canaan

GET TO KNOW

- Joshua, Caleb, Rahab, Deborah, Jael, Gideon, Samson, Delilah, Jephthah, Hannah, Eli, Samuel

CONSIDER

- What is heroism?

The Promised Land
Joshua, Judges, and 1 Samuel

The Book of Joshua begins with the Israelites at a turning point. After forty years of wandering in the wilderness, the people have reached the banks of the Jordan River. On the other side lies Canaan, the "land flowing with milk and honey" that God promised to the children of Israel. The people's joy and anticipation are tempered, however, by the deep sense of loss they feel at the death of Moses, the great leader who brought their parents and grandparents out of slavery in Egypt.

One comfort is the fact that their new leader was chosen by God and comissioned by Moses himself. Joshua was known for his courage and his military prowess. An even more important characteristic, from the biblical standpoint, was Joshua's undivided faithfulness to the covenant. Moved by his example, the people renewed their own commitment on the banks of the Jordan. They promised to follow Joshua and asked just one thing of him: "Only be strong and resolute!" *(Joshua 1:18).*

Joshua's first move was to send scouts ahead into the nearest Canaanite settlement, the walled city of Jericho. There the spies encountered a woman named Rahab, the earliest example in literature of the prostitute with a heart of gold. She symbolizes the potential for moral good no matter what reputation or past deeds may indicate.

Rahab, like others in Jericho, had heard of the Israelites' deliverance from Egypt. Unlike

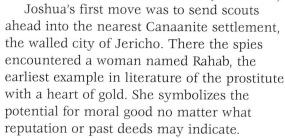

George Caleb Bingham's *Daniel Boone Escorting Settlers through the Cumberland Gap.* In the early years of the United States, settlers moving west identified with the Israelites crossing into the Promised Land. This painting was intended to call up biblical images of Joshua leading the Israelites across the Jordan.

the others, however, she had been converted by the news and vowed faithfulness to Israel's God. Rahab sheltered the Israelite spies in the inn she kept, hiding them under the sheaves of flax drying on the roof. In return, she received a pledge that she and her family would be spared during the siege of Jericho. She was to mark her house with a scarlet cord hung from the window.

On receiving the spies' report that "the Lord has delivered the whole land into our power," Joshua readied the people for the passage across the Jordan—a crossing reminiscent of the Israelites' crossing of the Red Sea. The Book of Joshua underlines the significance of the crossing by recounting a miracle associated with this passage:

> When the people set out from their encampment to cross the Jordan, the priests bearing the Ark of the Covenant were at the head of the people. Now the Jordan keeps flowing over its entire bed through the harvest season. But as soon as the bearers of the Ark reached the Jordan, and the feet of the priests bearing the Ark dipped into the water at its edge, the waters coming down from upstream piled up in a single heap a great way off. . . . The priests who bore the Ark of the Lord's Covenant stood on dry land in the middle of the Jordan, while all Israel crossed over on dry land, until the entire nation had finished crossing the Jordan.
>
> *Joshua 3:14–17 [NJPS]*

In this eighteenth-century woodcut illustrating a Jewish guide to the Holy Land, the artist has depicted the city of Jericho surrounded by seven walls.

God of Battles

In William Shakespeare's *Henry V,* the young king prays on the eve of the great battle between the English and the French at Agincourt. "O God of battles!" Shakespeare has his hero begin. When his captains seem daunted by the odds against them, Henry says, "We are in God's hands, brother, not in theirs." And when the bloody battle has ended in a victory by the greatly outnumbered English, Henry cautions his armies against taking the credit: "God fought for us."

The Book of Joshua is a book of battles, concerned as it is with the Israelites' struggle to enter a land already occupied by people who made their own claims to it. The Book of Joshua recounts one of the most famous victories celebrated in military lore: the Israelites' siege of Jericho, where "the walls came a-tumblin' down":

> The Lord said to Joshua, "See, I will deliver Jericho and her king and her warriors into your hands. Let all your troops march around the city and complete one circuit of the city. Do this six days, with seven priests carrying seven ram's horns preceding the Ark. On the seventh day, march around the city seven times, with the priests blowing the horns. And when a long blast is sounded on the horn . . . all the people shall give a mighty shout. Thereupon the city wall will collapse, and the people shall advance."
>
> *Joshua 6:2–5 [NJPS]*

The Book of Joshua is religious history, written from the Israelites' perspective. Had the people of Jericho written a history of this event, they might have had quite a different slant on what had happened—a slant that might even have claimed that they had been deserted by their gods.

The Book of Joshua gives God the credit for victory in battle but blames faithless humans for military defeat. Time and again, the Israelites learn that turning their backs on God and on the covenant will lead inevitably to loss and punishment—not at God's hands but at the hands of their enemies, not because God has deserted them but because they have deserted God.

THE BIBLE

AS **Literature**

Literary Structure of the Book of Judges

While this chapter focuses on the middle section of the Book of Judges, the entire book has a carefully formed structure. The main body of the book contains the accounts of the recurring cycles of apostasy (abandonment of one's religion or creeds), oppression, distress and deliverance.

There are typically five parts to this formula:

1. The Israelites do something offensive in the eyes of God.
2. God allows a foreign people to defeat and subjugate the Israelites.
3. Some time elapses and the Israelites cry out to God for help.
4. God then hears their cries and raises up a judge to deliver the people from the foreign oppressors.
5. Finally, the judge dies and the Israelites again commit apostasy, restarting the process.

The judges themselves provide a literary pattern. If you look at Gideon and his son Abimelech as the centerpieces, you see the stories positioned as mirror images:

A Ehud: Chapter 3.12–30, a lone hero from the tribe of Benjamin, who delivers Israel from oppression from the East

B Deborah: Chapters 4 and 5, a woman from one of the Joseph tribes that lived to the west of Jordan, who judges at a time when Israel is being overrun by a coalition of Canaanites

C Gideon: Chapters 6 through 8, the ideal judge

C′ Abimelech: Chapter 9, the opposite of what a judge should be

B′ Jephthah: Chapter 11 through 12:7, a man from the other tribe of Joseph, which lived east of the Jordan

A′ Samson: Chapters 13 through 16, a lone hero from the tribe of Dan who delivers Israel from oppression from the West

The Time of the Judges

The Book of Joshua comes to its conclusion long before the Israelites have established a successful presence in Canaan. The course of war has reflected the fluctuation in the people's resolve and commitment. When they were faithful, they succeeded. When they were unfaithful, they failed. As Joshua grew old and approached death, it was apparent that there was no charismatic figure to succeed him. Instead, authority would have to be shared among the leaders of the 12 tribes, who were ordered to secure the territories promised to them by God. Like Moses before him, Joshua rallied the people before his death. He recalled the great events of the Exodus and called the people to renew their commitment to the covenant.

> Choose this day whom you will serve, whether the gods your ancestors served in the region beyond the River or the gods of the Amorites in whose land you are living; but as for me and my household, we will serve the Lord.
>
> *Joshua 24:15 [NRSV]*

Joshua was right to be concerned. After his death, the central purpose and unity of the Israelites disintegrated rapidly into quarreling among the tribes. Left to their own devices, the people were more likely to choose the easy ways of their neighbors' gods and the comfort of assimilation over the strict ethical guidelines of the law, the hardships of battle, and the relative loneliness of being God's chosen ones. Life in the Promised Land grew to resemble life in the American "wild West"—lawless, violent, and dangerous. "In those days there was no king in Israel, and every man did that which was right in his own eyes" *(Judges 21:25)*.

Just as in the American West, the moral vacuum in which the Israelites found themselves gave rise, over the years, to legendary heroic figures. These were the men and women known as the biblical **judges.** The judges earned God's favor and the people's support by their outstanding personal character, and they provided brief interludes of peace in a time of anarchy. The judges (whose title should be understood more as "deliverers" than as legal authorities) were by no means perfect, but they exhibited particular **virtues,** or moral characteristics, that were prized in their time and situation.

Deborah

The first of the heroic figures introduced in the Book of Judges is notable for her gender as well as for her virtues. Deborah, whose name in Hebrew means "hornet" or "bee," was the only one of the biblical judges who actually served as a mediator of legal disputes. She held court under a palm tree on a main road. Deborah, like Moses' sister Miriam, was called a prophet—a sign that her wisdom was seen as divinely guided. But wisdom, though it is vitally important, was not Deborah's only virtue. She also demonstrated remarkable courage by going into battle at the head of the Israelite troops alongside their general, Barak. One of the Bible's most fascinating **canticles,** or songs, celebrates Deborah's role as the symbolic mother of her people:

> The inhabitants of the villages ceased, they ceased in Israel,
> until that I Deborah arose, that I arose a mother in Israel.
> *Judges 5:7 [KJV]*

The narrative of Deborah is associated with that of another, more morally ambiguous hero. To assist Barak and Deborah in their battle, a woman named Jael took it upon herself to lure the enemy general, Sisera—an ally of her husband—into her tent with the traditional nomadic offer of hospitality. When Sisera's guard was down, Jael killed him in a particularly gruesome way, by driving a tent peg into his skull. Although Jael, too, is celebrated as a hero in the canticle of Deborah, her action violated both the commandment against murder and the obligation of hospitality.

■ The narrative of Jael suggests that in certain extreme cases basic moral norms might be overridden. What might those cases entail? This is a very complex moral point that you might well enjoy debating.

Gideon

The forty years of peace that followed Deborah's victory ended when the Israelites once again were "offensive to the Lord." They had fallen under assault by the Midianites, who were stealing crops and ruining the land. An angel summoned a simple man named Gideon to come to the rescue. Gideon did not believe the angel was really from God, and so he put the angel to a series of tests. Finally, Gideon came to believe and went about blowing his trumpet to summon soldiers from all over the land to defend Israel.

Jael's vicious but liberating act was a popular subject for Renaissance painters, who saw it as a symbol of the rise of the individual against the tyranny of the feudal system. Pictured here is Jacopo Negretti's *The Death of Sisera.*

God did not want the might of all these soldiers to be a sign that they won a victory without God, so God instructed Gideon to send most of the army home. Gideon the nonsoldier went against the enemy with just 300 men.

Gideon won the battle by a bit of trickery. Three groups of one hundred soldiers each surrounded the Midianites' camp. They had torches hidden in jars and trumpets at the ready. When Gideon's group sent out a trumpet call, the soldiers broke their jars, blew their trumpets, and then shouted "For the Lord and for Gideon!" *(Judges 7:18).* The enemy fled in a panic. A judge who became heroic in spite of himself helped the Israelites win victory.

In *The Daughter of Jephthah,* the French painter Edgar Degas captures the moment when Jephthah comes to claim his daughter for the sacrifice.

Gideon was able to suspend his disbelief and the cynicism that was common in the land. He responded to God with willingness and humility.

Jephthah

After forty years of peace, the Israelites were in trouble again. This time, the judge who saved them hardly seems like the heroic type. Jephthah, the son of a prostitute, had been chosen to lead not because he was a good man but because he was a fierce fighter. In the war against the Ammonites, Jephthah wagered with God. In return for support, he promised to sacrifice the first living thing that greeted him when he arrived home. That turned out to be his daughter.

Commentaries disagree as to whether he actually had his daughter killed or committed her to God's service.

There is one darkly humorous incident on Jephthah's watch. Their fellow tribesmen, the Ephraimites, could not say certain words because of their accent, and so the accent could be used against them. Jephthah's men stopped all the deserting soldiers and asked them if they were Ephraimites. When they denied it, they were asked to say the word *shibboleth.* When they said "Sibboleth," they were killed at once—42,000 of them.

Jephthah at the very least showed a lack of faith in God's promises. His legacy was not one of peace like Gideon's but a legacy of strife:

> And the children of Israel did evil again in the sight of the Lord; and the Lord delivered them into the hands of the Philistines forty years.
>
> *Judges 13:1 [KJV]*

THE BIBLE

IN **Literature**

Hamlet and Jephthah

In Act 2, Scene 2 of *Hamlet,* Shakespeare compares Polonius to the Judge Jephthah. Polonius comes bustling in. Hamlet tells Rosencrantz and Guildenstern that Polonius is a "great baby," and tells them that he can tell, just from looking at Polonius, that he's come to announce the arrival of the players. Sure enough, that's what Polonius has on his mind, and Hamlet mocks him, although Polonius doesn't seem to notice until Hamlet suddenly calls him "Jephthah, judge of Israel." Hamlet's implication seems to be that Polonius, like Jephthah, has one daughter whom he claims to love "passing well," and that Polonius, again like Jephthah, sacrifices her for his own advantage.

HAMLET	O Jephthah, judge of Israel, what a treasure hadst thou!
LORD POLONIUS	What a treasure had he, my lord?
HAMLET	Why, 'One fair daughter and no more, The which he loved passing well.'
LORD POLONIUS	[Aside] Still on my daughter.
HAMLET	Am I not i' the right, old Jephthah?
LORD POLONIUS	If you call me Jephthah, my lord, I have a daughter that I love passing well.

HAMLET	Nay, that follows not.
LORD POLONIUS	What follows, then, my lord?
HAMLET	Why, 'As by lot, God wot,' and then, you know, 'It came to pass, as most like it was,'— the first row of the pious chanson will show you more; for look, where my abridgement comes.

Samson

Perhaps the most famous of the heroes to arise during the time of the judges was Samson. The biblical account of Samson's birth, life, and death epitomizes a hero narrative, common to many cultures. But although many of the elements of the account seem designed merely to entertain, this portion of the Book of Judges differs from heroic legends like those of the ancient Greek Hercules. The narrative of Samson carries a strong moral message about the responsibility of humans to control their own lives.

Samson's most notable characteristic was his physical strength, which the Bible tells us was rooted in his mother's vow to dedicate her unborn child to God's service as a **Nazirite,** a person set apart and bound by certain restrictions. It is easy to lose sight of the sacred dimension of Samson's power in the chronicle of his heroic deeds. There was something almost amoral about Samson. He was like a force of nature, forcing his way through human fortifications, the natural world, and the opposite sex with complete abandon and self-indulgence. He became Israel's hero because he was so like Israel in the days of the judges, full of potential but morally unconscious.

As in many ancient heroic legends, the secret to Samson's significance can be found wrapped in a riddle. After finding a honeycomb in the skull of the lion he had vanquished the year before, Samson entertained his father-in-law's household with this enigma:

> Out of the eater came something to eat,
> Out of the strong came something sweet.
>
> *Judges 14:14 [NJPS]*

Transformed by God's purposes, Samson's all-consuming self-indulgence would be turned into moral nourishment for the people, and the sweetness of deliverance would come from his strength, tempered in captivity.

Samson and Delilah

Like the heroes of classical Greece to whom he bears such a striking resemblance, Samson suffered a tragic fall. He became involved with a woman named Delilah, who was either herself a Philistine or a sympathizer with Israel's enemy. In return for a large amount of silver, Delilah agreed to discover the secret of Samson's strength in order to render him helpless.

Twice Delilah teased Samson to get an answer; twice he lied about the source of his strength; but the third time was the charm. Samson admitted that his strength came from God and was symbolized by the uncut hair of the Nazirite. This time, Delilah was successful in weakening the strong man. When she had his hair cut off, Samson could not shake off her hold and escape:

> Then [Delilah] said, "The Philistines are upon you, Samson!"
> When he awoke from his sleep, he thought, "I will go out as at
> other times, and shake myself free." But he did not know that the
> Lord had left him. So the Philistines seized him and gouged out
> his eyes. They brought him down to Gaza and bound him with
> bronze shackles; and he ground at the mill in the prison. But the
> hair of his head began to grow again after it had been shaved.
>
> *Judges 16:20–22 [NRSV]*

Samson's capture and his blinding by the Philistines are profoundly symbolic of the condition of the Israelites in the time of the judges. Taking God's presence and power for granted, the people had allowed themselves to be lulled into unconsciousness and lured by the temptations of strange gods. They were so blind that they were unaware that God's protecting presence had departed from them.

INTO EVERYDAY *language*

The word *shibboleth* is sometimes used to describe a code word that will distinguish spies or outsiders (who couldn't possibly know the code) from trusted insiders. In common language, the word has come to mean the jargon or clichés used by members of a group to help define their insider status.

Because the Philistine nation was described as crude and boorish, the word *philistine* has come into the language to describe an uncouth or uncultured person, perhaps one who is unappreciative or even destructive of artistic values.

The poet John Milton captured this spiritual blindness brilliantly in his dramatic poem *Samson Agonistes.* As the poem opens, the sightless hero is laboring at his millstone in Gaza. Milton, who lost his own sight before writing *Samson Agonistes,* turned the strong man's lament into a dirge for the loss of freedom and hope:

> O loss of sight, of thee I most complain!
> Blind among enemies, O worse than chains,
> Dungeon, or beggary, or decrepit age!
>
> In power of others, never in my own;
> Scarce half I seem to live, dead more then half.
> O dark, dark, dark, dark, dark, amid the blaze of noon,
> Irrecoverably dark, total eclipse
> Without all hope of day!

But in Milton's poem, as in the Book of Judges, Samson's blindness ironically grants him inner sight. Made a mockery in the temple of the Philistines' god, Samson calls upon God to grant just enough of his strength to return so he can take down the pillars of the temple, giving his own life in this final act of heroism. Depending on the viewpoint, Samson's final gesture can be seen as a heroic self-sacrifice or an act of revenge or suicidal terrorism.

Andrea Mantegna's *Samson and Delilah* differs from most representations of this scene in depicting Samson as a man of average proportions, looking exhausted, and Delilah as more a reluctant tool of Philistine patriotism than an evil seductress.

Samuel

The underlying message of the books of Joshua and Judges is that violence and warfare, however necessary they may appear to be to a people's survival and growth, come at a terrible cost. The thin line between the controlled mayhem of war and the chaos of anarchy is difficult to maintain, especially in

CULTURAL
CONNECTIONS

 usic

The Book of Judges has provided rich inspiration for composers of two forms of musical drama, the oratorio and its successor, the opera. As a form, the oratorio originated in seventeenth-century Italy. Philip Neri, a popular Catholic priest, drew crowds to the weekly musical entertainments he sponsored in the oratory, or chapel, of his parish church in Rome. These oratorios, as they came to be called, were two-act sung settings of biblical stories. The oratorio form later traveled to England, where it reached its peak in the works of George Friedrich Handel. *Messiah* is Handel's best-known oratorio, but he wrote many others, including works dramatizing the stories of Deborah, Jephthah, and Samson. Gradually, composers widened the oratorio form to include theatrical aspects of acting, costumes, and sets, giving rise to the opera. The French composer Camille Saint-Saëns originally intended his 1877 opera, *Samson*

et Dalila, to be an oratorio, and this popular vehicle for tenors like Placido Domingo (shown above in the role of Samson) retains many of the characteristics of the earlier form. Saint-Saëns's partner Ferdinand Lemaire, took liberties with the biblical text in his libretto, or script, for the opera, emphasizing the doomed love story of the central characters and the moral corruption of the Philistines.

the absence of a strong moral compass. The Israelites were without such moral guidance during the time of the judges, and life in the Promised Land was marred by horrific incidents of gang rape, tribal feuding, and mass murder.

This turmoil leads right into the First Book of Samuel. It is the story of yet another faithful family struggling with infertility. An Israelite woman named Hannah, shamed by barrenness and by the fertility of her husband's younger wife, dared to speak directly to God. She asked for a son and, in an act of startling selflessness, vowed to give the child into God's service. God granted Hannah's prayer, and she was true to her word:

> "It was this boy I prayed for, and the Lord has granted me what I asked of Him. I, in turn, hereby lend him to the Lord. For as long as he lives he is lent to the Lord."
>
> *1 Samuel 1:27-28 [NJPS]*

Hannah's son, Samuel, was chosen early in life to become Israel's moral compass.

While living at the tabernacle with the elderly high priest Eli, whose sons had corrupted their priestly inheritance, Samuel received a call from God. This was no longer the common event it had been in the time of the patriarchs and of Moses. "In those days the word of the Lord was rare; prophecy was not widespread" *(1 Samuel 3:1)*. Indeed, it took some time for the young Samuel and the aging Eli to interpret the event. But Samuel was immediately obedient:

> The Lord came, and stood there, and He called as before: "Samuel! Samuel!" And Samuel answered, "Speak, for Your servant is listening."
>
> *1 Samuel 3:10 [NJPS]*

After a long absence, the spirit of the Lord returned to Israel and rested on Samuel:

> And Samuel grew, and the Lord was with him, and did let none of his words fall to the ground. And all Israel from Dan even to Beersheba knew that Samuel was established to be a prophet of the Lord.
>
> *1 Samuel 3:19-20 [KJV]*

projects

Choose one or more of the projects below. Share the results with the class.

1. Develop a list of heroic character traits that are needed in today's society. Describe each trait and give examples from history or literature of characters that exhibit the trait.

2. Imagine you are commissioned to create an epic story that will give future generations a glimpse at your world today. What kind of story would you tell? How would you tell it?

3. Read the "Song of Hannah" *(1 Samuel 2:1-10)*. Compare and contrast it with the "Song of Moses" and the "Song of Miriam" found in Exodus 15.

Unit Feature
Exodus and Emancipation

The story of Exodus provided light for one of the darkest corners of American history—slavery. From the years when slaves were held captive in the South, through the time of abolition, and on to the ongoing struggle for civil rights, the Exodus story has provided inspiration, metaphor, and support to African Americans in their struggle for freedom. Just as the Hebrews who were slaves in Egypt escaped with God's help, and just as they eventually crossed the river Jordan into the Promised Land, so the African American slaves eventually were freed and have slowly struggled for civil rights.

Even though some Americans used the Bible to support slavery and segregation, the influence of the Book of Exodus on the struggle for emancipation and rights drowns out that use of the Bible. The echoes of the Exodus story can be heard in African American spirituals; abolitionist writings such as those the former slave Frederick Douglass; the life of Harriet Tubman, called "the Moses of her people"; and the speeches of Dr. Martin Luther King, Jr., who noted a parallel between his mission and that of Moses.

This painting illustrates the activities of the Underground Railroad. What conditions did the "conductors" of the Railroad work under?

Tell me where you're bound
Tell me where you're marching
"From Selma to Montgomery town"
www.negrospirituals.com/song.htm

SONGS OF FREEDOM

One of the indigenous art forms of America is the African American spiritual. "Spirituals" were songs originally composed by slaves who had become Christians. The songs incorporated elements from both African heritage and American folk music. The spirituals drew their themes from biblical sources, both the Hebrew Scriptures and the New Testament. The most common theme is the Exodus—from slavery in Egypt, to the escape through the Red Sea, through sojourn in the desert, and on into the Promised Land.

A few examples of spirituals that incorporated the Exodus story are "Go Down, Moses," "Didn't Old Pharaoh Get Lost?" "My Army Cross Over," "O the Dying Lamb," "Ride on Moses," and "Turn Back Pharaoh's Army."

Sometimes the words of traditional Negro spirituals were slightly changed and adapted to special events. For example, the words of "Joshua Fought the Battle of Jericho" were changed into "Marching 'round Selma."

Marching 'round Selma like Jericho,
Jericho, Jericho
Marching 'round Selma like Jericho
For segregation wall must fall
Look at people answering
To the Freedom Fighters call
Black, Brown and White American say
Segregation must fall.
Good evening freedom's fighters

THE MOSES OF HER PEOPLE

Harriet Tubman was a figure whose whole life and heroic actions evoke the Exodus story. Born into slavery, she married a free black, John Tubman, in 1844. When she learned she might be sold, she escaped to Philadelphia in 1849. After working and saving money for a year, she traveled to Maryland to lead her sister and her sister's two children to liberty as a conductor on the "Underground Railroad." This was the first of nineteen journeys she took to the South to free over 300 slaves. She was noted for her bravery and determination. For example, she carried a gun, and if slaves considered turning back, she would threaten them: "You'll be free or die." Her work was admired by fellow abolitionists such as John Brown, who called her "General Tubman," and Frederick Douglass, who said of her, "Excepting John Brown—of sacred memory—I know of no one who has willingly encountered more perils and hardships to serve our enslaved people than [Harriet Tubman]."

During the Civil War, she served the Union Army as a cook, nurse, scout, and spy. After the war, she founded a home for elderly poor blacks, and she died in 1913. Because of her work with the Underground Railroad, she came to be called "Moses."

www.pbs.org

SLAVE, ABOLITIONIST, PUBLIC SERVANT

Frederick Douglass was one of the greatest human rights advocates of nineteenth-century America. Born to a slave mother and a white father, Douglass was raised by his grandmother on a plantation in Maryland. When he was 8 years old, he was sent to Baltimore to be a house servant; and, when he told the lady of the house that he would like to be able to read the Bible, she taught him to read. In 1838, after serving in several jobs as a slave, he escaped to the North and became involved with the abolitionist movement.

Douglass wrote an autobiography about his life as a slave that has become a classic of American literature. After a speaking tour in Europe, he purchased his freedom and began an abolitionist newspaper, *North Star.* During the Civil War, he served as an advisor to President Lincoln; and, after the war, he became a government official, serving, among other positions, as U.S. minister and consul general to Haiti.

In his writings and speeches, Douglass demonstrated anger against those Americans who professed Christianity and allegiance to the Bible, yet perpetuated the institution of slavery. There are several specific references to Exodus in his writings. He criticized the use of terminology from Exodus by "Exodus movements" that proposed to move freed slaves out of the South to Africa:

It was contended that the Negro could never be free and flourish on American soil, that the Atlantic was his Red Sea, that Africa was his land of Canaan, the Colonization Society was his Moses, and that Divine Providence was leading him on to a land of safety. This African Exodus did much in its day to darken counsel, confuse the judgment, and benumb the national conscience, and make it regard the oppression and slavery of our country a necessary evil, inevitable, and beyond remedy.

Howard University Archives

This photo of Frederick Douglass was taken before the Civil War.

He likewise condemned the proposed Exodus movement to Kansas, saying about the freed slave:

He lines the sunny banks of the Mississippi, fluttering in rags and wretchedness, mournfully imploring hard-hearted steamboat captains to take him on board; while the friends of the emigration movement are diligently soliciting funds all over the North to help him away from his old home to the new Canaan of Kansas.

The Negro Exodus from the Gulf States

Douglas opposed this particular use of imagery from Exodus, as he felt that freed African Americans had a great deal to offer to the economy of the South and would be happier remaining there if they so chose.

However, Douglass applied imagery from Exodus in a positive way to describe the work of fellow abolitionist William Lloyd Garrison, with whom he worked for a time:

"You are the man—the Moses—raised up by God to deliver his modern Israel from bondage" was the spontaneous feeling of my heart, as I sat away back in the hall and listened to his mighty words; mighty in truth—mighty in their simple earnestness.

My Bondage and My Freedom

I SEE THE PROMISED LAND

A final example of a figure influenced deeply by the message of Exodus regarding slavery is Dr. Martin Luther King, Jr., the emblem of the civil rights movement of the 1960s. His last speech, given on the evening before he was assassinated, was entitled "I See the Promised Land." King mentions the Exodus story several times in this speech, referring to Pharaoh and the slaves. At the conclusion, he draws a parallel between the situation of Moses, who died before entering the Promised Land, and his own situation regarding the Civil Rights Movement:

Like anybody, I would like to live a long life—longevity has its place. But I am not concerned about that now. I just want to do God's will. And He's allowed me to go up to the mountain. And I've looked over. And I've seen the Promised Land. I may not get there with you. But I want you to know tonight, that we, as a people will get to the Promised Land. And I'm happy tonight. I'm not worried about anything. I'm not fearing any man. Mine eyes have seen the glory of the coming of the Lord.

www.edchange.org

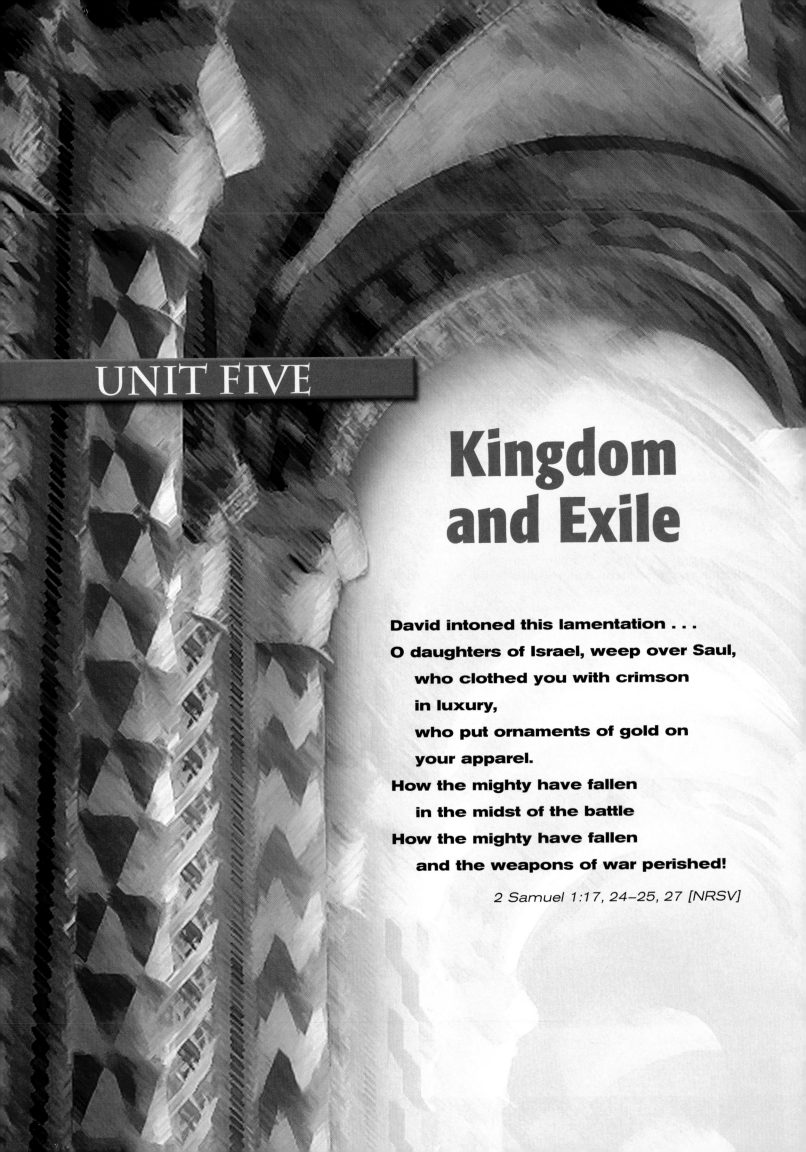

UNIT FIVE

Kingdom and Exile

David intoned this lamentation . . .

O daughters of Israel, weep over Saul,

who clothed you with crimson

in luxury,

who put ornaments of gold on

your apparel.

How the mighty have fallen

in the midst of the battle

How the mighty have fallen

and the weapons of war perished!

2 Samuel 1:17, 24–25, 27 [NRSV]

In this unit you will discover

- King David, one of the most influential figures in the Hebrew Scriptures

- The sagas and battles that formed the kingdom of Israel

- How that kingdom fell and its people were scattered in exile

KEY BIBLICAL TEXTS

■ 1 Samuel 1–4; 8:1–12:25; 15:1–16:23; 17:1–18:29; 19:1–24:22; 28:3–25; 31:1–13; 2 Samuel 1:1–27; 6:1–23; 11:2–12:24; 15:1–6; 18:1–19:8

DISCOVER

■ The Israelites' desire for a king and Samuel's attempt to talk them out of it

■ The rise and fall of Saul, Israel's first king

■ The reign of King David, a central character in the history of the chosen people

GET TO KNOW

■ Saul, Jesse, David, Goliath, the witch of Endor, Jonathan, Abigail, Michal, Uriah, Bathsheba, Absalom, Abishag

CONSIDER

■ What role do government leaders play in shaping the identity of a people?

David the King

The question of authority is central to all forms of government. Why should people accept someone else's decisions about matters that affect their lives? Why should anyone obey a policeman, a judge, or any other government official? And yet without authority of some kind, society can degenerate into chaos, "each doing what is right in his own eyes" *(Judges 17:6)* without regard for the rights and needs of others. The first and second Books of Samuel describe a set of wandering tribes, beset by hostile outsiders, struggling to become a nation. That nation must answer the question of who has authority to govern and why.

During the first centuries of their dwelling in the Promised Land, the Israelites had no centralized government. Authority rested in charismatic leaders such as the judges. As a judge, Samuel traveled across the land to settle controversies *(1 Samuel 7:15–16)*. Samuel was also a prophet who called the people of Israel to keep the laws of God and who rebuked and warned them when they failed. And Samuel was a priest who offered sacrifices to God on the people's behalf:

> So Samuel took a sucking lamb and offered it as a whole burnt offering to the Lord; Samuel cried out to the Lord for Israel, and the Lord answered him.
>
> *1 Samuel 7:9 [NRSV]*

"Give Us a King!"

People often seek a powerful central authority when they feel the need for protection from outside enemies. During the last part of the

In this illustration from the fifteenth-century Nuremberg Bible, Samuel anoints Saul with oil from a jar. In Biblical times, ointments made from olive oil mixed with sweet spices were used for healing wounds, strengthening the muscles of soldiers and athletes, and preserving the bodies of the dead. In addition to these natural associations, the anointing of a king symbolically conferred upon him divine approval and authority.

premonarchy period, the Israelites were under constant siege by the powerful Philistines, who were diverted only briefly by Samson's suicidal destruction of their temple. The low point came when a Philistine raiding party captured the ark of the covenant—the chief symbol of God's presence and of the people's identity. The daughter-in-law of Eli, the high priest, memorialized the grief of the Israelites by naming her son, born as the ark was carried away, Ichabod, a name meaning "glory is gone from Israel" *(1 Samuel 4:19–22 [NJPS]).*

The people turned to Samuel and begged him to find them an earthly king. According to the Bible, God told Samuel not to feel rejected by the people's request for a king. It was God's authority they were rejecting *(1 Samuel 8:7)*. That fact and Samuel's dire warnings about the consequences of monarchy seem to indicate that the request for a king was wrongheaded. And yet the monarchy took Israel to the next step in its development as a nation.

Reluctantly, God agreed to give the people a king and pointed out to Samuel a handsome young man from the tribe of Benjamin whose name was Saul. Samuel anointed Saul's head with oil, kissed him, and said to him:

In the painting *Saul and David,* attributed to Rembrandt, the young musician is a glowing figure in the lower right corner. Most of the painting is dominated by a thick, dark curtain, which the dejected king draws partly across his face.

> The Lord has anointed you ruler over his people Israel. You shall reign of the people of the Lord and you will save them from the hand of their enemies all around.
>
> *1 Samuel 10:1 [NRSV]*

Through Samuel, God gave Israel the government they wanted. Saul's reign began with several popular victories over the enemies of Israel. Very soon, however, it was apparent that the new king was a deeply troubled man. He was rash and impatient. He flew into jealous rages and sank into brooding depressions. He challenged Samuel's religious authority. He disobeyed Mosaic laws. He even plotted against his own family. Samuel's warning about the dangers of a monarchy began to ring true. Where would the people of Israel find a new (and improved) king?

David: Unlikely Hero

David was a shepherd boy, the youngest son of a man named Jesse whose flocks David tended. God sent Samuel secretly to anoint one of Jesse's sons as the new king-in-waiting. Seven brothers were presented to Samuel, but each was rejected, "for the Lord does not see as mortals see; they look on the outward appearance, but the Lord looks on the heart" *(1 Samuel 16:7 [NRSV]).*

Finally, Jesse called his son David in from the fields. To the amazement of Jesse's whole family (although not of the reader who is getting quite used to biblical surprises), Samuel anointed David as Israel's divinely chosen king.

The first meeting between Israel's first two kings came about because of the affliction of the one and the talent of the other. Saul had lost favor with God and was very depressed. His servants suggested that he might look for relief in someone skilled in music. David, known for his talent with a lyre, was called to play for Saul. Saul took a liking to the young man who would someday replace him as king and said to the boy's father, Jesse:

> "Let David remain in my service, for he has found favor in my sight." And whenever the evil spirit from God came upon Saul, David took the lyre and played it with his hand, and Saul would be relieved and feel better, and the evil spirit would depart from him.
>
> *1 Samuel 16:22–23 [NRSV]*

INTO EVERYDAY
language

A *Goliath* is a giant, a person or object of larger-than-average stature. A *David-and-Goliath situation* is one in which an underdog takes up the challenge of an opponent against all odds.

IN YOUR
journal

List the qualities that you think make a good friendship. How does the relationship between David and Jonathan meet (or fail to meet) your standards? Cite evidence from the text.

Goliath

Perhaps one of the best-known events in the life of David is his battle with the Philistine giant, Goliath of Gath. Goliath had taunted the Israelites to send out one man to take him on. Should that one champion defeat Goliath, the Philistines would cede victory to the Israelites. Of course, should that champion lose, the Philistines would crush the Israelites. Nobody accepted the challenge—nobody, that is, but David the son of Jesse.

David was delivering some cheese and grain to his brothers in Saul's army. He heard Goliath's taunting and volunteered to take on the giant. He refused Saul's armor, and chose some smooth stones for his sling. He announced his intentions to Goliath.

> You come to me with sword and spear and javelin; but I come to you in the name of the Lord of hosts, the God of the armies of Israel, whom you have defied.
>
> *1 Samuel 17:45 [NRSV]*

David killed Goliath with a well-aimed shot. He cut off Goliath's head with his own sword and took it to Jerusalem. This great plot has inspired writers, painters, sculptors, and poets from that time to this.

■ Read the whole account in 1 Samuel 17. Talk about what you read. What does it teach about decisions, about courage, about fighting against the odds?

A Memorable Friendship

David became a favorite of Saul's son Jonathan. The Bible describes their meeting in terms that make it clear that David and Jonathan were soul mates:

> When David had finished speaking to Saul, the soul of Jonathan was bound to the soul of David, and Jonathan loved him as his own soul.
>
> *1 Samuel 18:1 [NRSV]*

The bond between David and Jonathan was tested many times by the roles that the two played in carrying out God's plan for the Israelite monarchy. Jonathan made a covenant with David by giving to David his robe, his armor, his sword, his bow, and even his belt. This gesture symbolized Jonathan turning over his rights to the throne. Only this sworn friendship between Jonathan and David kept the murderous violence of Saul from bringing ruin to both families.

This illumination from the Nuremberg Bible (1483) shows both Saul's suicide and his beheading.

The American painter William Sidney Mount was inspired by theatrical staging in his composition of the encounter between Saul and Samuel's ghost. The witch, at left, is depicted, according to custom, as a woman with masculine features and the pointed nose and chin of a hag.

Despair and Death

In the end, boxed in by Philistine assaults, Saul chose a desperate strategy:

> "Seek out for me a woman who is a medium, so that I may go to her and inquire of her." His servants said to him, "There is a medium at Endor."
>
> *1 Samuel 28:7 [NRSV]*

This violated the very core of Israelite belief and Mosaic Law. Saul himself had only recently driven out of the country all those suspected of being mediums or wizards. He attempted to call up the spirit of Samuel, now dead, to plead for a return of the Lord's favor. The medium (in some translations she is referred to as the "witch of Endor") succeeded in reaching Samuel, but the prophet's message was one of inevitable doom. The First Book of Samuel ends with Saul surrounded by the bodies of his sons—including Jonathan—slain by the Philistine armies. And so, he took his own life to avoid capture.

As the Second Book of Samuel opens, David the shepherd boy has come to power as God intended, but not without paying a great price. Thousands of years later, David's song of mourning for Saul and Jonathan is still one of the most moving tributes ever offered:

> From the blood of the slain
>   from the fat of the mighty,
> the bow of Jonathan did not turn back,
> nor the sword of Saul return empty.
>
> Saul and Jonathan, beloved and lovely!
> In life and in death they were not divided;
> they were swifter than eagles,
>   they were stronger than lions.

INTO EVERYDAY *language*

Saul killed himself by falling on his sword. In contemporary language, *falling on one's sword* communicates how one person takes the full heat or the responsibility for an event or a consequence even though the fault could easily be spread around.

In this sixteenth-century Italian fresco, David dances wildly in front of the ark as an embarrassed Michal looks on from the palace window.

O daughters of Israel, weep over Saul,
who clothed you with crimson in luxury,
who put ornaments of gold on your apparel.

How the mighty have fallen
in the midst of battle!

How the mighty have fallen
and the weapons of war perished!
2 Samuel 1:22–25, 27 [NRSV]

A King and a Capital

Although anointed by Samuel, David did not assume the kingship of Israel at Saul's death. Saul's remaining heirs held tightly to their power. Meanwhile David went to Hebron, where he was anointed king over the territories of the tribe of Judah. After a number of costly battles, however, the people recognized that God's favor was with David, not with the house of Saul. And so, the Israelites eventually acclaimed him their king. David assumed the monarchy at age 30 and reigned for forty years.

One of David's first moves as monarch was to win himself a capital city—the hilltop fortification of Zion, in Jerusalem. David conquered the fortress and named it the City of David, a name Jews and Christians continue to use for Jerusalem to this day.

David's Wives

Like many other kings at that time, David had many wives and concubines. Among his wives were several remarkable women. One was Abigail, described as "a woman of good understanding, and of a beautiful countenance" *(1 Samuel 25:3 [KJV])*. When David first met Abigail, she was married to the miserly, evil Nabal. Nabal violated the laws of hospitality by denying food and shelter to David and his followers, who were on the run from Saul's army. (All in all, there were fourteen instances of David being on the run from Saul's army.) Abigail recognized the young man as Israel's future king and served him herself. After Nabal's death, Abigail married David and became one of his most trusted advisors *(1 Samuel 25)*.

Another of David's wives was Michal, the daughter of Saul. Saul had exacted a terrible dowry for Michal, asking David for the foreskins of one hundred Philistines. Of course, Saul was hoping that David himself would be killed. But David met the impossible demands. Michal, like her brother Jonathan, saved David from her father's wrath.

When David brought the ark of the covenant to Jerusalem he "danced before the Lord with all his might." Michal saw her royal husband dancing with the people and despised him: "Is this how a king acts?" Michal chastised David: "How the king of Israel honored himself today, uncovering himself today before the eyes of his servants' maids, as any vulgar fellow might shamelessly uncover himself!" David defended his celebration, reminding her that even the king is still a servant of God. "It was before the Lord, who chose me in place of your father and all his household, to appoint me as prince over Israel, the people of the Lord, that I have danced before the Lord. I will make myself yet more contemptible than this, and I will be abased in my own eyes; but by the maids of whom you have spoken, by them I shall be held in honor" *(2 Samuel 6:14–23 [NRSV])*.

Rembrandt's *Bathsheba* depicts the wife of the soldier Uriah in a moment of contemplation. Attended by her maid after the bath David has watched from his palace, Bathsheba holds the message David has sent inquiring about her.

Bathsheba

The narrative of David's adulterous passion for Bathsheba, the wife of Uriah, a brave soldier in David's army, is a cautionary tale of sin and repentance. The account is full of complex characterizations and rich with irony. King David, who had long desired Bathsheba, summoned her, "and she came to him and he lay with her." Afterward, she sent him a message: "I am pregnant" *(2 Samuel 11:3–5 NRSV])*.

What could King David do to protect the mother and child from the consequences of his actions? His adultery had left him with few or no honorable options. King David first resorted to trickery. He recalled Uriah from the field and told him to go and be with his wife. Then, David reasoned, Bathsheba could pretend that she was pregnant by her husband rather than by David. But even when drunk, Uriah followed the code of a good soldier and refused to go to his wife while his army was still in the field.

When that plan failed, King David sent Uriah back to the front with murderous orders: "Set Uriah in the forefront of the hardest fighting, and then draw back from him, so that he may be struck down and die" *(2 Samuel 11:15 [NRSV])*. This plan succeeded, and Bathsheba was now free. "When the mourning was over, David sent and brought her to his house, and she became his wife, and bore him a son" *(2 Samuel 11:27 [NRSV])*.

Within the account, and associated with it, are examples of two other important literary forms found in the Bible—the parable and the psalm. A **parable** is a very short story that conveys a moral or spiritual point. The prophet Nathan, successor to Samuel, confronted David with his sin by telling the king this parable:

> There were two men in a certain city, the one rich and the
> other poor. The rich man had very many flocks and herds; but
> the poor man had nothing but one little ewe lamb, which he
> had bought. He brought it up, and it grew up with him and
> with his children; it used to eat of his meager fare, and drink

This illumination from the Shah Abbas Bible shows scenes from the life of David's son Absalom.

from his cup, and lie in his bosom, and it was like a daughter to him. Now there came a traveler to the rich man, and he was loath to take one of his own flock or herd to prepare for the wayfarer who had come to him, but he took the poor man's lamb and prepared that for the guest who had come to him.

2 Samuel 12:1–4 [NRSV]

David was caught in Nathan's clever trap. He was so moved by the story that he cried out. "As the Lord lives, the man who has done this deserves to die!" Nathan said to David:

You are the man! Thus says the Lord, the God of Israel: I anointed you king over Israel, and I rescued you from the hand of Saul. I gave you your master's house, and your master's wives into your bosom, and gave you the house of Israel and of Judah. And if that had been too little, I would have added as much more.

2 Samuel 12:7–8 [NRSV]

■ Read all of 2 Samuel 12. What were the consequences of King David's adultery?

The other literary form associated with this account, the **psalm,** is a poetic prayer set to music. David, the skilled musician, is credited with composing many of the psalms collected in the Book of Psalms. Psalm 51, a prayer of repentance, is traditionally attributed to David in his time of grief and fasting after the death of Bathsheba's first child.

■ Read Psalm 51. According to the text, what kind of sacrifice for sin was most acceptable to God? What must David understand in order to receive God's forgiveness?

Absalom

Relationships between kings and their children are often complex. Ordinary family rivalries become dynastic struggles that intensify when children of different mothers compete for the father's throne. David's relationships with his children were no exception. His eldest son and heir, Amnon, raped and traumatized Tamar, Absolom's half-sister. Absalom, David's second son, saw that David indulged Amnon and would not punish him, so Absalom had Amnon killed to avenge Tamar's honor. David blindly mourned Amnon and condemned Absalom, who had no choice but to go into exile. Father and son were temporarily reconciled and for a time maintained an icy politeness. But Absalom was both vain and ambitious, and it wasn't long before he let himself be persuaded to lead a populist rebellion against his father. Only in hindsight, after Absalom's death in battle, did David mourn the son he had turned into an enemy:

The king was deeply moved, and went up to the chamber over the gate, and wept; and as he went, he said, "O my son Absalom, my son, my son Absalom! Would I had died instead of you, O Absalom, my son, my son!"

2 Samuel 18:33 [NRSV]

A Legacy

At the end of his life, King David, an old man confined to bed and perpetually cold, saw his surviving sons wrangling for his kingdom. He acceded to the wishes of Bathsheba that her son, Solomon, be named his heir. David lives on in Jewish and Christian tradition as the greatest of Israel's kings. He is reminiscent of the flawed hero found in almost all literature.

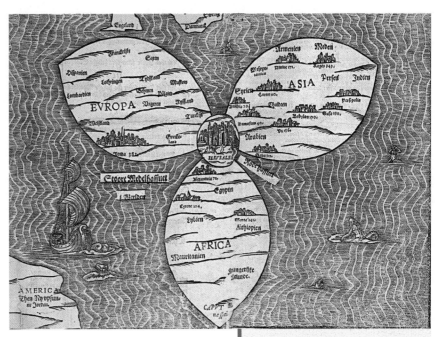

As this medieval map makes clear, Jerusalem has long been the religious center of the Western world.

The Hebrew prophets described the messiah, the anointed one promised by God, as the "Son of David." Later, the Christian Scriptures would afford that title to Jesus as he entered Jerusalem for the last time. (See Matthew 21:9.)

David's hold on the Western imagination lies both in his personal heroic charm and in his wholehearted commitment to the God who chose him. The difference between Saul and David is that David saw the error of his ways and repented. Although David was not permitted to build a temple for the Lord, he laid the foundations for Jerusalem, a city regarded as holy by three major faiths. And because David remained faithful to God, God remained faithful to him, never revoking the promise that out of David's line would come the eternal kingdom of God.

On his deathbed, David remembered this promise:

> Is not my House established before God?
> For He has granted me an eternal pact,
> Drawn up in full and secured.
> Will He not cause all my success
> And [my] every desire to blossom?

2 Samuel 23:5 [NJPS]

projects

Choose one of the projects listed below. You may want to work in teams to complete the project. Share the results with the rest of the class.

1. Prepare an art exhibit. Feature portrayals of King David in art and literature. Try to use both Jewish and Christian sources from various cultures.

2. The "Last Words of David" in 2 Samuel 23:1–7 have been given a wonderful musical setting by the composer Randall Thompson. Locate a recording of the work and listen to it with a small group. What does the music add to the text?

3. Read Deuteronomy 17:14–24. In this passage, God appears to tell about the coming of a king. Make a list of the qualities of a good king according to the passage. Report how David and Saul lived up to these qualities or failed to live up to them.

KEY BIBLICAL TEXTS

- 1 Kings 1:1–2:12; 3:3–28; 5:1–9:9; 10:1–13; 12:1–33; 16:29–19:21; 21:1–29; 2 Kings 2:1–25; 4:1–24; 5:1–27; 9:1–37; 17:7–23; 24:1–25:30

DISCOVER

- The reign of Solomon and his great gift
- The division of the kingdom and its collapse after the death of Solomon

- The role of Elijah and how he faced King Ahab and his queen, Jezebel
- The final fall of the kingdom

GET TO KNOW

- Solomon, the Queen of Sheba, Rehoboam, Jeroboam, Elijah, Jezebel, Ahab, Jehu, Elisha, Nebuchadnezzar

CONSIDER

- Why do governments rise and fall?

The Kingdom Falls

The reign of King David brought the combined kingdoms of Israel and Judah into statehood. The people were united under a human monarchy, and their allegiance to the covenant with God continued. The ark of the covenant, brought by David to Jerusalem, was still the heart of the people's identity. But with human rule came risks and challenges. Rather than relying on God's choice of a king, for example, the succession of power now depended on settling the claims of the dead monarch's contending heirs. With David this painful process began even before he died, as his son Adonijah overthrew his father's power. Only the pleas of Bathsheba on behalf of her son Solomon forestalled a civil war.

After Solomon was anointed David's heir, David called his son to his bedside and reminded Solomon of the covenant from which his power derived:

> I am about to go the way of all the earth. Be strong, be courageous, and keep the charge of the Lord your God, walking in his ways and keeping his statutes, his commandments, his ordinances, and his testimonies, as it is written in the law of Moses, so that you may prosper in all that you do and wherever you turn.
>
> *1 Kings 2:2–3 [NRSV]*

Solomon faced his new responsibilities in a time of turmoil and shifting alliances. In this confused time, according to 1 Kings, God appeared to Solomon in a dream and made an astonishing offer: Ask for anything, and it will be yours. Solomon requested wisdom.

The account of Solomon's judgment of the dispute between the two mothers is often depicted in art in palaces, courts, and other centers of authority, as with Raphael's version in the papal residence in Vatican City.

The Wisdom of Solomon

This gift of wisdom became Solomon's most memorable characteristic. Even today a person who makes wise decisions is called "like Solomon" or "a Solomon." The most convincing evidence of his wisdom is the way he handled the plight of two mothers, both claiming the same baby. Solomon declared he would cut the baby in half for the two women. The real mother pleaded for the life of the baby and conceded the child to the other woman. Solomon gave her the child. You can read the whole account of this wise decision in 1 Kings 3:16–28.

The House of the Lord

After the gift of wisdom, Solomon is best known for building the First Temple in Jerusalem. King David had wished to begin this task, but God cautioned that the time was not yet right. David was a man of war with blood on his hands. Under Solomon's rule, however, the kingdom was at first both peaceful and prosperous.

Wishing to complete his father's dream, Solomon sent word to Hiram, king of Tyre, who had supplied the materials for David's simple palace. With Hiram's assistance, Solomon began the work of building a magnificently elaborate dwelling place for the God's presence on earth. The finest materials were used for the temple and its furnishings. After many years, the costly project was completed, and Solomon presided over the dedication ceremonies. He declared:

> The Lord has chosen
> To abide in a thick cloud:
> I have now built for You
> A stately House,
> A place where You
> May dwell forever.

1 Kings 8:12–13 [NJPS]

This illustration of the temple in Jerusalem is taken from a color lithograph cover of an early twentieth century Haggadah (Passover narrative) from Hungary. The Hebrew text translates as, "Next year in Jerusalem," the final toast of the Passover feast.

CULTURAL
CONNECTIONS

*A*rchitecture

The construction of Solomon's Temple, as described in the Bible, inspired the designers of Gothic cathedrals and Renaissance basilicas. Bernini's *baldacchino,* or canopy, over the altar in Saint Peter's in Rome was inspired by the image of the great pillars of the temple.

Hiram was a bronze worker from Tyre. He is credited with fashioning the temple's two pillars. He became the patron of medieval guilds for stonemasons and master builders. They in turn were responsible for building most of the cathedrals in Europe. The masons and builders developed a complicated set of symbols that invested their work with mystical aspects. These symbols were incorporated into their work in wood, stone, and glass.

During the European Enlightenment, these symbols in turn were incorporated into the philosophy and practice of the Freemasons. Hiram's pillars, named Boaz ("strength") and Jachin ("stability"), appear frequently in Masonic imagery (as shown here on a Masonic apron).

The ark of the covenant was carried up to the temple in solemn procession and installed in the holy of holies. Sacrifices were offered. Solomon took a great risk in building the temple without the express command of the Lord, but his work was validated:

> The Lord appeared to Solomon a second time, as He had appeared to him at Gibeon. The Lord said to him, "I have heard the prayer and the supplication which you have offered to Me. I consecrate this House which you have built and I set My name there forever. My eyes and My heart shall ever be there."
>
> *1 Kings 9:2–3 [NJPS]*

For 400 years, until its destruction by the Babylonians, Solomon's Temple served as the center of Israelite public life and worship. Sacrifices and prayers were offered only there and nowhere else. The great annual feasts drew people from all over the united kingdoms to Jerusalem. With the temple, the Israelites had a house for their God that could compare with or even surpass the temples of their neighbors' gods. The ark of the covenant, the sign of Israel's special relationship with God, stood in splendor in the very midst of the nation.

■ What role did the temple play in the lives of the Israelites?

Solomon and Sheba

The First Book of Kings introduces one of the Bible's most compelling and mysterious characters:

> When the queen of Sheba heard of the fame of Solomon (fame due to the name of the Lord), she came to test him with hard questions.
>
> *1 Kings 10:1 [NRSV]*

Who was the Queen of Sheba, and why has she exercised such a powerful hold on the imaginations of artists and poets through the centuries? The First Book of Kings devotes only thirteen verses to the meeting between Solomon and the powerful woman who came to test his wisdom, but Jewish, Christian,

The view of the Queen of Sheba in an Ethiopian story panel.

and Islamic artists and storytellers have
embroidered and illustrated this account.
Tradition locates Sheba in sub-Saharan Africa,
specifically modern-day Ethiopia, and by
association connects the Queen of Sheba
with the "black and beautiful" beloved of
the biblical Song of Songs, a celebration of
the power of erotic passion traditionally
attributed to Solomon. This association has
helped cast the relationship of Solomon and
Sheba as a romance, although the account in
1 Kings gives no hint of such a liaison.

The place of the Queen of Sheba in Jewish
and Christian tradition is a factor not of her
glamour but of her thirst for true wisdom,
which is symbolic of the soul's thirst for God.
When Solomon gave the queen answers that
assured her of the authenticity of his wisdom,
she praised not only Solomon but also the
God of Israel, whose greatness was reflected in his gifts to the king. For her
ability to respond in faith, the Queen of Sheba takes her place among other
valiant, non-Israelite women who recognize Israel's God.

This rich and elaborate painting by Cornelis de Vos (1585–1651) associates Solomon's offerings to the idols with the excesses of a Renaissance court.

Unwise Choices

It would seem that Solomon, with his God-given wisdom and his devoted
building of the temple, would be just the ruler to inaugurate a long reign of
peace, unity, and prosperity for Israel. Unfortunately, however, Solomon did
not remain faithful to the covenant, as he had been advised to do by his father.
Like David before him, Solomon made unwise choices, carrying the acquisition
of wives and concubines to ridiculously excessive lengths. In his attempts to
secure alliances with neighboring nations, Solomon chose most of his wives
from outside Israel. This would not necessarily have been a problem, but
Solomon built temples where his wives and mistresses could worship their
gods and goddesses. Worse still, from the biblical standpoint, Solomon
abandoned the worship of Israel's God, turning away from the temple he built
in order to engage in the religious cults of other peoples:

> For when Solomon was old, his wives turned away his heart
> after other gods; and his heart was not true to the Lord his God,
> as was the heart of his father David.
>
> *1 Kings 11:4 [NRSV]*

The Kingdom Divided

Because of Solomon's religious infidelity, God told him that he had
forfeited his father's kingdom. For the sake of David, who had loved his
son, God allowed Solomon to retain power while he lived but foretold the
division and eventual destruction of the opulent state Solomon had built.

After Solomon's death, the people realized that all the warnings
Samuel had given them about kings were true. Solomon's glorious
building programs had been made possible only by forced labor and by
mortgaging the national treasury. When the people begged Solomon's
heir, Rehoboam, to treat them less harshly, he answered with all the
arrogance of a Pharaoh: "My father made your yoke heavy, but I will add
to your yoke; my father flogged you with whips, but I will flog you with

In *Elijah and the Ravens*, contemporary Chinese painter He Qi incorporates elements of Buddhist monasticism, including the traditional saffron robe, into his Cubist-inspired portrait of Elijah, the traditional founder of Western monastic practice.

scorpions" *(1 Kings 12:14 [NJPS]).* At this the ten tribes that made up the northern kingdom of Israel immediately seceded. They took Jeroboam as their king and left Rehoboam to be the scourge of the southern kingdom of Judah.

The fate of the divided kingdom for generations after the death of Solomon, as recounted in the biblical books of Kings and Chronicles, was an epic of bad government. The kings of Israel and Judah were, with rare exceptions, cruel, foolish, weak, and sinful. They exploited and abused the people from within and left them vulnerable to attacks from without.

Elijah

Hebrew Scriptures continually confirm God's providential care for the people. At a time when governmental ethics were at their lowest point, God sent the people a moral champion in the form of the great prophet Elijah the Tishbite. This rigorously righteous holy warrior took on the royal couple who epitomized all that was wrong with Israel in this dark time—the evil King Ahab and his Phoenician queen, Jezebel.

Ahab and Jezebel were flagrant murderers for gain. They had set up a man to be killed in order to inherit his property. Jezebel viewed the occasional Israelite prophets who dared to condemn Ahab's worship of her gods as just so many annoying flies to be swatted. In Elijah, however, she met her match.

According to Jewish tradition, the prophet Elijah lived in the northern kingdom in a cave on Mount Carmel where the present-day Israeli city of Haifa is located. The biblical accounts show how he tried to bring the nation back to righteousness by his preaching and by signs that were done in answer to his prayers.

CULTURAL
CONNECTIONS
*M*usic

Felix Mendelssohn (1809–1847), one of the nineteenth century's greatest musical composers, wrote and then conducted the premier performance of the oratorio *Elijah*. The *London Times* described the reception of the work: "Never was there a more complete triumph—never a more thorough and speedy recognition of a great work of art." In fact, in England only Handel's *Messiah* has remained as popular.

Elijah is a more traditional oratorio than *Messiah* in that it is a narrative of the events of the life of Elijah. It is interesting that Mendelssohn, a rather mild-mannered man, should choose as a subject the fiery prophet Elijah. Mendelssohn wrote a letter in 1836 to his collaborator on the libretto: "I imagined Elijah as a real prophet through and through, of the kind we could really do with today: Strong, zealous and yes, even bad-tempered, angry and brooding—in contrast to the riff-raff, whether of the court or of the people, and indeed at odds with almost the whole world—and yet borne aloft as if on angels' wings."

Queen Jezebel, a beautiful and yet immoral daughter of the Phoenician king, had brought likenesses of the idol Baal with her when she married King Ahab. She encouraged her husband to steal from the people to enrich their household. She sent her servants to kill Naboth so she could confiscate his vineyards.

The account says that God told Elijah to inform Ahab that there would be no more rain in the kingdom until Elijah called for rain. During the drought, God sent ravens to feed Elijah as he hid by a brook. When the brook dried up, he went to live with a poor widow and her son.

After three years without rain, Elijah arranged a showdown between himself and the prophets of Baal. In the showdown, 450 prophets of Baal put a sacrificial bull on an altar and prayed that their idol would consume the

Elijah by Peter Paul Rubens. Elijah's exit from earthly existence provides one of the Bible's most memorable images.

sacrifice with fire. They prayed for days and nothing happened. Elijah selected twelve stones to represent the twelve tribes of Israel and built an altar. He put a trench around the altar and filled it with water. He had water poured over the sacrificial bull.

At Elijah's prayer, fire came and consumed not only the sacrifice, but the altar and all the water as well. Elijah showed no mercy, and he had the prophets of Baal slain. And he foretold that Jezebel would receive terrible punishment for all her evil.

After Elijah had defeated the prophets of Baal, he was in fear for his very life and fled. He fell asleep under a broom tree and longed for death. On the strength of a cake and some water, he journeyed for forty days until he came to Horeb, the Mount of God. In the northern literature, Horeb was the mountain where Moses received the commandments (called Sinai in the southern literature).

According to the account, on that mountain Elijah received a message that echoes to this day:

> And, behold, the Lord passed by, and a great and strong wind rent the mountains, and brake in pieces the rocks before the Lord; but the Lord was not in the wind: and after the wind an earthquake; but the Lord was not in the earthquake: and after the earthquake a fire; but the Lord was not in the fire: and after the fire a still small voice.
>
> *1 Kings 19:11–12 [KJV]*

Elijah learned the lesson of Moses. He now understood that zeal and pyrotechnics were not enough to educate others. He needed patience and long-term commitment. The "still small voice" shows up time and again in literature as a true source of knowledge and understanding.

Elijah's ministry ended at the River Jordan, the symbolic boundary between slavery and freedom, life and death, earth and God's realm. According to the biblical account, Elijah was taken up in a fiery chariot. He handed on to his disciple Elisha his mission to keep Israel faithful.

Elijah holds an important place in modern Judaism. He is a symbolic guest at every bris, or circumcision. A space is reserved for him at every seder, or Passover meal. His return in the same chariot that took him away is a symbol of the hopes and longings of the Jewish people.

An anonymous English seventeenth-century needleworker telescoped time in her depiction of Jezebel's death and burial. The queen falls from the window toward her own head, hands, and feet, left by the hungry dogs.

INTO EVERYDAY language

Jezebel seduced Ahab away from his faith. She also exhibited quite a few quite nasty traits. In common language, a *jezebel* is an impudent, shameless, or morally unrestrained woman.

Jezebel's Fate

Queen Jezebel outlived both Ahab and Elijah, though she did not outlive the vengeance Elijah prophesied. An impetuous and violent royal steward, Jehu, known for driving his cart like a madman, killed Ahab's grandson and assumed the throne. Jezebel knew her days were numbered. She painted her eyes, dressed her hair, and looked out the window. When Jehu arrived at the palace, she was ready for him. She taunted him by addressing him as Zimri, a previous assassin—a kind of Israelite Benedict Arnold:

> As Jehu entered the gate, she called out, "Is all well, Zimri, murderer of your master?" He looked up toward the window and said, "Who is on my side, who?" And two or three eunuchs leaned out toward him. "Throw her down," he said. They threw her down; and her blood splattered on the wall and on the horses, and they trampled her. . . .
> So they went to bury her; but all they found of her were the skull, the feet, and the hands. They came back and reported to him; and he said, "It is just as the Lord spoke through His servant Elijah the Tishbite: The dogs shall devour the flesh of Jezebel in the field of Jezreel; and the carcass of Jezebel shall be like dung on the ground, in the field of Jezreel, so that none will be able to say: 'This was Jezebel.'"
>
> *2 Kings 9:31–33, 35–37 [NJPS]*

The Final Fall

The destruction of David's kingdom began with corruption from within and slowly slid into domination from without. Long before the events that would result in exile and captivity, the kings of Israel and Judah became mere puppets in charge of weak states doomed to pay tribute to the powerful empires of the Middle East. The long, slow slide finally culminated in destruction, as the people ignored the warnings of prophets and forgot the painful consequences of violating the covenant.

Israel, the northern kingdom, was the first to succumb. Weary of paying tribute to the Assyrians, the Israelite king Hoshea attempted a revolt. The uprising was crushed unmercifully; the northern kingdom of Israel was conquered, and many of its inhabitants were carried off into exile. These Israelites, the members of ten tribes (all but those of Judah and Benjamin and some members of the Levite tribe), never again emerged as identifiable peoples. They became assimilated into the cultures of their enforced or adopted new homes and are known today as the "lost tribes":

> The Lord rejected all the descendants of Israel; he punished them and gave them into the hand of plunderers, until he had banished them from his presence. When he had torn Israel from the house of David . . . Israel was exiled from their own land to Assyria until this day.
> *2 Kings 17:20–21, 23 [NRSV]*

Archaeological evidence of the dissolution of the biblical kingdoms is seen in a stone frieze found in present-day Iraq showing the Israelite King Jehu offering tribute to the Assyrian King Shalmaneser III.

Eventually it was the turn of the southern kingdom, Judah. The Babylonian emperor Nebuchadnezzar, famed for his cities of hanging gardens, wiped out Judean hopes of rebellion by invading and destroying Jerusalem. Solomon's great temple was looted of its treasures, including the ark, and burned to the ground. The people of Judah were carried off into captivity in Babylon. (Read 2 Kings 24:11–16.) There a small but enduring group kept alive the hope of return.

projects

Choose one of the projects below. You may want to work in small groups or with a partner. Be sure to report your results to the class.

1. Research some of the archeological explorations associated with Solomon's Temple, the Queen of Sheba, the Assyrian domination of Israel, or the Babylonian domination of Judah. Report on what you discover.

2. Obtain a CD of Mendelssohn's oratorio *Elijah.* Listen to it carefully. Most copies have translations you can follow. Write a review of your experience.

3. Immediately prior to the time Elijah was "caught up to heaven in the whirlwind," his younger understudy Elisha requested a double portion of Elijah's spirit *(2 Kings 2:9).* In a very interesting literary device, the Bible tells of fourteen wonders performed by Elijah and (to show the double portion of spirit) twenty-eight performed by Elisha. Try to locate all fourteen of Elijah's miracles and all twenty-eight of Elisha's. Make a chart of your findings.

Unit Feature
Exile and Return

In the Book of Deuteronomy, Moses gave a final speech before he anointed Joshua and went off to die. In that final speech Moses said:

> See, I have set before you today life and prosperity, death and adversity. If you obey the commandments of the Lord your God that I am commanding you today, by loving the Lord your God, walking in his ways and observing his commandments, decrees and ordinances, then you shall live and become numerous, and the Lord your God will bless you in the land that you are entering to possess. But if your heart turns away and you do not hear, but are led astray to bow down to other gods and serve them, I declare to you today that you shall perish; you shall not live long in the land that you are crossing the Jordan to enter and possess. I call heaven and earth to witness against you today that I have set before you life and death, blessings and curses. Choose life so that you and your descendants may live, loving the Lord your God, obeying him, and holding fast to him; for that means life to you and length of days, so that you may live in the land that the Lord swore to give to your ancestors, to Abraham, to Isaac, and to Jacob.

> *Deuteronomy 30:15–20 [NRSV]*

What does this all mean? There have been a number of passages in the Bible already, beginning in Genesis, where God has promised the land of Canaan to the people of Israel. Genesis reports that God said to Abraham "To your offspring, I will give this land . . . for all the land that you see I will give to you and to your offspring for ever. . . . And I will give to you, and to your offspring after you, the land where you are now an alien, all the land of Canaan, for a perpetual holding; and I will be their God" *(Genesis 12:7; 13:15; 17:8 [NRSV])*.

The northern and southern kingdoms fell, and the people of Israel lost their land. The First Temple was destroyed, and the people were scattered, with some even taken into captivity. What was next? Would there be a return to the land of promise?

THE FIRST RETURN

The prophets Jeremiah and Ezekiel had a message of hope for the people of Israel who were in captivity in the city of Babylon after the fall of Jerusalem and the fall of the southern kingdom. Jeremiah wrote from Jerusalem to the captives to urge them to

> Build houses and live in them; plant gardens and eat what they produce. Take wives and have sons and daughters; take wives for your sons, and give your daughters in marriage, that they may bear sons and daughters; multiply there, and do not decrease. But seek the welfare of the city where I have sent you into exile, and pray to the Lord on its behalf, for in its welfare you will find your welfare. . . . Only when Babylon's seventy years are completed will I visit you, and I will fulfill to you my promise and bring you back to this place. For surely I know the plans I have for you, says the Lord, plans for your welfare and not for harm, to give you a future with hope.

> *Jeremiah 29:5–7; 10–11 [NRSV]*

In approximately seventy years, Cyrus, the king of Persia, defeated the Babylonians. At that time, Cyrus allowed the people to return to Jerusalem, and they began to rebuild the temple that is now called the Second Temple. The return was not quite what was promised. The people who returned to the land were under foreign rulers—a condition that continued until the twentieth century. The destruction of the Second Temple and Jerusalem in the year 70 began a widespread scattering of Jews throughout the world. The term used for this scattering is the Greek word *Diaspora*. The Jews in the Diaspora continued to long for their promised homeland.

THE SECOND RETURN

Herein is a source of today's Middle East tensions. Without taking any sides in the issue, here are some of the facts to consider. The Jewish population of Palestine increased dramatically from the 25,000 Jewish inhabitants in 1800. Toward the end of World War II, it is estimated that there were 574,000 Muslims, 70,000 Christians (almost all Arab Christians), and almost 600,000 Jews. Today, Jews comprise 80.1 percent of the 5.8 million population of the area. Muslims, mostly Sunni, comprise 14.6 percent, while Christians comprise 2.1 percent and others 3.2 percent.

In 1948, Israel became an independent nation. The following events led up to the United Nations resolution that granted Israel statehood.

In 1917 Chaim Weizmann, a Jewish scientist, statesman, and Zionist, persuaded the British government to issue a statement favoring the establishment of a Jewish national home in Palestine. The statement, which became known as the Balfour Declaration, was, in part, payment to the Jews for their support of the British against the Turks during World War I. After the war, the League of Nations ratified the declaration and in 1922 appointed Britain to govern in Palestine. This came to be known as the Mandate Period.

The course of events caused Jews to be optimistic about the eventual establishment of a homeland. Their optimism inspired Jewish exiles to gather in Palestine. They came fleeing persecution by Arabs in the Middle East. They escaped Russian pogroms. They came from North Africa and Ethiopia. They emigrated from Germany when the Nazi persecutions began. And finally there came the survivors of the Holocaust. The arrival of many Jewish immigrants in the 1930s awakened Arab fears that Palestine would become a national homeland for Jews. By 1936 guerilla fighting had broken out between the Jews and Arabs. Unable to maintain peace, Britain issued a white paper in 1939 that restricted Jewish immigration into Palestine. The Jews, feeling betrayed, bitterly opposed the policy, and they looked to the United States for support.

Throughout the Roosevelt and Truman administrations, the U.S. Departments of War and State, recognizing the possibility of a Soviet–Arab connection and the potential Arab restriction of oil supplies to the United States, advised against American intervention on behalf of the Jews.

Britain and the United States, in a joint effort to examine the dilemma, established the "Anglo-American Committee of Inquiry." In April 1946, the committee submitted recommendations that neither Arabs nor Jews dominate Palestine. It concluded that attempts to establish nationhood or independence would result in civil strife; that a trusteeship agreement aimed at bringing Jews and Arabs together should be established by the United Nations; that full Jewish immigration be allowed into Palestine; and that two autonomous states be established with a strong central government to control Jerusalem, Bethlehem, and the Negev, the southernmost section of Palestine.

British, Arab, and Jewish reactions to the recommendations were not favorable. Jewish terrorism in Palestine antagonized the British, and by February 1947 Arab–Jewish communications had collapsed. Britain, anxious to rid itself of the problem, set the United Nations in motion, formally requesting on April 2, 1947, that the U.N. General Assembly set up the Special Committee on Palestine (UNSCOP). This committee recommended that the British mandate over Palestine be ended and that the territory be partitioned into two states. On November 29, 1947, the partition plan was passed in the U.N. General Assembly.

U.N. Resolution 181 defined the outline of a settlement in Palestine, creating both a Jewish and a Palestinian homeland. Unfortunately, the U.N. plan never went into effect. War broke out between the Arabs and the Jews living in Palestine, and Israel declared itself an independent nation in May 1948. Since then, there have been three more wars and continual hostilities, although some progress has been made toward peace.

EXODUS, THE NOVEL

In 1958 Leon Uris wrote a historical novel that soon outsold *Gone with the Wind.* His novel focused on the history of the Israeli people up to the founding of the state of Israel. The modern historical novel is a fairly recent invention that some scholars trace to the works of Sir Walter Scott (1771–1832). His stories about his native Scotland unleashed a passion for the form among readers and writers.

There had been a gulf between history and fiction that was thought to be unbridgeable. In his *Poetics,* Aristotle separated the two on the grounds that "historical events were unique and happened once and once only, whereas poetic events seemed to be eternally relevant, happening anew each time" (*The Literary Encyclopedia,* www.LitEncyc.com).

In *Exodus,* Uris melted away the gulf and created a story that conveyed both the uniqueness of the history and the timelessness of poetry. People who read his book had an emotional response to the plight of the exiles who sought to return to the land of promise, who struggled in fear, who suffered and died, but who dreamed of being home.

Uris described how the Holocaust affected the lives of his major characters who are concentration camp survivors. They fled from Europe and were held in a British detention camp on Cyprus waiting for permission to sail to British Palestine on a boat renamed *Exodus.*

Calling to mind the words of Moses to Pharaoh in the biblical exodus, the characters ask the British authorities to "let my people go." The novel aligns the biblical exodus with various historical episodes of anti-Semitism, the European persecution of the Jews, and the Nazi "final solution." The context and the result is the fight for freedom in a land of their own.

Each section of the novel is prefaced by a passage from Hebrew Scripture. The final scene depicts the celebration of the Jewish Passover—the cornerstone of the novel. Uris told the Associated Press in a 1988 interview that *Exodus* became the Bible of the Jewish dissident movement in the Soviet Union, where it was called simply "the book."

Leon Uris

United Artists made the book into a movie directed by Otto Preminger. Some of the leading actors of the day starred in the film— Paul Newman, Eva Marie Saint, Lee J. Cobb, Peter Lawford, and Sal Mineo. The *New York Times* rated the film "the blockbuster of 1960."

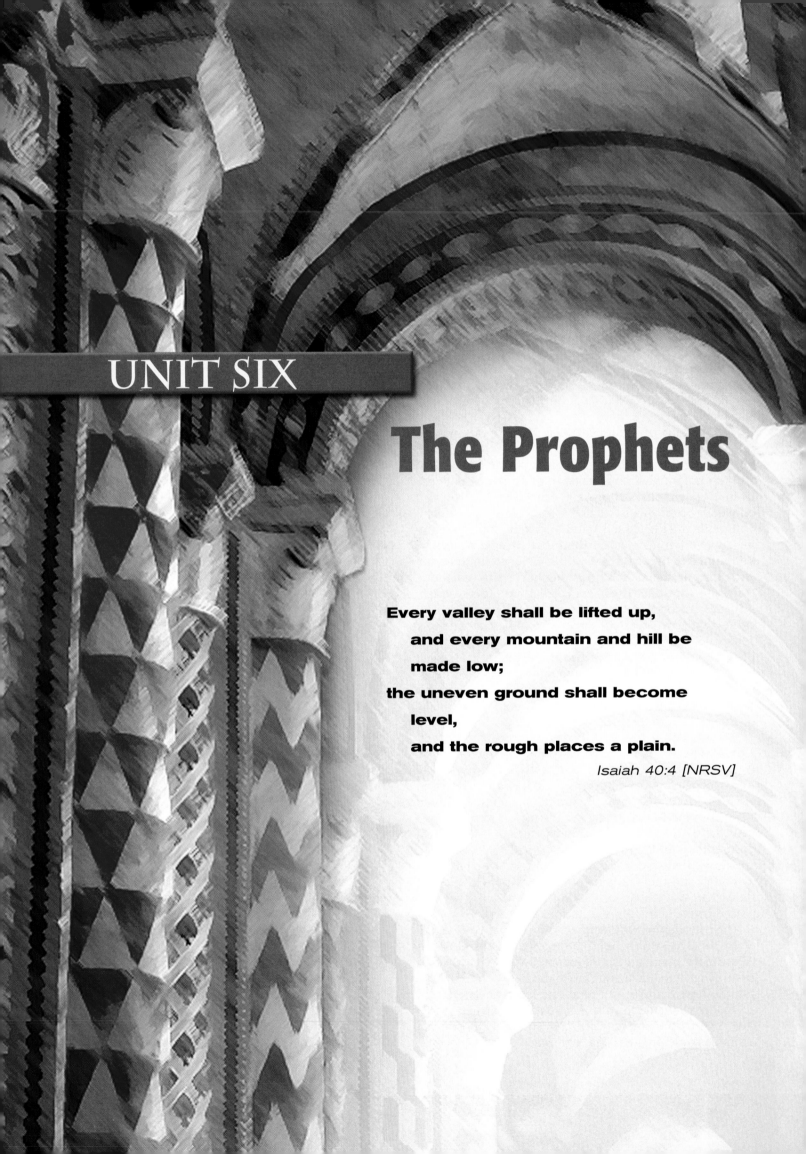

UNIT SIX

The Prophets

Every valley shall be lifted up,
    and every mountain and hill be
    made low;
the uneven ground shall become
    level,
    and the rough places a plain.

Isaiah 40:4 [NRSV]

In this unit you will discover

- That the literature of the prophets contains messages of universal challenge and comfort

- That the twelve minor prophets bore messages of social justice and reform

- That a recurring theme in prophetic literature is a thirst for justice

Isaiah was a member of a priestly family, married to a woman who was a prophet in her own right. Isaiah was already disturbed by the unfaithful and unjust actions of his countrymen when God called him in a stunning vision at the death of the popular King Uzziah:

> In the year that King Uzziah died, I saw the Lord sitting on a throne, high and lofty; and the hem of his robe filled the temple. **Seraphs** were in attendance above him; each had six wings: with two they covered their faces, and with two they covered their feet, and with two they flew. And one called to another and said:
>
> "Holy, holy, holy is the Lord of hosts;
> the whole earth is full of his glory."
>
> And I said: "Woe is me! I am lost, for I am a man of unclean lips, and I live among a people of unclean lips; yet my eyes have seen the King, the Lord of hosts!"
>
> Then one of the seraphs flew to me, holding a live coal that had been taken from the altar with a pair of tongs. The seraph touched my mouth with it and said: "Now that this has touched your lips, your guilt has departed and your sin is blotted out." Then I heard the voice of the Lord saying, "Whom shall I send, and who will go for us?" And I said, "Here am I; send me!"
>
> *Isaiah 6:1–3, 5–8 [NRSV]*

Isaiah began taking the people to task for their abandonment of their covenant with God. He issued a series of angry condemnations of the surrounding nations whose ways the Israelites have adopted and told them the inevitable consequences of Israel's infidelity—conquest and exile. Yet, at the heart of Isaiah's message are a deep and abiding optimism and hope. The prophet gave two of his children names symbolic of God's faithfulness—Immanuel ("God-with-us") and Shear-Jashub ("a remnant shall return"). Isaiah placed his trust in this "remnant," a small but powerful group of people who remained faithful. From them God would bring forth a messianic, eternal reign of peace and justice.

The Book of Isaiah contains some of the most optimistic and hopeful visions of the future to be found in all of literature. Faced with ample evidence of humanity's inhumanity, injustice, and violence, Isaiah granted his audience (and the countless generations to come) a vision of unshakeable peace:

> And he shall judge among the nations, and shall rebuke many people: and they shall beat their swords into plowshares, and their spears into pruning hooks: nation shall not lift up sword against nation, neither shall they learn war any more.
>
> *Isaiah 2:4 [KJV]*

These words are engraved on a stone façade known as the Isaiah Wall that faces the world headquarters of the United Nations in New York City, and both the monument and the words on it have traditionally provided a rallying point for peace activists of all faith traditions and political affiliations.

Isaiah may have been called, as he said, to bear God's message to "a people of unclean lips," but that message was overwhelmingly one of hope in the midst of the terrible consequences of the people's sins:

> Comfort, O comfort my people
>   says your God.
> Speak tenderly to Jerusalem,
>   and cry to her
> that she has served her term,
>   that her penalty is paid,
> that she has received from the Lord's hand
>   double for all her sins.
>
> *Isaiah 40:1–2 [NRSV]*

This bronze statue entitled *Let Us Beat Swords into Plowshares* was presented to the United Nations in 1959 by the country then known as the Soviet Union.

The Book of Isaiah contains memorable images of spousal and maternal love, the relationship between an artisan and his artwork, and the wonders of nature to assure the people that God has not forgotten them and that the time of brief suffering will lead to great and lasting joy.

■ **Find an example of one of these hopeful images used by Isaiah.**

But the future was not to be transformed solely out of God's providence, or generous care. The people had a responsibility, too. In line with the biblical role of the prophet as social critic, Isaiah reminded the people of their responsibilities under the covenant, which God had never dissolved. According to Isaiah, God was looking for a different kind of religious commitment in the glorious future to come. They were to live as a universal sign of justice and righteousness, a "light to the nations":

> No, this is the fast I desire:
> To unlock the fetters of wickedness,
> And untie the cords of the yoke
> To let the oppressed go free;
> To break off every yoke.
> It is to share your bread with the hungry,
> And to take the wretched poor into your home;
> When you see the naked, to clothe him,
> And not to ignore your own kin.
> Then shall your light burst through like the dawn.
> *Isaiah 58:6–8 [NJPS]*

American folk artist and Quaker preacher Edward Hicks painted more than one hundred variations of this painting, called *Peaceable Kingdom.* They all illustrate Isaiah 11:6–9. Many, like this one, include a background scene showing the negotiation of a peace treaty between William Penn and the Delaware peoples of the Pennsylvania colony.

One Vision—Differing Interpretations

The Book of Isaiah contains a group of passages that are clearly related in tone, message, and genre. The four passages, including a famous passage in Chapter 53, collectively are referred to as "The Suffering Servant Songs." Who is the suffering servant? First of all, on their own merit, the servant songs speak to anyone who endures suffering for the sake of others. For many Jews, however, the songs have deeper meaning. For them the suffering servant is the nation of Israel. Still other Jews read the songs as telling about Isaiah himself.

In general, Christians see in the servant songs a specific foreshadowing of Jesus and his sufferings. They see explicit parallels between these texts and events in the Gospels of the New Testament.

Jews often read the suffering servant as a portrait of Israel as a whole. Others, because the servant is depicted suffering for the sins of others rather than their own, view the servant as a portrayal of the "remnant" who remain faithful to God despite exile. Some Jews do see the suffering servant as a description of the Messiah (this interpretation figures in the sixth-century Babylonian Talmud, where the suffering servant is referred to as the "leper scholar," and also in the biblical commentary of the twelfth-century rabbi and philosopher Moses Maimonides), but others do not.

In either interpretation, the portrayal of the suffering servant invites reflection on the purpose of suffering, deepening the message of Genesis (suffering as the consequence of sin) and Job (suffering as a test of faith) with a new suggestion that suffering may purify a community.

THE BIBLE
IN Literature

PROPHECY AND POETRY

The prophets always wrote with a sense of urgency. Scolding and warnings, comfort and consolation, promise and fulfillment were conveyed as a matter of life and death. Sometimes, the only way to lift the writing above the daily grind was to use poetry. The language of poetry gave the prophetic message more power, more meaning, and more staying power. Messages meant for Israel at the moment became, through poetry, messages for the ages.

Look at a two-verse example from Isaiah. He was the master of the poetry of redemption. He took a single simple metaphor and in three lines gave an unforgettable message. The translator for these verses is Professor Robert Alter:

> As I pour water on parched ground, rivulets on dry land,
> I will pour my spirit on your seed, my blessing on your offspring
> And they will sprout from amidst the grass like willows by streams of water.

People living in the Middle East with the shocking contrast between desert and oasis were well aware what happened when water was poured on parched ground. A wasteland could be turned overnight into a flower-carpeted garden. And so the power of Isaiah's poetry is clear. And in the second line, God is doing the same with his spirit, or breath: pouring that blessing like water onto the seed, the offspring, of Israel. And in the last line, both bring forth a wonderful growth of grass.

This tiny bit of poetry shows a great deal of symmetry. It starts with water and ends with water, and in the middle there is a transition from physical water to the water of blessing.

Like the prophets themselves, their prophecies can have redemptive value and hope as the passage above does. Or their words can be used to give warning or reproof. In any case, the power of the prophetic poetry has been grabbing readers for thousands of years and wrapping them in timeless truth.

The Authorship of Isaiah

The question of who wrote the Book of Isaiah is a point where faith traditions diverge. Most Orthodox Jews and Evangelical Christians tend to look at the Book of Isaiah as a single book written by the Prophet Isaiah in the eighth century B.C.E. The argument for one book is based, among other things, on the unity of Isaiah in the usage of the word "The Holy One of Israel," a title for God that occurs twelve times in Chapters 1–39 and fourteen times in Chapters 40–66. Outside of Isaiah, it appears in Hebrew Scriptures only six times. Also, there are at least twenty-five Hebrew words or forms found in Isaiah that occur in no other prophetic writing [NIV Study Bible].

However, liberal Jews, mainline Protestant Christians, and Roman Catholics see the Book of Isaiah in three parts written by three different people at three different times. Chapters 1–39 are considered the original or First Isaiah and are dated at about 150 years before the exile. The writings contained in Isaiah 40–55 are thought to come from an unknown author who was one of the exiles living in Babylon about fifty years after the exile—almost two centuries after the First Isaiah.

Second Isaiah's writings expressed the hope and promise that the deliverance of the exiled people of Israel from Babylon was at hand. Second Isaiah expressed his prophetic calling through the mind and heart of a poet. He envisioned God's action on the basis of what he observed and probably expressed his searching awareness in writing more than in speech.

These faith traditions hold further that a third Isaiah wrote Chapters 56–66. This person is thought to be a disciple or disciples of the Second Isaiah who wrote the concluding chapters of the book some forty years after Second Isaiah.

Jeremiah

You've probably seen cartoon or movie depictions of the **prophet of doom,** a shaggy-bearded individual in ragged robes, ranting from a soapbox or wearing a sandwich board sign that reads, "The end is near!" These caricatures for the most part are based on the figure of Jeremiah, the original biblical prophet of doom. It was Jeremiah's destiny to be called to prophecy in a time of relative prosperity and peace for Judah just before the fall of Jerusalem and the destruction of the First Temple. It was a time when the people and their leaders were smugly comfortable in their mistreatment of the poor and their adoption of **pagan** religious practices.

Jeremiah, a young man at the time of his calling, probably had a sense of just how poorly a message of reform and a prediction of disaster would go over with such an audience when he tried politely to refuse his mission:

A fifteenth-century French painter depicted the prophet Jeremiah in a cardinal's robes. The shelf above the prophet contains symbolic objects mentioned in Jeremiah's oracles.

> Now the word of the Lord came to me saying,
>> "Before I formed you in the womb
>>> I knew you,
>> and before you were born
>>> I consecrated you;
>> I appointed you a prophet
>>> to the nations."
> Then I said, "Ah, Lord God! Truly I do not know how to speak, for I am only a boy." But the Lord said to me,
>> "Do not say, 'I am only a boy';
>> for you shall go to all
>>> to whom I send you,
>> and you shall speak whatever
>>> I command you.
>> Do not be afraid of them,
>> for I am with you to deliver you,
>>> says the Lord."
> Then the Lord put out his hand and touched my mouth; and the Lord said to me,
>> "Now I have put my words in your mouth.
>> See, today I appoint you over
>>> nations and over kingdoms,
>> to pluck up and to pull down,
>> to destroy and to overthrow,
>> to build and to plant."
>
> *Jeremiah 1:4–10 [NRSV]*

Giving in to the inevitable, Jeremiah used his formidable gifts of eloquence and imagery to sting the conscience of the people. God's words literally rolled from Jeremiah's mouth in a series of pointed attacks on idolatry and injustice, seasoned with terrible premonitions of devastation to come.

■ Find some of the symbols Jeremiah used to express his message of coming destruction.

INTO EVERYDAY *language*

A *jeremiad* is a rant—a mournful or fiercely critical speech, editorial, or other communication targeting social or political ills. The jeremiad set to a stirring rhythm is a common feature of Jamaican reggae music.

CHAPTER 13

KEY BIBLICAL TEXTS

- Hosea 1–11; Amos 5; Jonah; Micah; Haggai; Zechariah 7:1–8:23; Malachi

DISCOVER

- The message and method of some of the minor prophets
- The call to faithfulness of Hosea
- The journey of Jonah
- The struggles to call for justice and restoration of Amos and Micah
- The need for renewal in Israel

GET TO KNOW

- Hosea, Gomer, Jonah, Amos, Micah, Haggai, Zechariah, Malachi

CONSIDER

- What qualities mark a just society?

Called to Account

Major Messages from Minor Prophets

If you've ever played a computer game that lets you design a simulated society, you know what it's like to try to build a better world. Even without that kind of gaming experience, however, you have probably had occasion to notice an injustice or a social problem in the world around you. Maybe it made you angry. Maybe you wanted to draw other people's attention to what you saw. Maybe you were moved enough to try to make a difference. If so, you have something in common with the biblical prophets, especially those referred to as "the twelve" or the **"minor prophets."**

These prophets received the name *minor* not because they were any less important in their prophetic roles than were Isaiah, Jeremiah, and Ezekiel, but because the books that bear their names are relatively short. Like Isaiah, Jeremiah, and Ezekiel, these prophets experienced themselves as called to speak God's word. Most of these prophets were active before or during the exile. Their central message—the importance of remaining faithful to the covenant—is similar to that of Isaiah, Jeremiah, and Ezekiel. Because of the brevity of these books, however, the message is concentrated into dramatic visions and pointed rebukes.

The visions of the prophet Joel (shown here in Michelangelo's Sistine Chapel portrait) have become part of the Jewish Passover Haggadah and the Christian liturgy of Pentecost.

CULTURAL
CONNECTIONS
usic

Like Jeremiah and Ezekiel, several of the prophets are known for their vivid prophecies of doom. Images from one of these passages in Zephaniah *(Zephaniah 1:2–18)* made their way into the Roman Catholic funeral mass or requiem in the form of a hymn called *Dies Irae* (Latin for "day of wrath"). For centuries, classical composers have *quoted* the musical setting of *Dies Irae* by Thomas of Celano (thirteenth century). (*Quoting* is a process comparable to sampling in today's popular music recording.) The choral setting of *Dies Irae* by composers

Wolfgang Amadeus Mozart (eighteenth century) and Giuseppe Verdi (nineteenth century) are two well-known examples that quote the original.

Listen to one or both of these musical settings of the *Dies Irae*. You may be surprised at how familiar these melodies are. Film and TV producers frequently incorporate musical references to the *Dies Irae* in their soundtracks, counting on the power of the music to communicate to audiences quickly and wordlessly the message of impending doom. The next time you hear this music in the background, look out!

Webster's New World Dictionary of Music

These prophets speak with eloquence of **the day of the Lord,** the forthcoming judgment that will punish the society for its infidelity to the commandments. To sum up the underlying message of the minor prophets:

> For I desire goodness, not sacrifice;
> Obedience to God, rather than burnt offerings.
> *Hosea 6:6 [NJPS]*

Hosea

While unrelenting in their condemnation of ethical violations, these prophets are not without their words of consolation. These are often framed in moving metaphors of God's **mercy.** In the Book of Hosea, for example, the prophet uses memorable images of marriage and parenthood to express God's unconditional love.

In a key metaphor, God asked Hosea to marry a prostitute named Gomer and to remain faithful to her even when she strayed, as God had remained faithful to Israel despite the people's fondness for other gods. In Hosea, sexual fidelity in marriage is symbolic of faithfulness to the covenant.

God spoke to Israel as Hosea spoke to Gomer, pledging unconditional love:

> I will take you for my wife forever; I will take you for my wife
> in righteousness and in justice, in steadfast love, and in mercy.
> I will take you for my wife in faithfulness; and you shall know
> the Lord.
> *Hosea 2:19–20 [NRSV]*

The children of Hosea and Gomer were given Hebrew names that described the state of estrangement that existed between Israel and the Lord in Hosea's day. Later, another domestic moment took on prophetic symbolism. The image of beloved children, learning to walk with the help of a patient parent, was used to emphasize God's inability to abandon the wayward Israel (called Ephraim) and Judah.

These tender images are in sharp contrast with other parts of the Book of Hosea, which promise harsh judgment for infidelity to the covenant. Yet, throughout, the familial imagery suggests the unbreakable bond between God and the people of Israel.

■ **What purpose might the domestic metaphors in the Book of Hosea serve in conveying the prophet's message?**

Hosea offered a message of hope even while proclaiming a searing and total punishment that would end the nation's habit of promiscuity. Hosea saw beyond the wrath of God to a love that would not let people be wiped out. The very judgment itself would take Israel back into the wilderness for a new beginning, a new covenant, and a new gift of love in a second history of reconciliation and regeneration.

Hosea pointed to the steadfast love, or covenant love, that God had for his people. Even though Israel would suffer a punishment for her unfaithfulness to the covenant agreement, God would still restore and renew her because of this steadfast love.

Jonah

There is one minor prophet with whom you are probably familiar, no matter how limited your previous exposure to the Bible might be. The narrative of Jonah has been extraordinarily popular throughout the ages and is the subject of countless children's books. However, you may have noticed some interesting differences between the Jonah of the children's books and the Jonah of the Bible—as well as some differences between the Book of Jonah and those of the other prophets.

In contrast with the other biblical prophets, Jonah is written in prose, as a third-person narrative. Its form is a short story, only forty-eight verses long. In that sense, Jonah resembles those children's picture books you may remember.

Jonah is also distinguished from the other prophets in that his primary audience is neither Israel nor Judah, but Nineveh, the capital city of wickedness, the heart of Israel's oppressors, the Assyrians. Yet his message is the same as that of the other prophets: repent, stop abusing your fellow humans, or be destroyed by the wrath of God.

For this fourteenth-century fresco, the Italian painter Giotto chose the most dramatic moment from the Book of Jonah. The image of God's hand clutching Jonah's robe recalls Psalm 139:9–10.

It's this paradox that lies behind the drama of Jonah. All the biblical prophets are initially reluctant, but Jonah carried his reluctance to extremes. Jonah was not interested in saving Nineveh, which was a brutally militaristic nation not unlike Hitler's Germany. Jonah was angry. As a loyal Israelite, Jonah wanted the hated Assyrian capital destroyed. He felt that his message to them might bring the people of Nineveh to repentance and thus assure their continuance.

Thus, rather than carry out God's command, Jonah took matters into his own hands and hopped a ship heading in the opposite direction from Nineveh to Tarshish, a seaport in Spain. This action alone was enough to indicate how unhappy Jonah was with his mission, because the desert-dwelling Israelites feared the strange and powerful ocean more than anything else in the natural world.

A ferocious storm struck, and the ship began to sink. The captain called Jonah on

THE BIBLE

AS **Literature**

THE LITERARY STRUCTURE OF THE BOOK OF JONAH

The overall narrative of Jonah is tightly constructed in three chiasms, or inverted parallelisms. The chart will help you see the chiasms when you read Jonah.

PARALLELISM 1
Jonah flees his mission:
Chapters 1–2

A Jonah's commission and flight
    (1:1–3)
B The endangered sailors cry out to
    their god   (1:4–6)
C Jonah's disobedience exposed
    (1:7–10)
D Jonah's punishment and
    deliverance   (1:11–2:10)

Jonah reluctantly fulfills his mission:
Chapters 3–4

D′ Jonah's renewed commission and
     obedience   (3:1–4)
C′ The endangered Ninevites'
     repentance   (3:5–9)
B′ The Ninevites' repentance
     acknowledged   (3:10–4:4)
A′ Jonah's deliverance and rebuke
     (4:5–11)

PARALLELISM 2 IN CHAPTER 1

A   Narrative—fear   (4, 5a)
B   Prayer of sailors   (5b)
C   Narrative   (5c, 6a)
D   Speech of captain   (6b)
E   Speech of sailors   (7a)
F   Narrative   (7b)
G   Speech of sailors   (8)
H   Proclamation of Jonah—fear
     (9, 10a)
G′ Speech of sailors   (10b)
F′ Narrative   (10c)
E′ Speech of sailors   (11b)
D′ Speech of Jonah   (12)
C′ Narrative   (13)
B′ Prayer of sailors   (14)
A′ Narrative—fear   (15, 16a)

PARALLELISM 3 IN CHAPTER 4

A   Speech of Jonah   (2, 3)
B   Speech of God   (4)
C   Act of Jonah   (5)
D   Act of God   (6a, b)
E   Jonah happy   (6c)

The Pivotal Act of God (7, 8a)

E′ Jonah unhappy   (8b)
D′ Speech of Jonah   (8b)
C′ Speech of God   (9a)
B′ Speech of Jonah   (9b)
A′ Speech of God   (10, 11)

deck and the sailors cast lots—a custom widely used in the ancient Near East—to determine who was responsible for the calamity. The lot fell on Jonah who admitted that he was a Hebrew who worshiped the "God of heaven, who made the sea and the land," in other words, the God over everything. Jonah volunteered to be thrown overboard. Immediately the seas calmed. The calm put fear into the hearts of the sailors, and they made sacrifices and vows to God. The somewhat ironic point is that the Gentile sailors showed more fidelity than the prophet.

Just when Jonah was on the point of drowning, a big fish scooped him up. There is no whale in the Book of Jonah, even though it is difficult to say "Jonah and the big fish." The notion of a whale emerged from the story being told over and over again.

Though the big fish may be memorable, what happened next is even more memorable. First, Jonah offered up a prayer of thanksgiving to God for deliverance from death in the sea and an acknowledgment of who God is. His gratitude was increased by his knowledge that he deserved to die, but God showed him mercy.

Jonah was then vomited out to the dry land by the big fish at the command of God. Now it was time for Jonah to honor a second command from God, to go to Nineveh and proclaim the message God has given him.

Jonah went this time, and the Ninevites repented, including the king, who issued a proclamation. Jonah was, however, greatly displeased and angry. In a

INTO EVERYDAY
language

A *jonah* is a jinx or unlucky person, especially aboard ship. The name comes from Jonah's shipmates' awareness that Jonah was the cause of the storm.

THE BIBLE

IN **Literature**

As a young man, American novelist and poet Herman Melville (1819–1891) worked on New England whaling ships. He came to share the fascination and terror the whalers felt toward the great beast they hunted. In his classic novel *Moby-Dick,* the crew of the whaler *Pequod* hears a sermon and sings a hymn based on Jonah. Father Mapple, in giving the sermon, recounts the narrative with a number of embellishments that are worth reading.

Beloved shipmates, clinch the last verse of the first chapter of Jonah—"And God had prepared a great fish to swallow up Jonah."

Shipmates, this book, containing only four chapters—four yarns—is one of the smallest strands in the mighty cable of the Scriptures. Yet what depths of the soul does Jonah's deep sealine sound! What a pregnant lesson to us is this prophet! What a noble thing is that canticle in the fish's belly! How billow-like and boisterously grand! We feel the floods surging over us; we sound with him to the kelpy bottom of the waters; sea-weed and all the slime of the sea is about us! But what is this lesson that the book of Jonah teaches? Shipmates, it is a two-stranded lesson; a lesson to us all as sinful men, and a lesson to me as a pilot of the living God. As sinful men, it is a lesson to us all, because it is a story of the sin, hard-heartedness, suddenly awakened fears, the swift punishment, repentance, prayers, and finally the deliverance and joy of Jonah. As with all sinners among men, the sin of this son of Amittai was in his willful disobedience of the command of God—never mind now what that command was or how conveyed—which he found a hard command. But all the things that God would have us do are hard for us to do—remember that—and hence, he oftener commands us than endeavors to persuade. And if we obey God, we must disobey ourselves; and it is in this disobeying ourselves, wherein the hardness of obeying God consists.

The Hymn
The ribs and terrors in the whale,
Arched over me a dismal gloom,
While all God's sun-lit waves rolled by,
And lift me deepening down to doom.
I saw the opening maw of hell,
With endless pains and sorrows there;
Which none but they that feel can tell—
Oh, I was plunging to despair.

In black distress, I called my God,
When I could scarce believe him mine,
He bowed his ear to my complaints—
No more the whale did me confine.
With speed he flew to my relief,
As on a radiant dolphin borne;
Awful, yet bright, as lightning shone
The face of my Deliverer God.

My song forever shall record
That terrible, that joyful hour;
I give the glory to my God,
His all the mercy and the power.

dialogue with God, God asked, "But Nineveh has more than a hundred and twenty thousand people who cannot tell their right hand from their left, and many cattle as well. Should I not be concerned about the great city?" Thus, the focus of the Book of Jonah is not so much the evil of the Assyrians as it is the judgmental attitude of Jonah, who symbolized those Israelites who thought God's mercy belonged only to the chosen people.

For Jews, the Jonah narrative is a reminder that each person is responsible for answering God's call and turning away from evil. That is why this most ironic of Hebrew texts is read aloud in the synagogue on the most solemn Jewish holy day, Yom Kippur. Christians find in Jonah the message that the covenant extends to the Gentiles, and they see in Jonah's three days and nights in the fish's belly a metaphor for Jesus' time in the tomb.

The Book of Jonah expresses the universal mercy of a compassionate God, which stands in contrast to the human tendency to do otherwise. Jonah's reluctance stemmed from his personal recognition that God was "a gracious God and merciful, slow to anger, and abounding in steadfast love, and ready to relent from punishing" *(Jonah 4.2 [NRSV]).*

Amos and Micah

The call to balance justice with mercy that is at the heart of the prophets is sounded strongly in Amos and Micah. These two prophets draw upon a shared rural background. Amos called himself a herdsman, although there is evidence that he was broadly educated, and Micah was a shepherd. These two prophets used vivid images from animal husbandry and agriculture to indict the smug injustices practiced by the leaders of society. The writings of Micah and Amos epitomize the role of the prophet, which is to comfort the afflicted and afflict the comfortable.

IN YOUR
journal

Describe one solution to a major injustice you see in the world.

Justice

Amos's message was direct and uncompromising. Over and over again, Amos announced to the people of Israel that because of their social injustice and religious arrogance, God would punish them by means of total military disaster. His addresses typically made a logical connection between Israel's unjust actions—past and present—and God's judgment.

Amos appealed over and over again to traditions that he and his listeners had in common. Among these was the belief that God brought Israel out of Egypt and granted the people the land of Canaan. Amos's words expressed a strong belief in God as the only God. For Amos, God's concern and control were not limited just to Israel but encompassed all the nations. Amos spoke of a God who was insistent upon social justice and who discounted formal rites and sacrifices where they appeared to be a substitute for obedience to God's covenant. Amos was simply holding the people accountable for transgressions.

Amos's message was one of righteous anger and a mixture of colorful curses hurled at the enemies of justice and hallucinatory visions of the punishments to come. At the center was the heartfelt cry:

But let justice roll down like waters,
and righteousness like an ever-flowing stream.
Amos 5:24 [NRSV]

The Civil Rights Memorial in Montgomery, Alabama, features words from a speech by Dr. Martin Luther King, Jr., paraphrasing Amos 5:24. What does the memorial's flowing water symbolize?

...UNTIL JUSTICE ROLLS DOWN LIKE WATERS AND RIGHTEOUSNESS LIKE A MIGHTY STREAM

MARTIN LUTHER KING JR

In his *Letter from Birmingham Jail,* written to other ministers after having been jailed for civil disobedience while protesting segregation, Martin Luther King, Jr., invoked Amos as a role model. "Was not Amos an extremist for justice?" King asked, when questioned about the appropriateness of mixing religion with social action. "So the question is not whether we will be extremists but what kind of extremists we will be. Will we be extremists for hate or for love?" The "creative extremism" of Amos, as King called it, is a continuing theme in American history. It is seen in the lives of social reformers who sought to bring to life Amos's vision of the perfect society.

Restoration

Micah the shepherd was more restrained than Amos the herdsman, though he unhesitatingly condemned idolaters and false religious leaders, comparing them to drunken preachers. Micah echoed many of the same themes, and even the same language, as Isaiah, offering a promise of comfort in the midst of affliction. Like the other minor prophets, Micah contrasted the elaborate ritual practices adopted from other religions with the true covenant. In a phrase often quoted, he delivered the Lord's message:

> **And what does the Lord require of you**
> **but to do justice, and to love kindness,**
> **and to walk humbly with your God?**
>
> *Micah 6:8 [NRSV]*

The final theme of the book of Micah is restoration—the return to wholeness that accompanies repentance and rededication to the covenant. This set the tone for the works of the final three minor prophets. The sufferings of exile, predicted and explained by the prophets, eventually ended. But the need to remind the surviving remnant of their ethical and religious obligations, the thirst for an ever-flowing stream of justice, would go on.

Passover Feast in Russia. The unknown artist painted this scene on cardboard. It shows a vision of Elijah arriving to share the seder table with the family.

Renewal

Two prophets, Haggai and Zechariah, arose in the post-exilic period to carry on the role of afflicting and comforting the people during the period of the rebuilding of the temple. They were most concerned with helping the people refocus on the religious practices associated with the temple, ridding them of the elements of local Canaanite religions and Babylonian and Persian rituals that had crept in over the long years of the exile. Additionally, Zechariah took time to remind the people of the ancient prophetic theme of social justice, explaining that even the purest temple sacrifice is meaningless when not accompanied by charity toward those in need.

The prophet Malachi came to prominence after the temple had been rebuilt, some think at the time of Nehemiah. He gave voice to the longings of the post-exilic community, who were only too well aware that earthly temples and kingdoms were transitory. Malachi's visions exhorted the people to look forward to the coming of God's perfect reign, which would be heralded by messengers (the name *Malachi* in Hebrew means "messenger") including the prophet Elijah, who had been taken up in the fiery chariot. To this day, faithful Jews pour a cup of wine for Elijah at the Passover meal and open the door to welcome him in anticipation of the coming of the messianic kingdom.

Haggai, Zechariah, and Malachi were the last prophets of the Hebrew Scriptures. After Malachi, in Jewish tradition, the scriptural prophetic voice fell silent. Judah survived as a subject kingdom, first of the Persians, later of the Greeks and Syrians, and still later as the Roman-occupied province of Judea. Because only Judah remained, the Israelites were now called Jews. Repeated raids on the temple, and its final destruction in the year 70, took their toll on Judaism as a priestly and prophetic tradition. Jewish religious life became increasingly more centered on the teachings of rabbis and scribes who interpreted the tradition. The focus of spiritual life gradually shifted from the temple to the synagogue and to the home.

Choose one of the two projects below to continue your study of the twelve, or minor, prophets:

1. Read one of the prophets not covered in this chapter—Joel, Obadiah, Nahum, Habakkuk, or Zephaniah. Summarize the message of your chosen prophet in your own words.

2. With a small group, create a short play, tableau, video, or other creative medium to express the message of either Micah or Amos in contemporary culture and language.

Unit Feature
Thirst for Justice

The biblical prophets are characterized by a thirst for justice. Some of the prophets, such as Amos and Jeremiah, had a keen sense of the plight of the poor, and they had the need to speak out for social justice. Although biblical prophecy came to an end, the need for prophets persists. The biblical prophets have inspired individuals and organizations to step up and speak up for justice, for peace, and for true freedom.

A prophetic message is hardly ever easy to hear. Prophetic words and prophetic actions are aimed most often at the powerful in society. They can be threatening to comfort and ignorance. One of the values of studying the messages of the biblical prophets is developing the ability to recognize and appreciate the prophetic voices that come forward in each generation to challenge conventional wisdom and to speak for those who have no voice.

This feature highlights three prophetic voices—two individuals and one group—that have echoed the words of Isaiah, Jeremiah, Ezekiel, Hosea, Amos, Micah, and the rest of the prophets.

Cesar Chavez

1. A TWENTIETH-CENTURY AMOS

Cesar Estrada Chavez was born on March 31, 1927, near his family's farm in Yuma, Arizona. He became, as Robert F. Kennedy noted, "one of the heroic figures of our time." A second-generation American, he saw his family lose their farm during the depression, and he spent his youth as a migrant farm worker in Arizona and California. He saw firsthand the injustices of farm workers' lives. He married and settled in the East San Jose barrio of *Sal Si Puedes* ("Get Out if You Can!"). In 1952, he joined the Community Service Organization, a prominent Latino civil rights group. While with the group, Chavez coordinated voter registration drives and conducted campaigns against racial and economic discrimination. He eventually became the organization's national director.

But Chavez's passion was to create an organization to protect and serve farmworkers, whose poverty and alienation he had shared. He left the security of a regular paycheck and began the United Farm Workers of America. His tireless work for the farmworker resulted in 1975 in the California Agriculture Labor Relations Act. It remains as the only law in the nation that protects the farmworkers' right to form unions. Chavez was a strong believer in nonviolence, in the tradition of Martin Luther King and Francis of Assisi. He effectively used peaceful tactics such as fasts, boycotts, strikes, and pilgrimages. In 1988, at the age of 61, he endured a thirty-six-day "Fast for Life" to highlight the harm caused by pesticides to farmworkers and their children.

He was a deeply spiritual man who drew his strength from silence and reflection and the reading of the Bible. He died in 1993, and over 50,000 people attended his funeral. He was awarded the Presidential Medal of Freedom. Chavez's life cannot be measured in material terms; he never owned a house and never earned more than $6,000 a year, but his personal motto is also his legacy: *"Se si puede!"* —"It can be done!"

2. NEVER EVER FORGET

"To remain silent and indifferent is the greatest sin of all." These words of Elie Wiesel echo the words of the prophets. Elie Wiesel was born in Romania on September 30, 1928. An otherwise traditional Jewish upbringing was shattered in 1944 when his entire village was deported. Wiesel survived the Nazi death camps of Auschwitz, Buna, Buchenwald, and Gleiwitz. After the liberation of the camps, he spent a few years in a French orphanage. He began working as a journalist and was influenced by the writer François Mauriac to break his silence about the Holocaust.

For all his life, in his novels and plays and memoirs, Wiesel has been a prophetic voice reminding everyone that the Holocaust can never be forgotten. In 1986, Wiesel received the Nobel Peace Prize. In awarding him the prize, the Nobel committee said of him: "Wiesel is a messenger to mankind; his message is one of peace, atonement and human dignity. His belief that the forces fighting evil in the world can be victorious is a hard-won

Elie Wiesel

belief. His message is based on his own personal experience of total humiliation and of the utter contempt for humanity shown in Hitler's death camps. The message is in the form of a testimony, repeated and deepened through the works of a great author."

In his book *Night,* Wiesel wrote in words that could have come from the mouths of the prophets one of the most renowned passages in all of Holocaust literature:

> Never shall I forget that night, the first night in camp, which has turned my life into one long night, seven times cursed and seven times sealed. Never shall I forget that smoke. Never shall I forget the little faces of the children, whose bodies I saw turned into wreaths of smoke beneath a silent blue sky. Never shall I forget those flames which consumed my faith forever. Never shall I forget that nocturnal silence which deprived me, for all eternity, of the desire to live. Never shall I forget those moments which murdered my God and my soul and turned my dreams to dust. Never shall I forget these things, even if I am condemned to live as long as God himself. Never.

3. STUDY WAR NO MORE

The American Friends Service Committee was founded in 1917 to provide young Quakers and other conscientious objectors an opportunity to serve civilian casualties of war instead of fighting during World War I. All throughout its history, the AFSC has worked for peace and justice in the world. Members of the AFSC have focused on programs designed to relieve the ten-

sions that often lead to war. Their message is strong and relentless and very frequently unpopular. Their message is in the spirit and tone of the words of Isaiah in filling up valleys, making crooked ways straight, and lowering hills in the cause of beating swords into plowshares. In its own words the organization says of itself:

> We seek to understand and address the root causes of poverty, injustice, and war. We hope to act with courage and vision in taking initiatives that may not be popular. We are called to confront, nonviolently, powerful institutions of violence, evil, oppression, and injustice. Such actions may engage us in creative tumult and tension in the process of basic change. We seek opportunities to help reconcile enemies and to facilitate a peaceful and just resolution of conflict. We work to relieve and prevent suffering through both immediate aid and long-term development and seek to serve the needs of people on all sides of violent strife.

In 1947, the American Friends Service Committee received the Nobel Peace Prize. In the presentation, the chair of the Nobel Committee, Gunnar Jahn, said, "It is through silent assistance from the nameless to the nameless that they have worked to promote the fraternity between nations cited in the will of Alfred Nobel."

A TRADITION OF PROPHECY

The literature of the biblical prophets continues to be a part of the words and actions of people who strive to help others. Great traditions of volunteering, charitable giving, advocacy, protest, leadership, public service, and even respectful dissent have their roots in the books of the prophets.

Members of the American Friends Service Committee caring for the refugees of World War II

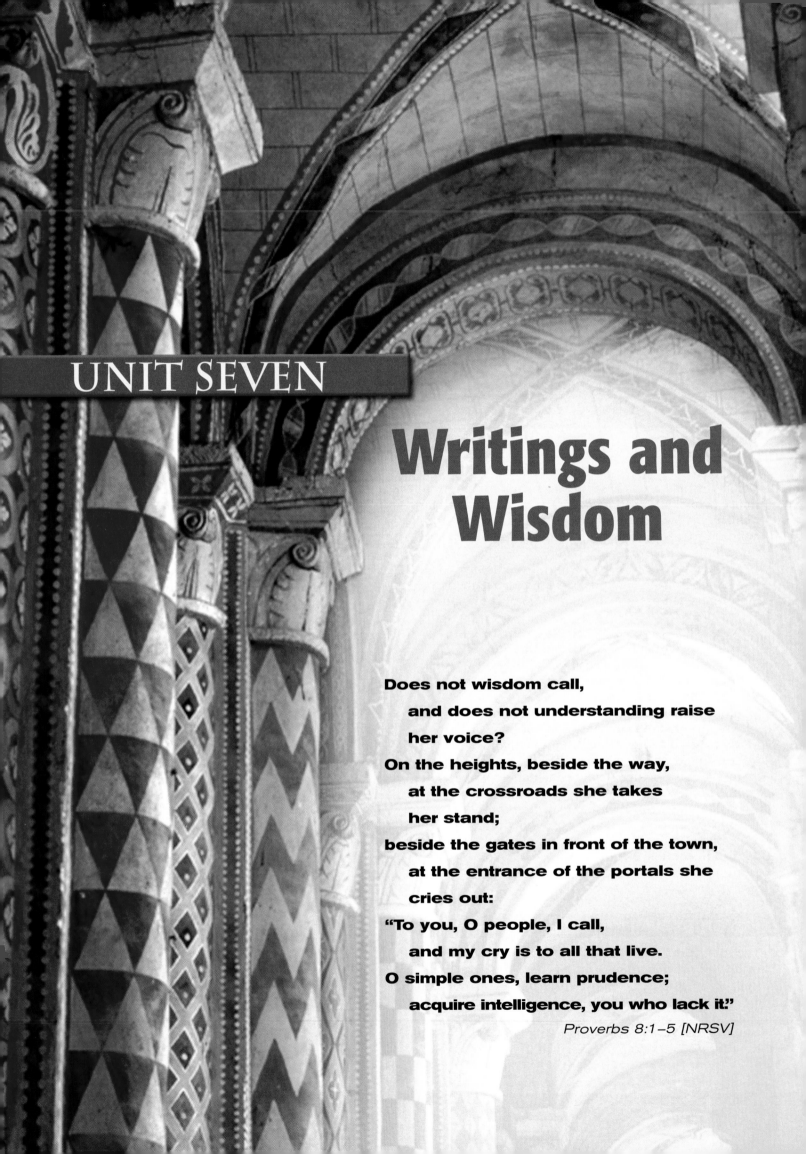

UNIT SEVEN

Writings and Wisdom

Does not wisdom call,
      and does not understanding raise
      her voice?
On the heights, beside the way,
      at the crossroads she takes
      her stand;
beside the gates in front of the town,
      at the entrance of the portals she
      cries out:
"To you, O people, I call,
      and my cry is to all that live.
O simple ones, learn prudence;
      acquire intelligence, you who lack it."

Proverbs 8:1–5 [NRSV]

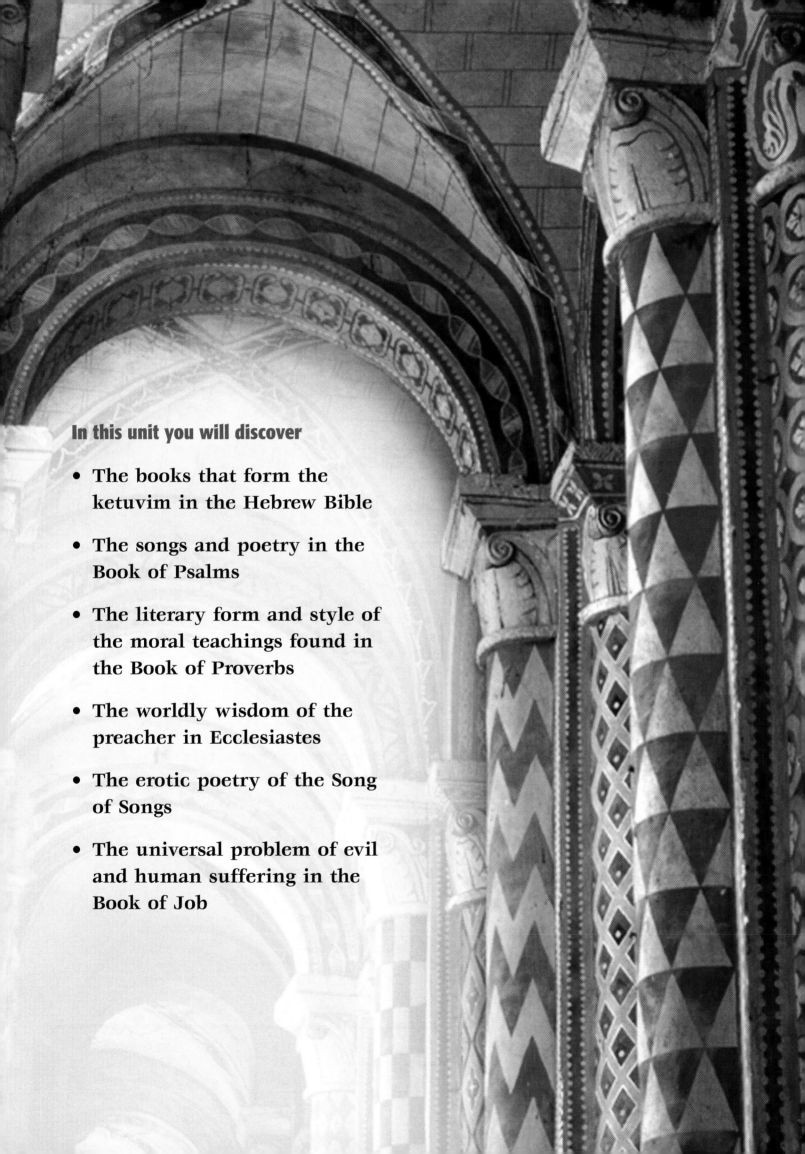

In this unit you will discover

- The books that form the ketuvim in the Hebrew Bible

- The songs and poetry in the Book of Psalms

- The literary form and style of the moral teachings found in the Book of Proverbs

- The worldly wisdom of the preacher in Ecclesiastes

- The erotic poetry of the Song of Songs

- The universal problem of evil and human suffering in the Book of Job

KEY BIBLICAL TEXTS

- Psalms 1, 8, 17, 19, 21, 22, 23, 24, 27, 34, 42, 43, 46, 51, 55, 63, 69, 79, 84, 90, 91, 95, 96, 100, 103, 104, 115, 119, 120, 121, 122, 126, 127, 128, 131, 133, 137, 139, 145, 146, 147, 150

DISCOVER

- That the Book of Psalms contains what for Jews and Christians are the "Top 150" songs of all time

- That the psalms convey a depth and variety of human emotion
- How the poetry in the psalms works
- How the psalms are different from other poetry of the time
- How translations of the psalms have influenced the English language, culture, and music

CONSIDER

- What role does music play in your life?

Songs and Poetry The Psalms

When people want to express depth of feeling and strong emotion they often turn to music. All you need to do is examine the role music plays in your life. How important is your collection of songs? What do the lyrics mean to you? How does your music help you communicate with your friends? How does it help to identify you? All your answers to those questions are reflected in the role of the Book of Psalms in the lives of Jews and of Christians. The psalms are songs, and they are meant to be sung. The psalms are poetry—just as the lyrics to great songs often stand on their own as poetry.

The psalms convey all human emotion—joy and happiness, longing and grief, anger and impatience, patriotism and solidarity, love, fear, and hope. In addition, the psalms give a sense of the Israelites' close personal relationship with their God. The "lyrics" of the psalms affirm that those who keep that covenant relationship attain happiness:

Happy is the man who has not followed the counsel of
    the wicked,
  or taken the path of sinners,
  or joined the company of the insolent;
  rather, the teaching of the Lord is his delight,
  and he studies that teaching day and night.

He is like a tree planted beside streams of water,
  which yields its fruit in season,
  whose foliage never fades,
  and whatever it produces thrives.

The artist Marc Chagall, in his painting *King David on Red Ground*, shows the influence of the psalms on the people.

CULTURAL
CONNECTIONS

The Music of the Psalms

The poetry collected in the Book of Psalms was designed to be sung. There are many references in the psalms themselves to musical instruments and even to methods of singing. Although the original music has been lost, Jewish communities around the world maintained a method for chanting the psalms that still echoes in synagogues today.

As Christianity moved westward, the psalms were sung in the musical styles of Constantinople and Rome. The most common chant was called Gregorian chant, named for Pope Gregory I (590–604), who sanctioned the style of chant for singing the psalms. Much later, great composers such as Bach and Mozart also rendered versions of the psalms.

With the Protestant Reformation came a renewed emphasis on congregational singing of the psalms. That gave rise to the creation of many popular hymns, most of which were based on the

Isaac Watts

psalter (another term for the Book of Psalms).

Isaac Watts (1674–1748) and Charles Wesley (1707–1788) were two of the most prolific hymn writers, and much of their work was based on or inspired by the psalms. Watts composed over 600 hymns; his first hymnbook was *The Psalms of David*, published in 1719. Wesley wrote over 6000 hymns. Many of the hymns of Watts and Wesley are still sung today around the world.

Charles Wesley

Hebrew poetry also inspired the moving folk tunes of a process known as shape-note singing. Early British immigrants brought this haunting chant to the United States. It is alive today in many small Appalachian communities. Perhaps the most widely recognized hymn tune in English-speaking countries is "Old Hundredth," the melody for the hymn "Praise God from Whom All Blessings Flow" (based on Psalm 100). Hebrew poetry continues to inspire musicians today as they put translations of the psalms to music.

Not so the wicked;
   rather, they are like chaff the wind blows away.

Therefore the wicked will not survive judgment,
   nor will sinners, in the assembly of the righteous.

For the Lord cherishes the way of the righteous,
   but the way of the wicked is doomed.
                   Psalm 1 [NJPS]

The psalms offer an insight into the way the Israelites perceived their relationship with God. Although there is an abundance of nature imagery used in the psalms, as in other ancient literature, there is an important difference. The psalms always acknowledge the sovereignty of God over creation. The God of the psalms is not a personification of the forces of nature but rather the master of these forces. Conversely, human beings

The psalms have a unique view of nature as under God's control and for human benefit. "You cause the grass to grow for the cattle, and plants for people to use, to bring forth food from the earth, and wine to gladden the human heart, oil to make the face shine, and bread to strengthen the human heart" *(Psalm 104:14–15 [NRSV])*.

Psalm 68 is one of the most memorable personal laments, comparing the psalmist's trials to being overcome by rising floodwaters.

are not at the mercy of their God's whims. They are partners in creation, and they are invited into a relationship with their God:

> When I look at your heavens, the work of your fingers,
> the moon and the stars that you have established;
> What are human beings that you are mindful of them,
> mortals that you care for them?
> Yet you have made them a little lower than God,
> and crowned them with glory and honor.
>
> *Psalm 8:3–5 [NRSV]*

As many of the psalms demonstrate, the Israelites' relationship with God was deeply personal. It was so personal, in fact, that they did not hesitate to remind God of promises made or even seemingly to shame God into fulfilling them:

> How long, O Lord? Will you be angry forever?
> Will your jealous wrath burn like fire?
>
> *Psalm 79:5 [NRSV]*

> Not to us, O Lord, not to us, but to your name give glory,
> for the sake of your steadfast love and your faithfulness.
> Why should the nations say, "Where is their God?"
> Our God is in the heavens; he does whatever he pleases.
>
> *Psalm 115:1–3 [NRSV]*

There are many more emotions in the poetry of the Psalms—gratitude, praise, grief over the unreliability of human friendships and political alliances, sorrow for wrongdoing, hope for the future. Often several of these seemingly conflicting emotions surface within the same psalm. That is why the poems and prayers of the Book of Psalms cannot be rigidly categorized by theme. Traditional Jewish thought recognizes three kinds of psalms: 1) hymns (songs of praise to God), 2) **elegies** or **laments** (poetry of personal or communal sorrow), and 3) didactic (teaching) poems. Biblical scholars have identified other groupings, useful for comparison. The most commonly used categories are listed in the chart below.

CATEGORIZING THE PSALMS		
TYPE	**IDENTIFYING FEATURES**	**EXAMPLE**
Praise	Praise of God's power and might, acknowledgment of the universality of God's reign	**Psalm 24**
Thanksgiving	Personal or national gratitude for God's help in a specific time of distress or war, contrast of God's power with that of other gods	**Psalm 115**
Nature	Celebration of God's actions in creation or use of natural images to describe God's power	**Psalm 104**
Trust	Humble surrender to God's care, statement of faith in God's providence, contentment	**Psalm 23**
Pilgrimage	Longing for the temple, praise of Jerusalem as the city of David, celebration of liturgical gathering, invocation of peace	**Psalm 122**
Royal	Praise of Israel's king as a representative of the divine kingship of God, invocation of God's help for the ruler	**Psalm 21**
National Lament	Cry for God's attention, description of the nation's unjustified suffering at the hands of enemies, plea for God's help, promise to return to faithfulness	**Psalm 79**
Personal Lament	Vivid description of the speaker's distress, reminder of the covenant, protestation of innocence, condemnation of evildoers, profession of faith in God's ability to save	**Psalm 22**
Confession	Admission of personal or national wrongdoing, plea for forgiveness, promise of conversion	**Psalm 51**
Didactic Poem	Recounting of God's past actions on behalf of Israel, reminder of the wisdom of keeping the covenant, contrast of good and evil or wisdom and foolishness	**Psalm 145**

The Psalms as Poetry

If you are familiar with poetry in English, you may find it difficult to identify the psalms as poems. Hebrew poetry does not rely on rhyme or familiar metrical rhythms. Many of the characteristics of Hebrew poetry are recognizable only when the psalms are read in their original language. Alliteration, wordplay such as puns, and the use of acrostics are lost in translation. Psalm 119, for example, is an acrostic in Hebrew. Each of its verses begins with a letter of the Hebrew alphabet, in sequence. That technique is especially appropriate for this psalm, which celebrates the power of God's word in the Scriptures.

In English translation, however, you can get some idea of the structural technique known as **parallelism** and the rich use of figures of speech that mark the poetry of the psalms. Hebrew poetry often features verses made up of pairs of lines that parallel one another, echoing or extending the same thought in slightly different language or using inversion for contrast. Here are two examples, from Psalm 19:

Echo:

[A] The heavens declare the glory of God,
    [B] the sky proclaims His handiwork.

Extension/Inversion:

[A] Day to day makes utterance,
    [B] night to night speaks out.

Psalm 19:1-2 [NJPS]

Another form of parallelism that is frequently used in Hebrew poetry is called **chiasm:** inverting the structure of a sentence to form a mirror image rather than a simple echo. For example, "So God created humankind in his image, in the image of God he created them" *(Genesis 1:27 [NRSV])*, and, "Whoever sheds the blood of a human, by a human shall that person's blood be shed" *(Genesis 9:6 [NRSV])*. An example of chiasm in the psalms is "We have escaped like a bird from the snare of the fowlers; the snare is broken, and we have escaped" *(Psalm 124:7 [NRSV])*. As you can see from these examples, sometimes the "mirror" phrase is a restating of the first phrase, as in Psalm 124, while other times the "mirror" adds to and changes the sentence's meaning, as in Genesis 9.

The Book of Psalms abounds in the figures of speech that make poetry such a powerfully concentrated form of language. The limits of human language are

THE BIBLE

AS **Literature**

THE BIBLE'S INFLUENCE ON LANGUAGE

In English translation, especially the King James Version, the Book of Psalms has produced hundreds of phrases that recur in literature and even in everyday conversation. The list below shows some of the most familiar. Take a few moments to leaf through the psalms to see if you can uncover more:

- Out of the mouths of babes (Psalm 8:2)
- The apple of the eye (Psalm 17:8)
- All they that go down to the dust (Psalm 22:29)
- The valley of the shadow of death (Psalm 23:4)
- My cup runneth over (Psalm 23:5)
- A thousand years in thy sight are but as yesterday (Psalm 90:4)

- We spend our years as a tale that is told (Psalm 90:9)
- A lamp unto my feet (Psalm 119:105)
- Gone astray like a lost sheep (Psalm 119:176)
- The wings of the morning (Psalm 139:9)
- Put not your trust in princes (Psalm 146:3)

stretched in search of adequate metaphors and similes for a God who is larger than words and who cannot be pictured. In addition, because Hebrew poetry depends so much on parallelism and figures of speech (not on rhyme or rhythm), it is relatively easy to translate without losing the poetic flavor of the Hebrew.

In his book *The Art of Biblical Poetry,* Robert Alter, a Hebrew scholar and professor of comparative literature at the University of California at Berkeley, points out that Hebrew poetry is one of the wellsprings of Western literature. Unlike other ancient poetry, Hebrew writers used verse primarily for celebrating prophecy and liturgy in song. They also used the form to highlight or summarize prose narrative. In a way, Hebrew poetry breaks out of narrative the way music breaks out in a Broadway play. Hebrew poetry did not tell epic tales, as did Greek or Latin poetry.

Hebrew poetry did, however, thrive on parallelism, which gives it much of its shape and changes the perception of its audience.

Hebrew poetry is not exclusive to the psalms but can be found in the books of Job, the Prophets, and Proverbs. Professor Alter diagramed five predominant techniques that Hebrew writers used in poetry. The five techniques and the symbols are as follows:

=   Synonymity: The first part of a verse is roughly the equivalent of the second.

(=) Synonymity with nearly verbatim repetition

{}   Complementarity: The first part of a verse is complementary to the second.

>   Focusing, heightening, and intensifying the first part of a verse in the second

±   Consequentiality: The second part of the verse shows a consequence of the first.

Here are examples of the techniques as adapted from Professor Alter's translation of 2 Samuel 22:

1. God, my rock where I shelter; = my shield, my saving horn

2. The snares of the Pit encircled me; (=) the traps of death sprung on me.

3. The earth and heaven shuddered; {} heaven's foundations shook, they heaved, for he was incensed.

4. The breakers of death washed over me. > The torrents of the underworld around me terrified me.

5. Smoke went up from his nostrils. ± Consuming fire came from his mouth and coals blazed forth from Him.

■ Look up two or three different psalms. Try to find an example of each technique. While you are at it, look for similes and metaphors for God (such as *rock* or *fortress*). Remember that a simile usually includes the word *like*.

Psalm 23

The Twenty-Third Psalm is one of the most familiar psalms and, according to surveys, the favorite. It is often recited at funerals because it is seen as a message of hope that God will be with the departed and the departed with God or as a message of consolation for the surviving members of the family.

Studying this psalm can help with an understanding of the poetry of all the psalms. First, read the psalm in the King James Version:

> The Lord is my shepherd; I shall not want.
>
> He maketh me to lie down in green pastures;
> he leadeth me beside the still waters.
>
> He restoreth my soul:
> he leadeth me in the paths of righteousness for his name's sake.
>
> Yea, though I walk through the valley of the shadow of death,
>
> I will fear no evil; for thou art with me;
> thy rod and thy staff, they comfort
> me.
>
> Thou preparest a table before me in the
> presence of mine enemies;
> thou anointest my head with oil; my
> cup runneth over.
>
> Surely goodness and mercy shall follow
> me all the days of my life,
> and I will dwell in the house of the
> Lord forever.
> *Psalm 23:1–6 [KJV]*

The structure of the psalm is a poem with three stanzas that use as a literary device the personification of a sheep depending on the shepherd. The psalm is short, concise, and power-packed:

1. *The Shepherd:* The first stanza uses the Lord as shepherd as a metaphor of hope. The personified sheep is the speaker. The sheep trusts the shepherd implicitly to provide everything needed for life.

2. *The Peril:* In the second stanza, there is a shift from a sheep grazing in a pasture to the perils that befall the speaker. Still, that speaker relies entirely on the protection of the shepherd and the shepherd's staff to ward off the enemies.

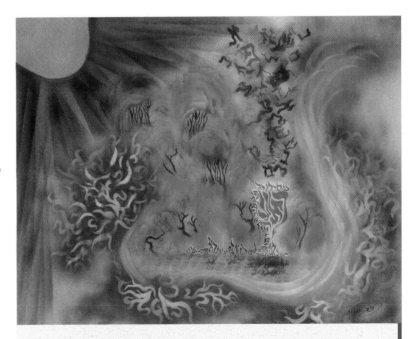

Contemporary Israeli artist Moshe Tzvi Berger painted this representation of the Twenty-Third Psalm, which hangs in the Museum of Psalms in Jerusalem. The artist left a message for the viewers of the painting. "Friend! Whoever you may be, listen in awe to this perfect poem and, if you have a moment to contemplate this image, may it communicate the deepest insights of this psalm to you."

THE BIBLE
IN Literature

PSALM 23

John Bunyan (1628–1688) wrote one of the most popular books of the seventeenth century, *The Pilgrim's Progress.* It was particularly popular in the American colonies, where the colonists identified with its theme of spiritual pilgrimage. Below is a reflection on the Twenty-Third Psalm from Bunyan's work:

John Bunyan

> Now at the end of this Valley was another, called the Valley of the Shadow of Death, and Christian must needs go through it, because the way to the Celestial City lay through the midst of it. Now, this Valley is a very solitary place. The Prophet Jeremiah thus describes it: A wilderness, a land of deserts and of pits, a land of drought, and of the shadow of death, a land that no man (but a Christian) passeth through, and where no man dwelt.
>
> The pathway was here also exceeding narrow, and therefore good Christian was the more put to it; for when he sought, in the dark, to shun the Ditch on the one hand, he was ready to tip over into the mire on the other; also, when he sought to escape the mire, without great carefulness he would be ready to fall into the Ditch. Thus he went on, and I heard him here sigh bitterly; for, besides the dangers mentioned above, the pathway was here so dark, that oft-times, when he lifted up his foot to set forward, he knew not where, or upon what he should set it next.
>
> One thing I would not let slip; I took notice that now poor Christian was so confounded that he did not know his own voice; and thus I perceived it; just when he was come over against the mouth of the burning Pit, one of the wicked ones got behind him, and stepped up softly to him and whisperingly suggested many grievous blasphemies to him, which he verily thought had proceeded from his own mind. This put Christian more to it than anything that he met with before, even to think that he should now blaspheme Him that he loved so much before; yet, if he could have helped it, he would not have done it; but he had not the discretion neither to stop his ears, nor to know from whence those blasphemies came.
>
> When Christian had traveled in this disconsolate condition some considerable time, he thought he heard the voice of a man, as going before him, saying, "Though I walk through the Valley of the Shadow of Death, I will fear no evil, for thou art with me."

The Pilgrim's Progress, Part I,
Fourth Stage, passim

3. *Blessings and Benefits:* The third stanza pulls back the veil on the metaphor and shows a mature member of society who has a seat at the table, who receives blessings and benefits in the sight of his enemies, and who is singled out for fulfillment. And this fulfillment entails dwelling in the house of the Lord, being included in that family and being protected by its master.

The Bible designates this psalm as "a Psalm of David." King David started out as a shepherd. He traveled a dangerous path through many dark valleys. And he was anointed with oil to be the leader of the chosen people.

The image of God as shepherd is a prevalent one in the Bible. In addition to this Psalm, it is very evident in the Book of Ezekiel. In Chapter 34 of Ezekiel, the prophet tells of shepherds who do not care for the flock. God sends a message through the prophet, "I will save my flock, and they will no longer be plundered. I will judge between one sheep and another. I will place over them one shepherd, my servant David, and he will tend them. He will tend them and be their shepherd" (*Ezekiel 34:22–24*).

For Christians, this psalm takes on even greater meaning because Jesus identified himself as the good shepherd who cares for the flock (read John 10:11). All in all, this one poetic song has captivated and consoled people for 3000 years.

Public Worship/Private Prayer

The Book of Psalms plays a central role in Jewish and Christian religious life. Both traditions incorporate psalms in their public worship and in customs of private prayer. The psalms are included in ritual texts for liturgy such as the Jewish *Siddur,* the Roman Catholic Lectionary, and the Anglican Book of Common Prayer. The medieval Christian monastic custom of chanting certain psalms at certain hours of the day—known as the "divine office" or "liturgy of the hours"—grew out of the Jewish practice of reciting the psalms in a weekly or monthly cycle of personal prayer. Beautifully illuminated "books of hours" contained the texts of the psalms in calligraphy with miniature illustrations and gold-leaf ornamentation. They were produced for use by medieval clergy and wealthy laypeople.

However popular the psalms continue to be as a form of personal meditation or private prayer, a primary purpose remains that of offering musical praise to God in collective worship. The words of Psalm 150, which closes the Book of Psalms, evoke the "joyful noise" the psalms were meant to be:

> Hallelujah.
> Praise God in His sanctuary;
>   praise Him in the sky, His stronghold.
> Praise Him for His mighty acts;
>   praise Him for His exceeding greatness.
> Praise Him with blasts of the horn;
>   praise Him with harp and lyre.
> Praise Him with timbrel and dance;
>   praise Him with lute and pipe.
> Praise Him with resounding cymbals;
>   praise Him with loud-clashing cymbals.
> Let all that breathes praise the Lord.
>   Hallelujah.

Psalm 150 [NJPS]

projects

Choose at least one of the projects listed below. Work alone or with a partner. Be sure to provide some record of your work that can be shared with the class.

1. Read through a few of the psalms and select one strong emotional statement. Based on that statement, create your own song or poem to convey that same emotion. Be sure to incorporate some of the features and techniques of Hebrew poetry, such as parallelism and colorful figures of speech.

2. Do some research on the sound of the psalms today. Find recordings of hymns based on the psalms or of contemporary music inspired by the psalms. Compare what you discover with contemporary popular music.

KEY BIBLICAL TEXTS

- Proverbs 1:1–33, 3:1–20, 6:6–11, 8:1–10:2, 13:12–25, 15:1–5, 16:18–19, 20:11–12; 22:1–6, 25:20–22, 26:1–14, 27, 28, 29:18–20, 30:15–28, 31:9–31

DISCOVER

- The practical wisdom found in the Book of Proverbs
- The contrast that exists between wise people and foolish people

- The seven collections of wise sayings that make up the Book of Proverbs
- The praise of the good wife

CONSIDER

- Where do you turn for good advice?

Bits of Wisdom
Proverbs

According to the Bible, when Solomon was offered any gift in the world, he chose wisdom. It only takes one glance at a newspaper's advice columns, or a stroll through the self-help section of your local bookstore, to see that people today are still in search of Solomon's gift. The range of topics and questions is enormous. Humans obviously long for and will pay for good advice on how to be happy and healthy, how to maintain good marriages and friendships, how to raise children, how to succeed in a career, and how to make sound and ethical choices.

In 1992, the Associated Press evaluated 4000 self-help books. They concluded that the oldest and best of the how-tos of happiness are in the oldest self-help book—the Bible. Wisdom literature focuses on the search for order and truth amid life's mysteries.

Proverbs

The Book of Proverbs distills wisdom into a wealth of short, memorable statements. In Hebrew, the word used for **proverb** is *mashal,* meaning "to rule" or "to govern." Thus, proverbs are not just wise sayings but rules covering a broad range of topics that govern life. They are rules to live by if one is to enjoy life. The Book of Proverbs is attributed to Solomon. The First Book of Kings notes that Solomon's wisdom "excelled all the wisdom of Egypt"—the acknowledged source of much ancient wisdom—and credits him with composing 3000 proverbs *(1 Kings 4:30, 32).*

Solomon, shown here as a wise and learned medieval nobleman, is traditionally credited with the authorship of many of the wisdom texts collected in the Bible.

You can probably recite a number of proverbs from your own family and cultural traditions. Here are some of well-known examples from the Book of Proverbs, the Bible's most widely quoted book:

- Those who trouble their households will inherit wind *(11:29)*.
- Hope deferred makes the heart sick, but a desire fulfilled is a tree of life *(13:12)*.
- Those who spare the rod hate their children, but those who love them are diligent to discipline them *(13:24)*.
- A soft answer turns away wrath, but a harsh word stirs up anger *(15:1)*.
- A glad heart makes a cheerful countenance, but by sorrow of heart the sprit is broken *(15:13)*.
- Pride goes before destruction, and a haughty spirit before a fall *(16:18)*.
- Wine is a mocker, strong drink a brawler, and whoever is led astray by it is not wise *(20:1)*.
- If you close your ear to the cry of the poor, you will cry out and not be heard *(21:13)*.
- Train children in the right way, and when old, they will not stray *(22:6)*.
- If your enemies are hungry, give them bread to eat; and if they are thirsty, give them water to drink; for you will heap coals of fire on their heads *(25:21–22)*.
- Like a dog that returns to its vomit is a fool who reverts to his folly *(26:11)*.
- The wicked flee when no one pursues, but the righteous are as bold as a lion *(28:1)*.

The Poetry of Proverbs

Much of the Book of Proverbs is set in Hebrew poetic form. You will recognize the characteristic parallel line structure. The use of inversion for contrast is clearly apparent in the composition of the proverbs, because one of the chief purposes of this biblical text is to stress the differences between wisdom and folly. The parallelism "The wise man [*does something*]/But the fool [*does something else*]" appears over and over.

Other poetic and literary forms are also employed by the Book of Proverbs to convey information about wisdom and foolishness. Lists of related objects or activities, usually grouped in threes and fours, serve to make them easier to recall:

> Three things are beyond me;
> Four I cannot fathom:
> How an eagle makes its way over the sky;
> How a snake makes its way over a rock;
> How a ship makes its way through the high seas;
> How a man has his way with a maiden.
> *Proverbs 30:18–19 [NJPS]*

The parable, or teaching story, also appears in the Book of Proverbs, as in this famous admonition addressed to the "lazybones"—the biblical embodiment of foolishness:

> Go to the ant, you lazybones;
>   consider its ways, and be wise.
> Without having any chief
>   or officer or ruler,
> it prepares its food in summer,
>   and gathers its sustenance in harvest.
> *Proverbs 6:6–8 [NRSV]*

Virtues and Vices

In today's bookstores, self-help and religion constitute separate, often even contradictory, sections. For the people of the biblical world that gave rise to the Book of Proverbs, however, such a distinction would be unimaginable. All wisdom, in the Bible, was by nature religious, because all wise behavior was rooted in doing the will of God. To the biblical mind, there was no happiness, health, or success outside the covenant. The central thesis of Proverbs is that all wisdom comes from respecting God. "The fear of the Lord is the beginning of knowledge," says Proverbs 1:7. Here "the fear of the Lord" does not mean cowering in fright before God, but having respect for God's wisdom, justice, and love. In Proverbs, God is the source and example of wisdom. Trying to appear righteous is foolish as "the eyes of the Lord are everywhere, keeping watch over the wicked and the good" *(Proverbs 15.3)*.

The Book of Proverbs offers what many people would agree is a model of commonsense morality. The basic values underlying Proverbs reflect a common thread that runs throughout Western culture.

"Hinge" Virtues

In its simplest form, the Book of Proverbs contrasts right and wrong, good and evil. It praises certain character traits and condemns others. The biblical response to the perennial human questions of what is right and what is wrong influenced the medieval notion of **cardinal virtues** and **deadly sins,** a distinctly Christian tradition celebrated in art and literature and present, in one form or another, in almost every self-help book or advice column or character education course today.

In Western art, the cardinal virtues are traditionally personified as female figures holding symbolic objects. Left to right, the images depict "Prudence," from a fresco by Piero del Pollaiolo; "Justice," as shown in a fresco by Veronese; "Fortitude," from a panel by Botticelli; and "Temperantia," a watercolor by Sir Edward Burne-Jones.

The cardinal virtues (from the Latin word for "hinge")—so called because they are the habits upon which other moral behavior hinges—are four in number. They are often personified as female figures holding symbolic objects:

- **Prudence** is applied wisdom, the habit of guiding one's choices through the use of reason, forethought, and self-control.
- **Justice** is the habit of fairness and honesty, as well as a willingness to consider the needs of others equally with, or even ahead of, one's own desires.
- **Temperance** is the habit of moderation and balance, qualities prized in all cultures. It is the "middle path" steered between austerity and excess.
- **Fortitude** is the habit of courage in choosing what is right even in the face of peer pressure or persecution. It is the moral stamina to live by one's convictions.

Deadly Sins

In contrast to the cardinal virtues are cardinal **vices**—in Christian understanding, the "seven deadly sins." Each of these evils was roundly condemned in the Book of Proverbs. Christian tradition culled out these vices and described them as enemies of the human ability to love and choose what is good—and therefore "lethal":

- **Pride** is an exaggerated sense of one's own worth that looks down on others and rejects the demands of legitimate authority.
- **Envy** is a refusal to acknowledge or to enjoy one's gifts, while constantly yearning for more and resenting what others have.
- **Anger** is unjustified or unrestrained hatred, rage, and violence.
- **Lust** is mindless sexual appetite or illicit sexual behavior.
- **Sloth** is spiritual and intellectual laziness, the lack of will to do what is right or to change for the better.
- **Avarice** is the unjust coveting or acquisition of money, property, and material goods.
- **Gluttony** is overindulgence in food and drink.

■ How are the virtues praised by the Book of Proverbs important character traits for society today?

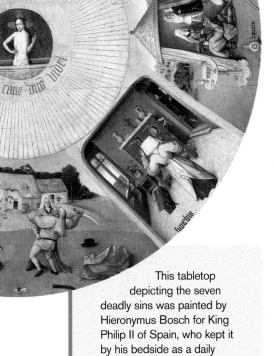

This tabletop depicting the seven deadly sins was painted by Hieronymus Bosch for King Philip II of Spain, who kept it by his bedside as a daily reminder of behaviors to avoid.

CULTURAL
CONNECTIONS
*W*ise Sayings

Collections of wise sayings have always been an important part of American popular literature. The best known of these collections is *Poor Richard's Almanac,* an annual treasury of practical advice issued by the American author, inventor, and founding father Benjamin Franklin between the years 1732 and 1757. Franklin invented the persona of "Poor Richard" Saunders for this publishing venture, which both satirized and expanded upon the tradition of wisdom literature:

- Early to bed and early to rise, makes a man healthy, wealthy, and wise.
- Three may keep a secret, if two of them are dead.
- Fish and visitors stink in three days.
- God helps them that help themselves.
- Don't throw stones at your neighbors, if your own windows are made of glass.
- A true friend is the best possession.
- 'Tis easier to prevent bad habits than to break them.
- Haste makes waste.
- The noblest question in the world is, *What Good may I do in it?*

Literary Collections

The Book of Proverbs is made up of at least seven different literary collections. They are separated by internal titles, and each of them has a slightly different literary form:

1. *The Proverbs of Solomon, Son of David, King of Israel:* This collection extends from 1:1–9:18. It is made up mostly of long poems. Much of the rest of the book is made up of short sayings. The style of this collection is quite like that of a parent admonishing a child.
2. *The Proverbs of Solomon:* This section extends from 10:1–22:16. The sayings in this collection are connected by catchwords (like "the wise" and the "foolish," as was explained earlier). The literary style consists of brief and somewhat disconnected sayings. Chapter 25:1–Chapter 29:27 are also part of this collection.
3. *The Words of the Wise:* This collection extends from 22:17–23:11. There is a distinct change in style and content in this collection as well. Many of the sayings are found in the writings of a famous Egyptian sage.
4. *The Sayings of the Wise:* This collection extends from 23:12–24:34. The style here is that of slightly longer poems with similes and metaphors. The collection also gets into some strong moral issues.
5. *The Words of Agur:* This collection is found in Chapter 30. The literary form in this collection is that of an oracle, a series of riddlelike sayings to force the listener to think along with the speaker.
6. *The Words of King Lemuel:* This collection is contained in 31:1–9. The literary style here is "an oracle that his mother taught him."
7. *Praise for the Good Wife:* The final collection is found in 31:10–31. The style here is an acrostic poem in Hebrew.

The Strong Woman

The last verses of the Book of Proverbs provide a poem of praise for the good wife. The words of this poem, though written many centuries before feminism, do not portray a woman who is passive or who is a pawn of men:

The Fiancés, by Mark Chagall, is reminiscent of the closing verses of the Book of Proverbs.

> A capable wife who can find?
>   She is far more precious than jewels.
>
> She is like the ships of the merchant;
>   she brings her food from far away.
>
> She considers a field and buys it;
>   with the fruit of her hand she plants a vineyard.
>
> She girds herself with strength,
>   and makes her arms strong.
>
> She perceives that her merchandise is profitable.
>   Her lamp does not go out at night.
>
> She opens her hand to the poor,
>   and reaches out her hands to the needy.
>
> Strength and dignity are her clothing,
>   and she laughs at the time to come.
>
> She opens her mouth with wisdom,
>   and the teaching of kindness is on her tongue.
>
> Charm is deceitful, and beauty is vain,
>   but a woman who fears the Lord is to be praised.
>
> Give her a share in the fruit of her hands,
>   and let her works praise her in the city gates.
>   *31:10, 14, 16–18, 20, 25–26, 30–31 [NRSV]*

■ How does this poem sound in light of today's society and its concerns about the role of women?

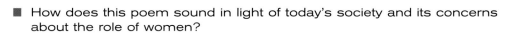

projects

Choose one of the following projects. If you choose the first one, do the work alone. The second project demands group work.

1. Write an advice column. Write letters seeking advice. Base them on real situations in your school, your friendships, or in your home. Answer the letters with verses from the Book of Proverbs. You can use other biblical words of wisdom as well.

2. Create a sitcom that shows wisdom and folly. The situation should set up the folly. The solution to the situation should reveal the wisdom. If everyone is willing, perform what you have created for the class.

More Wisdom
Ecclesiastes and Song of Songs

You don't have to spend too much time spinning the radio dial or channel surfing on the television before you bump into two phenomena, the cynical and worldly wise talk-show host and the exaltation of erotic love in music and in film. The Bible has a character that would make a great host for talk radio. The Bible also has one whole book dedicated to celebrating human, erotic love. The radio star is Koheleth, the "leader of the assembly" in the Book of Ecclesiastes. And the Song of Songs is an unbridled poetic look at the wonders of erotic love that would be at home on MTV.

Ecclesiastes

In the whole canon of biblical literature, no book is more modern in tone than the Book of Ecclesiastes. Nowhere else in the Bible—or, perhaps, in all of Western literature—are the joys of human life and the sorrows of human mortality so sharply and memorably contrasted.

The Book of Ecclesiastes is another of the wisdom books attributed to Solomon, but its first-person speaker is better known as Koheleth, a Hebrew title that means " leader of the assembly" and which the King James Version translates as "the preacher." The title "Ecclesiastes" comes from the Greek word meaning "member of the assembly."

Whether or not this book is, as Jewish tradition suggests, the work of an older, wiser King Solomon, it is certain that the preacher's voice is one of the most distinctive in the Bible. The preacher claims that looking over one's life experience reveals that the traditional path to happiness is meaningless. The preacher also asks the kinds of ultimate questions about justice and meaning that can be heard in late-night college discussion groups.

Koheleth acquires wisdom through observation, noting everything that goes on "under the sun." Koheleth's observations do not always confirm his beliefs. Here are some of Koheleth's most startlingly "modern" comments:

All You Need to Know by contemporary artist Colin Bootman. The artist used images from his own community to depict the wisdom of Solomon.

- There is nothing new under the sun *(1:9 [NRSV]).*
- For in much wisdom is much vexation, and those who increase knowledge increase sorrow *(1:18 [NRSV]).*
- The lover of money will not be satisfied with money; nor the lover of wealth, with gain. *(5.10 [NRSV]).*
- Surely there is no one on earth so righteous as to do good without ever sinning *(7:20 [NRSV]).*
- Again I saw that under the sun the race is not to the swift, nor the battle to the strong, nor bread to the wise, nor riches to the intelligent, nor favor to the skillful; but time and chance happen to them all *(9:11 [NRSV]).*
- Of making many books there is no end, and much study is a weariness of the flesh *(12.12 [NRSV]).*

One Hebrew word dominates Ecclesiastes: *hevel.* The word is most often translated "vanity." This translation gives the impression of someone who frets about clothing or sits in front of a mirror all day. *Hevel* means "vapor" or "wisp of smoke." It is used over and over again to show that life and its joys are fleeting. Death is inevitable, the great equalizer that does not respect class, fame, or power:

> All go to one place; all are from the dust, and all turn to dust again.
> *Ecclesiastes 3:20 [NRSV]*

> Whatever your hand finds to do, do with your might; for there is no work or thought or knowledge or wisdom in Sheol, to which you are going.
> *Ecclesiastes 9:10 [NRSV]*

Koheleth tries to find meaning in life in traditional ways: through wisdom, riches, buildings, and love. But he finds that the pursuit of each is *hevel.* He is also disturbed by the injustices he sees in the world: people oppressed without hope of relief *(4.1),* the wicked prospering while the righteous perish *(7.15),* and noble acts that are soon forgotten *(9.15):*

> There is nothing better for mortals than to eat and drink, and find enjoyment in their toil. This also, I saw, is from the hand of God; for apart from him who can eat or who can have enjoyment? For to the one who pleases him God gives wisdom and knowledge and joy; but to the sinner he gives the work of gathering and heaping, only to give to one who pleases God. This also is vanity and chasing after wind.
> *Ecclesiastes 2:24–26 [NRSV]*

Moderation is the Key

It is important to remember that Ecclesiastes lacks the concepts of personal immortality that entered later forms of Judaism and became so central to Christianity. For the Jews of Koheleth's day, death ended humanity's brief existence. The spirits of the dead, like the shades dwelling in the classical Greek underworld, passed into the abyss of **Sheol.** Compared with the inevitability of death, the preacher observed, life holds little that is truly meaningful:

> Vanity of vanities, says the Teacher, vanity of vanities! All is vanity.
> *Ecclesiastes 1:2 [NRSV]*

How is a person to find meaning in life? Koheleth's message, though sometimes bleak, should not be taken for complete **nihilism,** or the denial of all meaning. Cynics are often disappointed idealists, and Koheleth is a good example of that process. There is a message of faith and hope in the Book of Ecclesiastes, even though it cannot be supported by observation. One source of hope lies in the importance of enjoying fully the gifts of life, including human relationships, instead of taking them for granted:

> Two are better than one, because they have a good reward for
> their toil. For if they fall, one will lift up the other; but woe to
> one who is alone and falls and does not have another to help.
> *Ecclesiastes 4:9–10 [NRSV]*

> So I commend enjoyment, for there is nothing better for
> people under the sun than to eat, and drink, and enjoy
> themselves, for this will go with them in their toil through the
> days of life that God gives them under the sun.
> *Ecclesiastes 8:15 [NRSV]*

In the enjoyment of blessings, Koheleth sees evidence of God's mysterious providence, which provides a sense that there is a larger intelligence at work in the universe. "Go," Koheleth instructs his audience, "eat your bread in gladness, and drink your wine in joy; for your action was long ago approved by God" *(Ecclesiastes 9:7 [NJPS]).*

Finally, the Book of Ecclesiastes, like Proverbs, finds solace and wisdom in the way of moderation and balance, celebrating a life in which all things have their appropriate place. The words of Koheleth were turned into a song by Pete Seeger, "Turn, Turn, Turn." The song became immensely popular in a version recorded by the folk-rock group the Byrds in 1966:

The preacher's most cynical—and memorable—utterance inspired a whole genre of painting known as the vanity, or *memento mori* (Latin for "remember mortality"), of which three examples are shown here: Evert Collier's *Vanitas Vanitatum et Omnia Vanitas,* Cezanne's *Still Life with Skull,* and Trophime Bigot's *Allegory of Vanity.*

> To every thing there is a season, and a time to every
>   purpose under the heaven:
> A time to be born, and a time to die: a time to plant,
>   and a time to pluck up that which is planted;
> A time to kill, and a time to heal; a time to break
>   down, and a time to build up;
> A time to weep, and a time to laugh; a time to mourn,
>   and a time to dance;
> A time to cast away stones, and a time to gather
>   stones together; a time to embrace,
>   and a time to refrain from embracing;
> A time to get, and a time to lose; a time to keep, and a time to
>   cast away;
> A time to rend, and a time to sew; a time to keep silence, and a
>   time to speak;
> A time to love, and a time to hate; a time of war, and a time of
>   peace.
>
> *Ecclesiastes 3:1–8 [KJV]*

Although life may at times seem meaningless, Koheleth concluded that God "has made everything suitable for its time; moreover he has put a sense of past and future into their minds, yet they cannot find out what God has done from the beginning to the end. I know that there is nothing better for them than to be happy and enjoy themselves as long as they live" *(Ecclesiastes 3:11–12 [NRSV]).*

Koheleth later provides a recipe for how happiness and enjoyment are reached:

> The end of the matter; all has been heard. Fear God, and keep
> his commandments: for that is the whole duty of everyone. For
> God will bring every deed into judgment, including every
> secret thing, whether good or evil.
>
> *Ecclesiastes 12:13–14 [NRSV]*

The Song of Songs

Of all the popular songs you listen to and all the poetry you read, clearly the most popular topic is love. Something about the romantic relationships humans form with one another seems to give rise to music and poetry, whether celebrating the joys of love or mourning its loss. The Bible, as you have seen, does not shy away from this mysterious and compelling experience, which Genesis describes as built into human nature from the very beginning. The Hebrew Scriptures include many tales of human love, from "marriages made in heaven" (Isaac and Rebekah, Jacob and Rachel) to love gone wrong (Samson and Delilah). So it is no surprise that the Bible would contain love poetry as well as love stories.

What is surprising about the book known as the Song of Songs (in some versions, the Song of Solomon or Canticle of Canticles), however, is not its topic but its tone and content. Modern readers unfamiliar with this Hebrew text are often taken aback by its explicit, ecstatic celebration of erotic love. In an intoxicating swirl of images both earthy and sublime, the Song of Songs unfolds as a dramatic dialogue between a lover and a beloved, with occasional comments addressed to an admiring chorus of friends. The perspective shifts back and forth between genders, sometimes in mid-verse, stressing the melding of the sexes in love. The lovers of the poem linger over rich descriptions of each other's physical attributes. The language is as vivid and memorable as that of any love poetry in history:

This painting is entitled *The Song of Songs.* The artist, He Qi of Nanjing, China, combines the elements of Chinese folk art with Western and Medieval themes.

Let him kiss me with the kisses of his mouth!
For your love is better than wine!

I am black and beautiful, O daughters of
     Jerusalem,
like the tents of Kedar, like the curtains of
     Solomon.

I am a rose of Sharon, a lily of the valleys.

He brought me to the banqueting house, and his
intention toward me was love.

My beloved speaks and says to me:
     "Arise, my love, my fair one, and come away;
for now the winter is past, the rain is over and gone.
The flowers appear on the earth; the time of
     singing has come,
and the voice of the turtledove is heard in our land.

I opened to my beloved,
     but my beloved had turned and was gone.
My soul failed me when he spoke.
I sought him, but did not find him;
     I called him, but he gave no answer.

I am my beloved's and my beloved is mine;
     he pastures his flock among the lilies.
You are beautiful as Tirzah, my love, comely as
     Jerusalem,
     terrible as an army with banners.
                    Song of Solomon 1:2, 5; 2:1, 4, 10–12;
                              5:6; 6:3–4 [NRSV]

It is striking that the Song of Songs contains no mention of God, who is otherwise the main character of the Hebrew Scriptures and never offstage for more than a few verses. If you are puzzled about how this book found its way into the Bible, you are among good company. Throughout the centuries, many Jewish and Christian scholars have had difficulty justifying the inclusion of the Song of Songs in the biblical canon.

Yet, Judaism has always celebrated the body as God's good creation, and marital sexuality as both a sign and an example of the covenant between God and humans. Though Christianity has been influenced by more austere philosophies that made some Christian groups less comfortable with the body than were their Jewish ancestors, Christianity, too, sees marriage as a holy relationship. For this reason selections from the Song of Songs are often incorporated into the readings at Jewish and Christian wedding ceremonies.

Marriage as Metaphor

On one level, the Song of Songs is about two people in love. On another, however, readers throughout the centuries have found in its lush poetry an evocative allegory of the love between God and the chosen people of Israel, God and the Church, or God and any human soul. Some Jewish commentators find an allegory for the Jewish people's love of the Torah. Some even read the bridegroom as a representation of the person who seeks wisdom, with wisdom itself as the bride. These interpretations need not cancel out the basic, obvious reading. The Song of Songs may be both human love story and divine love story.

A detailed Jewish reading of the Song of Songs is found in the **Targum** (an Aramaic language translation and commentary of the Torah compiled in the

Many Jewish couples choose wedding rings inscribed in Hebrew *Ani l'dodi v'dodi li* ("I am my beloved's and my beloved is mine"), echoing the lover's vow in Song of Songs 6:3.

early Middle Ages). The Targum links different episodes in the Song of Songs to moments in Israel's history, as if the whole book were an allegory.

As an example, Chapter 1:2, "Let him kiss me with the kisses of his mouth: for thy love is better than wine" [KJV] is described as a reference to God's gift of the Torah. The gift of the books of the Law is like a "kiss from God." Another example is found in 5:2–6. Here the beloved is gone, and the bride is left anguished and alone, beaten in the streets by sentinels. The Targum sees this as a metaphor for the Babylonian exile.

Christian scholars often use an allegorical reading of the text to show a relationship between Jesus and the Church. No matter how the book is interpreted, it has greatly influenced Western art and literature. The extravagant language of the poem influenced the language of the troubadours and their songs of courtly love. A popular French medieval poem, "The Romance of the Rose," drew heavily on the Song of Songs. Medieval mystical poets, especially Juan de la Cruz, used the language of Song of Songs to describe the soul's desire for union with Jesus.

Despite all that, the Song of Songs stands on its own as a remarkable testament to the power of human love in its most awesome form, a love so fiercely possessive that it partakes in the immortal nature of God:

> Set me as a seal upon your heart,
>   as a seal upon your arm;
> for love is strong as death,
>   passion fierce as the grave.
> Its flashes are flashes of fire,
>   a raging flame.
> Many waters cannot quench love,
>   neither can floods drown it.
> If one offered for love
>   all the wealth of one's house,
>   it would be utterly scorned.
>
> *Song of Solomon 8:6–7 [NRSV]*

IN YOUR journal

Copy the lyrics of your favorite love song or love poem into your journal. What view of love does the song or poem express? How does this view compare with the perspective expressed in the Song of Songs?

projects

Choose one of the following projects. Work with a partner or with a small group. Report the results to the class.

1. Listen to a random hour of music on the radio or watch an hour of music television. During that hour, try to discover images or metaphors that are also found in the Song of Songs.

2. Read the editorial pages or the op-ed pages of your local newspaper. You can also listen to talk radio. How many of the concerns you see there are reflected in the Book of Ecclesiastes?

3. Choose one verse in either Ecclesiastes or Song of Songs and create a visual presentation of that verse. (That means you cannot use any words to express the content of the verse.)

KEY BIBLICAL TEXTS

■ Job 1:1–2:13, 3:1–26, 8:1–22, 9:1–10:22, 13:1–28, 19:1–29, 29:1–25, 31:1–40, 38:1–39:30, 42:1–17

DISCOVER

■ How the Book of Job tackles the problem of human suffering

■ The arguments for and against a good God who lets bad things happen

■ Your own view of good and evil in the world

GET TO KNOW

■ Satan, Job, Job's wife, Job's friends

CONSIDER

■ What kinds of questions does human suffering raise?

The Problem of Suffering
The Book of Job

Illness, natural disaster, crime, financial crisis, failure, loss of love, death—these are all facts of human life. And though tragedy often seems to strike randomly, out of the blue, most people struggle to find some meaning or explanation for terrible events, even if it's only to cast blame. The Book of Job is one of the most enduring explorations of these questions in all literature, perhaps because it puts God on trial for the mysteries of human suffering.

Named for its central character, the Book of Job consists of a series of poetic exchanges set within a narrative framework. The narrative has a test for the hero and a reversal of fortunes that is itself later reversed. This account addresses one of the most pressing human riddles: If God is all-powerful, why do terrible things happen? And if God allows evil things to happen, can God honestly be described as good?

This puzzle remains essentially unsolved, though various believers in various times have developed their own ways of resolving or living with the paradox. There is a technical term for the struggle with good and evil, **theodicy,** which means literally "the defense of God." The Book of Job promotes the value of remaining steadfast in the face of horrible circumstances and personal suffering.

Catastrophic events such as the terrorist attacks of September 11, 2001, often cause people to search for the meaning of suffering and tragedy. The Book of Job is evidence that such a search for meaning has always been a part of the human condition.

Job and His Family, William Blake, 1821.

Prologue

The narrative of Job opens with a description of the protagonist's prosperity and piety. Job was the quintessential good man. He was as prosperous as anyone in Hebrew Scriptures, with seven sons, three daughters, 7000 sheep, 3000 camels, 500 pairs of oxen, 500 donkeys, and many servants. He was so concerned with keeping his family in God's good graces that he offered sacrifices on behalf of his children, just in case they went a little astray out of carelessness. Yet, one can almost hear the ominous music building on the soundtrack of his life. Through no fault of his own, things were about to change for the worse.

The narrative switches locations to the court of heaven, where God was surrounded by his heavenly beings. One of them was Satan, literally, the "Accuser" or "Prosecutor" (not the devil—a much later meaning of the term):

> The Lord said to Satan, "Where have you come from?" Satan answered the Lord, "From going to and fro on the earth, and from walking up and down on it."
>
> *Job 1:7 [NRSV]*

Why Me?

With God's permission, Satan brought about a series of catastrophes that quickly reduced Job to ruin. But God protected Job's life. Satan could only go so far. Job's flocks, the source of his wealth, were stolen. Job's servants were killed, and his children were lost when the house in which they were feasting was destroyed by a whirlwind. Job mourned these staggering blows. He tore his robe, shaved his head, and fell on the ground—all signs of extreme sorrow and grief. But his faith was firm. Job's response was everything God could want:

> Naked I came from my mother's womb, and naked shall I return there; the Lord gave, and the Lord has taken away; blessed be the name of the Lord.
>
> *Job 1:21 [NRSV]*

Satan set up a second test by inflicting a hideous skin disease on Job himself. Made unclean by the boils that scarred his body, Job had to leave

INTO EVERYDAY *language*

Job's comforters are people who make you feel worse in a time of tragedy by judging or criticizing you under the guise of offering sympathy.

society and dwell outside the town limits, literally in the town dump, where he used a piece of broken pottery to scratch the unbearable itching of his sores. Yet still he remained faithful. Job's wife, on the other hand, who also suffered these tragedies, had another response. She blamed God and probably Job, too:

> Then his wife said to him, "Do you still persist in your integrity? Curse God, and die."
>
> *Job 2:9 [NRSV]*

Job's stoic endurance in the face of great suffering has earned him a reputation for impressive fortitude, making him a role model for those in similar circumstances. "The patience of Job" is proverbial. But as the narrative goes on, Job experienced many of the same emotions a less patient victim might. He plunged into deep depression, shot through with a flickering of righteous indignation. His words have come to the minds of thousands of people over the years as they also find themselves in despair:

> Let the day perish in which I was born,
>   and the night that said," A man-child is
>   conceived."
>
> Let the day be darkness!
>   May God above not seek it, or light shine on it.
>
> Why did I not die at birth,
>   come forth from the womb and expire?
>
> Truly the thing that I fear comes upon me,
>   and what I dread befalls me.
>
> I am not at ease, nor am I quiet:
>   I have no rest; but trouble comes.
>
> *Job 3:3–4, 11, 25–26 [NRSV]*

> A mortal, born of woman,
>   few of days and full of trouble,
> comes up like a flower and withers,
> flees like a shadow and does not last.
>
> For there is hope for a tree,
>   if it is cut down, that it will sprout again,
>   and that its shoots will not cease.
>
> But mortals die, and are laid low;
>   humans expire, and where are they?
>
> *Job 14:1–2, 7, 10 [NRSV]*

And though he steadfastly refused to curse God or die, the hopelessness he felt moved Job to dare the kinds of questions that do not occur to a happy man. Against everything he stood for, Job allowed himself to wonder, "Why me?"

Job and His Wife by Georges de La Tour, c. 1650.

Answers and Questions

Even before Job began questioning his fate, there were people around him ready to provide explanations for his sufferings. In addition to the bitterness of his wife, Job had to deal with the well-meaning but utterly useless advice of his three friends—Eliphaz the Temnite, Bildad the Shuhite, and Zophar the Naamathite. Each of the three, seeking some explanation for Job's sufferings, found a different way to blame the victim.

Three times Job's friends spoke, and three times he had to defend himself. The more his friends piled on their "windy words," the more Job was moved to voice questions of his own. Job's questions, however, were neither rhetorical nor addressed to his friends. In the tradition of the Bible's righteous men, Job went right to the source. He put his questions to God:

> If I have sinned, what have I done to You,
> Watcher of men?
> Why make me Your target,
> And a burden to myself?
> Why do You not pardon my transgression
> And forgive my iniquity?
>
> *Job 7:20–21 [NJPS]*

Although Job acknowledged that "man cannot win a suit against God; if he insisted on a trial with Him, He would not answer one charge in a thousand" *(Job 9:2–3 [NJPS])*, his questions did indeed put God on trial. It was Job's unshakeable faith in God's essential goodness, not his doubt and despair, that drove the questioning. Job even enlisted God as his advocate, his prosecuting attorney as it were, against God's own self. In one of the Bible's best-known passages, Job declared:

> For I know that my Redeemer lives,
>   and that at the last he will stand upon the earth;
> and after my skin has been thus destroyed,
>   then in my flesh I shall see God.
>
> *Job 19:25–26 [NRSV]*

The Hebrew word *go'el,* translated as "redeemer" in some Christian translations, is translated as "vindicator" in the NJPS Tanakh. Under Mosaic Law, this is the title given to a relative, literally a "next of kin," whose sworn duty it is to defend the family's honor by paying ransom, restoring damage to reputation, and avenging wrongs. Remarkably, Job turned the tables and was testing God, with God as his lawyer.

Job recognized the risk he was taking, but he insisted on the right to try his suit. "He may well slay me; I may have no hope; yet I will argue my case before Him" *(Job 13:15 [NJPS]).* After he did so, as eloquently as possible, Job rested his case: "The words of Job are ended" *(Job 31:40).* Word of Job's audacious challenge spread, and he drew the anger of a pious young man named Elihu, who—as if things weren't bad enough for Job already—arrived to read the riot act to his elder. Elihu considered himself God's defense counsel, and his "opening statement" goes on for six chapters.

This medieval illumination makes disturbingly clear how far Job has fallen in the world. His skin condition has made him ritually unclean, and his poverty leaves him no option but to dwell on a dunghill, literally a heap of human and animal waste outside the town limits.

■ What points did Job make in his case against God? What was the nature of Elihu's defense of God?

God Takes the Stand

The most astonishing moment in the Book of Job comes when Elihu was in mid-sermon, seemingly ready to go on for hours. With all the drama of the last act of a *Law and Order* episode, the defendant (God) suddenly arrived to testify:

> Then the Lord answered Job out of the whirlwind:
> "Who is this that darkens counsel
>   by words without knowledge?
> Gird up your loins like a man.
>   I will question you, and you shall declare to me.
>
> *Job 38:1–3 [NRSV]*

William Blake's engraving, *Then the Lord Answered Job Out of the Whirlwind*, illustrating the Book of Job, brings the biblical texts to life in dramatic detail.

IN YOUR *journal*

How do people today explain why "bad things happen to good people"? Using news accounts, TV and radio talk shows, and discussions with family members and friends, come up with a list of common attempts to explain tragedy and suffering.

Ignoring Elihu and the three comforters, God spoke directly to Job, turning the tables yet again. Instead of defending himself, God cross-examined his accuser:

Where were you when I laid the foundation of the
    earth?
Tell me, if you have understanding.
Who determined its measurements—surely you
    know!
Or who stretched the line upon it?
On what were its bases sunk, or who laid its
    cornerstone
when the morning stars sang together
    and all the heavenly beings shouted for joy?
                            Job 38:4–7 [NRSV]

At first, Job remained unimpressed. Pushed to respond to God's questions, he did the biblical equivalent of taking the fifth:

See, I am of small worth; what can I answer You?
I clap my hand to my mouth.
I have spoken once, and will not reply;
Twice, and will do so no more.
                            Job 40:4–5 [NJPS]

As God pressed on, cataloging deeds of divine power, he mentioned two creatures that have left their mark on the Western imagination:

Look at Behemoth, which I made just as I made you;
    it eats grass like an ox. . . .
Can you draw out Leviathan with a fishhook,
    or press down its tongue with a cord?
Can you put a rope in its nose,
    or pierce its jaw with a hook?
                    Job 40:15, 41:1 [NRSV]

In Hebrew legend, Leviathan is a sea monster—a kind of serpent or dragon. Behemoth is a huge, oxlike beast. Readers have traditionally associated these names with nonmythical animals. Leviathan is sometimes shown as a giant crocodile or as a whale. Behemoth is sometimes associated with the hippopotamus.

Happily Ever After?

At the end of God's testimony, Job spoke. In essence, he dropped the charges, revoking his suit. Although Job expressed repentance, God made no move to punish him for his audacity. Instead, God turned his wrath on the miserable comforters, for giving bad advice. The ever-righteous Job offered sacrifices on their behalf, as he had once done for his children. In another profound reversal, Job was actually rewarded with even more wealth and even more wonderful children than he had lost.

The Lord blessed the latter days of Job more than his
beginning.
                           Job 42:12 [NRSV]

This ending, though pleasing in some ways, has failed to satisfy various readers over the centuries. The questions of theodicy, after all, remain unanswered, and

Job on Stage

The American poet Archibald MacLeish won the Pulitzer Prize for his verse play *J.B.,* a reworking of the biblical text that makes Job a twentieth-century businessman. MacLeish's Satan, depicted as a circus vendor named Nickles, poses the dilemma of theodicy in song: "If God is God, He is not good; / If God is good, He is not God." The play foregoes the biblical happy ending. MacLeish's protagonist is unsatisfied by God's defense, but finds a kind of hope in the words of his wife:

Sarah: You wanted justice, didn't you?
There isn't any. There's the world . . .
Cry for justice and the stars
Will stare until your eyes sting. Weep,
Enormous winds will thrash the water.
Cry in sleep for your lost children,
Snow will fall . . .
      Snow will fall . . .
J.B.: Why did you leave me alone?
Sarah: I loved you.
I couldn't help you any more.
You wanted justice and there was none—
Only love.
J.B.: He does not love. He Is.
Sarah: But we do. That's the wonder.

MacLeish seems to suggest that although modern people can no longer easily put their faith in a God who is a "distant voice," the urge to believe, to hope, and to love—even in the face of tragedy—may be miracle enough.

although the wealth was probably welcome, most parents know that lost children are not replaceable. The happy ending can strike modern readers as a little too pat or contrived, a little too much like the cavalry arriving just in time in the last reel of a Western movie.

Job is one of the most difficult books in the Bible in that it provides no clear-cut moral or answer to Job's situation. Job is not condemned, but neither is there a logical or legal answer given to why Job has suffered. It remained a mystery to Job, although the reader is ready for Job's restoration in the epilogue because of the heavenly vantage point of the prologue earlier on. Perhaps one of the points is that which Job made when he said:

> See, he will kill me; I have no hope;
>   but I will defend my ways to his face.
> This will be my salvation,
>   that the godless shall not come before him.
>   *Job 13:15–16 [NRSV]*

Job and His Daughters, an engraving by William Blake, c. 1823. Among the rewards given to Job after his fortunes were restored are three daughters whose loveliness was unsurpassed in all the land. These young women are notable both in being mentioned by name and in sharing equally with their brothers in their father's inheritance.

THE BIBLE

IN Literature

Herman Melville's 1851 novel *Moby-Dick, or The Whale* is generally ranked among the greatest American literature. The seemingly simple story of a New England whaling ship's last voyage is layered with symbolism and rich with biblical allusion. At the novel's core is the obsession of the *Pequod's* captain with vengeance against the legendary white whale named Moby-Dick, which Captain Ahab believes is responsible for destroying his life.

Moby-Dick may be read as a uniquely American, inverted version of the Book of Job. The connection is signaled early in the novel, when we learn that one of the *Pequod's* prosperous, smug backers is a hypocritical Christian named Bildad. Like the "comforter" of Job with whom he shares a name, Melville's Bildad favors a harsh and judgmental interpretation of the Scriptures. "For a pious man, especially for a Quaker, he was certainly rather hard-hearted, to say the least."

Melville follows the traditional association of the biblical leviathan with the whale. *Moby-Dick's* narrator, the young sailor Ishmael, often digresses from the tale to discuss the natural history of leviathan and wonders at his own audacity in hunting the whale:

> To grope down into the bottom of the sea after them; to have one's hands among the unspeakable foundations, ribs, and very pelvis of the world; this is a fearful thing. What am I that I should assay to hook the nose of this leviathan! The awful taunting in Job might well appall me.

Moby-Dick's inversion of the biblical text centers on Captain Ahab, who can be seen as a kind of anti-Job. Where Job questions and complains but never succumbs to his wife's injunction to "curse God and die," Ahab defiantly rejects any authority but his own mad will. Where Job eventually concedes God's power and repents his lack of humility, Ahab refuses to bend before the whale, who has become both god and devil to him. In answer to the first mate, Starbuck, who accuses the captain of **blasphemy,** Ahab rages:

> All visible objects, man, are but as pasteboard masks. But in each event—in the living act, the undoubted deed—there, some unknown but still reasoning thing puts forth the moldings of

A *Moby-Dick* book illustration by the American artist Isaac Walton Taber.

its features from behind the unreasoning mask. If man will strike, strike through the mask! How can the prisoner reach outside except by thrusting through the wall? To me, the white whale is that wall, shoved near to me. Sometimes I think there's naught beyond. But 'tis enough. He tasks me; he heaps me; I see in him outrageous strength, with an inscrutable malice sinewing it. That inscrutable thing is chiefly what I hate; and be the white whale agent, or be the white whale principal, I will wreak that hate on him. Talk not to me of blasphemy, man; I'd strike the sun if it insulted me.

Moby-Dick ends where the Book of Job begins, in violent destruction and death. The novel's last words are Ishmael's. He is the sole survivor of the *Pequod,* and he prefaces the end of his story with the words of the messenger of doom from Job 1:16: "I alone have escaped to tell you."

CULTURAL
CONNECTIONS

Philosophy

The English philosopher Thomas Hobbes (1588–1679) lived during an era of political and religious turmoil. He spent much of his life longing for security and stability. Hobbes's description of chaotic times has much in common with Job's complaint: "continual fear and danger of violent death, and the life of man solitary, poor, nasty, brutish, and short."

As a political philosopher, Thomas Hobbes is best known for the work from which that memorable description comes, the 1651 *Leviathan*. Hobbes uses the biblical description of leviathan, the great beast subject to God alone, as a metaphor for the power of the state, the only institution he believes is capable of offering security and stability in a troubled world.

When people are living in a state of war, whether literal or symbolic, Hobbes suggests that their only recourse is to confer all their power and strength upon one person, or upon one assembly of people, that may reduce all their wills, by plurality of voices, into one will. This done, the multitude so united in one person is called a **commonwealth**, in Latin *civitas*. This is the generation of that great leviathan, or rather, to speak more reverently, of that "mortal god," to which we owe under the "immortal God" our peace and defense.

Hobbes's vision, though pessimistic and subject to exploitation by dictatorial sovereigns and states, paved the way for later theories of the social contract, which influenced the development of American forms of democracy.

projects

This special book of the Bible deserves a special project. Everyone in the class should do the project. Sharing the results is important.

1. *The Setup:* Many students, although aware of good and evil, have not thought deeply about it. In the Judeo-Christian tradition, God is considered to be all good, all knowing, and all powerful. Yet this view presents a problem. Where does all the evil in the world come from? How could all-good God let something like the Holocaust happen? Why would God let innocent children suffer?

2. *The Quick Answer:* The traditional response to this dilemma is that people have free will. They are free to choose to do evil. If God stepped in, there would be no freedom. People would be little more than fleshy robots. So, human freedom brings evil.

3. *Your Task:* This could be a very interesting and important project for you. First reflect and

examine your own view of good and evil. The task should last about a week to ten days. Interview at least three people, eliciting their opinions on the nature of good and evil—a family member, a faculty member, and a fellow student. In the interview, explore and record the responses to the following:

a. *What is good?*
b. *What is evil?*
c. *Do absolute good and evil exist?*
d. *Are only humans evil, or is there evil in nature?*
e. *How do you support your views?*

4. *The Follow Through:* When you have digested your research and the interviews, compare what you discovered with what you read in the Book of Job. Then write a personal reflection on your findings and attach it to the record of your findings. Be prepared to share the results with the class.

KEY BIBLICAL TEXTS

■ The Book of Ruth; the Book of Esther

DISCOVER

■ How Ruth's actions are signs of faithfulness and selflessness

■ Why Esther is considered a savior of the Jewish people

■ The importance of these two books and of other women in the Bible and their influence on women's struggle for equality

GET TO KNOW

■ Ruth, Naomi, Boaz, Esther, Mordecai, Haman

CONSIDER

■ Upon what factors does women's role in society depend?

Women of Valor Ruth and Esther

The Bible has more than its share of male heroes, ranging from the strong but stupid Samson to the wily and complicated trickster Jacob to King David. Biblical women, however, tend to fall into two categories: resilient and wily matriarchs (Sarah, Rebekah, Rachel, Hannah) and evil temptresses (Delilah, Jezebel). The exception—a woman painted with individuality and complexity, one who transcends social and religious generalizations—stands out all the more clearly for her rarity. A few of these remarkable women have already been discussed: Rahab, the Canaanite prostitute who sheltered the Israelite spies; Deborah, the judge and general; the wise Queen of Sheba. The two books of the Hebrew Scriptures that bear the names of women introduce two of the best-known women of valor and virtue, Ruth and Esther. Each in her own way played a pivotal role in the growth and protection of the Jewish people, though neither fits any stereotype.

Ruth

It's interesting to note that one of the Bible's most memorable portrayals of loving kindness celebrates the bond between two people stereotypically at odds—a mother-in-law and a daughter-in-law. And the daughter-in-law, Ruth, was not even born Jewish. In

Ruth's commitment to her mother-in-law is a favorite subject in Western art. William Blake's watercolor-embellished engraving (above) shows Orpah returning in tears (but possibly with some relief) to Moab, while Ruth clings to Naomi. The contemporary English painter Simon Palmer transposes the scene (below) to a twentieth-century dream landscape, where a scarecrow in female attire looks on as Naomi and Ruth make their weary way.

fact, she was a Moabite, one of those "foreign women" the prophets were always warning Israelite men against. So how did this unlikely woman become a heroine of the Hebrew Scriptures?

The first chapter of the brief Book of Ruth set the scene. "In the time of the judges," famine, that great motivator of migration, struck Israel. Seeking fertile land for his family, a Jewish man named Elimelech took his wife, Naomi, and his two young sons to Moab. Over the course of their stay, Elimelech died. The two sons grew to adulthood and married Moabite women. When disease took the two sons before they had children of their own, the grieving widow Naomi then decided to return to her native land, hoping to find some Israelite relative who would take her in. Naomi's daughters-in-law accompanied her part of the way, but she sent them back, knowing they would be better off among their own people. One daughter-in-law, Orpah, tearfully bade farewell to Naomi. But the other, Ruth, refused to be parted from the mother-in-law she had come to think of as a best friend and beloved relative. In words that have become synonymous with the commitment to loving relationship, Ruth said to Naomi:

Jean-Francois Millet's popular painting, *The Gleaners*, presents a romanticized image of what was in reality backbreaking, sweaty labor that resulted in perhaps a few stalks of substandard grain, trampled into the mud by workers' boots and horses' hooves. The practice of gleaning continues in one form or another even today.

> Do not press me to leave you
>   or to turn back from following you!
> Where you go, I will go;
>   where you lodge, I will lodge;
> your people shall be my people,
>   and your God my God.
> Where you die, I will die—
>   there will I be buried.
> May the Lord do thus and so to me,
>   and more as well.

Ruth 1:16–17 [NRSV]

In Jewish tradition, Ruth is considered the prototype of the model convert to Judaism.

■ What does Ruth promise to do if Naomi will allow her to accompany her back to Israel?

Though Naomi was certainly moved by Ruth's plea—there is evidence throughout the narrative that their affection was mutual—she must have been worried, as well. The position of a widow with no children was a precarious one in Israelite society, and Ruth's foreign status only complicated things. The famine had ended, but there was no guarantee that Naomi and Ruth would find relatives to care for them. There was a distant cousin, Boaz, but Naomi did not want to presume on his kindness.

The two women returned to Naomi's hometown of Bethlehem at the time of the barley harvest. Naomi, whose name means "pleasant" in Hebrew, asked the townspeople to call her Mara, meaning "bitter," "for the Almighty has dealt bitterly with me" *(Ruth 1.20 [NRSV])*. Ruth, familiar with the established custom of the Middle East, volunteered to put bread on the table by **gleaning,** gathering up the stalks of grain left behind for the poor when the reapers had finished harvesting a field. By chance, Boaz, an older, wealthy, and unmarried man, owned the field Ruth chose to visit. Drawn to the young woman, at first by her beauty and then by her loyalty to Naomi, Boaz ordered his field workers to leave extra grain for Ruth. He politely offered her water and a shady place to rest. He instructed her to glean only in his field. There he protected her from the unwanted attentions of the rowdy laborers. Ruth was astonished at—and a bit suspicious of—such generosity:

> "Why have I found favor in your sight, that you should take notice of me, when I am a foreigner?"
> But Boaz answered her, "All that you have done for your mother-in-law since the death of your husband has been full told me, and how you left your father and mother and your native land and came to a people that you did not know before. May the Lord reward you for your deeds, and may you have a full reward from the Lord, the God of Israel, under whose wings you have come for refuge!"
>
> *Ruth 2:10–12 [NRSV]*

The Redeeming Kinsman

Naomi was overjoyed when Ruth returned with the grain and the news of her meeting with Boaz. In fact, she asked Ruth to carry out an action that was truly puzzling to a Moabite, though to her credit she carried out Naomi's request

French painter Nicolas Poussin places the meeting between Ruth and Boaz (depicted in the foreground) in a lush panorama.

without a protest. Naomi told Ruth to dress herself in her best clothes, to find the place where Boaz would be sleeping in his field, to lie down at his feet, and to ask him to throw his cloak over her. Naomi wasn't just trying to help Ruth find herself a husband by flaunting her feminine charms. The actions Naomi outlined were the established process for approaching a "redeeming kinsman." Under a tradition known as **levirate marriage,** when a married man died without children, the closest unmarried male relative (usually a brother if he had one) was obliged to marry the widow and father a child. That child would be, legally and religiously, the heir of the dead man. For Boaz to throw his cloak over Ruth, signifying engagement to marry her, would also indicate his willingness to perform this family obligation.

As it happened, Boaz was more than willing. He was even more impressed by Ruth's devotion to Naomi, which had been demonstrated by her choosing to continue her mother-in-law's family lineage by marrying an older man instead of the young, handsome suitor she might have attracted on her own. There was, however, one hitch—another male relative with a closer family tie. Boaz tilted the negotiations in his own favor by making a marriage to Ruth sound like a burden with little financial reward. The other man then surrendered his claim over her by removing his sandal and handing it to Boaz in the marketplace:

> Then all the people who were at the gate, along with the elders, said, "We are witnesses. May the Lord make the woman who is coming into your house like Rachel and Leah, who together built up the house of Israel. May you produce children in Ephrathah and bestow a name in Bethlehem; and, through the children that the Lord will give you by this young woman, may your house be like the house of Perez, whom Tamar bore to Judah."
>
> So Boaz took Ruth and she became his wife. When they came together, the Lord made her conceive, and she bore a son. Then the women said to Naomi, "Blessed be the Lord, who has not left you this day without next-of-kin; and may his name be renowned in Israel! He shall be to you a restorer of life and a nourisher of your old age; for your daughter-in-law who loves you, who is more to you than seven sons, has borne him."
>
> Then Naomi took the child and laid him in her bosom, and became his nurse. The women of the neighborhood gave him a name, saying, "A son has been born to Naomi. They named him Obed; he became the father of Jesse, the father of David."
>
> *Ruth 4:11–17 [NRSV]*

In this way Ruth, a foreigner, became the great-grandmother of David, Israel's greatest king. According to Christian tradition, Ruth was an ancestor of Jesus, who came from the line of David. Almost unique among biblical characters, Ruth has been depicted as completely without fault or character flaw. Her love for Naomi—and later for Naomi's God and Naomi's relative Boaz—was selfless and wholehearted, earning her the compliment, unheard of in the male-centered Israelite culture, that she was better for Naomi than seven sons. And so, the narrative of a woman who asked to be called bitter has a sweet ending.

The Book of Ruth concludes with a short genealogy from Perez to David. The genealogy is a sign of peace and prosperity and contrasts with the famine and turbulence that started the book. Just as Naomi was brought from emptiness to fulfillment through the selfless love of Ruth, so Israel came from famine and difficulty to prosperity in the reign of David.

THE BIBLE

AS **Literature**

There is marvelous symmetry throughout the Book of Ruth. The action moves from a briefly sketched account of distress (1:1–5), 71 words in Hebrew, through four episodes to a concluding account of relief and hope that is drawn with equal brevity (4:13–17), 71 words in Hebrew. The crucial turning point occurs exactly midway in line 2:20, where it states that the Lord's "kindness has not forsaken the living or the dead!"

The opening line of each of the four episodes signals its main theme: verse 1:6, the return; 2:1, the meeting with Boaz; 3:1, finding a home for Ruth; 4:1, the decisive event at the gate. The closing line of each episode facilitates transition to what follows.

Contrast is also used to good effect. Naomi's name means "pleasant," but she is bitter (1:20) and empty (1:21), although she becomes full at the end. Another contrast is the living and the dead. Most striking is the contrast between the two main characters—Ruth and Boaz. Ruth is a young foreigner who is a childless and destitute widow while Boaz is a middle-aged, well-to-do Israelite securely established in his home community.

All aspects of the narrative keep focused on the central theme—the passage from emptiness to fullness through the selfless acts of Ruth and Boaz. In the process, Naomi moves from bitterness to fullness.

NIV Study Bible

This painting is a theater illustration showing a costume designed for a play about Esther by the French dramatist Jean Racine. He was commissioned to write the play by the wife of Louis XIV, Madame de Maintenon, who, like Esther, was a commoner who married a king.

Esther

The Book of Esther is remarkable among the Hebrew Scriptures not only for focusing on a woman, but because it (like the Song of Songs) contains no mention of God. The rabbis who argued for the book's inclusion among the canonical writings, however, made the case that this narrative, on one level merely a Jewish variation on a common Middle Eastern theme, is filled throughout with evidence of God's saving presence. Salvation is worked out, as it often is in the Bible, through the actions of an otherwise unlikely person—in this case, a beauty queen.

The Beauty Queen

At the beginning of the Esther narrative, it seems as though Esther was going to be famous only for her beauty:

It happened in the days of King Ahasuerus—that Ahasuerus who reigned over a hundred and twenty-seven provinces from India to Ethiopia. . . .

In the fortress of Shushan lived a Jew by the name of Mordecai, son of Jair son of Shimei son of Kish, a Benjaminite. Kish had been exiled from Jerusalem in the group that was carried into exile along with King Jeconiah of Judah, which had been driven into exile by King Nebuchadnezzar of Babylon. He was foster father to Hadassah—that is, Esther—his uncle's daughter, for she had neither father nor mother. The maiden was shapely and beautiful.

Esther 1:1, 2:5–7 [NJPS]

In this altar panel by the Renaissance painter Filippino Lippi, three scenes from the life of Esther are collapsed into one composition. Esther (in rose, middle left) is seen entering the court of Ahasuerus for the first time as Vashti (in yellow, middle right) is led away.

Esther moved from the house of a Jewish exile to the harem of a Persian king named Ahasuerus, whose name in Greek is Xerxes. The king, having a bit of a problem controlling his wine consumption, had flown into a drunken rage at his queen, Vashti, because she had refused to let him parade her charms in front of his intoxicated banquet guests. Vashti was dismissed, and the king held a beauty contest for a replacement. But the rules were slightly different from those of a modern beauty contest. Contestants were given beauty treatments—for a year. Yet, there were no speeches, no talent shows, no eveningwear competition, just a night with the king in his bedroom. The king was looking for a more compliant woman, one who was lovely but without a troublesome mind of her own. In a fine twist of irony, however, he chose Esther, who was blessed with both beauty and brains. Mordecai had encouraged Esther to hide the fact that she was a Jew. (Note that the word *Israelite* does not appear in this book.)

THE BIBLE

IN Literature

John Keats (1795–1821) was the epitome of the English Romantic poet. A man of heightened sensitivity, passionate intelligence, and frail health (he suffered from consumption—tuberculosis—which was at that time inevitably fatal), Keats was always attuned to the undercurrent of melancholy that seemed to flow through the natural world. As a literary device, this sense that all nature is in sympathy with the human heart is known as the *pathetic fallacy,* and Keats employed it often. His 1819 poem "Ode to a Nightingale" describes the night bird's song as one of unbearable sweetness and sorrow, longing and loss. In this verse from the poem, Keats projects his own melancholy mood onto the figure of Ruth. Though the Bible never mentions that Ruth suffered homesickness, Keats's striking image lives on, summing up the universal human experience of being "a stranger in a strange land," even at home.

> Thou wast not born for death, immortal Bird!
>   No hungry generations tread thee down;
> The voice I hear this passing night was heard
>   In ancient days by emperor and clown:
> Perhaps the self-same song that found a path
>   Through the sad heart of Ruth, when, sick for home,
>   She stood in tears amid the alien corn.

In Rembrandt's depiction of Esther's banquet, the queen's goodness is illuminated by the lamplight while Haman the villain lurks in the shadows.

Haman the Wicked

The Book of Esther has its villain, and he was completely without redeeming qualities. Haman, the king's steward, is introduced as "the foe of the Jews." His family lineage marked him as a descendant of the Amalekites, the worst enemies of the Israelites from the time of their entrance into the Promised Land. (See Exodus 17:14–16.)

Haman had been raised to hate the Jews. For his part, Mordecai refused to bow to an enemy of his people, and so gave Haman a personal target for his prejudice. For Mordecai's insolence, Haman vowed to destroy all the Jews and brought the matter before the king. Taking advantage of the king's perpetual tipsiness, Haman filled the king's head with rumors of treachery by "a certain people," carefully omitting whom he meant. The king signed Haman's edict dooming the Jews of Persia, and he gave Haman the funds to carry out the plan. Haman, to prolong the agony, left the date of the massacre to chance, drawing lots called *purim* in Hebrew to choose the appointed day.

When Mordecai, whose position at the palace gate positioned him at the center of the news, heard Haman's plan, he mourned, tore his clothes, and put on sackcloth and ashes. He approached his foster child, Esther, and asked her to use her influence with King Ahasuerus to stop the massacre. Esther was reluctant. She knew that entering the king's presence without being summoned was punishable by death. But Mordecai drew on Esther's loyalty to her people and offered her the chance to be their deliverer. The phrase "from another quarter" has been interpreted to be an indirect reference to God—the only such reference in the entire book:

> Do not imagine that you, of all the Jews, will escape with your life by being in the king's palace. On the contrary, if you keep silent in this crisis, relief and deliverance will come to the Jews from another quarter, while you and your father's house will perish. And who knows, perhaps you have attained to royal position for just such a crisis.
>
> *Esther 4:13–14 [NJPS]*

The Jewish feast of Purim, or Lots, celebrates Esther's defeat of Haman's genocidal plot. The megillah, or scroll, of the Book of Esther (lower right) is read in its entirety in the synagogue on that day, and the members of the congregation hiss, boo, and rattle noisemakers whenever Haman's name is mentioned. Purim is traditionally a day of masquerade, costume, merrymaking, carnival games, and giving food to friends and to the poor (right).

The Plan

The suggestion may have been Mordecai's, but the plan was Esther's own. Once decided, she demonstrated a shrewd knowledge of royal politics and of ordinary human vanity. "I will go to the king, though it is against the law; and if I perish, I perish" *(Esther 4:16 [NRSV]).*

Esther did go to the king, who welcomed her and offered her whatever she wanted. Instead of asking outright for what she wanted, she asked if the king and Haman might join her for dinner. The king agreed. At dinner the king again offered Esther anything she wanted. Esther shrewdly asked for another dinner with the same guests the following day. Haman, thinking that this meant a promotion might be imminent, was thrilled. As he boasted of this special honor to his friends that evening, he complained that the one thing robbing him of complete joy was Mordecai, who still refused to bow to him. His wife and friends convinced Haman to build a gallows outside his house so that he could watch Mordecai hang on the day the edict took effect.

A twist occurs in the narrative when the king discovered that Mordecai had once saved his life and had never been rewarded. When Haman arrived the next morning, the king asked what he would recommend as a reward for someone the king wants to honor. Haman, believing that he was that someone, advised the king to give the man fancy clothes and jewelry and have him ride on the king's horse through the city while a high official went before him declaring, "This is what is done for the person whom the king wants to honor." To his horror, Haman learned that the honoree was not to be him, but Mordecai. To make matters worse, the king asked Haman to lead Mordecai through the streets shouting Haman's own line. Haman was furious but had to comply.

In a second dinner party that night, the king asked once again for a chance to fulfill Esther's desire. Esther, to everyone's surprise, begged the king to preserve her life and that of her people. When asked by the king who was threatening her, Esther replied "This vile Haman!" The king became furious and left the room. Haman fell on the couch beside Esther pleading for his life.

THE BIBLE
AS Literature

In the Book of Esther, feasting is a prominent theme and setting for important plot developments. There are ten banquets: (1) 1:3–4; (2) 1:5–8; (3) 1:9, (4) 2:18; (5) 3:15; (6) 5:1–8; (7) 7:1–10; (8) 8:17; (9) 9:17; (10) 9:18–32. The three pairs of banquets that mark the beginning, middle, and end of the narrative are particularly prominent. Two are given by the king, two are prepared by Esther, and one is the double celebration of Purim.

The phrase *the whole megillah* is directly related to the Book of Esther. *Megillah* is the Hebrew word for scroll. The words refer to the fact that the entire scroll of Esther is read aloud at the feast of Purim and have come to mean a long or involved story or account.

When the king returned and saw Haman on the couch next to his wife, he interpreted this as an attempted seduction. The king bemoaned that he did not have any gallows ready to hang Haman. Then, one of the king's officials pointed out that a newly built gallows could be found in front of Haman's house. So, Haman was hanged on the gallows he himself had built.

A new royal edict permitted the Jews to defend themselves in the face of Haman's decree. The narrative ends with the proclamation of a great feast, encouraging all Jews to observe this day as a holiday, which was given the name *Purim,* or "lots," after the lots used by Haman to determine the day on which he would kill the Jews.

The Bible and Women

In spite of the example of loving and courageous women like Ruth and Esther, the Bible—at least as traditionally interpreted and applied in everyday modern life—has not always been presented as friendly to women. Biblical pronouncements about women's "place" in the world have often been used to justify second-class citizenship.

When the first wave of American women's suffragists were engaged in the struggle for the right to vote in the mid-1800s, for example, some of their fiercest opposition came from clergymen seeking to invoke the Bible against them. The feisty suffragist Elizabeth Cady Stanton met them on their own ground, even publishing her own version of the Bible. Other women in the suffragist, abolitionist, and temperance movements drew inspiration, not frustration, from the biblical tradition. Anna Howard Shaw, an ordained Methodist minister and medical doctor, drew on biblical tradition to stir American women to take up prophetic roles for social change:

> This, then, is God's lesson to you and to me. He opens before our eyes the vision of a great truth, and for a moment He permits our wondering gaze to rest upon it; then He bids us go forth. Jacob of old saw the vision of God's messengers ascending and descending, but none of them were standing still.

The enduring popularity of the biblical stories of Ruth and Esther is demonstrated by these paintings. In Frank Topham's *The Story of Ruth and Boaz,* a father looks over his daughter's shoulder as she reads; they sit in a field that could be the place where Ruth met Boaz. Dora Holzhandler's *The Story of Esther* depicts a Purim celebration with the girls, as is traditional, costumed as Queen Esther.

Although appeals are often made to biblical tradition to limit women's power and authority, the narratives of Ruth and Esther are proof that the biblical message cannot be so easily reduced. Neither Ruth nor Esther was a "traditional" woman. Ruth was a foreigner who chose the Jewish faith out of devotion to her mother-in-law and wound up the great-grandmother of King David, the most famous king in Hebrew Scriptures. Esther was as beautiful as any biblical heroine, and she violated tradition by marrying a pagan king, but she used her intelligence to save her people. Both are numbered among the "women of valor" whose praises are sung in the Book of Proverbs:

> Her children rise up and call her happy;
>   her husband too, and he praises her:
> "Many women have done excellently,
>   but you surpass them all."
> Charm is deceitful, and beauty is vain,
>   but a woman who fears the Lord is
>   to be praised.
> Give her a share in the fruit of her hands,
>   and let her works praise her in the city
>   gates.

A monument in Seneca Falls, New York (top right), site of the first women's suffrage convention, recalls the moment when Elizabeth Cady Stanton and Susan B. Anthony first met, initiating a partnership that would change American life. A caricature of feminist leaders Stanton and Anthony (right) draws on religious imagery to depict them as the patron saints or guardian angels of the women's suffrage movement.

projects

Choose one of the following projects to learn more about the women of the Hebrew Scriptures:

1. Leaf through the Hebrew Scriptures and find ten women who are given substantial space. Make a chart. In the first column put the women's names. In the second column put a one- or two-sentence summary of the women's roles. In the third column, write the significance of the women's account for today's world.

2. Do some research to learn more about the Purim festival. What are some of the customs? What role does this festival play in the life of the Jewish community? Share what you find out.

KEY BIBLICAL TEXTS

■ The Book of Daniel 1:1–7:28; 12:1–13

DISCOVER

■ That apocalyptic writing provides a message of hope in times of persecution

■ That the Book of Daniel is written in a kind of code that its readers would understand but that enemies would not

■ That visionary writing gives the sense that things will turn out all right

■ That the visions of Daniel still resonate in today's language and culture

GET TO KNOW

■ Daniel, Nebuchadnezzar, Shadrach, Meshach, Abednego, Gabriel, Michael

CONSIDER

■ What do you read or watch to give you a sense that things are going to turn out for the best?

Visions of the Future
Daniel

Under the most incredible stress, enduring physical torment, psychological chaos, and spiritual torment, the human psyche has unexpected powers of survival. When people undergo long periods of persecution or oppression, their collective spirit may demonstrate the same kind of persistence, expressing itself in works of art that convey hope and look forward to a transformed future. Such works of art, literature, and music often rely heavily on codes and symbolism that mask the true message of liberation from the oppressor.

During the years of slavery in the American South, for example, enslaved Africans used the conventional language of the Bible as a code to express their longing for freedom, singing spirituals that spoke of "crossing Jordan" and looked forward to "that great gettin'-up morning" when all oppressive power structures would be overthrown.

The Book of Daniel is an example of the kind of literature that uses elaborate codes to provide hope to people in distress. Such writing is known as

The famed Hanging Gardens of Babylon, one of the seven wonders of the ancient world, were evidence of the technological and aesthetic sophistication of the Babylonian empire, which made many contributions to Western culture. From the Bible's point of view, however, the knowledge and power of the Babylonians were put to evil use in the service of false gods and the oppression of captives.

THE BIBLE
IN Literature

Percy Bysshe Shelley (1792–1822) was part of the English Romantic movement that also included John Keats and George Gordon, Lord Byron. Shelley's reputation for radical behavior began when he was dismissed from Oxford for distributing pamphlets advocating atheism. Shelley's sonnet "Ozymandias" echoes Nebuchadnezzar's dream of the idol with feet of clay. Both the poem and the dream (as interpreted by Daniel) warn that earthly empires, no matter how powerful, must eventually fall:

> I met a traveler from an antique land
> Who said: Two vast and trunkless legs of stone
> Stand in the desert . . . Near them, on the sand,
> Half sunk, a shattered visage lies, whose frown,
> And wrinkled lip, and sneer of cold command,
> Tell that its sculptor well those passions read
> Which yet survive, stamped on these lifeless things,
> The hand that mocked them and the heart that fed;
> And on the pedestal these words appear:
> "My name is Ozymandias, king of kings;
> Look on my works, ye Mighty, and despair!"
> Nothing beside remains. Round the decay
> Of that colossal wreck, boundless and bare
> The lone and level sands stretch far away.

apocalyptic literature, from the Greek word *apocalypse,* which means "revelation." To those familiar with the code, the narratives and visions contained in Daniel reveal a message of hope and transformation.

Who were the people to whom this revelation was addressed? Most scholars think Daniel was written to offer encouragement to the Jews undergoing persecution under the reign of Greek Syrian emperors. That would make it the most recent of the Hebrew Scriptures. Others suggest that the Book of Daniel actually comes from a much earlier time in which its story is set—during the first years of the Babylonian exile. In either case, Daniel's powerful visions have given hope to people for millennia. The theme of the book is God's sovereignty: "The Most High God is sovereign over the realm of man" *(Daniel 5:21 [NJPS]).*

Prologue

The Book of Daniel begins with an introduction to its central character, the young Jew named Daniel. With his three companions, Daniel was carried off to captivity by Nebuchadnezzar's armies. In Babylon, the young men were chosen—for their looks, intelligence, and cultural refinement—to be trained as servants of the king:

> In the third year of the reign of King Jehoiakim of Judah, King Nebuchadnezzar of Babylon came to Jerusalem and besieged it. . . . Then the king commanded his palace master Ashpenaz to bring some of the Israelites of the royal family and of the nobility, the young men without physical defect and handsome, versed in every branch of wisdom, endowed with

INTO EVERYDAY language

An idol with *feet of clay* is a hero who suffers from a fault or weakness that brings him or her down to the level of ordinary mortals. The metaphor comes straight from Daniel, Chapter 2.

CULTURAL
CONNECTIONS

usic

At the height of its popularity, grand opera was the music of the people, known and loved by all ages and social classes. In fact, one particular opera chorus has inspired political revolutions, given hope to captives, and served as an unofficial national anthem of oppressed peoples everywhere.

Giuseppe Verdi's 1842 opera *Nabucco* was an immediate sensation. Its story, loosely based on the lives of the Jewish captives in Babylon under Nebuchadnezzar, was romantic and appealing. The central chorus, *"Va, pensiero"* ("The Chorus of the Hebrew Slaves"), married a stirring melody with moving lyrics based on Psalm 137 to create an instant hit. Italian nationalists, struggling at the time against Austrian oppression and occupation, quickly adopted Verdi's chorus of patriotic longing as their own anthem, where it served to unite the *Risorgimento* movement. The song's popularity spread throughout Europe and America. When Verdi died, thousands of people walking in his funeral procession spontaneously broke into this beloved chorus. During World War II, *"Va,*

pensiero" was an anthem of homesickness and hope that echoed through prison camps. And when the State of Israel declared its independence in 1948, the occasion was marked by a heartfelt rendition of Verdi's chorus, whose sorrowful lyrics are belied by the triumphant melody:

Fly, my thoughts, on golden wings!
Fly, settle on the cliffs and hills
Where the warm, soft breezes carry
The sweet fragrance of my native land.

Bear my greetings to the banks of the Jordan,
To the desolate towers of Zion.
O my homeland, so beautiful and so lost!
O remembrances, so dear and so deadly!
Golden harps of our prophets and poets,
Why do you hang silent on the willows?

Rekindle our hearts with memories;
Sing to us of the days that are no more.
Remembering the fate of Jerusalem,
Play us a harsh lament,
Or let God use you to inspire in us
The courage to endure our suffering!

---

knowledge and insight, and competent to serve in the king's palace; they were to be taught the literature and language of the Chaldeans. . . .

Among them were Daniel, Hananiah, Misael, and Asariah, from the tribe of Judah. The palace master gave them other names: Daniel he called Belteshazzar, Hananiah he called Shadrach, Misael he called Meshach, and Asariah he called Abednego. . . . In every matter of wisdom and understanding concerning which the king inquired of them, he found them ten times better than all the magicians and enchanters in his whole kingdom.

Daniel 1:1, 3–4, 6–7, 20 [NRSV]

Interpreter of Dreams

The first five chapters of the Book of Daniel contain two narratives of Daniel's adventures as an interpreter of dreams. These narratives recall the account of one of Israel's great patriarchs, Joseph. Like Joseph, Daniel was a captive in a foreign and hostile land. Like Joseph, Daniel attracted the attention and favor of the ruler and was given a position of importance. And, like Joseph, Daniel had the gift of interpreting dreams. This was a prophetic role that in Jewish tradition is synonymous with revealing God's will. When he explained to his companions why he had been given the gift denied to the Babylonian magicians and astrologers, Daniel explained it this way:

> Blessed be the name of God from age to age,
>> for wisdom and power are his.
> He changes times and seasons,
>> deposes kings and sets up kings;
> he gives wisdom to the wise
>> and knowledge to those who have understanding.
> He reveals deep and hidden things;
>> he knows what is in the darkness, and light dwells in him.
>>> *Daniel 2:20-22 [NRSV]*

It happened that Nebuchadnezzar had a most disturbing dream, and he sent for his magicians to interpret it for him—or they would die. The king would not tell the magicians what the dream was but told them, in effect, that if they were so smart, they would know both the dream and its interpretation. Predictably, they failed. So the king ordered the magicians executed.

God revealed to Daniel both the dream and the interpretation. So, Daniel said to the executioners, "Do not destroy the wise men of Babylon, bring me in before the king and I will give the king the interpretation" *(Daniel 2:24 [NRSV])*.

The king had dreamed of a great statue that had a head of gold, a chest of silver, arms and legs of iron, and feet partly of iron and partly of clay. The statue came apart and was destroyed. Daniel interpreted the dream as a political prophecy. The four substances symbolized four kingdoms (probably Babylon, Media, Persia, and Greece). These kingdoms would be destroyed. But the one God of heaven would set up a kingdom that would never be destroyed, that would last forever.

After King Nebuchadnezzar heard the interpretation, he fell on his face and said to Daniel, "Truly, your God is God of gods and Lord of kings and a revealer of mysteries, for you have been able to reveal this mystery" *(Daniel 2:47 [NRSV])*. The king then placed Daniel in a high position, lavished many gifts upon him, and made him governor over the entire province of Babylon, placing him in charge of all its wise men.

Besides serving as an eloquent testimony to divine wisdom, Daniel's words could be understood by the persecuted community as a reminder that earthly might and knowledge were transitory and that God would bring to light all the secret crimes of the oppressors. This same message is buried in all Nebuchadnezzar's dreams.

King Nebuchadnezzar had a second dream. Daniel predicted that the King would be humiliated when he reached his greatest moment. This happened a year later when King Nebuchadnezzar was driven away from human society into the wilderness. When this period was over, Nebuchadnezzar, instead of complaining, praised God and God's "everlasting sovereignty" and then was restored to kingship.

The Fiery Furnace

Between the two dreams is the narrative of the fiery furnace. For all his apparent sophisticated charm, Nebuchadnezzar has been revealed to the reader as a petulant tyrant capable of inhuman cruelty. He fashioned a huge golden idol and commanded everyone in the land to fall down and worship it at the sound of a musical cue. Only Daniel's three companions refused, calmly insisting on their right to worship only their own God.

The king had shown special favor to these Hebrew captives, appointing them administrators over the province of Babylon at Daniel's request. And so he was embarrassed and enraged. He prepared a hideous punishment for the three young men. But the Book of Daniel demonstrates that the oppressor never triumphs, and that God will always deliver his chosen ones. Cast into a fiery

The "three Hebrew children in the fiery furnace" were a hugely popular subject of medieval art and drama. In this fifteenth-century German illustration, the three young men stand calmly praying in the flames while Nebuchadnezzar's servants (armed with the pitchforks associated with devils in Christian images of hell) are overcome by the heat.

Unit Feature

The Bible and Shakespeare

William Shakespeare (1564–1616) is perhaps the most recognized figure in English literature. His plays and poetry are as alive today as they were in the late sixteenth and early seventeenth century when they were first performed. He was first and foremost a secular writer who captured the quirks and weaknesses of kings and of buffoons, of tragic heroes, and of merciless villains.

What about the Bible and the Bard of Avon? Do his broad comedies, his dark tragedies, or his epic histories have anything at all to do with the Bible? In fact, they do. Shakespeare used over 1300 documented biblical references in his thirty-seven plays written from 1589 through 1613. Why is there so much of the Bible in Shakespeare? The answer is really quite simple. People of all walks of life in England read the Bible, and so the contents of the Bible were a ready source of material for Shakespeare. And he was more than willing to rely on his audiences to understand how he put the words, sentiments, and characters of the Bible to dramatic use.

Some of the biblical references are very clear, such as the names of persons or verses that parallel lines from the Bible. Others are less obvious. Often, Shakespeare took images found in the Bible and developed them for his own purposes. In either case, Shakespeare presupposed that his audience—from queen to commoner—knew the Bible well enough to see just what the bard was doing.

BIBLICAL REFERENCES

A few scholars, beginning with Walter Whiter in 1794, have examined the biblical references in the works of Shakespeare in detail. Some devoted much time and energy to the subject. For example, Bishop Christopher Wordsworth wrote *Shakespeare's Knowledge and Use of the Bible* in 1864. Much more recently, Naseeb Shaheen, of the University of Memphis and perhaps the world's foremost authority on Shakespeare and the Bible, documented an average of forty biblical references per play.

Some of the biblical references are direct both as to names and as to narrative. The creation, the temptation, the fall, the narrative of Cain and Abel, the flood, the narrative of the patriarchs, Job, Pharaoh, Samson, David, Solomon, and many other figures in the Bible are contained in Shakespeare's plays. The scholar Carl Ackermann, author of *The Bible in Shakespeare,* points out "from Adam to Christ and his apostles scarcely an important person is omitted and in addition a large number of the stories connected with their lives have been presented at least in their broader outlines." The following is just a sampling of allusions collected by Carl Ackermann.

CREATION

Teach me how
To name the bigger light, and how the less,
That burn by day and night.

The Tempest (1.2)

And God made two great lights; the greater light to rule the day, and the lesser light to rule the night.

Genesis 1:16 [KJV]

ABEL AND CAIN

Which blood, like sacrificing Abel's cries,
Even from the tongueless caverns of the earth,
To me for justice and rough chastisement

Hamlet (3.3)

And the Lord said, "What have you done? Listen; your brother's blood is crying out to me from the ground!"

Genesis 4:10 [NRSV]

ABRAHAM

Sweet peace conduct his sweet soul to the bosom
Of good old Abraham!

Richard II (4.1)

The sons of Edward sleep in Abraham's bosom.

Richard III (4.3)

And it came to pass, that the beggar died, and was carried by the angels into Abraham's bosom.

Luke 16:22 [KJV]

JOB

I am as poor as Job, my lord; but not so patient.

Henry IV, Part 2 (1.2)

Ye have heard of the patience of Job.

James 5:11 [KJV]

DANIEL

A Daniel come to judgment! Yea, a Daniel!
O wise young judge, how I do honor thee!

The Merchant of Venice (4.1)

. . . for Daniel had convicted them of false witness by their own mouth. . . . And Daniel became great in the sight of the people from that day, and thenceforward.

Daniel 13:61, 64 [Douay Old Testament]

BARABBAS

Would any of the stock of Barabbas
Had been her husband rather than a Christian!

The Merchant of Venice (4.1)

Then cried they all again, saying, Not this man, but Barabbas. Now Barrabas was a robber.

John 18:40 [KJV]

PILATE

How fain, like Pilate, would I wash my hands
Of this most grievous guilty murder done!
Richard III (1.4)

So when Pilate saw that he could do nothing,
but rather that a riot was beginning, he took
some water and washed his hands before the
crowd, saying: "I am innocent of this man's
blood; see to it yourselves."
Matthew 27:24 [NRSV]

THE PRODIGAL SON

I had a hundred and fifty tattered prodigals
lately come from swine-keeping, from eating
draff and husks.
Henry IV, Part 1 (4.2)

And he went and joined himself to a citizen of
that country; and he sent him into his fields
to feed swine. And he would fain have filled
his belly with the husks that the swine
did eat.
Luke 15:15, 16 [KJV]

THE BIBLE AND SHAKESPEARE PARALLELS

Some of Shakespeare's verses directly parallel biblical
verses, as if the poet's mind were saturated with biblical
verses. Here are just a few samples of these parallels. It
can be fun to look up the Bible references to see just
how completely parallel the verses are.

Blessed are the peacemakers on earth.
Henry VI, Part 2 (2.1) and Matthew 5:9 [KJV]
Forbear to judge, for we are sinners all.
Henry VI, Part 2 (3.3) and Romans 3:23 [KJV]
Art thou, like the adder, waxen deaf?
Be poisonous too . . .
Henry VI, Part 2 (3.2) and Psalm 58:4 [KJV]
My name be blotted from the book of life.
Richard II, Part 1 (1.3) and Psalm 69:28 [KJV]
Dying so, death is to him advantage.
Henry V (4.1) and Philippians 1:21 [KJV]
What his heart thinks his tongue speaks.
Much Ado about Nothing (3.2) and
Matthew 12:34 [KJV]
Give every man thine ear, but few thy voice;
Take each man's censure, but reserve thy judgment.
Hamlet (1.3) and James 1:19 [KJV]
Cherish those hearts that hate thee.
Henry VIII (3.2) and Matthew 5:44 [KJV]

COMMON ISSUES

Shakespeare's plays are predominantly secular in nature.
Even so, Shakespeare grappled with issues found in
Genesis, Psalms, Proverbs, Job, the Gospels, Paul, and so
forth. Justice, suffering, mercy, sin, and redemption are

Professor Naseeb Shaheen teaches Shakespeare, English
Renaissance literature, and the Bible as literature. He is an
internationally known authority on Shakespeare, having published
five books on biblical references in Shakespeare and Spenser. His
most recent volume, *Biblical References in Shakespeare's Plays*,
is probably the most quoted book about Shakespeare in print.
Shaheen has also published over thirty articles, mainly on
Shakespeare, many of them published by Oxford and Cambridge
University Presses. His personal collection of pre-King James Bibles
is one of the largest in the world. (*Memphis University Catalog*)

among the many issues that fill Shakespeare's plays. Carl
Ackermann believes that Shakespeare's works are so full
of these issues because "he studied [the Bible] until its
thought and teachings, its story and personalities, had
fairly burned themselves into his memory, and became a
part of his being."

Three plays in particular—*Measure for Measure, Othello,*
and *The Winter's Tale*—demonstrate a particular biblical
worldview. *Measure for Measure* deals with the difference
between the law in the person of the obsessed Angelo and
grace in the person of the Duke who sweeps in to remedy
the situation. In *Othello*, the tragic hero, when given the
choice between good and evil, chooses evil, although his
decision was shaped in large part by the machinations and
temptations of the devilish Iago. *The Winter's Tale*, the last
play Shakespeare wrote, moves from a very bleak beginning to a positive but bittersweet ending. Shakespeare's
romances combined tragedy with a good ending, making
the eventual happiness more deeply appreciated because
it came through trial. At the heart of Shakespeare's plays
are the sentiments that creation is good, that life will go
on, and that things will get better.

Carl Ackermann asks, "What would Shakespeare have
been without the Bible? No doubt his genius would have
found expression in some other field of thought if he had
not been so fortunate as to be permitted to peruse carefully the pages of the Bible. However, I cannot but express
the conviction that without the Bible, [Shakespeare] would
have been shorn of much of his power."

Shakespeare's mind was filled with the language and
images of the Bible. He fully expected that those who
saw his plays would be able to grasp the level of meaning in his use of that language and those images brought
to the drama.

Another Covenant

Do not think that I have come to abolish the law or the prophets; I have come not to abolish but to fulfill. For truly I tell you, until heaven and earth pass away, not one letter, not one stroke of a letter, will pass from the law until all is accomplished.

Matthew 5:17-18 [NRSV]

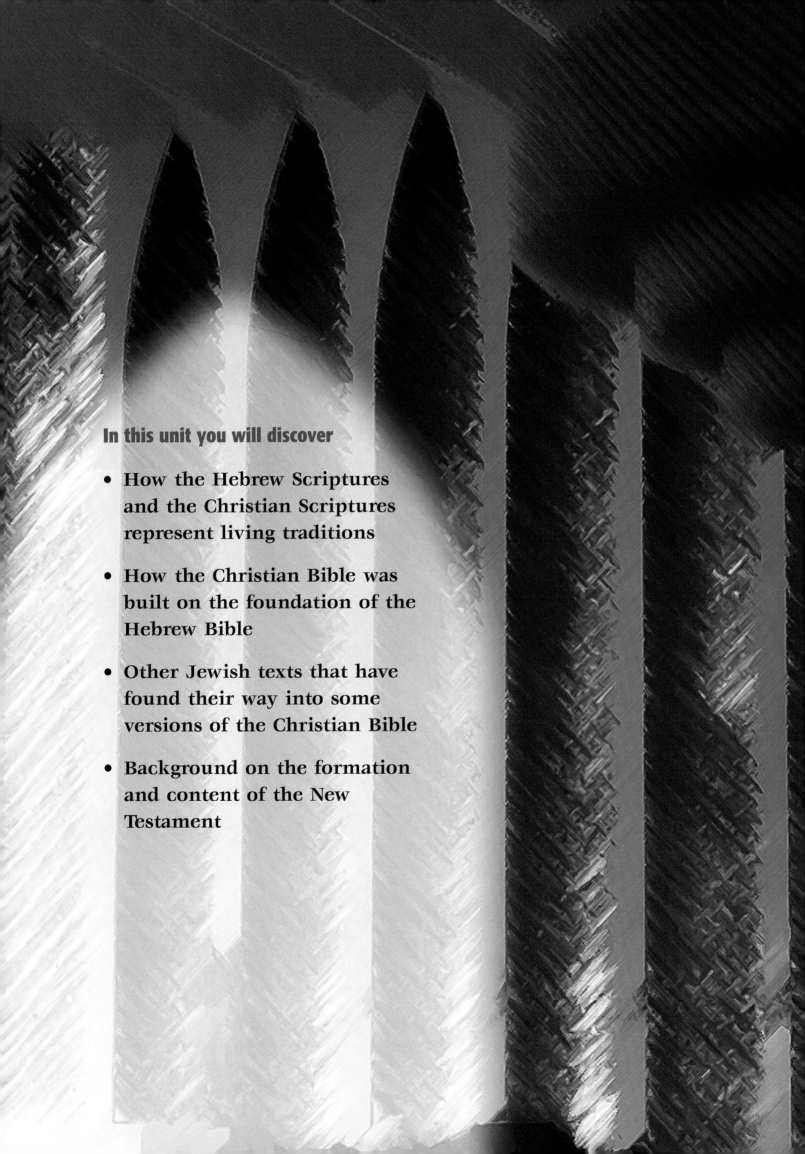

In this unit you will discover

- How the Hebrew Scriptures
  and the Christian Scriptures
  represent living traditions

- How the Christian Bible was
  built on the foundation of the
  Hebrew Bible

- Other Jewish texts that have
  found their way into some
  versions of the Christian Bible

- Background on the formation
  and content of the New
  Testament

Living Tradition

Before setting out on an overview of the Christian Bible and its New Testament, it is important to realize that for Jews and Christians the Bible is a document for living. Within these two traditions, the serious study of the Bible and the use of the Bible in daily life are precious and important. Even while learning about the Bible as literature and the Bible in literature, it is important to understand what kind of literature it is and how its influence has been used.

This textbook is divided into two parts, the Hebrew Bible and the Christian Bible. As you have already learned, the Christian Bible includes the Hebrew Scriptures. In the Christian Bible, the Hebrew Scriptures are called the Old Testament. To lay a solid foundation for understanding the literature of the Christian Bible, it is a good idea to keep some factors in mind:

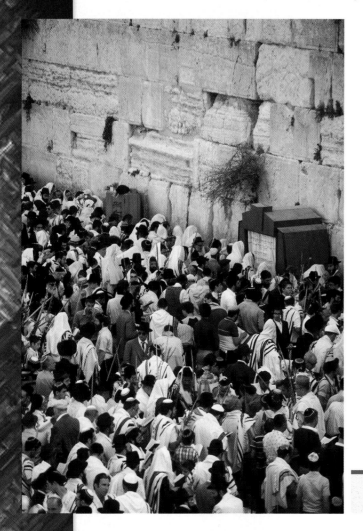

1. *The Jewish tradition continued.* The Jewish tradition did not come to a stop when Christianity and the Christian Bible began to take shape in the first century. Judaism and its relationship with the Hebrew Bible constitute a living tradition that continues unbroken through the centuries. It is a tradition that was traumatized by the destruction of the temple in Jerusalem in the year 70 and gradually became a rabbinic, or teaching, tradition rather than a temple religion. It is a tradition that has changed and grown, has suffered greatly, has been divided by differing approaches, but is still dynamic and alive.

2. *The law and the prophets are the foundation of Christian tradition.* The words of Jesus are quite clear: "Do not think I have come to abolish the law or the prophets; I have come not to abolish but to fulfill. For truly I tell you, until heaven and earth pass away, not one letter, not one stroke of a letter, will pass from the law until all is accomplished" *(Matthew 5:17–18 [NRSV]).* The statement of Jesus is a dramatic demonstration that the Hebrew Scriptures have not become outdated. In fact, without the Hebrew Bible, the New Testament would be unintelligible—a plant deprived of its roots and destined to dry up and wither.

Many Jews pray at the Western Wall for the coming of a Messiah.

3. *There are two views of how the Hebrew Scriptures look to the future.* For Christians, everything in the Old Testament is seen through the lens of the birth, life, teaching, suffering, death, and resurrection of Jesus. For Christians, the narratives and accounts in the Hebrew Scriptures are seeded with promises of a Messiah, a new age, and a new relationship with God. All of this they see as coming to pass in Jesus. The narratives and prophetic literature of the Hebrew Bible were written first to help the Israelites understand their own times from God's point of view. That same literature took on a new and quite different meaning for Christians.

4. *There are promises to be fulfilled.* Both Christians and Jews are waiting for promises to be fulfilled. Today, for example, many Jews pray at the "Wailing Wall" of the temple ruins in Jerusalem. They are praying and longing for a messianic age. Christians believe that age has come in Jesus Christ. Still, they know that what they see as accomplished in Jesus has yet to be fulfilled in the minds and hearts of the people. They are awaiting a second coming of Jesus. And so, both traditions have great expectations of promises yet to be fulfilled.

It is important to remember that although both Jews and Christians share a common body of writing, the two traditions do not view the Hebrew Scriptures or the Christian Old Testament in the same way. The way Christianity today views and uses the Hebrew Bible differs from Judaism. The narratives, prophecies, and poetry are the same, but in the two living traditions, the interpretation, the use, and the purpose are often quite different.

Giotto's portrait showing the infant Jesus with a scroll in his hand.

The Bible in Apostolic Times

Christianity began in Judaism. Jesus and his first disciples were Jews. When the writers of the New Testament refer to "the scriptures," almost without exception, they mean the Hebrew Scriptures. Christians see Jesus as a teacher who set a new course. For Christians Jesus is the Christ, from the Greek word for "messiah," or "anointed one."

Early Christian understanding of an old covenant and new covenant come from an interpretation of the words of the prophet Jeremiah in the Hebrew Scriptures. Jeremiah was writing at the time of the destruction of Jerusalem and the First Temple:

> Behold, the days come, saith the Lord, that I will make a new covenant with the house of Israel, and with the house of Judah:
> Not according to the covenant that I made with their fathers in the day that I took them by the hand to bring them out of the land of Egypt; which my covenant they brake, although I was an husband unto them, saith the Lord.
> *Jeremiah 31:31–32 [KJV]*

In his First Letter to the Corinthians, written around the year 54, the apostle Paul described what Jesus did at the Last Supper. Paul wrote about Jesus taking a cup of wine and saying:

> This cup is the new covenant in my blood. Do this, as often as you drink it, in remembrance of me.
>
> *1 Corinthians 11:25–26 [NRSV]*

Chapters 9 and 10 of the Letter to the Hebrews go into more detail and interpretation of this new covenant. The letter quotes the words of the prophet Ezekiel:

> A new heart I will give you, and a new spirit I will put within you; and I will remove from your body the heart of stone and give you a heart of flesh. I will put my spirit within you, and make you follow my statutes . . .
>
> *Ezekiel 36:26–27 [NRSV]*

For Christians, this new heart and new spirit are signposts of their new covenant. Jesus drew these sentiments and longings and hopes into a summary of the commandments in the Hebrew Scriptures:

> "You shall love the Lord your God with all your heart, and with all your soul, and with all your mind." This is the greatest and first commandment. And a second is like it: "You shall love your neighbor as yourself." On these two commandments hang all the law and the prophets.
>
> *Matthew 22:37–40 [NRSV]*

Serious Differences

To understand the ways the authors of the New Testament write about the Hebrew Bible, it is important to understand two fairly technical terms. The first is a term you have already learned, **midrash,** that is, interpretation, or exposition. The second technical term is **polemic,** or strong, formal, and persistent argument—in short, a dispute. First of all, the New Testament interprets major events in the Hebrew Bible very differently than does Jewish tradition—then and now. This includes, for example, the Genesis account of Adam and Eve, the sacrifice or binding of Isaac, the scapegoat of Leviticus, the kingship of David, and the interpretation of the suffering servant of Isaiah and of the other prophets and of the writings. When you read about the Hebrew Scriptures in the New Testament, you are getting this new "midrash," this new interpretation. As the Christian community grew, it rejected or altered many of the Jewish interpretations.

Second is the idea of a polemic. For the most part, the first-century Jewish community rejected the Christian interpretations of the scriptures as pointing to Christ as the fulfillment of the prophetic literature and the subject of the writings. The Christian community stood up to that rejection, and a dispute was born. At times in the dispute each side took issue with the claims of the other. A residue of that dispute is found in the New Testament. It is important to recognize that the dispute existed and to remember its context when reading the New Testament.

This was the scene as the branches of the biblical tree separated from the single trunk of the Hebrew Bible. An awareness of these conditions will help in two ways. First, it enables a broader understanding of the literature of the Bible. Second, it aids in an understanding of why the Christian Bible is made up of an Old and a New Testament and is not just "the New Testament part."

CULTURAL
CONNECTIONS
*H*andel's *Messiah*

A SAMPLE OF SCRIPTURE FOUND IN *MESSIAH*

1 PROPHECY AND PROMISE OF THE REDEEMER

Air for Tenor:

Every valley shall be exalted, and every mountain and hill made low; the crooked straight, and the rough places plain *(Isaiah 40:4)*.

Chorus:

And the glory of the Lord shall be revealed, and all flesh shall see it together: for the mouth of the Lord hath spoken it *(Isaiah 40:5)*.

2 THE SUFFERING OF THE LAMB WHO REDEEMS

Air for Tenor:

Thou shalt break them with a rod of iron; thou shalt dash them in pieces like a potter's vessel *(Psalm 2:9)*.

Chorus:

Hallelujah: for the Lord God omnipotent reigneth. The kingdom of this world is become the kingdom of our Lord, and of his Christ; and he shall reign forever and ever. King of Kings, and Lord of Lords *(Revelation 19:6, 11:15, 19:16)*.

3 THANKSGIVING FOR THE DEFEAT OF DEATH

Duet for Alto and Tenor:

O death, where is thy sting? O grave, where is thy victory? The sting of death is sin, and the strength of sin is the law *(1 Corinthians 15:55–56)*.

Chorus:

But thanks be to God, who giveth us the victory through our Lord Jesus Christ *(1 Corinthians 15:57)*.

George Friedrich Handel

One cultural example of how the Hebrew Bible is interpreted by Christians as predicting and presenting Jesus as the savior of the world is George Friedrich Handel's oratorio *Messiah*.

Unlike the majority of Handel's works, which rose and fell in popularity, *Messiah* has endured. This particular oratorio was written in three acts, much like an opera. The libretto of *Messiah* is made up almost entirely of verses from the Old and New Testaments from the King James Version of the Bible. Charles Jennens (1700–1773), who was a Shakespeare scholar, pulled the verses together into three parts: (1) The promise and birth of the Messiah; (2) the suffering, death, and rising of Jesus; (3) and finally, a thanksgiving for the defeat of death.

The first performance of *Messiah* was in Dublin in 1742. At once the work was a popular success. Handel's gift for blending English church music, German symphonic traditions, and the style of the Italian opera made his oratorios an important musical form in England.

The Dublin premiere was staged for charity, and Handel continued to donate proceeds from his performances of *Messiah,* especially to London's Foundling Hospital. At first the reception in England was subdued. Some thought it improper for Bible verses about Christ to be sung in a theatrical setting by opera singers. But King George II is said to have been so moved by the music that when the first "Hallelujah" rang out, he rose to his feet and remained standing until the last note of the chorus was sung. This began the tradition of standing up for the Hallelujah Chorus, still customary today. In ensuing years *Messiah* gained in recognition and acclaim. Partial perfomances were presented in New York in 1770. America's first complete performance of *Messiah* took place on Christmas Day, 1818, in Boston.

Every year at Avery Fisher Hall at Lincoln Center in New York, there is a sing-along performance of Handel's *Messiah*. Three thousand people bring their own music, and without rehearsal they sing a performance of *Messiah*.

Conflict

The Acts of the Apostles outlines the early growth of Christianity from Jerusalem to Rome. In that narrative is the basic conflict between the Jewish Christians and the larger Jewish community. That conflict was quite "out in the open" as Paul and the disciples spread their message that the messiah had come and that he had established a new covenant. Jews who did not accept that Jesus was the messiah were not at all happy about the claim that God had established a new covenant. Not surprisingly, this was the source of extreme tension. Gradually Paul and ultimately Christianity expanded their focus to include the other nations—the Gentiles, or non-Jews. No longer did one have to become a Jew to be a Christian. The strong conflict has influenced relationships between the Christians and Jews for two thousand years. It has led to abuses and to persecution on both sides. The story of Cain and Abel has often been played out in the relationship between Jews and Christians.

It seems that neither side acknowledged the great scope of the practices, rituals, attitudes, and ideals that are common to synagogue and church. It is important to remember, however, that early Christian leaders clung to the Hebrew Bible and forcefully resisted any attempts to separate the Hebrew Scriptures from the New Testament writings. They asserted that both collections of books were and always will be sacred literature for Christians. Therein lies an opportunity for growth in mutual understanding.

Recently, through initiatives, dialog, and shared study, what is common in the two Bibles is becoming a starting point for conversation between Christians and Jews. Some Christians are beginning to see the lasting value of God's covenant with the people of Israel. Some Jews are beginning to appreciate how the church kept safe within the Christian Bible the hopes and longings of Israel. Pope John Paul II, who was pope for twenty-six years and who lived under both Nazi and Communist rule, extended a hand of reconciliation to the Jews. He apologized for any anti-Semitism, and he called Judaism "the elder brother" of Christianity.

Just as it is impossible for Christians to fully understand their tradition without knowledge of the Hebrew Bible, so Jews can benefit from a knowledge of the Christian Bible to see how much of their own heritage has been preserved and nourished in its literature.

■ What are your current perceptions of the relationship between the Hebrew Bible and the Christian Bible?

A Note on Literary Development

The literature of the New Testament could not be more different from that of the Hebrew Scriptures. The Old Testament is written in classic Hebrew. It was compiled and edited over more than a thousand years. It includes history, law, prophecy, speeches, prayers, poetry, and song.

The New Testament was written in popular, or *koine,* Greek. This was the language of the markets and seaports. It was written within a period of not quite a century. It is less than one-third the size of the Hebrew Scriptures, and it centers upon the life and impact of one person. Yet, for Christians, the two collections of writings together reveal God's word and set forth the ideals upon which much of civilization, its literature, and its culture have been formed.

Saint Augustine: A detail from a Botticelli fresco painted in 1480.

An Example from Genesis

You have already seen some of the diverse interpretations of the Hebrew Scriptures, for example, the "binding of Isaac." Another important example from Genesis is the interpretation of the fall of Adam and Eve. They were given a command from God. They disobeyed that command and ate of the fruit of the forbidden tree. They were subsequently ushered out of the garden (see Genesis 3.) For many Christians, this sin was an **original sin** that infected the whole human race and was handed on through conception and birth. Such an interpretation is the foundation for a belief in the need for a redeemer who would make it possible to shed that original sin.

There is no concept of original inherited sin in rabbinic Judaism. Instead, the fall is seen as the result of the first people's attempt to become like God. Through that attempt they were forced to leave the garden and toil for their living, sacrificing their ease and privilege.

The writings of Augustine, one of the more influential writers in Western Christian thought, interpreted Genesis in the light of what he read in the letters of Paul the apostle. He developed from them the concept of original sin

KEY BIBLICAL TEXTS

- 1 Maccabees 1–4; 2 Maccabees 6–7, 12:43–45; Wisdom 2:23–24, 3:10, 8:7, 18:15–16; Sirach 44:1–10; Tobit 4–12; Judith 8–15; Daniel 13 [Susanna]

GET TO KNOW

- Alexander, Antiochus, Mattathias, Judas Maccabeus, Eleazar, Hannah, Tobit, Tobias, Raphael, Judith, Susanna

DISCOVER

- The importance of some Jewish texts that are not in the Hebrew Bible
- Some accounts and narratives that are fresh, interesting, and exciting literature on their own merits
- The value of these special texts to understanding the New Testament

CONSIDER

- What role do hero stories play in your life?

Other Jewish Texts in the Christian Bible

A family of heroes putting down an evil ruler, wise sayings, a guardian angel leading a couple to marriage, and a valiant woman tricking and decapitating an enemy king—all this you will find in a group of books in the Bible called the Deuterocanonical books, or the Apocrypha. Most of these books were originally written in Greek or were written in Hebrew and translated into Greek. They were part of the **Septuagint,** a Greek translation of Hebrew Scriptures made two hundred years after the exile.

The common people in Palestine no longer spoke Hebrew. Hebrew was the language of scholars. The spoken languages were Aramaic and Greek. The Hebrew Scripture quoted in the New Testament is the Septuagint. This Greek version of the Scriptures contains not only the thirty-nine books of the Hebrew Scriptures, but also a number of additional books.

Even though the stories and accounts in the books are part of Jewish lore, the books themselves are not part of the canon of the Hebrew Bible (which was established about the year 90). The books, however, became part of the Christian tradition because the

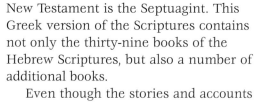

In this painting by the seventeenth-century artist Caravaggio, Jerome translates the Bible into Latin. It was he who first placed the Apocrypha in the Christian Bible.

DEUTEROCANONICAL/APOCRYPHAL WORKS		
CATHOLIC CANON	**ORTHODOX CANON**	**PROTESTANT APOCRYPHA**
Tobit	Tobit	Tobit
Judith	Judith	Judith
Additions to Esther	Additions to Esther	Additions to Esther
1–2 Maccabees	1–3 Maccabees	1–2 Maccabees
Wisdom	Wisdom	Wisdom
Sirach (Ecclesiasticus)	Sirach (Ecclesiasticus)	Sirach (Ecclesiasticus)
Baruch	Baruch	Baruch
Letter of Jeremiah	Letter of Jeremiah	Letter of Jeremiah
Additions to Daniel	Additions to Daniel	Additions to Daniel
	1 Esdras	1 Esdras
	2 Esdras (not universal)	2 Esdras
	Psalm 151	Prayer of Manasseh
	4 Maccabees (appendix)	
	Prayer of Manasseh (sometimes in appendix)	

Christians were reading the Greek Bible. Jerome was reluctant to put these books into his Latin translation because they were not present in the Hebrew, but the tradition of the Greek Bible prevailed. In the Protestant Reformation, Protestant Christians rejected these books, calling them **apocrypha** (meaning "hidden"). The Anglican tradition considered them "a collection of additional Books written by people of the Old Covenant and used in the Christian Church." Roman Catholic and Eastern Orthodox Christians, however, still accept these books as canonical scripture, but call them **deuterocanonical** (from the Greek for "second canon") because they were accepted after the first canon of Scriptures was set.

History

The Books of the Maccabees provide a historical bridge between the Hebrew Scriptures and the New Testament. These books deal with the history of the Jewish people during the period of Greek domination prior to the New Testament era.

First Maccabees begins with a description of the conquests of the Greek ruler Alexander the Great and the rulers who succeeded him. The focus in the early part of the book is the ruler Antiochus Epiphanes, one of the most notorious enemies in Jewish history. Antiochus entered Jerusalem and plundered the temple. A few years later, he took control of Jerusalem itself, destroying property and livestock and taking women and children captive. But this was only the beginning of troubles for the Jewish people. Next, Antiochus demanded that everyone in his realm profess the same religion. He sought to suppress the Jewish religion by forbidding circumcision and the keeping of the Sabbath, by ordering the sacrifice of unclean animals, and by setting up idols in worship places. He decreed that anyone who did not obey his decrees would die (see 1 Maccabees 1:50).

Antiochus, in a move that horrified the Jewish people even more, set up a statue of the Greek god Zeus on the altar of burnt offering in the courtyard of the tabernacle in the temple. Like the holy of holies, this altar was a particularly sacred place. In response to the action of Antiochus, the family of Mattathias went into mourning, tearing their garments and wearing sackcloth as when a loved one dies.

The Triumph of Judas Maccabeus by Peter Paul Rubens.

When Mattathias discovered that the king's army had slaughtered a thousand Jews who withdrew to the wilderness to escape, he and his family and friends made a decision: "Let us fight against anyone who comes to attack us on the Sabbath day; let us not all die as our kindred died in their hiding places" *(1 Maccabees 2:41 [NRSV])*. Mattathias and his family formed an army made up of other Jews opposed to the rule of Antiochus. They went through the land tearing down the pagan altars and forcing boys to be circumcised *(1 Maccabees 2:45–48)*.

After the death of Mattathias, his son Judas Maccabeus, for whom the book is named, succeeded him as leader of the rebel army. Eventually, the deeds of Judas came to the attention of Antiochus, who sent an enormous army, which included Syrian and Philistine troops, under the command of Lysias, to destroy the Jewish forces. In preparation for battle, the army of Judas fasted and prayed. Judas encouraged his frightened troops, reminding them of how God delivered their ancestors from Egypt. Once again, they were victorious, killing 3000 and scattering the rest. Another returning detachment approached from the hills. When the soldiers saw that Judas was burning the camp, they fled.

The following year Lysias attacked again, this time with 60,000 men, against Judas's 10,000 men. Again, Judas was victorious. After this, Judas and his men went to Jerusalem to cleanse and rededicate the temple. They tore down the profaned altar of sacrifice, built a new one, offered sacrifice, and for eight days celebrated the rededication. Judas proclaimed that this celebration should occur each year, and this is the origin of the Jewish Feast of Hanukkah.

The Second Book of Maccabees is largely a repetition of the story of 1 Maccabees but has a different style and some additional elements. This book includes references to a number of beliefs that became pivotal in the Christian tradition:

1. The resurrection of the dead *(2 Maccabees 7–8)*
2. Reward and punishment after death *(2 Maccabees 6:26)*
3. The creation of the world out of nothing *(2 Maccabees 7:28)*
4. Saying prayers for the dead *(2 Maccabees 12:39–45)*

Another way that 2 Maccabees was influential was in its portrait of the Jewish martyrs in Chapters 6 and 7. They became models for both Jewish and Christian martyrs. Chapter 6 tells the story of the elderly scribe Eleazar who, in the days of persecution just before the Maccabean revolt, refused to eat pork when threatened with death. Though the soldiers, who had grown to know and respect him, told him he could simply pretend to eat it, Eleazar refused because of the bad example this would provide. He was then beaten to death. "So in this way he died, leaving in his death an example of nobility and a memorial of courage, not only to the young but to the great body of his nation" *(2 Maccabees 6:31 [NRSV])*.

Chapter 7 tells the heroic story of Hannah and her seven sons. Her entire family was arrested and ordered under torture to eat the flesh of swine in violation of the dietary laws and as an explicit rejection of their God. The family was subjected to horrifying tortures, and all died for their beliefs. Just

CULTURAL
CONNECTIONS

anukkah

The Jewish festival of **Hanukkah** (also called the "Feast of Lights") celebrates the military success of Judas Maccabeus and his army over Antiochus and the rededication of the Jerusalem Temple by Judas Maccabeus. The word Hanukkah means "dedication."

The practice of lighting a **menorah,** a candlestick with eight branches, traces its origin to the Talmud. According to the Talmud, Judas Maccabeus could find only a small jar with a one-day supply of oil to light the lamps of the temple. However, so the legend says, the lamps continued to burn for eight days, after which more oil was found. During the festival, an additional candle is lit each night until the whole menorah is lighted.

Hanukkah traditions include eating foods fried in oil such as potato pancakes *(latkes)* and doughnuts *(sufganiyot)* to recall the miraculous oil. Children are given gifts of gold-foil-wrapped chocolate coins *(gelt)* to celebrate the Jewish nation that was formed after the Maccabean victory *(1 Maccabees 15:6),* and they play with a top called a *dreidel* on the sides of which are the Hebrew letters for the phrase "a great miracle happened here."

Contemporary artist Dora Holzhandler's painting shows the lighting of the menorah during Hanukkah.

before dying, one of the sons said to his executioner, "You accursed wretch, you dismiss us from this present life, but the King of the universe will raise us up to an everlasting renewal of life, because we have died for his laws" *(2 Maccabees 7:9 [NRSV]).* The mother, speaking valiantly to her dying sons, said, "The Creator of the world will in his mercy give life and breath back to you again, since you now forget yourselves for the sake of his laws" *(2 Maccabees 7:23 [NRSV]).* The mother also died.

Prophetic Literature

Prophecy is another genre presented in the Apocrypha or Deuterocanonical books. Included in both the Catholic and Orthodox canons are the Book of Baruch and the Letter of Jeremiah. Baruch was the secretary of the prophet Jeremiah.

Though it was probably written some time later, the setting of Baruch is the Babylonian exile. This book includes prayers, poems, and a hymn to wisdom and gives a good understanding of Jewish worship within one to two hundred years before the birth of Jesus. All of the exiles are asked as a collective nation to acknowledge their sins and repent *(Baruch 5:1–2).*

The Letter of Jeremiah, often included as the sixth chapter of Baruch, consists of seventy-three verses and is supposed to be a letter written by the prophet Jeremiah to the exiles in Babylon. It reflects many of the themes of the Book of Jeremiah, including the condemnation of the worship of idols and false gods.

IN YOUR
journal

Read the entire text of the account of the woman and her seven sons in 2 Macabees 7:1–41. Write your reactions to what you have read.

The Judith narrative demonstrates God's commitment to the survival of the Jewish people and the importance of the people's faith. This narrative has greatly influenced Western culture, inspiring literature (the Old English poem "Judith"), music (Antonio Vivaldi's *Juditha Triumphans*), and paintings (Caravaggio's *Judith and Holofernes*).

The story of Susanna is found in the thirteenth chapter of the Book of Daniel (one of three additions to Daniel). Set during the Babylonian exile, the story tells how a beautiful, pious, married Jewish woman was desired by two corrupt judges who spied on her as she bathed. They told her that if she would not have sexual relations with them, they would tell her husband that she had committed adultery with a young man (an offense meriting death under the existing Jewish law). Susanna, though, chose to deny them:

> I am completely trapped. For if I do this, it will mean death for me; if I do not, I cannot escape your hands. I choose not to do it; I will fall into your hands, rather than sin in the sight of the Lord.
> *Daniel 13:22–23 [NRSV]*

So the corrupt judges accused Susanna of adultery with a young man, and she was condemned to death.

An angry Daniel said he would not take part in shedding the woman's blood:

> Are you such fools, O Israelites, as to condemn a daughter of Israel without examination and without learning the facts? Return to court, for these men have given false evidence against her.
> *Daniel 13:48–49 [NRSV]*

CULTURAL
CONNECTIONS

usic

The American Opera *Susannah*

Only a few twentieth-century operas have earned a place in the standard repertoire of the world's great opera houses, mainly works early in the century by Puccini and Richard Strauss, plus a handful of post–World War II works by Benjamin Britten and Francis Poulenc. The sole American opera in the repertoire is *Susannah*, by Carlisle Floyd. A lifelong southerner, Floyd set the story in an American Bible Belt community of the 1930s and portrayed Susannah and her brother as marginalized members of the close-knit community—social outcasts.

His first full-length opera, *Susannah*, premiered in 1955 at Florida State University when Floyd was just 28 years old. It combined the features of *verismo* (operatic concentration on the stark and sometimes ugly trials of ordinary people) with those of folk opera. It included music reminiscent of hymns, folk songs, and square dances. Floyd wrote his own libretto, as he did for all of his eleven operas. Here he borrowed the narrative of Susannah and the Elders but set the tale in the mountains of Tennessee. The seduction of Susannah by Reverend Blitch and the avenging of her dishonor by her brother, who killed Blitch, depicted the consequences of a conflict between narrow religious dogma and straightforward folk honesty.

Despite its immediate success, and some 700 productions since then, *Susannah* was not considered a legitimate part of the standard repertory until staged in 1993 by the Lyric Opera of Chicago and in 1999 by the Metropolitan Opera in New York.

Daniel then interrogated each of the judges separately and caught them in an inconsistency regarding the tree under which they said they had discovered Susanna and her alleged lover. The two judges were then convicted of giving false evidence and were put to death for their evil deed.

The account of Susanna has delighted people for twenty-two centuries, in part because it is entertaining. At the same time, Susanna was both an alluring woman and the most chaste of heroines set upon by two vicious villains. Her virtue and a courageous young hero saved her. This narrative influenced European literature as almost no other biblical narrative has. There are sixty-seven dramas of Susanna, including twenty-eight in German, ten in Italian, six in Dutch, four in Spanish, and several in English, such as the Scottish poem, "The Pistill of Swete Susan." Handel created an opera on Susanna, as did the American composer Carlisle Floyd.

This painting, *Susannah and the Elders* by Frans Floris, clearly shows the lust of the elders and the chaste strength of Susanna.

In the sixty succinct sentences averaging less than twenty-five words, short enough to be read in one sitting, Susanna is power packed with contrasts of the characters' reversals throughout. Unlike other women in the Bible—Jael, who drove a tent peg into Sisera's head; the clever Esther, who won the beauty contest when she slept with the king; the judge Deborah, who led her people into war; or Miriam, who danced before God—Susanna was heroic in a conventional way in her culture. She was a shy, beautiful wife who was quiet, meditative, and retiring. But when she was challenged, there was the firmness of a character made of stern stuff. She drew upon the strength of God to successfully deal with her dire situation.

projects

Choose one of the following projects to learn more about the Apocrypha, or deuterocanonical, books:

1. Locate more artworks based on the books of Tobit, Judith, or Macabees. If possible, make copies of the images to share. Give a brief oral report on how these works of art reflect both the biblical texts and the culture of the times in which they were created.

2. Read the entire story of Susanna (Chapter 13 of Daniel in Roman Catholic and Orthodox translations or all by itself in the Apocrypha section of the NRSV). Analyze the account using what you know of contemporary literature. Look for the devices of paradox and reversals. Share your analysis.

New Testament Background

The New Testament took quite a long time to develop. Most of the writing in the New Testament took place during the years 45 to 95 and was in wide circulation. Yet, it was not until the second half of the fourth century that the number and contents of the books were finally settled; and even then, it was a couple more centuries before the New Testament was universally accepted as twenty-seven books.

Forming a Canon

The Greek word *kanon* means a "straight rod," a "bar," or a "rule"—in other words, a "standard." The canon of books in either the Hebrew Bible or the New Testament is the accepted standard. The formation of the canon of the New Testament began with the collecting of the letters of the apostle Paul, such as his letters to the Romans, the Corinthians, the Ephesians, and the Philippians.

There were a number of gospels, or narratives about the life of Jesus, written in the first two centuries after Christ. Some of them, such as the Coptic gospel of Thomas, were discovered in Egypt in the twentieth century. Quite a few gospels competed with Matthew, Mark, Luke, and John in the early church, but these four gained a general acceptance very early on.

The drive to create a canon of Christian writings was given urgency by the preaching of a bishop named Marcion in the second century. Marcion taught that the gospel of Christ was all about love to the complete rejection of any law. He advocated that the entire Hebrew Bible should be eliminated as having nothing to do with Christianity. Marcion proposed that the Christian canon be limited to the letters of Paul and a version of Luke's gospel. Marcion's short canon would have erased Christianity's link to Judaism. His attempts were soundly defeated. While Marcion was trying to limit the Christian Scriptures, other groups, such as the **Gnostics,** were seeking to enlarge it to include all sorts of writings.

To fight off the pressures, church leaders gradually developed some criteria to judge what writings were going to be included in the Christian Scriptures:

1. **Apostolic Origin:** The book or letter should be attributed to and based on the teaching of the first-generation apostles or their close companions.
2. **General Acceptance:** The major communities in the early Christian world should have acknowledged it as authentic.

Athanasius, Bishop of Alexandria.

3. **Public Use:** The book or letter should have been read publicly when early Christian communities gathered for weekly worship.
4. **Consistent Message:** The work should contain an outlook or message similar to or complementary to other accepted Christian writings.

It still took quite a while longer for the canon to be established—more than two hundred years longer. In point of fact, the canon of the New Testament was not so much formed as it was *recognized*. The writer Tertullian (c. 160–225) was the first to use the words "New Testament." During his time, the New Testament was about 80 percent established.

The Holy Mountain—Mount Athos in Greece—where monks from very early days copied and preserved manuscripts.

At Easter time in the year 367, Athanasius, the bishop of Alexandria in Egypt, wrote a festal letter. In it he listed twenty-seven books as making up the scriptures of the New Testament. Jerome, who translated the books into Latin, followed him. And, finally, the Church councils of Hippo in 393 and Carthage in 397 settled the matter once and for all.

Most scholars agree that even with its problematic passages and its often untraceable origins, the New Testament is the result of a good deal of "common" sense—the common sense of its links to the apostles, the common sense of its use in the community, and the common sense of its acceptance by the Christian churches.

The Christian Bible in the Early Church

From the earliest days of the Christian church, the Bible was read publicly. At times, narratives were acted out with movements and gestures. This tradition of public proclamation helped the early Christians master the content of the Bible. Of course, the primary venue for the reading was during the public worship of the Christian community.

The listeners, whether or not they could read themselves, remembered what they heard. Memory and rote repetition were valued tools in learning the Bible. The Talmud described the good disciple as a "plastered cistern that loses not a drop." That is to say, the listener's task is to remember the words accurately.

The reading and interpretation of the New Testament was complicated by the ancient manuscripts themselves. Ancient manuscripts did not have spaces between words or punctuation that divided sentences or clauses within sentences. The reader provided those. Consider the text about King Herod and the Magi from the gospel of Matthew. If this had been written in modern English, the text might look like this:

An example of how a papyrus manuscript looks in the original Greek. Notice the lack of separation and punctuation.

```
WHENHERODSAWTHATHEHADBEENTRICKED
BYTHEWISEMENHEWASINFURIATEDANDHESEN
TANDKILLEDALLTHECHILDRENINAN
DAROUNDBETHELEHEMWHOWERETWOYEAR
SOLDORUNDERACCORDINGTOTHE
TIMETHATHEHADLEARNEDFROMTHEWISEMEN
THENWASFULFILLEDWHATHADBEENSPOKEN
THROUGHTHEPROPHETJEREMIAHAVOICEWAS
HEARDINRAMAHWAILINGANDLOUDLAMENTATION
SRACHELWEEPINGFORHERCHILDRENSHEREFUSED
TOBECONSOLEDBECAUSETHEYWERENOMORE
```

Anyone reading an ancient text in Greek had to supply the spaces and the punctuation. Such ancient readers would have been familiar with the text—probably from hearing it read or recited. A messenger carrying a letter often presented it orally. The New Testament letters were often not only presented orally to the congregation to whom they were addressed but also circulated to other congregations.

When William Tyndale began to translate and publish the Bible in English in 1526, the text was printed in a form that we are used to today, with separation between words and punctuation. Here is the same passage from Matthew:

> When Herod saw that he had been tricked by the wise men, he was infuriated, and he sent and killed all the children in and around Bethlehem who were two years or under, according to the time that he had learned from the wise men. Then was fulfilled what had been spoken through the prophet Jeremiah:
>
> > "A voice was heard in Ramah,
> > wailing and loud lamentation:
> > Rachel weeping for her children;
> > she refused to be consoled,
> > because they are no more."
>
> *Matthew 2:16–18 [NRSV]*

A Quick Tour

The rest of this chapter will give a quick overview of the New Testament by looking at the character of Paul and at the gospels of Matthew, Mark, Luke, and John. Note: The Gospel of Mark comes second in the New Testament line-up, but because it is the shortest gospel it will be treated first in this book. That way, you will have an opportunity to read an entire gospel. The chapters on the other gospels will focus on the differences or the special characteristics of each.

About Paul

While not an original disciple of Jesus before his death, Paul became a disciple shortly afterward. Paul was a Jewish scholar—a Pharisee—who was very devout, so devout that he at first persecuted Christians. An intense personal experience led him to join the Christian community. Paul was a witness to many events after Jesus' death:

> He [Jesus] appeared to Cephas [Peter], then to the twelve. Then he appeared to more than five hundred brothers and sisters at one time, most of whom are still alive, though some have died. Then he appeared to James, then to all the apostles. Last of all . . . he appeared also to me.
>
> *1 Corinthians 15:5–8 [NRSV]*

Paul wrote a number of letters that were relatively close in time to the events of Jesus' life and death. In fact, they are some of the earliest writings in the New Testament. Scholars will argue, based on such things as literary style, that Paul did not in fact write some of the letters attributed to him. One letter that most scholars now agree was not written by Paul is the "Letter to the Hebrews." For some 1200 years from the year 400 to 1600, the Letter to the Hebrews in the Bible was commonly called "The Epistle of Paul to the Hebrews." Indeed, the King James Version of the Bible has this title. Since the time of the Reformation, it has been widely recognized by nearly all scholars that Paul could not have been the writer. There is no disharmony between the teaching of Hebrews and that of Paul's letters, but the specific emphases and writing styles are markedly different.

Despite the fact that the authorship of some letters is disputed, many key letters, such as the two letters to the Corinthians and the letter to the Romans, which have been formative to Christianity, are undisputedly Paul's.

THE LETTERS OF PAUL			
DATE WRITTEN	**LETTER**	**WHERE WRITTEN**	**AUTHORSHIP**
51	1 Thessalonians	from Corinth	Paul
51–52	2 Thessalonians	from Corinth	Disputed*
55	1 Corinthians	from Ephesus	Paul
55	2 Corinthians	from Macedonia	Paul
57	Romans	from Cenchrea or Corinth	Paul
60	Ephesians	from Rome	Disputed*
60	Colossians	from Rome	Disputed*
60	Philemon	from Rome	Paul
61	Philippians	from Rome	Paul
63–65	1 Timothy and Titus	from Philippi	Disputed*
67–68	2 Timothy	from the Mamertine	Disputed*

NIV Study Bible

*Evangelical Protestants for the most part assert that Paul wrote the letters. Mainline Protestants and others believe that they may have been written not by Paul but by followers of Paul.

What Is a Gospel?

It is important to understand that within the New Testament, a gospel is a unique literary form. A gospel is not a biography of Jesus and is not intended to be. Nor is a gospel a reporter's account of events. *Gospel* is an Anglo-Saxon word that translates the Greek word *evangelion*—literally "good tidings" or "good news." In many ways, the gospels are proclamations of the early church. They describe the life and teaching of Jesus as seen through the eyes of faith—as the life and teachings had come to be understood in the community.

There are four different gospels in the New Testament. All the gospels have common material. Three of the gospels—Matthew, Mark, and Luke—are called the *synoptic* (from the Greek for "seen together") gospels because their general outline and approach can be "looked at together." Each gospel is a presentation of the life, teaching, death, and resurrection of Jesus for a specific audience. The gospels are not histories—certainly not as history is defined today. They describe events, journeys, parables, and the suffering and death of Jesus looking backward from a conviction that Jesus was risen from the dead and he was the Messiah. And so, the gospels are a type of sacred history that interprets events and relates them to the prophecies of the Hebrew Scriptures.

Before any academic study of the gospels, it is important to realize what kind of writing they are. For Christians each of the gospels and all the gospels together provide a faith-filled look at Jesus and the salvation and kingdom he taught about. You are not picking up a newspaper account, an eyewitness report, or even a memoir. Preachers and teachers shared the contents of the gospels, and the events and teachings were told and retold within the Christian community. They were shared from city to city and from person to person long before they were written down. That process of development gives them their own literary character.

Although the gospels can be compared to other forms of writing and literature, no one literary form fully explains the gospels. A quick thumbnail of each of the gospels will help you keep them organized as you learn about each. As you read the thumbnails, remember that the very nature of this kind of writing makes assigning authorship or ascertaining the date a gospel was written very difficult. Very early in their development, the Christian churches attributed the gospels in the New Testament to Matthew, Mark, Luke, and John. It is important for you to understand that scholars disagree about the meaning of this attribution—whether the authors named actually penned the

INTO EVERYDAY *language*

The word *gospel* itself is frequently used beyond its biblical meaning to signify something that provides truth or guiding principles. "He took his boss's suggestions as gospel." "She spread the gospel of recycling."

CULTURAL
CONNECTIONS

Gospel Attitudes toward the Jews

In the gospels of Matthew and John, the respective writers lay blame for Jesus' death on the Jews. In one passage in John, the text says, "the doors of the house where the disciples had met were locked for fear of the Jews" (John 20:19 [NRSV]). The writers were reacting to the increasing separation and hostility between the Jewish community and the followers of Jesus—most of whom, according to the text, were Jews. While this started before the year 70 when the temple in Jerusalem was destroyed by the Romans, it increased immediately afterward.

Throughout history, this language and the attitude the language betrays have been used to lay blame for the death of Jesus on all Jews. Most scholars point out that it was really the religious authorities and Romans who put

Jesus to death. In fact, Jesus' execution required Roman sanction, and there is little doubt that the Romans, too, were interested in removing a threat to Roman peace, no matter how innocent the threat might have been. The Contemporary English Version—a recent English translation of the Bible—recognizes this point by translating the Greek word for *Jews* in John 20:19 as "Jewish leaders."

Nonetheless, it is true that, down through the centuries, passages from the New Testament have been used to justify and even encourage anti-Semitism. It is important, however, to recognize that much of contemporary Christianity is working to overcome this unhappy fact in its history. Dialog and study among Jews and Christians are part of the struggle to eradicate the crime of anti-Semitism wherever it occurs.

In art and architecture, the four evangelists are often shown symbolically. The symbols are taken from Ezekiel 1:1–14, from Daniel 8:1–8, and from Revelation 4:7. Matthew is shown as an angelic man, Mark is shown as a lion, Luke is shown as a winged ox, and John is shown as an eagle. This plate showing the symbols is from the Book of Kells.

gospels. There is also a wide range of opinion regarding when a specific gospel reached its final form. What is given here represents a fairly narrow range of opinion, but the information will help you categorize each gospel.

Matthew

Author: Matthew was one of the apostles, also called Levi. He was a Jew from Capernaum. He was supposedly a tax collector. **Audience:** This gospel was addressed to the Jews. There are sixty references to Jewish prophecies and forty quotations from the Hebrew Scriptures. **Date:** There is some uncertainty whether Matthew or Luke was written first (both were later than Mark), but a good estimate is between 60 and 70. (Some argue for an even later date.) **Purpose or Theme:** The gospel was written to demonstrate that Jesus of Nazareth was the messiah and king promised by the Hebrew Scriptures. It nonetheless contains some harsh words of judgment on the Jewish community.

Mark

Author: John Mark was the son of Mary of Jerusalem. His Jewish name was John, but his Roman name was Mark. He is thought to be a disciple of the apostle Peter. **Audience:** This gospel was written for Roman Christians. The explanations of Jewish words and customs indicate that the author wrote to foreigners. **Date:** The gospel was written around 50 or as late as 60. It was the first of the four written. Both Matthew and Luke borrow from it. **Purpose or Theme:** The gospel portrays Jesus as Christ, the servant of others. **A Note about Style:** Mark's gospel is vivid and filled with action. It focuses on some of the wondrous actions of Jesus and shows his power over nature, demons, and death.

Luke

Author: Luke, it seems, was a Greek and a native of Antioch. He was a companion of Paul. Paul's influence is seen in the work. **Audience:** The gospel is addressed to an individual, Theophilus, who was a high-ranking Greek. The fact that Jewish customs are explained and Greek names are substituted for the Hebrew ones further demonstrates that the gospel was for a Greek audience. **Date:** The gospel was written near the date of Matthew's gospel—between 60 and 70 (again, some argue for a later date). **Purpose and Theme:** This gospel tries to give an orderly narrative of Jesus' life. It also portrays Jesus as "the Son of Man."

John

Author: John is identified as a son of Zebedee and the brother of the apostle James. He had been a disciple of John the Baptist before he followed Jesus of Nazareth. **Audience:** John's gospel was written for the Christian Church—already formed and functioning. **Date:** John's is the very last gospel written. The most acceptable date is between 90 and 100. **Purpose and Theme:** From beginning to end, the Gospel of John is designed to show Jesus Christ as divine—as the son of God. John's gospel also visits stern judgment on the Jewish community.

This ninth-century vellum of the French school shows the evangelists' symbols surrounding a symbolic lamb.

Summary

Armed with the information in this unit, you are now ready to learn some of the specific themes and literary genres found in the New Testament. You will see that these twenty-seven relatively brief books have influenced literature, painting, music, and theater. The rhetoric, themes, and teachings are still influencing writers and artists, filmmakers and musicians. These same brief books have also inspired revolutions, helped form democracies, and motivated men and women to lead lives of heroic self-sacrifice.

projects

Choose one of the following projects to further explore some background to the New Testament:

1. Do a library or Internet search to find out more about how ancient texts were written and how they were handed down. Try to discover some of the oldest texts that exist. (*Hint:* You might key into your search engine the words "Thucydides," "Herodotus," or "Dead Sea Scrolls.") Report on your findings.

2. Research some of the traditions of reciting and performing material from the gospels. Make a brief report on your discoveries.

Unit Feature
A Summary of Literary Genres in the Bible

Now is a good time to review and summarize the various literary genres in the Bible. The Bible is full of literary genres that engage the reader and relay the message in many different literary forms.

THE NARRATIVE

In the epigraph to his book *Gates of the Forest*, Elie Wiesel wrote "God made people because God loves stories." Henry R. Luce, founder of *Time Magazine*, quipped, "*Time* didn't start this emphasis on stories about people; the Bible did." The narrative is the most common literary form in the Bible. A good narrative invites the reader to participate in the action, to share the experience with the characters. Here is a brief checklist of narrative elements in the Bible:

1. *The Setting:* Physical, temporal, and cultural elements that support the narrative
2. *Characters:* A cast of engaging individuals or groups to carry the story forward
3. *Plot:* The movement of the story from a beginning to an end
4. *Conflict:* The elements that interrupt and even derail the movement of the story
5. *Suspense:* An element of uncertainty about the outcome
6. *Reality:* Even in the most fantastic of tales, a grounding in the familiar and the accessible
7. *Unity and Coherence:* The clues and dialog and action that make the story intelligible
8. *Choice:* Even in the most fatalistic of tales, the choices and decisions of the protagonist and the other characters that drive the story forward
9. *Transformation:* Change in situations and people by the end of the narrative
10. *Spice:* Foils, dramatic irony, poetic justice, and other elements that enhance the experience
11. *A Point of View:* The overall positioning of the narrative to get the reader invested in the experience and to bring his or her own thought and imagination to it

Here are a few recognizable narrative forms:

1. *The Heroic Narrative:* This kind of story is structured around the life and exploits of a protagonist. Such narratives are strongly biographical. The narrative of David in Hebrew Scriptures, for example, is one of the longest narratives in all of ancient literature.

2. *The Epic:* An expansive story that sums up a whole age. Epics tend to have a strong nationalistic interest, and they deal with the destiny of a whole nation. The most obvious epic work in the Bible is Exodus. For literary purposes, the key narrative sections are Exodus 1–20 and 32–34; Numbers 10–14, 16–17, and 20–24; and Deuteronomy 32–34.
3. *The Comedy:* The word here is used in the technical dramatic sense. It does not mean a series of jokes or a funny situation. This narrative form is most often a story that begins in prosperity, descends into a series of trials and troubles, and rises again to provide a "happy ending." In literary terms, for all its misery, the Book of Job can be considered a comedy, as can the Book of Jonah.
4. *The Tragedy:* This term, too, is used in the dramatic sense. This form has much in common with some of the Greek dramas in that a flawed hero starts out well and then gradually is at the center of great personal and even national deterioration. The ending is usually catastrophic. This form is less pervasive in the biblical narratives, but it is an important form. The most dramatic example of a tragedy is the account of King Saul.

POETRY

Next to the narrative, poetry is the most prevalent type of writing in the Bible. Some of the books of the Bible are entirely poetic in form: Psalms, Song of Solomon, Proverbs, and Lamentations. Many others are mainly poetic: Job, Ecclesiastes (in which even the prose passages achieve poetic effects), Isaiah, Hosea, Joel, and numerous other prophetic books. There is no book in the Bible that does not require the ability to interpret poetry to some degree, because every book includes imagery and figurative language.

Poetry is the language of images. It uses many comparisons and is concentrated and more highly patterned than ordinary discourse. Poets do things with language and sentence structure that people do not ordinarily do when speaking. Poetry is used to intensify feeling or insight.

PROVERBS

Biblical proverbs, or short moral sayings, play upon both imagination and human experience. Proverbs are striking and memorable, simple, and profound. They

Michelangelo's famous fresco of the Last Judgment over the altar in the Sistine Chapel in Rome is perhaps the most famous portrayal of biblical visionary literature. It weaves together the visions and symbols into a powerful visual statement as strong as, if not stronger than, the written word.

can be specific or quite general. They are often written in poetic form.

The Book of Proverbs arranges its sayings according to categories, such as the drunkard, 23:29–35; the king, 25:2–7; or the sluggard, 26:13–16. Chapters 1 through 9 of the Book of Proverbs focus on instruction unified by a common theme—wisdom, common images and characters, and an interesting counterpoint between wisdom and folly. The proverb form is found throughout the Bible.

PARABLE

Within the gospels are short stories that teach by using specific and concrete examples from everyday life. Jesus taught with parables to put his message about God's reign into language that all his hearers would grasp immediately.

When Jesus was asked, "And who is my neighbor?" he did not give an explanation but told a story—a parable. He told of a man going down the road from Jerusalem to Jericho who is beaten, stripped, and left for half-dead by a group of robbers. The story is graphic. The robbers, those that take money from the unidentified presumably Jewish man, are contrasted with a Samaritan—a foreigner—who gives money to the innkeeper to take care of this unidentified man. At the end of the narrative, Jesus poses a question to the questioner: "And of these, who proved to be a neighbor?" The parable led the hearers to a new and important conclusion.

EPISTLES

The word *epistle* is used to describe letters that were addressed to churches and circulated from one church to another. The epistle is a dominant literary genre in the New Testament. An epistle combines literary and expository features. A good epistle weaves together the best characteristics of private correspondence and public address. In order to follow the logical flow of ideas, to interpret figurative language, and to be sensitive to the effects of artistic and stylistic patterns, a reader needs to keep in mind a simple five-part structure:

1. An opening or salutation
2. A thanksgiving—including such features as a prayer for spiritual welfare, remembrance of the recipients, and the like
3. The body of the letter
4. Moral exhortations
5. A closing and a benediction

VISIONARY LITERATURE

A particularly fascinating genre is the apocalypse or visionary literature. In such literature, descriptions are often symbolic rather than literal. Events are described that have not happened. Such writing engages the imagination of the reader. Visionary literature is an assault on familiar patterns of thought in an effort to shake the reader out of complacency with the normal flow of things. Visionary literature is a revolutionary genre. It announces an end to the way things are and opens up alternate possibilities. At the same time, these visions provide comfort in times of crisis.

The Book of Daniel in Hebrew Scriptures is visionary literature, as is the Book of the Revelation. Both contain visions of God in a time to come. There are other characteristics of such apocalyptic literature:

- *Symbolic Visions:* Apocalypses often present visions or dreams filled with elaborate symbols. These symbols can be of strange animals, numbers, or cosmic events.
- *A Heavenly Mediator:* Usually apocalyptic writing has a figure that explains the visions. This could be an angel or, as in the beginning of the Book of Revelation, Christ.
- *The End of the World:* One major theme of such literature is the end of time. This is particularly evident in the Book of Revelation.

Adapted from *How to Read the Bible as Literature* by Leland Ryken

The Four Gospels

You are the light of the world. A city built on a hill cannot be hid. No one after lighting a lamp puts it under the bushel basket, but on the lampstand, and it gives light to all in the house. In the same way, let your light shine before others, so that they may see your good works.

Matthew 5:14–16 [NRSV]

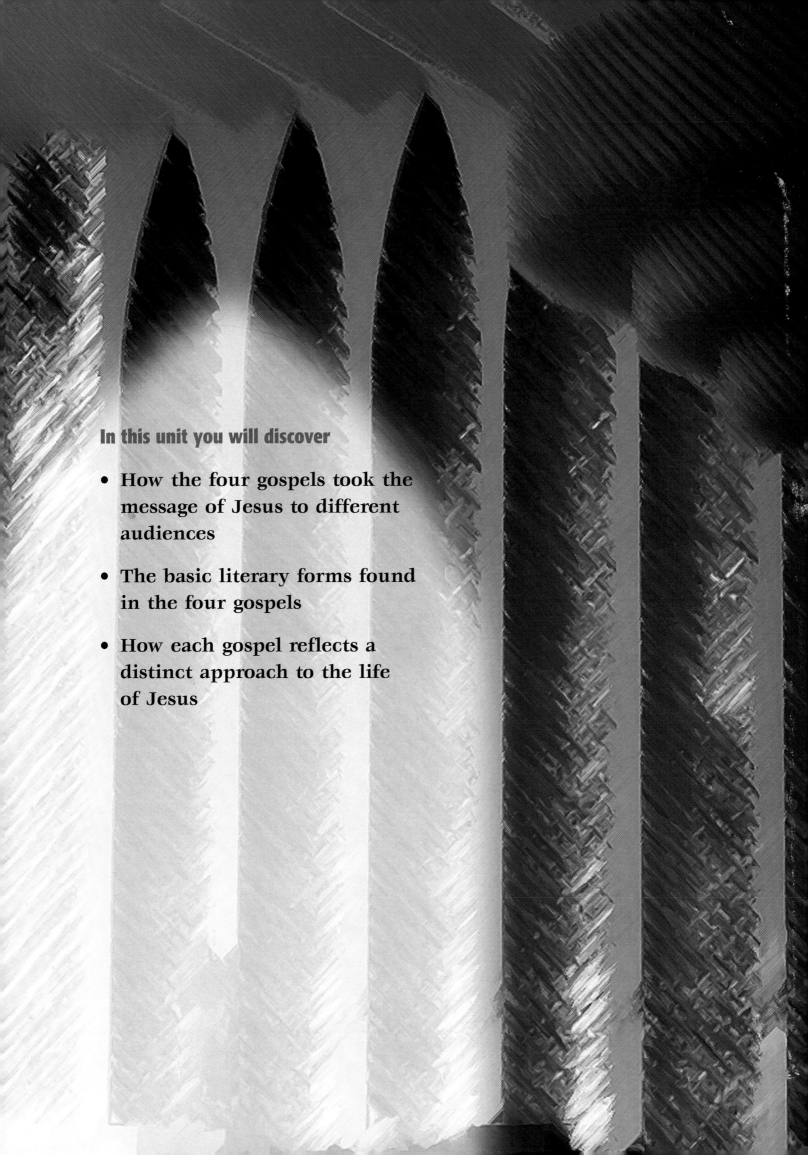

In this unit you will discover

- How the four gospels took the message of Jesus to different audiences

- The basic literary forms found in the four gospels

- How each gospel reflects a distinct approach to the life of Jesus

KEY BIBLICAL TEXTS

■ The entire text of Mark

DISCOVER

■ The fast-paced style of Mark
■ Mark's portrayal of Jesus as a servant
■ How Mark shows Jesus as having power over nature
■ The manuscript discrepancies that give Mark an alternate ending

GET TO KNOW

■ The cast of Mark's gospel

CONSIDER

■ What do you think about when you hear someone referred to as a "servant"?

Mark

If you have any familiarity with the Christian Bible, you are probably aware that the gospels line up as Matthew, Mark, Luke, and John. Why start an overview of the gospels with Mark? There are three reasons for this. First, Mark is the shortest of the four gospels. It is a work that can be read in a single sitting. Second, this gospel was probably the first compiled. Finally, Mark's gospel provides much of the source material for Matthew and Luke.

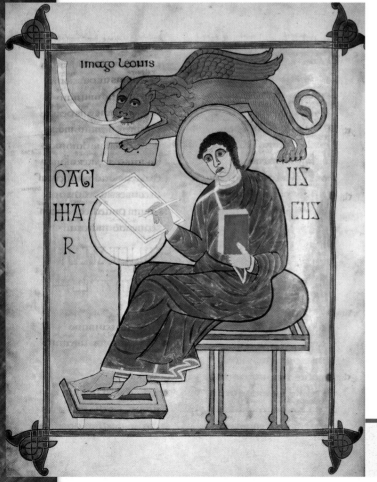

Imago Leonis

OAGI HA R

US CUS

This page from the Lindisfarne Gospels depicts Mark. Note the symbol of the lion.

A Journalistic Style

If you were to buy a copy of four newspapers on the same day—*The New York Times, The Washington Post, USA Today,* and your local newspaper—and read about a national event, would the articles be exactly the same? Each paper tries to focus on details that are important to its particular readers. For example, factors such as the demographics and the political leanings of the paper's readership would affect how the story was presented.

The gospels in the Christian Bible are hardly newspaper reports, yet each gospel was tailored to its anticipated readership. If any one of the gospels has a newspaper "feel" to it, it is Mark's. It is the shortest gospel and the most journalistic of the four. Remember, however, that unlike a journalist, the author is not describing recent events as an eyewitness.

You will begin your study of the gospels by reading the whole of Mark's gospel. (In subsequent chapters, you will examine specific aspects of the

A detail from the sixteenth-century Flemish artist Joachim Patenier's depiction of Jesus' baptism.

other three gospels.) Much of this chapter functions as a reading guide. It doesn't make any difference which translation you choose to read. All the passages cited in this chapter, however, will be from the New Revised Standard Version.

Although Mark mentions no author's name, the early Church attributed it to the John Mark who is mentioned elsewhere in the New Testament. This brief gospel delves into the mystery of who Jesus was and what his mission was. In the style of a journalist, Mark breathlessly connects short passages (called **pericopes**) to form a unified narrative of Jesus' work as a teacher, a healer, and a miracle worker. However, Mark's narrative points ahead to the death of Jesus. For Mark, Jesus is first and foremost a suffering servant.

The Prologue

The Gospel of Mark begins like classical epics—such as *The Iliad* and *The Odyssey*—in the middle of the action. Rather than providing details about the background of Jesus, Mark begins with Jesus' public life. At the outset, he makes a clear statement of his view of Jesus' identity: "The beginning of the good news of Jesus Christ, the Son of God" *(Mark 1:1)*. During the rest of the gospel, the identity of Jesus is a question that must be answered by his followers and his opponents alike.

John the Baptist is the first character to appear. Mark cites the Hebrew prophets Malachi and Isaiah about the messenger who will prepare the Lord's way *(Mark 1:2–3)* and then introduces John with the implication that he is that messenger. The opening verses show that Mark had knowledge of the Hebrew Scriptures. Mark, however, seems in this gospel to be addressing an audience of non-Jews. He translates Aramaic words and explains Jewish customs to communicate more clearly with a Gentile readership.

Jesus enters into the picture right after John. The scene is Jesus' baptism by John in the Jordan River. "And just as he was coming up out of the water, he saw the heavens torn apart and the Spirit descending like a dove on him.

INTO EVERYDAY
language

The expression *a house divided will not stand* (Mark 3:25) was used by Abraham Lincoln in a speech presented in Springfield, Illinois, on June 16, 1858, at the Republican State Convention, which nominated Lincoln as a candidate for the U.S. Senate. In it, he opposed the U.S. Supreme Court's Dred Scott decision, which prevented Congress from excluding slavery in the new U.S. territories.

And a voice came from heaven, 'You are my Son, the Beloved; with you I am well pleased'" *(Mark 1:10–11).*

Next, Mark, using as he often does the adverb "immediately," tells of Jesus' temptation in the wilderness. After this brief prologue, Mark moves directly into Jesus' public life.

The Public Life of Jesus

The first chapter of the gospel introduces all three of the actions for which Jesus is noted: teaching with authority, healing, and **exorcism** (the driving out of evil spirits). Indeed, there are more exorcisms in Mark than in any other gospel.

The second chapter of Mark gives a sense of Jesus already moving toward suffering and death. For example, the scribes, after witnessing the healing of a paralytic during which Jesus said, "your sins are forgiven," believed he was **blaspheming,** that is, he was claiming the attributes of the deity: "Who can forgive sins but God alone?" *(Mark 2:7).*

Again and again throughout Mark, there are instances that build a "case" for Jesus' condemnation and ultimately his execution. In Chapter 3, as Jesus was about to heal on the Sabbath, he received a rebuke from the Pharisees. Jesus went on with the healing nonetheless. Mark points out that "the Pharisees went out and immediately conspired against him, how to destroy him" *(Mark 3:6).*

After calling twelve followers, or **disciples,** Jesus continued with his ministry of healing. In Chapters 3 and 4, he began to teach in parables, short stories bearing spiritual truths. Among the most famous parables is that of the sower.

Usually gospel parables come without any explanation or interpretation. An intriguing aspect of the parable of the sower is that Jesus explained it to his disciples when he was alone with them. Before he explained the parable, Jesus, according to the text, told why he taught in parables: "To you has been given the secret of the kingdom of God, but for those outside, everything comes in parables; in order that they may indeed look, but not perceive, and may indeed listen, but not understand; so that they may not turn again and be forgiven" *(Mark 4:11–12).*

This lack of perception and understanding is characteristic of the disciples in the Gospel of Mark. The parable was of a sower who sowed seed on several different kinds of ground: a footpath, rocky ground, thorns, and good soil. You can read the explanation in verses 14 through 22.

Notice the references in this passage to "affliction and persecution." Some scholars think this refers to the suffering that would be experienced during the Jewish revolt leading up to the destruction of the temple in the year 70.

Chapter 4 concludes with another feature of Mark's gospel: a **nature miracle,** that is, a wondrous event involving the forces of nature. While Jesus and his followers were crossing a lake, a severe windstorm arose. Jesus was sound asleep. When the frightened disciples awakened him, he commanded the wind, "Peace! Be still!" *(Mark 4:39).* He then said to his disciples, "Why are you afraid? Have you still no faith?" *(Mark 4:40).*

Narratives within Narratives

Chapter 5 begins with the account of a man possessed by demons. According to the text here and in other places, the demons recognized Jesus as "the Son of the Most High." Jesus called out the demons and cast them into a herd of pigs that then ran into the water and drowned. This set of events, according to the text, greatly disturbed those in the area, and the people begged Jesus to leave. A reader might wonder what a herd of pigs was doing in a land where eating pork was not kosher. The pigs were probably there to feed the

Roman legions. It might not be a coincidence that the account refers to the devils as "Legion."

Mark introduces another one of his characteristic forms of teaching: **intercalation.** Mark sandwiches one narrative in the midst of another. In this instance, he begins to tell the narrative of the daughter of Jairus, a leader of the synagogue. The child was dying, and Jairus begged Jesus to come and heal her. Then Mark notes that while Jesus was traveling to Jairus's house amidst a teeming crowd, a woman who had had a hemorrhage for twelve years came up behind him to touch his garment. "If I but touch his clothes, I will be made well," she thought to herself *(Mark 5:28)*. Jesus, according to the text, "feels that power has gone out of him" and asked who touched him. The woman came to him fearfully, as hemorrhaging produced a state of ritual impurity that entailed social restrictions or exclusions. Yet Jesus said to her, "Daughter, your faith has made you well; go in peace, and be healed of your disease" *(Mark 5:34)*.

Finally, Jesus arrived at Jairus's home and was taken to the little girl's body. "He took her by the hand and said to her, 'Talitha cum,' which means, 'Little girl, get up!' And immediately the girl got up and began to walk about (she was twelve years of age). At this they were overcome with amazement" *(Mark 5:41–42)*.

Loaves and Fishes

After telling how Jesus sent his followers on a mission, Mark recounts John the Baptist's execution by King Herod. Next, as Jesus was teaching a large crowd of people, they got hungry. Jesus' disciples wanted to send the people away so that they could buy food to eat. But Jesus suggested his disciples feed them. They answered, "Are we to go and buy two hundred denarii [i.e., a sum of money beyond reach] worth of bread, and give it to them to eat?" *(Mark 6:37)*. Jesus asked his disciples how many loaves of bread there were. When they found out there were five loaves and two fishes, Jesus ordered his disciples to get all the people to sit down in groups. The account continues:

> Taking the five loaves and two fish, he looked up to heaven, and blessed and broke the loaves, and gave them to his disciples to set before the people; and he divided the two fish among them all. And all ate and were filled; and they took up twelve baskets full of broken pieces and of the fish. Those who had eaten the loaves numbered five thousand men.
>
> *Mark 6:41–44*

Mark describes a number of other miracles and the escalating controversy between the Pharisees and Jesus. In Chapter 8, Jesus confronted his disciples with a question of his identity. The disciples, so often confused in this gospel, rose to the occasion, with Peter's declaration: "You are the Messiah" *(Mark 8:29)*.

Just after Peter's affirmation, Jesus began to openly discuss his coming ordeal with his followers, and Peter objected. Jesus replied, "Get behind me, Satan! For you are setting your mind not on divine things but on human things" *(Mark 8:33)*. This is known as the first prediction of the Passion. Jesus then spoke of the indispensable role of suffering in the life of all who follow him *(Mark 8:34–38)*.

This painting by James Jacques Joseph Tissot illustrates the account of the exorcism of the man possessed by an evil spirit.

In Chapter 12 of Mark, Jesus sat near the temple treasury; and, while rich people put in money, a widow came and put in two coins, translated in the King James Version as "mites." Jesus praises her action: "She out of her poverty has put in everything she had, all she had to live on" *(Mark 12:44)*. The term the *widow's mite* has entered the everyday language to signify a small contribution of great value.

Leonardo da Vinci's *Last Supper* is one of the most famous depictions of this gospel account. It is a mural in the refectory of the Dominican convent in Milan. The mural was recently restored to its original condition.

A Transfiguration

In Chapter 9, Mark notes that six days after the pivotal scene revealing Jesus' identity as a suffering Messiah, Jesus and three of his closest followers—Peter, James, and John—went up a mountain. In the words of the account: "And he was transfigured before them, and his clothes became dazzling white, such as no one on earth could bleach them. And there appeared to them Elijah with Moses, who were talking with Jesus" *(Mark 9:2–4)*. From the heavens, a voice spoke: "This is my Son, the Beloved; listen to him!" *(Mark 9:7)*. After this experience, Jesus spoke to his three disciples about the resurrection, just as he had spoken to them about the Passion in the previous chapter: "As they were coming down the mountain, he ordered them to tell no one about what they had seen, until after the Son of Man had risen from the dead" *(Mark 9:9)*.

Up to Jerusalem

Almost immediately after the transfiguration, Mark gives an example of the disciples' lack of understanding, so characteristic of Mark's gospel. A person brought his possessed son to Jesus for healing because the disciples of Jesus had failed. Jesus became exasperated with the disciples: "You faithless generation, how much longer must I be among you? How much longer must I put up with you?" *(Mark 9:19)*. Jesus then spoke with the father of the child and noted that all things can be done for one who believes. "Immediately, the father of the child cried out, 'I believe; help my unbelief!'" *(Mark 9:24)*. The tension between unbelief and belief is a major theme in the gospel of Mark.

Shortly after, Jesus again predicted his betrayal, death, and resurrection; and, again, his disciples failed to understand what he was talking about. A long teaching section follows. Then, as Jesus and the disciples made their way to Jerusalem, Jesus made a third and very specific prediction of his death, "See, we are going up to Jerusalem, and the Son of Man will be handed over to the chief priests and the scribes, and they will condemn him to death; then they will hand him over to the Gentiles; they will mock him, and spit upon him, and flog him, and kill him; and after three days he will rise again" *(Mark 10:33–34)*.

CULTURAL CONNECTIONS

Jesus Christ Superstar

Andrew Lloyd Webber and Tim Rice's rock opera *Jesus Christ Superstar* was originally released as a recording because producers were afraid to take a chance on such a daring stage production. *Jesus Christ Superstar* eventually premiered on Broadway in 1971 and ran for 720 performances. The musical tells the story of the last seven days in the life of Jesus. *Superstar* dramatizes Jesus' entry into Jerusalem, the unrest caused by his preaching and popularity, his betrayal by Judas, the trial before Pontius Pilate, and his crucifixion. The musical was made into a film in 1973, and a revival of the stage musical was broadcast on public television in 2001.

Jesus Christ Superstar Rocks Broadway

TIME Magazine, October 25, 1971.

The Final Week

With Chapter 11, Mark begins to narrate the final week of Jesus' life, starting with his entry into Jerusalem on a colt, with people spreading cloaks and branches before him, praising him with quotations from the Hebrew Scriptures. However, on the next day, the tone changed when Jesus went to the temple and drove out merchants, turning over their tables—one of the few scenes of Jesus' overt and righteous anger in the gospels.

The rest of Chapters 11 and 12 cover various teachings of Jesus, punctuated by clashes with the authorities in Jerusalem. Then, Chapter 13 provides an example of apocalyptic literature, which points forward to the end of the world. As part of his predictions, Jesus also said that his followers would suffer a great deal *(Mark 13:9–13)*. But as to the end of the world, he indicated that no one knows the exact time *(Mark 13:32–33)* and thus counseled his disciples to "Keep awake" *(Mark 13:37)*.

With Chapter 14, the events of the Jesus trial and execution begin to unfold. First of all, a woman came and anointed Jesus' feet with expensive ointment. Jesus defended her action, saying she had anointed his body for burial. After a brief account of Judas's betrayal of Jesus, Mark presents his version of the Last Supper—Jesus' last meal with his disciples while he was alive. The meal is presented as a celebration of the Jewish Passover. Notice the similarity between the words used by Jesus regarding the bread and the words used during the multiplication of loaves.

After the Last Supper, Jesus and his disciples went to the Mount of Olives and into the Garden of Gethsemane. Jesus pointed out to them that they all would deny him. There is a subtle reminder of the garden in Genesis as then Jesus wrestled with God about the coming ordeal.

In Mark's fast-paced account, Judas came with a group of priests, scribes, and elders to arrest Jesus, after which the disciples all deserted him. Jesus was taken to the high priest and other authorities, and the high priest asked him if he was the Messiah. Jesus replied, drawing on the Books of Daniel and Psalms: "I am," and "you will see the Son of Man seated at the right hand of the Power," and "coming with the clouds of heaven" *(Mark 14:62)*. The group accused Jesus of blasphemy.

The Yellow Christ by Paul Gauguin (1889). Peasant women kneel to pray at a wayside crucifix in the Breton countryside. The humanity of the Christ figure expresses just how real the experience is to the women. Yet the color is totally unreal–the yellow body of Christ and the red trees both stress the otherworldliness of the scene. The childlike drawing with its strong black outlines is deliberately reminiscent of medieval stained glass.

HISTORICAL
CONNECTIONS

Crucifixion in the Ancient World

The Jewish historian Josephus described the hanging of a person on a cross until that person died as "the most wretched of deaths." The Roman Seneca argued that suicide was better than this form of punishment, called crucifixion.

This cruel and humiliating form of execution was first practiced by the Persians. Alexander the Great and his generals brought the practice to the Mediterranean world.

The Romans developed a high degree of skill and efficiency in this form of punishment. It was used not only for criminals but to stem potential rebellions or simply to satisfy bloodlust. For example, during the reign of Roman Emperor Caligula (37–41), Jews were tortured and crucified in the amphitheater in Alexandria for the entertainment of the citizens. In the Roman Empire, crucifixion required approval from the local Roman governor. Roman citizens were not subject to this form of execution.

In Chapter 15, Jesus was brought before the Roman governor Pontius Pilate, who tried to release him. In the account, the crowd preferred that Pilate release a criminal, Barabbas. The crowd urged Pilate to crucify Jesus. Pilate did what they asked. Mark notes that a passerby, Simon of Cyrene, was forced to carry the cross for Jesus.

Mark notes that Jesus was put on the cross at 9:00 in the morning, and at 3:00 in the afternoon Jesus called to God in Aramaic, "Eloi, Eloi, lema sabachthanai?" which Mark translates for his Gentile readers: "My God, my God, why have you forsaken me?" *(Mark 15:34).* The words were taken from the first verse of Psalm 22. After a final cry, Jesus died. Afterward, a Roman soldier stated, "Truly this man was God's Son!" *(Mark 15:39).*

At the conclusion of the Passion narrative, Joseph of Arimathea, a member of the Jewish council, asked Pilate for the body of Jesus, wrapped the body in linen, laid it in a rock tomb, and rolled a stone before the entrance.

THE BIBLE
IN Literature

Countee Cullen
(1903–1946)

Simon of Cyrene is a character who appears in Mark's gospel. He was pressed into service to help Jesus carry the cross. Because of his place of origin, he is often considered to be of dark complexion.

Countee Cullen was an African American poet who was part of the movement called the Harlem Renaissance in the 1920s. In this movement, the work of a number of African American artists, writers, and musicians came to prominence. In the poem "Simon the Cyrenian Speaks," Cullen imagines what Simon of Cyrene's sentiments might have been as a black man who has suffered:

He never spoke a word to me,
    And yet He called my name;

He never gave a sign to me,
    And yet I knew and came.

At first I said, "I will not bear
    His cross upon my back;

He only seeks to place it there
    Because my skin is black."

But He was dying for a dream,
    And He was very meek,

And in His eyes there shone a gleam
    Men journey far to seek.

It was Himself my pity bought;
    I did for Christ alone

What all of Rome could not have wrought
    With bruise of lash or stone.

THE BIBLE

IN **Literature**

HEMINGWAY'S *The Old Man and the Sea*

Ernest Hemingway's last published work was *The Old Man and the Sea*. A number of gospel images can be found in the final pages of the book. First of all, the image of the fish recalls an ancient Christian symbol.* The Old Man's bleeding hands recall the nails in Jesus' hands. The way the Old Man holds the line across his back is reminiscent of Jesus carrying the cross. The Old Man collapses carrying the mast and boom (shaped like a cross) in much the same way that Jesus fell on his way to crucifixion. The Old Man lies on his bed with his hat cutting into his head. That suggests the crown of thorns. The Old Man's name, Santiago, is Spanish for Saint James—an apostle and a fisherman. And finally, the fish itself ends up a mangled and hideous sight.

Hemingway understood that the images of Christ's crucifixion were a part of the intellectual background readers would bring to his book. By using those images, he evoked feelings for the Old Man and caused the reader to invest personal biblical memories into what he or she was reading. In short, Hemingway was counting on the biblical literacy of his readers to increase the impact of his story.

Ernest Hemingway (1899–1961)

* The Greek word for fish is *ichthus*. Christians in hiding used the symbol as a visual acronym for Jesus Christ, God's Son, the Savior.

An Empty Tomb

Mark's gospel comes to a rather quick ending. Chapter 16 tells about the resurrection of Jesus from the dead and his appearance to the disciples. As you read Chapter 16, you will notice that there are two endings—a short one that ends with verse 8, and a longer ending that goes all the way to verse 20. Read the explanation for these two endings in the version of the Bible you are using. One thing the alternate endings show is how the manuscripts for the gospels grew and developed. Even though the longer ending was written later, its style is typical of the rest of Mark's gospel.

projects

Choose one or both of the projects to expand your knowledge of Mark's gospel:

1. Analyze the literary structure and flow of Mark's gospel. Show the devices Mark uses to advance the story, to keep readers interested, to make points, to identify Jesus for the readers, and the like. Share your analysis.

2. Find one or two examples of investigative reporting in the newspaper or a news magazine. Contrast and compare the style in the articles with the style of Mark's gospel. Describe the difference between journalistic style and actual journalism.

KEY BIBLICAL TEXTS

■ Matthew 1–2; 5–7; 10; 16:13–23; 18; 28

DISCOVER

■ That Matthew focuses on Jesus as the expected Messiah
■ That Matthew features information on the infancy of Jesus
■ How Matthew uses a discourse technique to present the teachings of Jesus

GET TO KNOW

■ Joseph, Mary, the wise men, Herod, the apostles

CONSIDER

■ When you get to know someone, do you ever ask who his or her family or ancestors are?

Matthew

Matthew's gospel focuses on Jesus as the fulfillment of the prophecies of the Hebrew Scriptures. In Matthew, Jesus is the son of David, the longed-for Messiah. The gospel contains a great deal of Christian **typology.** This is a technical term to describe how things in Christian Scriptures are predicted or symbolized by people or events in the Hebrew Scriptures.

Matthew is placed first in the canon and traditionally has been called "the first gospel." It is also sometimes called "the gospel of the church," because it devotes a good deal of time to discussing the church and has been used in the Christian liturgy from the earliest centuries. Indeed, in the early church, it was considered the most important gospel. It provides an abundance of Jesus' teaching. Unique features of Matthew include the genealogy, the infancy narrative, the great discourses of Jesus, and parts of the resurrection narrative.

Prologue of Matthew

Matthew begins with a genealogy, or list of the ancestors of Jesus. The very first verse, like that of Mark, projects a view of Jesus' identity: "An account of the genealogy of Jesus the Messiah, the son of David, the son of Abraham" *(Matthew 1:1 [NRSV]).*

"Messiah" is a Jewish concept, and Matthew is written primarily for an audience of the Jewish followers of Jesus. In the genealogy, Matthew traces the ancestry of Jesus in three

This detail of a stained-glass window from Chartres Cathedral in France illustrates Christ's ancestors and is called a Jesse Tree in honor of David's father.

THE BIBLE
IN Literature

A well-known twentieth-century poem that imaginatively develops the story of the three wise men is T. S. Eliot's "The Journey of the Magi." The narrator is one of the wise men, reflecting on the experience years later:

A cold coming we had of it,
Just the worst time of the year
For a journey, and such a long journey:
The ways deep and the weather sharp,
The very dead of winter.
And the camels galled, sore-footed, refractory,
Lying down in the melting snow.
There were times we regretted
The summer palaces on slopes, the terraces,
And the silken girls bringing sherbet.
Then the camel men cursing and grumbling
And running away, and wanting their liquor and women,
And the night-fires going out, and the lack of shelters,
And the cities hostile and the towns unfriendly
And the villages dirty and charging high prices:
A hard time we had of it.
At the end we preferred to travel all night,
Sleeping in snatches,
With the voices singing in our ears, saying
That this was all folly.

Then at dawn we came down to a temperate valley,
Wet, below the snow line, smelling of vegetation;
With a running stream and a water-mill beating the darkness,
And three trees on the low sky,
And an old white horse galloped away in the meadow.
Then we came to a tavern with vine-leaves over the lintel,
Six hands at an open door dicing for pieces of silver,
And feet kicking the empty wine-skins.
But there was no information, and so we continued
And arrived at evening, not a moment too soon
Finding the place; it was (you may say) satisfactory.

All this was a long time ago, I remember,
And I would do it again, but set down
This set down
This: were we led all that way for
Birth or Death? There was a Birth, certainly,
We had evidence and no doubt. I had seen birth and death,
But had thought they were different; this Birth was
Hard and bitter agony for us, like Death, our death.
We returned to our places, these Kingdoms,
But no longer at ease here, in the old dispensation,
With an alien people clutching their gods.
I should be glad of another death.

---

sections reflecting three major stages in the history of the people of Israel: from Abraham to Jesse; from David to the Babylonian exile; and from the exile to Jesus. The genealogy is also a key to understanding the Gospel of Matthew. The genealogy begins with Abraham, who is sometimes called "the father of the Jews." However, Abraham was also called "a father of many nations" *(Genesis 17:4 [KJV])*. Several women are mentioned in the genealogy as well: Tamar, Rahab, Ruth, and Bathsheba. All of these women were in some sense outsiders—either Gentiles or related to Gentiles. The genealogy itself reveals a literary tension in Matthew. Although it is rooted in a Jewish view of Jesus, it strives to demonstrate that Jesus is for all peoples.

The Birth of Jesus

The first major event in the Gospel of Matthew is Jesus' birth, which scholars call an **infancy narrative.** This narrative begins with an account of an unwed woman surprised but accepting of an unusual pregnancy—Mary, the mother of Jesus. The narrative, however, is told from the viewpoint of Joseph, Mary's fiancé. When he discovered that Mary was pregnant, he decided to "dismiss her quietly," but he had a dream. An angel gave him the following message: "Joseph, son of David, do not be afraid to take Mary as your wife, for the child conceived in her is from the Holy Spirit. She will bear a son, and you are to name him Jesus, for he will save his people from their sins" *(Matthew 1:20–21 [NRSV])*.

Bartolo di Fredi's *Adoration of the Magi* from the 1380s. The gifts of gold, incense, and myrrh are literary symbols. Gold was a gift fit for a king. Frankincense was used to honor the deity. Myrrh was used in the preparation of a body for burial. The narrative uses the symbols to suggest a realization on the Magi's part that Jesus was a king and God and that he would suffer death.

Sermon on the Mount by Fra Angelico.

Matthew follows this account immediately with a bit of typology, quoting Isaiah 7:14. The verse predicts that a virgin would bear a son. This verse, in addition to being an example of typology, is also a **fulfillment citation.** Such citations are used throughout Matthew's gospel in order to prove that Jesus fulfilled the expectations of the Hebrew Scriptures. The original word in Isaiah translated here as *virgin* can mean young girl or virgin. As it is cited in Matthew, however, it forms the basis for the Christian belief in the **virgin birth.** That tradition states that Mary was a virgin when she conceived and bore Jesus.

Chapter 2 presents another unique aspect of Matthew's infancy narrative: The wise men from the East are sometimes referred to with the Latin term **magi.** The wise men were all Gentiles. And so, according to Matthew, the first people to offer homage to Jesus were Gentiles.

A rather dark aspect of this chapter is the exchange between King Herod and the wise men and its results. Herod, alarmed at the wise men's announcement that a new king is being born, sought to kill Jesus and thus had all of the baby Jewish boys murdered. This has come to be called the "slaughter of the innocents." Jesus escaped the fate of the innocents because Joseph was warned in a dream to go to Egypt, and he, Jesus, and Mary remained there until Herod died, after which they settled in Nazareth of Galilee. This account is a not-so-subtle allusion to the story of Moses: When Moses was an infant, he was saved from slaughter in Egypt.

The Church of the Beatitudes was built in the late 1930s on a spot near Tabgha, Israel, traditionally believed to be the site of the Sermon on the Mount.

The Sermon on the Mount

The core of the Gospel of Matthew consists of narrative sections interspersed with long sermons or discourses. There are five major discourses in Matthew, framed with narrative sections. Some scholars see in these discourses another link to the Hebrew Scriptures. Just as there were five books in the Torah (Genesis, Exodus, Leviticus, Numbers, and Deuteronomy), so Jesus, like a "new Moses," teaches his followers in five discourses.

The Discourses of the Gospel of Matthew

- The Sermon on the Mount—Matthew 5–7
- The Missionary Discourse—Matthew 10
- The Parable Discourse—Matthew 13
- The Church Order Discourse—Matthew 18
- The Discourse on the End Times—Matthew 24–28

This chapter covers only three of the discourses. The first and most famous of the discourses is referred to as the "Sermon on the Mount," because the text notes that Jesus ascended a mountain to preach to the people. Again, there is a similarity between Jesus and Moses. Just as Moses delivered the Ten Commandments from Mount Sinai, so Jesus delivered this sermon, consisting largely of ethical guidelines, from a mountain.

The first section of the Sermon on the Mount has come to be called the **beatitudes,** from the Latin word for "happiness" or "blessedness." This section consists of nine qualities that Jesus considered characteristics of "blessedness" (*Matthew 5:3–11*).

After the beatitudes, Jesus used two strong metaphors to challenge his followers:

> You are the salt of the earth; but if salt has lost its taste, how can its saltiness be restored? It is no longer good for anything, but is thrown out and trampled under foot. You are the light of the world. A city built on a hill cannot be hid.
>
> *Matthew 5:13–14*

The notion of a city on a hill has captured the American imagination from colonial times. Governor John Winthrop used the phrase in a speech aboard the flagship *Arabella* in 1630. And President Ronald Reagan used the phrase during his farewell address in 1989.

The Kingdom Theme

The most prevalent and the most complex theme in the gospels is the *kingdom*—a translation of the Greek word *basilieva*. The word appears fifty times in Matthew, fourteen times in Mark, thirty-nine times in Luke, and five times in John. The reign of God was an essential element in the accounts of Jesus' teaching and was at the heart of his message. For most scholars, the kingdom theme has both a present and a future aspect.

The Gospels describe Jesus as proclaiming the kingdom as something that was coming about at the present moment and not merely a future reality (see Mark 1:15). The reported activity of Jesus in healing diseases, driving out demons, teaching a new ethic for living, and offering a new hope in God to the poor was understood to be a demonstration of that kingdom. The kingdom of God also referred to the changed state of heart or mind within disciples *(Luke 17:20–21)*. For many there is also a future aspect to the kingdom—a time when God would rule the earth. And there is a tension between the present and the future dimensions. Traditionally, Roman Catholics, many Protestants, and Pentecostals have tended to emphasize the present aspect, while evangelical Christians have emphasized the future aspect.

Historian, social commentator, and author H. G. Wells wrote, "This doctrine of the kingdom of heaven, which was the main teaching of Jesus, and which plays so small a part in the Christian creeds, is certainly one of the most revolutionary doctrines that ever stirred and changed human thought."

The common phrase *turn the other cheek* is derived from the Sermon on the Mount. Jesus says: "If anyone strikes you on the right cheek, turn the other also" *(Matthew 5:39 [NRSV])*. To turn the other cheek has come to mean being patient with wrongdoers rather than seeking revenge.

Also from the Sermon on the Mount, it is common to refer to a person with solid, traditional values as the "salt of the earth." *Give the shirt off your back* is a modern variation of Matthew 5:40. *Go the extra mile* is from 5:41. *Cast your pearls before swine* is from 7:6.

Church Discipline

Another discourse is found in Chapter 18. This discourse is sometimes called the "church order" or "church discipline" discourse, because it provides guidelines for the Christian community. Jesus presented the example of a child as the greatest in the kingdom of heaven. He later gave rules for how to deal with persons in the church who sin against the other members. He concluded this section with a famous teaching on prayer: "For where two or three are gathered together in my name, there am I in the midst of them" *(Matthew 18:20 [KJV])*.

Jesus also told of the necessity of mercy. Peter asked him if one must forgive someone seven times. Apparently he thought of the Jewish tradition of forgiving three times, which Peter doubled and added one more for good measure. Jesus answered, "Not seven times, but, I tell you, seventy-seven times" *(Matthew 18:22 [NRSV])*. Jesus then illustrated his teaching on mercy with a parable occurring only in Matthew (18:23–35). A merciful king forgave a servant a very large debt, but the same servant refused to forgive a man who owed him a much smaller sum of money. The parable ends with the following words of the king and Jesus' commentary:

> "You wicked slave! I forgave you all that debt because you pleaded with me. Should you not have had mercy on your fellow slave, as I had mercy on you?" And in anger his lord handed him over to be tortured until he would pay his entire debt. So my heavenly Father will also do to every one of you, if you do not forgive your brother or sister from your heart.
> *Matthew 18:32–35 [NRSV]*

The Resurrection

There are significant differences in the resurrection narrative in Matthew (Chapter 28). The account begins with an earthquake and a vision of an angel who rolled the stone away from the tomb. The angel so frightened the soldiers guarding the tomb that they seemed to be dead. The angel told the women not to fear, that Jesus had been raised. They were to go to Galilee to see him. The women were also afraid, but they were filled with joy as well. Jesus appeared to them and directed them to tell the disciples to meet him in Galilee.

After some intrigue on the part of the chief priests, the disciples went to Galilee and encountered Jesus on a mountain. Jesus then gave them what is called the great commission: "All authority in heaven and on earth has been given to me. Go therefore and make disciples of all nations, baptizing them in the name of the Father and of the Son and of the Holy Spirit, and teaching them to obey everything that I have commanded you" *(Matthew 28:18–20 [NRSV])*.

This verse shows the origin of the missionary thrust of Christianity, which seeks to spread its "good news" to all people. Likewise, the Christian ritual of baptism is mentioned, which from New Testament times has been the ritual of initiation into the Christian community. Finally, the mention of the Father, the Son, and the Holy Spirit is a demonstration that the foundational Christian doctrine of the **Trinity** was a part of the community's faith by the time this gospel was written.

The gospel of Matthew ends with a word of great encouragement and hope for the disciples: "And, lo, I am with you always, even unto the end of the world" *(Matthew 28:20 [KJV])*.

CULTURAL
CONNECTIONS
*T*he Missionary Spirit

The great commission at the end of Matthew's gospel has stirred many Christians to missionary activity. Interestingly, it also stirred a spirit of exploration. The desire to evangelize opened Christians to a desire to discover ends of the earth where the gospel had not yet been preached.

In the nineteenth century, Dr. David Livingstone (1813–1873) was moved to take the gospel message to the deepest parts of Africa. Under the sponsorship of the London Missionary Society, Livingstone set sail for Africa.

Livingstone was shocked by the slave trade that still flourished in Africa. He was convinced that if he could find easier routes of trade and communication with the African interior, it would lead to increased honest trade and an end to the human suffering of slavery. In November of 1855, Livingstone became the first European to see Mosi-o-Tunya ("the smoke that thunders")—Victoria Falls. His book *Missionary Travels* was an instant best seller.

Livingstone was driven by the passion of an evangelist and the vision of an explorer. On his last journey through Africa, it seemed as though the interior of the continent had swallowed him up. *The New York Herald* dispatched the journalist H. M. Stanley to find him. In what has become one of the most famous meetings in history, Stanley encountered Livingstone In the village of Ujiji with the words, "Dr. Livingstone, I presume?"

projects

Choose one of the following projects to learn more about the gospel according to Matthew:

1. In 1964, the avowed atheist Pier Paolo Pasolini was inspired by his reading of Matthew's gospel. He made a film to capture what he saw as powerful drama, using all amateur actors. The film is entitled, simply, *The Gospel According to Saint Matthew.* Rent a copy of the film and view it in a group. Record your reactions. How does the film increase your understanding of Matthew's gospel? It might be helpful to do a little Internet study of the film before viewing it.

2. Read one of the discourses from Matthew not covered in the text and write a brief report on what you read. Share the results with the class.

3. The Golden Rule is found in some form or another in most religious traditions. Try to discover how it is used in two or more religious traditions. How are the sentiments similar to what was written in Matthew? How are they different?

Luke

The Gospel of Luke could be called, "Luke: Volume One." Luke's work consists of two volumes, the gospel and the Acts of the Apostles. Luke traced not only the life, teaching, death, and resurrection of Jesus, but also the beginnings of the Christian community. There are many parallels between the two works.

Though sharing a similar structure and much material with Mark and Matthew, the gospel of Luke has several unique and distinguishing features. The infancy narrative from the perspective of Mary, the mother of Jesus; an emphasis on meal sharing; a focus on mercy and healing; a long teaching section using parables; and the resurrection narrative are all characteristically Luke. Luke, the author of this gospel, appears several times in the New Testament (Colossians 4:14, Philemon 24, 2 Timothy 4:11). Luke's gospel is structured as follows:

- Prologue
- Infancy narrative
- Ministry in Galilee
- Journey to Jerusalem
- Ministry in Jerusalem
- Passion
- Resurrection

Prologue of Luke

Though other gospels have prologues, Luke's is unique in setting forth the purpose of his work:

In *St. Luke Painting the Virgin*, Rogier van der Weyden depicts Luke painting the Virgin Mary and the child Jesus, following a tradition that Luke was an artist. This also reflects the traditional association of Luke with Mary, the mother of Jesus.

Since many have undertaken to set down an orderly account
of the events that have been fulfilled among us, just as they
were handed on to us by those who from the beginning were
eyewitnesses and servants of the word, I too decided, after
investigating everything carefully from the very first, to write
an orderly account for you, most excellent Theophilus, so that
you may know the truth concerning the things about which
you have been instructed.

Luke 1:1–4 [NRSV]

Luke addressed this gospel to Theophilus, but who is Theophilus? The word
means "lover of God" in Greek, and most scholars feel Theophilus was either a
name for a patron who financed the gospel or perhaps a generic name
indicating any reader of the gospel.

Rather than beginning his gospel with the birth of Jesus, Luke began the
infancy narrative with the birth of John the Baptist, the cousin of Jesus.
Indeed, throughout the infancy narrative, Luke created a parallel between
Jesus and John.

Luke grounded his gospel in history, pointing out that it begins "in the days
of King Herod of Judea" *(Luke 1:5 [NRSV])*. He tells the account of Zechariah
and Elizabeth, an elderly and childless couple. Zechariah, a priest, had a vision
of an angel who gave him the following news:

Do not be afraid, Zechariah, for your prayer has been heard.
Your wife Elizabeth will bear you a son, and you will name him
John. You will have joy and gladness, and many will rejoice at
his birth, for he will be great in the sight of the Lord. . . . Even
before his birth he will be filled with the Holy Spirit. He will
turn many of the people of Israel to the Lord their God. With
the spirit and power of Elijah he will go before him . . . to make
ready a people prepared for the Lord.

Luke 1:13–17 [NRSV]

CULTURAL
CONNECTIONS

Las Pastorelas

Luke's infancy narrative has given rise to many
cultural celebrations. The visit of the shepherds to
the infant Jesus took the form of community dramas
in Spain. These shepherds' plays, or *pastorelas*,
were taken from Spain to Mexico by sixteenth-
century missionaries. The *pastorelas* present the
story of the shepherds' vision of the angel and their
journey to visit the Christ child. However, they also
include imaginative details not contained in Luke's
account, such as a demonic figure who tempts the
shepherds not to continue and a lazy shepherd
who won't accompany the group.

Every year in Orange County, CA, the children perform *Las Pastorelas* on
December 13.

This painting of the annunciation account by Fra Angelico (1387–1455) shows a beam of light representing the Holy Spirit.

Zechariah had trouble believing the angel's words, and as a punishment he was struck temporarily mute. But when he returned home, the angel's words were fulfilled.

This opening passage demonstrates some of the characteristics that occur again and again in Luke's gospel. For example, the tone of "joy and gladness" is something found not only in the infancy narrative, but also throughout Luke's gospel.

Another Announcement

Luke tells of Jesus' conception and birth. Just as an angel announced the birth of John, so did the angel Gabriel announce the birth of Jesus to his mother Mary. "Greetings, favored one! The Lord is with you" *(Luke 1:28 [NRSV])*.

And now, you will conceive in your womb and bear a son, and you will name him Jesus. He will be great, and will be called the Son of the Most High, and the Lord God will give to him the throne of his ancestor David. He will reign over the house of Jacob forever, and of his kingdom there will be no end.

Luke 1:31–33 [NRSV]

Mary was concerned about his words, as she was still a virgin. But the angel explained that the conception of this child would be by the Holy Spirit. The angel also told her that Elizabeth had conceived a child. Mary accepted his words: "And Mary said, Behold the handmaid of the Lord; be it unto me according to thy word" *(Luke 1:38 [KJV])*. This structure of this announcement (often referred to as the *annunciation*) parallels the announcement to Zechariah, but Mary's response was quite different from his.

Mary then hurried to visit her cousin Elizabeth, whose baby stirred in her womb at Mary's approach. Elizabeth said, "Blessed are you among women, and blessed is the fruit of your womb. And why has this happened to me, that the mother of my Lord comes to me?" *(Luke 1: 42–43 [NRSV])*.

Mary responded to Elizabeth with a long prayer, which has come to be called the "Magnificat," the first word of the prayer in Latin *(Luke 1:46–55)*. This prayer, known also as a canticle, or song, is the first of several such canticles in Luke's infancy narrative. Luke's canticles have been incorporated into the worship services of many Christian churches. The prayer has as its literary model Hannah's prayer in 1 Samuel 2:1–10.

Notice that Mary said of God, "He has scattered the proud in the thoughts of their hearts. He has brought down the powerful from their thrones, and lifted up the lowly; he has filled the hungry with good things, and sent the rich away empty" *(Luke 1:51–53 [NRSV])*. These verses show how Luke's Gospel emphasizes the poor and the lowly.

Another famous canticle is presented in the very next scene, when Zechariah took his newborn baby John to the temple to be circumcised. Zechariah was suddenly able to speak again after being mute since the angel's revelation to him; he uttered the canticle known as the "Benedictus," again named for the first word of the canticle in Latin *(Luke 1:68–79)*.

The final verse of this chapter states that John "grew and became strong in spirit, and he was in the wilderness until the day he appeared publicly to Israel" *(Luke 1:80 [NSRV])*.

CULTURAL
CONNECTIONS
J.S. Bach

Perhaps no other New Testament text has provided a richer source of inspiration for composers than the Magnificat. The Magnificat appears as a song in the earliest Christian liturgies and has been set to music by hundreds of composers, the most famous of whom is Johann Sebastian Bach (1685–1750). Bach's Magnificat was written for the Christmas service of 1723 at St. Thomas's Church in Leipzig.

The form of Bach's music is the cantata, a genre of vocal chamber music in the Baroque period and a key part of the German Lutheran service. In Germany, the cantata was primarily a form of sacred music based on an actual biblical text or a paraphrase. Outside Germany, cantatas were primarily secular works and used contemporary poetry for text. Since the late eighteenth century, the term *cantata* has been applied to a wide

Johann Sebastian Bach

variety of works, sacred and secular, mostly for chorus and orchestra.

Bach was a deeply religious man who signed his cantatas "S.D.G.," which stands for *Soli Deo Gloria*—"to God alone the glory."

The Birth of Jesus

Luke tells of Jesus' birth in the second chapter of his gospel. Again, he grounded the account in the events of the times: "In those days a decree went out from Emperor Augustus that all the world should be registered. This was the first registration and was taken while Quirinius was governor of Syria" *(Luke 2:1–2 [NRSV])*. The account goes on to explain that Joseph and Mary went to Bethlehem, the city of David, who was Joseph's ancestor. "And so it was, that, while they were there, the days were accomplished that she should be delivered. And she brought forth her firstborn son, and wrapped him in swaddling clothes, and laid him in a manger; because there was no room for them in the inn" *(Luke 2:6–7 [KJV])*.

Luke's account of the visit of the shepherds *(Luke 2:8–20)* provides another example of Luke's continual emphasis on the lowly, the poor, and outcasts throughout his gospel. According to Luke, an angel appeared to a group of shepherds tending their flocks. The angels announced the birth of Jesus: "But the angel said to them, 'Do not be afraid; for see—I am bringing you good news of great joy for all the people: to you is born this day in the city of David a Savior, who is the Messiah, the Lord'" *(Luke 2:10–11 [NRSV])*. Notice that in this account, as earlier in the infancy narrative, there was a tone of joy. After the angel told

The Adoration of the Shepherds is a topic popular with painters through the ages. Georges de La Tour uses dramatic lighting in this version to highlight the infant Jesus.

THE BIBLE
AS Literature

LITERARY FEATURES IN THE GOSPEL OF LUKE

There are a number of storytelling techniques that are well developed in the Gospel of Luke. Luke used a travel motif for his account with the overall theme of a journey from Jesus' birth in an inconsequential town of Nazareth to his death in the capital Jerusalem. The gospel weaves the account of events in Jesus' journey with parables that Jesus told along the way.

Luke put together a gallery of memorable portraits that show compassion for the poor and the importance of women and other marginalized people. He heightened the contrasts between people such as Mary and Martha in one event and between the prodigal son and his older brother in a parable that Jesus told. These contrasts were rendered with simplicity and realism of style in a dramatic setting with a feel for the beauty and momentousness of the commonplace. Luke's flair for descriptions made this gospel a favorite among painters.

INTO EVERYDAY language

Two parables in Luke's gospel have left a trail in everyday language. The first is the story of the *good Samaritan.* Anybody who takes a risk to help others is labeled a good Samaritan. Some states even have good Samaritan laws to protect people who help out at a scene of an accident, for example, from being sued should something go wrong.

The other phrase is *Prodigal Son.* The phrase is used both to describe someone who wastes the family's money or resources as well as someone returning to the fold of the family. When the long-estranged uncle comes home for a family wedding, he might be greeted with, "Well, the prodigal son returns!"

the shepherds where to find the baby, an even more startling event occurred: "And suddenly there was with the angel a multitude of the heavenly host praising God, and saying, Glory to God in the highest, and on earth peace, good will toward men" *(Luke 2:13–14 [KJV]).* The angels' song is another example of music in Luke. Like the Magnificat and the Benedictus, this song forms the basis of a text known as the "Gloria," used for centuries in the worship services in the Christian church. It has likewise been the basis of musical compositions by great composers such as Antonio Vivaldi, whose *Gloria* is still frequently performed today.

Luke next describes how Jesus' parents brought him to Jerusalem to be presented in the temple. A man named Simeon approached them, took the baby in his arms, and recited a canticle *(Luke 2:29–32).* Like the other canticles, this one has been incorporated into Christian liturgy. Called the "Nunc Dimittis" after the first Latin words of the song, this canticle notes that Jesus is to be "A light to lighten the Gentiles, and the glory of thy people Israel" *(Luke 2:32 [KJV]).* The passage shows the universal aspect of Luke's gospel, which interprets the mission of Christ as directed not only to the Jewish people, but to non-Jews as well.

The Journey to Jerusalem

Luke contains a long travel narrative that takes Jesus to Jerusalem *(Luke 9:2–19:28).* This narrative has been compared to a similar travel narrative in Deuteronomy. You will find similar journey narratives in Luke, Volume 2: The Acts of the Apostles. It is during the journey that many of the themes unique to Luke's gospel are played out, including the themes of healing, the meal narratives, and events centered on women and on the parables.

When Jesus sent out his twelve disciples, he sent them to "preach the kingdom of God and to heal the sick" *(Luke 9:2).* After that, Jesus sent out seventy-two disciples to "Heal the sick who are there and tell them the kingdom of God is near" *(Luke 10:9).* Considering all the training modern-day doctors and nurses have, it is interesting that in sending out the twelve and then the seventy-two, there is no training session noted. The disciples are simply told to "heal the sick." When they came back, they were amazed at what had happened and said to Jesus, "Even the demons submit to us in your name" *(Luke 10:17).*

Many, if not most, of the wonders performed by Jesus were the healing of diseases of mind and body (including the driving out of evil spirits). For Luke, these healings were lessons about the kingdom of God, part of Jesus' saving mission. Luke is the only synoptic gospel in which Jesus is called "savior," and it is the only gospel in which Jesus claims he has come to seek out and save the lost.

Women in the Gospel of Luke

Throughout Luke's gospel, the reader encounters a number of women, some prominent and some less so. This inclusion of women is another characteristic of Luke. It follows his general emphasis on the lowly because of the status of women in his day. In fact, the prominence of women in Luke's gospel is truly remarkable. In the Roman Empire at the time of Jesus, women were second-class citizens. For example, under Roman law women could not be witnesses in a court of law. Their fathers and husbands had all the legal rights of the family and controlled all the money and property. In the Jewish synagogue, women were not allowed to sit with the men. Rabbis generally did not have women as disciples. The chart mentions some of the women featured in Luke.

This painting of Jesus in the House of Martha and Mary is believed to be the first work of the Dutch artist Jan Vermeer.

Women in the Gospel of Luke

Woman	Mentioned by Luke
Mary, the mother of Jesus	Infancy Narrative
Elizabeth	Chapter 1
Anna	Chapter 2
The Sinful Woman	Chapter 7
The Widow of Nain	Chapter 7
Female Disciples	Chapters 8, 23, and 24
Mary Magdalene	Chapters 8, 23, and 24
Joanna	Chapters 8 and 24
Martha and Mary	Chapter 10

In the course of the journey, Jesus visited two friends, the sisters Martha and Mary. While Jesus was teaching in their home, Martha was very busy preparing food for the guests, while Mary simply sat at Jesus' feet and listened to his teaching. Martha became irritated and asked Jesus to make Mary help her. He replied, "Martha, Martha, you are worried and distracted by many things; there is need of only one thing. Mary has chosen the better part, which will not be taken away from her" (Luke 10:41 [NRSV]).

Jesus as Storyteller

The rest of this section of Luke is a long teaching sequence, consisting largely of a group of parables. Often in answer to a question from the crowd, Jesus, rather than answering directly, taught in parables. For example, a lawyer asked Jesus, "Who is my neighbor?" and Jesus answered with one of the most famous parables of the Bible, that of the good Samaritan (Luke 10:29–37).

Another follower said to Jesus, "Teacher, tell my brother to divide the family inheritance with me." Jesus responded with the parable of the rich fool (Luke 12:13–21). When he was asked about the kingdom of God, Jesus answered with the short parables of the mustard seed and the yeast (Luke 13:18–19 and 13:20–21). When a guest desired a place of honor, Jesus told the parable of the wedding banquet (Luke 14:7–14). Another similar kingdom parable is the parable of the great dinner (Luke 14:15–24). As Jesus and his followers neared Jerusalem, Jesus presented another kingdom parable: the parable of the talents (Luke 19:11–27).

IN YOUR *journal*

Describe a time when a short story has taught you a lesson or made you stop and think. Does the story still have the same impact on you? Why or why not?

Titian's *Resurrection of Christ.*

Jesus was criticized for welcoming sinners. In answer, he told three parables about loss: the parables of the lost sheep *(15:3–7),* the lost coin (15:8–10), and the famous parable of the prodigal son *(15:11–32).*

Another group of parables concerns justice. For example, the parable of the dishonest manager *(16:1–13)* and the parable of Lazarus and the rich man *(16:19–31)* both chide rich people who neglect the poor. In the latter parable, a poor man named Lazarus lived at a rich man's gate and was ignored by the rich man. Though the parable gives no name to the rich man, he has traditionally been called *Dives,* Latin for "rich man." After death, the rich man went to Hades (Hell), while the poor man went to Abraham (Heaven).

The rich man begged Abraham to send someone from the dead to warn his family, but Abraham said, "If they do not listen to Moses and the prophets, neither will they be convinced even if someone rises from the dead" *(Luke 16:31 [NRSV]).*

Other parables in this section concern prayer. In the parable of the unjust judge, Jesus emphasized the need for persistent prayer *(18:1–8).* In the parable of the Pharisee and the tax collector *(18:9–14),* he praised the humble tax collector who prayed, "God, be merciful to me, a sinner!" *(Luke 18:13 [NRSV]).*

The Road to Emmaus

The descriptions of Jesus' arrival in Jerusalem and his suffering, death, and resurrection in Luke do not differ substantially from those in Matthew. But there is one event in Luke's resurrection account that has proven to be a significant inspiration for artists and writers. A unique element in Luke's narrative is the

Rembrandt's *Supper at Emmaus,* 1648.

account of two disciples traveling to the village of Emmaus, discussing the death of Jesus and his reported resurrection. Jesus appeared and walked with them, but they did not realize it was he. Jesus scolded them for their lack of faith and insight, and Luke notes "beginning with Moses and all the prophets, he interpreted to them the things about himself in all the scriptures" *(Luke 24:27 [NRSV]).*

In the evening, the disciples invited Jesus to stay with them, and Luke describes their dinner, which began with the traditional Jewish blessing of the bread: "When he was at the table with them, he took bread, blessed and broke it, and gave it to them. Then their eyes were opened, and they recognized him; and he vanished from their sight" *(Luke 24:30–31 [NRSV]).* The disciples hurried to Jerusalem to tell the apostles of their encounter with Jesus, only to learn that he had appeared to Peter as well.

The resurrection narrative concludes with an appearance of Jesus to all of the disciples, after which Jesus ascended to heaven. The final verse of Luke notes: "And they worshipped him, and returned to Jerusalem with great joy; and they were continually in the temple blessing God" *(Luke 24:52–53 [NRSV]).*

THE BIBLE

AS **Literature**

PARABLES

One of the most common forms of expression in the Christian Scriptures is the parable, which comes from the Greek word meaning "comparison." Parables are quite different from fables (like those of Aesop) and from allegories with layers and layers of meaning. Parables are usually taken from ordinary life. The story has a relatively simple meaning in itself but also demonstrates some quality or lesson that the storyteller wants to impart. Because of the timeless nature of the parable, it can be heard over and over again, casting both the story and its meaning into a kind of literary immortality.

Luke's gospel contains the most parables—twenty-eight. Matthew has twenty-four. Mark has nine. Traditionally, commentators have placed parables into one of two categories, ethical or theological. Under the first heading belong those parables that seek to teach a type of behavior or attitude that ought to be emulated. An example of this kind of parable is the story about new cloth on an old garment and new wine in old wineskins

(Matthew 9:16–17; Mark 2:21–22; Luke 5:36–38). The second category includes parables that explain something about the way people and God ought to relate. An example of this kind of parable is that of the unmerciful servant *(Matthew 18:23–35).* Some parables, such as that of the prodigal son, can fit into both categories.

Parables also can be divided into two main literary forms, narratives and sayings. In the narrative type, one finds renowned parables such as those of the good Samaritan, the prodigal son, and the sower. These familiar parables are set in a language that any first-century Galilean would have easily understood. Narrative parables express an ethical or theological idea through metaphor and simile. The second form, sayings, include "To what should I compare the kingdom of God? It is like yeast that a woman took and mixed in with three measures of flour until all of it was leavened" *(Luke 13:20–21).* These sayings resemble those found in the Book of Proverbs.

projects

Choose one of the projects to explore the impact Luke's gospel has had on language and literature:

1. By yourself or with a small group, locate musical compositions based on the canticles found in Luke. Bring recordings to the class to share. Talk about what you hear.

2. Make a handy reference list of some of Luke's parables. Then monitor the media—newspapers, magazines, and television—to see if any references to these parables crop up in reports or stories. Report on whatever you discover. (Don't be shy about reporting other biblical references, even if they are not to Luke's parables.)

KEY BIBLICAL TEXTS

- John 1:1–18; 2:1–3:21; 4:1–5:9; 6; 8–11; 13–17; 20–21

DISCOVER

- How John's gospel differs in style and substance from the other gospels
- The literary device of the seven signs that guide the reader through the life of Jesus

- The "I am" statements of Jesus, as recorded in John

GET TO KNOW

- Nicodemus, Lazarus, the beloved disciple, Mary Magdalene, Thomas

CONSIDER

- What are some different kinds of signs? What is their use?

John

Have you ever struggled to understand someone? Many people in the gospel of John struggled to understand Jesus. John writes: "In the beginning was the Word, and the Word was with God, and the Word was God" *(John 1:1 [KJV])*. These words also announce that this gospel is going to be different from those of Matthew, Mark, and Luke—the synoptics.

The Christian community has traditionally attributed this book to John, one of Jesus' twelve apostles, the son of Zebedee and the brother of James. In fact, John has traditionally been believed to be the author not only of this book, but also of four other New Testament documents: the three letters and the Book of Revelation. Some see this John as the unnamed "beloved disciple" who appeared several times in the gospel of John *(13:21–28; 19:26–27; 20:2–10; 21:4–8; 21:20–24)*. John seems to have been writing to a Greek-speaking audience and apparently a primarily Gentile one, as the author sometimes explains Jewish customs.

Like the other three gospels, this gospel focuses on the life, teaching, works, and passion of Jesus. Nonetheless, there are characteristics of John that make this gospel one of a kind. Almost all of the material in this fourth gospel occurs *only* in John.

There are some interesting differences between John's gospel and the other three. In the other gospels, Jesus made one significant trip to Jerusalem at the end of the gospel, and there he was crucified and rose again. But in the gospel of John, Jesus was constantly traveling back and forth between Galilee and Jerusalem. Also, certain events are recorded in a different order in John than in the synoptic gospels. For example, the cleansing of the temple occurred in John near the beginning of Jesus' public life, whereas the others record it as a prelude to the Passion. The other gospels include many parables, but John contains none at all. Instead, Jesus taught by means of long, philosophical discourses or sermons, and most of these concern the nature and mission of Jesus. In John, Jesus' work was focused in a group of **signs,** works performed to bring about belief in him. Only one of the signs (the feeding of the 5000) is found in the other gospels.

This page from the ninth-century Gospels of MacRegol depicts Saint John the Evangelist. Notice the eagle symbol traditionally associated with John.

Prologue

In the beginning was the Word, and the Word was with God, and the Word was God. He was in the beginning with God. All things came into being through him, and without him not one thing came into being. What has come into being in him was life, and the life was the light of all people. The light shines in the darkness, and the darkness did not overcome it.

He was in the world, and the world came into being through him; yet the world did not know him. He came to what was his own, and his own people did not accept him. But to all who received him, who believed in his name, he gave the power to become children of God, who were born, not of blood or of the will of the flesh or of the will of man, but of God.

And the Word became flesh and lived among us, and we have seen his glory, the glory as of a father's only son, full of grace and truth.

John 1:1–5, 10–14 [NRSV]

Veronese's painting depicts the wedding at Cana in a setting more like that of Italian Renaissance nobility than a humble setting in first-century Palestine.

In these opening words, reminiscent of the first lines of the Book of Genesis, John clearly reveals Jesus' divine nature. First of all, John writes that Jesus was God, present at the creation of the world and all things. Secondly, Jesus was flesh, that is, a human being. This view of Jesus as both God and man would become a foundational belief of the Christian community regarding Jesus. In later centuries, church councils such as that of Nicea in the year 325 would formulate this belief into written **creeds.** More than perhaps any other New Testament work, these verses, and indeed the entire gospel of John, very clearly begin to articulate the Christian doctrines of the incarnation (that God took flesh in Jesus) and the Trinity (one God in three divine persons: Father, Son, and Holy Spirit) as they developed during the first century.

Scholars see two main divisions in the gospel: The first part is called the Book of Signs, and the second part is called the Book of Glory.

The Book of Signs

The first part of John's gospel is built on seven miracles or signs. The signs are seen as pointers to the identity of Jesus and they reveal his divinity.

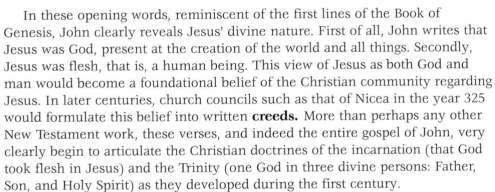

THE SIGNS	
1. Water Changed to Wine at the Wedding at Cana	2:1–11
2. Healing of a Royal Official's Son	4:46–54
3. Healing of a Paralytic at the Sheep Gate Pool	5:2–18
4. Feeding of the 5000	6:1–14
5. Walking on the Water	6:16–21
6. Healing of a Blind Man	9:1–41
7. Raising of Lazarus	11:1–44

CULTURAL CONNECTIONS

The Seven Last Words

For centuries, various musical settings have been composed for the "seven last words" of Christ from the cross. Among the most famous of these musical compositions is Joseph Haydn's *Seven Last Words of the Redeemer on the Cross.* Commissioned by the Cathedral of Cádiz in Spain for its Holy Week service, it was first performed in 1787. Haydn wrote it originally as an orchestral work but later published a version for string quartet. He also produced a version for choir and orchestra. Cellist Julian Armour has called it "a uniquely subtle and sublimely beautiful" piece of music—one of "such universal profundity that it speaks to musicians and music lovers of all nationalities and religions."

The "seven last words" are a compilation of the seven last sentences of Jesus recorded in all four Gospels:

1. Father, forgive them; for they do not know what they are doing *(Luke 23:34).*
2. My God, my God, why have you forsaken me? *(Matthew 27:46; Mark 15:34; Psalm 22:1).*
3. Woman, here is your son. Here is your mother *(John 19:26, 27).*
4. I am thirsty *(John 19:28).*
5. Truly, I say to you today you will be with me in paradise *(Luke 23:43).*
6. It is finished *(John 19:30).*
7. Father, into your hands I commend my spirit *(Luke 23:46).*

The High Priestly Prayer

Chapter 17 of John has traditionally been called the "high priestly prayer," for in it, Jesus switched from speaking to the disciples to speaking directly to God in the manner of the priests. He talked about his coming death and about his followers. The opening words of the prayer, according to the text, indicate once again Jesus' understanding of his relationship to God: "I glorified you on earth by finishing the work that you gave me to do. So now, Father, glorify me in your own presence with the glory that I had in your presence before the world existed" *(John 17:4-5 [NRSV]).* He first of all prayed for his disciples, saying, among other things: "And now I am no longer in the world, but they are in the world, and I am coming to you. Holy Father, protect them in your name that you have given me, so that they may be one, as we are one" *(John 17:11 [NRSV]).*

The Resurrection

In John's account of the resurrection, Mary Magdalene was the first to discover the empty tomb. She was followed by Peter and "the disciple whom Jesus loved" (traditionally believed to be John himself). As John notes, "Then the other disciple, who reached the tomb first, also went in, and he saw and believed; for as yet they did not understand the scripture, that he must rise from the dead" *(John 20:8-9 [NRSV]).* This

This painting by Titian (1512) is entitled *Noli Me Tangere* from the Latin for "Do not touch me," Jesus' words to Mary Magdalene when meeting her in the garden after his resurrection. Paintings depicting this meeting are traditionally given this name.

editorial comment by John is typical of this gospel. Then, Mary Magdalene met the risen Christ and mistook him for a gardener:

> "Sir, if you have carried him away, tell me where you have laid him, and I will take him away." Jesus said to her, "Mary!" She turned and said to him in Hebrew, "Rabbouni!" (which means Teacher). Jesus said to her, "Do not hold on to me, because I have not yet ascended to the Father."
>
> *John 20:15–17 [NRSV]*

Later that evening, Jesus appeared to the disciples and gave them the following commission:

> "Peace be with you. As the Father has sent me, so I send you." When he had said this, he breathed on them and said to them, "Receive the Holy Spirit."
>
> *John 20:21–22 [NRSV]*

A Third Encounter

In the final chapter of the gospel, the disciples were fishing and saw a man on shore who had built a fire. The man asked them to bring some of their catch, cooked the fish for them, and gave it to them, along with bread. When Peter recognized the man as Jesus, he immediately jumped into the water and swam ashore.

After the meal, Jesus had a conversation in which he asked Peter three times if he loved him. With each affirmative answer, Jesus gave an instruction to Peter: "Feed my lambs" *(21:15)*, "Tend my sheep" *(21:16)*, and "Feed my sheep" *(21:17)*. He then made a prediction about Peter's death *(21:18–19)*.

After this third encounter, John's gospel concludes in an unusual way. "But there are also many other things that Jesus did; if every one of them were written down, I suppose that the world itself could not contain the books that would be written" *(John 21:25 [NRSV])*.

INTO EVERYDAY *language*

John's gospel tells the story of the apostle Thomas, who was not present when Jesus first appeared to the disciples. He refused to believe their reports unless he got to touch the wounds in Jesus' hands, feet, and side. The following week Thomas was given the chance to do just that. He responded, "My Lord and my God!"*(John 20:28 [NRSV])*. Jesus said to Thomas, "Have you believed because you have seen me? Blessed are those who have not seen and yet have come to believe" *(John 20:29 [NRSV])*.

This apostle has been memorialized in everyday language; anyone with an incredulous attitude is called a *doubting Thomas*.

projects

Choose one of the projects below to expand your knowledge of John's gospel:

1. Do a quick scan of the whole of John's gospel. Make a list of five phrases that are familiar to you. Explain why they sound familiar. Compare your list with the lists others have made. Talk about how John's gospel has influenced language and even thought.

2. Select and read one of the seven signs in John's gospel. Then use that sign as inspiration for an artistic image. You can use drawing, modeling, photography, or poetry. Share and be willing to explain (if necessary) what you have done.

Unit Feature
Parables of Mercy

Perhaps the two best-known parables are those of the prodigal son *(Luke 15:11–32)* and the good Samaritan *(Luke 10:25–37)*. Many scholars consider them companion pieces in that both work on every level as stories of great mercy. The parable of the prodigal son is the story of a father who can rise above personal insult to welcome home a wayward son. The Samaritan rises above ethnic boundaries and national enmity to show compassion to a man beaten by highwaymen.

THE PRODIGAL SON

The prodigal son was a young man who asked his father for his inheritance and then left home for "a far country, and there wasted his substance with riotous living." As his money ran out, a famine occurred, and he went to work tending pigs; but even then he could not get enough to eat. He returned home, knowing that he had given up his right to be treated as his father's son but hoping that his father would accept him as a hired servant on the farm. Seeing the prodigal son coming from a distance, the father rejoiced and ordered the fatted calf to be slaughtered for a feast to celebrate his son's return.

The prodigal son's elder brother returned from the fields while the feast was going on and was angry. He complained that he had never been treated to such a feast, though he had remained and worked diligently for his father while his brother was away. The father reassured him, saying that the elder son would still get his inheritance, but it was right to celebrate the return of the prodigal son: "For this thy brother was dead, and is alive again; and was lost, and is found."

The structure of the parable can be analyzed as a chiasm, or inverted parallelism, in six parts as follows:

1 "Father, give me my share" —a son is lost
2 Wasted his share in extravagant living—gifts are squandered
3 A great famine arose in the country and he began to be in want—everything has been lost
4 Son hired himself out to feed the pigs—great sin (pigs are unclean animals)
5 No one gave him anything—total rejection
6 Came to himself—a change of mind
6' Will say to the father "I have sinned against heaven and before you and am no longer worthy to be called your son"—a change of mind
5' Returned; father saw him and embraced him—total acceptance
4' Said to father, "I have sinned against heaven and before you and am no longer worthy to be called your son"—great repentance
3' Father commanded servants to bring best robe, to put on ring, and to give shoes—gains everything
2' Fatted calf is killed for a great party—goods used in joyful celebration
1' "'For this my son was dead and is alive; he was lost and is found.' And they began to make merry"—a son is found

THE GOOD SAMARITAN

The story is well known. A man on a journey is beaten and robbed. People pass him by, but a Samaritan who—despite the mutual antipathy between his people and the Jews—cares for the man, takes him to an inn, pays for him, and leaves the innkeeper with instructions to do what was needed to get the man well again.

The story is told within the context of a forced confrontation between a lawyer and Jesus. One way to analyze the parable is to see it as another form of parallelism. The debate can be divided into eight exchanges that fall into two rounds of questions and answers. In each round there are two questions and two answers. The formal structure of each scene is identical:

Round One:
A lawyer stood up to put Jesus to the test.

Question 1:	Lawyer—"What must I do to inherit eternal life?"
Question 2:	Jesus—"What does the law say?"
Answer 1:	Lawyer—"Love God and love your neighbor."
Answer 2:	Jesus—"Do this and you shall live."

Round Two:
The lawyer wanted to justify himself.

Question 3:	Lawyer—"Who is my neighbor?"
Question 4:	Jesus—He told the story to set up the question: "Which one proved to be a neighbor to the man who fell into the hands of the robbers?"
Answer 3:	Lawyer—"The one who took pity."
Answer 4:	Jesus—"Go and do likewise."

LESSONS TO BE LEARNED

On the surface these two parables work as moral tales. As in most of Jesus' teaching, however, there were layers of meaning:

1. In the Prodigal Son: Although his parable is in the tradition of "lost son" stories—Jacob and Joseph or

David and Absalom—the purpose of the story is to show God as father and forgiver.

- The younger son came back. He greatly offended his father by asking for his inheritance, which in effect said to his father, "I wish you were dead." And yet upon his return, the father went out and embraced the son and welcomed him back. Furthermore, the father celebrated the son's return by inviting the villagers to share in his joy. Forgiveness of sins by a merciful God is a message hiding just beneath the surface.

- The father fell on his son's neck and kissed him (a scene right out of the Hebrew Bible) before hearing the son's prepared speech. The father did not demonstrate love in response to his son's confession. Rather, out of his own mercy, he ran to reconcile with his estranged son.

- In the Hebrew Scriptures, God is already presented as a father who also acts with the tender compassion of a mother *(Deuteronomy 32:18; Psalm 131; Isaiah 42:14, 66:13)*. The Dead Sea Scrolls describe God with the same imagery. More than 200 times Jesus called God "Father." In 1 John, the believer is described as "born of God." Thus, God "gives birth" in the New Testament even as he does in Hebrew Scriptures *(Deuteronomy 32:18)*. In this parable, the father appeared to take on the attributes of a compassionate and merciful God.

2. **In the Good Samaritan:** The principal disputes the Jews—especially the Pharisees—had with the Samaritans centered on the proper place for worship and the interpretation of the Torah. Jesus' presence in Samaria (the conversation with the Samaritan woman) and his use of a Samaritan in this parable demonstrate *inclusivity*—especially in an argument with a lawyer.

- The parable also demonstrates that neighborliness is based not on any entitlement (as those who past the beaten man may have had) but on mercy and compassion (demonstrated by the foreigner).

- It is important to note that the story's target audience, the Pharisees, despised Samaritans as **apostates.** Thus the parable, as told originally, might have had a significant theme of nondiscrimination and interracial harmony. But as the Samaritan population dwindled to near-extinction, this aspect of the parable became less and less discernible. Fewer and fewer people ever met or interacted with Samaritans or even heard of them in any context other than this one. To address this problem with the unfamiliar analogy, the story is often retold in more recognizable modern settings where the characters are ones in equivalent social groups known to not interact comfortably.

THE RETURN OF THE PRODIGAL SON

Henri Nouwen (1932–1996), a well-known twentieth-century writer, wrote this reflection on Rembrandt's painting in *The Return of the Prodigal Son* in 1994:

> The longer I look at "the patriarch," the clearer it becomes to me that Rembrandt has done something quite different from letting God pose as the wise old head of a family. It all began with the hands. The two are quite different. The father's left hand touching the son's shoulder is strong and muscular. The fingers are spread out and cover a large part of the prodigal son's shoulder and back. I can see a certain pressure, especially in the thumb. That hand seems not only to touch, but, with its strength, also to hold. Even though there is a gentleness in the way the father's left hand touches his son, it is not without a firm grip.

> How different is the father's right hand! This hand does not hold or grasp. It is refined, soft, and very tender. The fingers are close to each other and they have an elegant quality. It lies gently upon the son's shoulder. It wants to caress, to stroke, and to offer consolation and comfort. It is a mother's hand. . . .

The Early Christian Community

All who believed were together and had all things in common; they would sell their possessions and goods and distribute the proceeds to all, as any had need. Day by day, as they spent much time together in the temple, they broke bread at home and ate their food with glad and generous hearts.

The Acts of the Apostles 2:44–46 [NRSV]

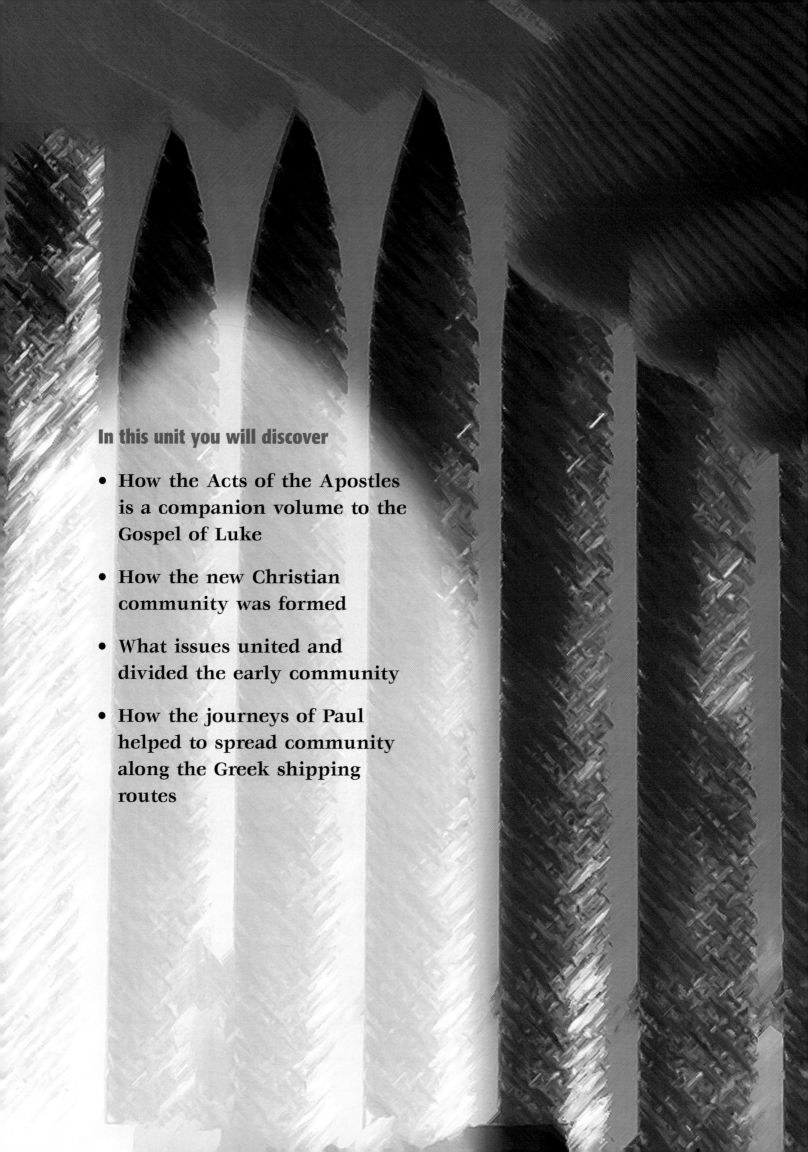

In this unit you will discover

- How the Acts of the Apostles is a companion volume to the Gospel of Luke

- How the new Christian community was formed

- What issues united and divided the early community

- How the journeys of Paul helped to spread community along the Greek shipping routes

KEY BIBLICAL TEXTS

- Acts 1–7

DISCOVER

- The relationship between the Gospel of Luke and the Acts of the Apostles
- The phenomenon known as Pentecost
- How the early members of the Church led a communal, or common, life

GET TO KNOW

- Gamaliel, Ananias and Sapphira, Stephen

CONSIDER

- Of what communities are you a member? How were these communities formed?

The Birth of the Church

The opening words of the Acts of the Apostles ("In the first book") signal the uniqueness of this book in the New Testament. (All quotations from this chapter are from the NRSV.) This book of the Christian Bible is presented as a companion volume to another book of the New Testament—the Gospel of Luke. The book is also addressed to Theophilus, as was Luke's gospel. In point of fact, the Acts of the Apostles closely resembles the gospels in its literary form.

The Acts of the Apostles picks up the threads and literary forms begun in the Gospel of Luke by chronicling the beginning of the Christian Church. Acts places strong emphasis on the power of the Holy Spirit, and it focuses on the preaching of the apostles. Healings and other signs are recorded at some length. The apostles' message is how God's covenant with the Hebrew people continued to be fulfilled in the life of the church through the holy spirit separately from the rabbinic Jewish community that continued in its own interpretation and practice of the Jews' original covenant with God.

Acts continues the journey account begun in Luke's gospel. That first journey moved from Nazareth, an inconsequential rural village, to the capital in Jerusalem. In Acts, the journey begins in Jerusalem with the establishment of a church and follows Paul's somewhat circuitous route to Rome, the capital of the empire. In Acts, Luke mentions thirty-two countries, fifty-four cities, and nine Mediterranean islands. Acts is a journal of the expansion of the early church along the Greek shipping routes.

Besides the journey theme (see Acts 19:21 and Luke 9:51, for example), there are other important parallels between Acts and Luke. There are parallel healings and the raising of people from the dead. Even within Acts there are parallels between speeches of Peter and those of Paul (look up, for example, Acts 3:12–26 and Acts 13:16–33).

The scene above is a tenth-century portrayal of the ascension from the *Benedictional of St. Aethelwold.* The painting below, dating from the twelfth century, is taken from a Catalan altarpiece. The two represent ways used throughout Christian history to portray the ascension.

Prologue

In the opening words of Acts, Luke summarizes what the community believed and proclaimed about Jesus' death and resurrection and adds an account of Jesus being taken up to heaven, which has come to be called the **ascension.** (Luke is the only one of the four gospel writers to mention this event, although there is a hint of an ascension in the longer ending of Mark's gospel.) Luke repeats Jesus' words commanding his followers to remain in Jerusalem to await the "baptism of the Holy Spirit." The apostles are anxious to know when the kingdom of Israel will be restored. This reflects a great concern of the first generations of Christians. Jesus' response to them sets the agenda for the Acts of the Apostles:

> It is not for you to know the times or periods that the Father has set by his own authority. But you will receive power when the Holy Spirit has come upon you; and you will be my witnesses in Jerusalem, in all Judea and Samaria, and to the ends of the earth.
>
> *Acts 1:7-8*

After speaking these words, Jesus, according to Acts, was lifted into heaven, and as his followers watched him, two men in white robes said to them:

> Men of Galilee, why do you stand looking up toward heaven? This Jesus, who has been taken up from you into heaven, will come in the same way as you saw him go into heaven.
>
> *Acts 1:11*

El Greco's painting *Pentecost* depicts the descent of the Spirit in Acts.

Pentecost

Shavuot, the feast of weeks, is a Jewish festival celebrated fifty days after Passover. It commemorates the occasion of God giving the law to Moses on Mt. Sinai, fifty days after escaping from Egypt. The Greek name for this festival is *Pentecost,* meaning "fiftieth." Acts describes how the apostles, while gathered for this feast, received the gift of the Holy Spirit, which Jesus had promised:

> And suddenly from heaven there came a sound like the rush of a violent wind, and it filled the entire house where they were sitting. Divided tongues, as of fire, appeared among them, and a tongue rested on each of them. All of them were filled with the Holy Spirit and began to speak in other languages, as the Spirit gave them ability.
>
> *Acts 2:2-4*

This account is often portrayed as a reversal of the Tower of Babel story in Genesis, during which the languages of people were confused and they were unable to understand one another.

Peter then told the assembled Jews about Jesus' death and resurrection. When Peter's hearers wondered how they should respond to this news, Peter answered: "Repent, and be baptized every one of you in the name of Jesus Christ so that your sins may be forgiven; and you will receive the gift of the Holy Spirit" *(Acts 2:38)*.

According to the text, approximately 3,000 people were baptized. The account establishes, along with the mentions of baptism in the gospels, the origin of the Christian ritual of baptism as the means of initiation into the Christian community. It is interesting to note in Peter's speech

THE BIBLE

IN Literature

The contemporary poet and winner of the Nobel Prize for Literature Derek Walcott uses imagery from the scene in Acts in his poem, "Pentecost":

Better a jungle in the head
than rootless concrete.
Better to stand bewildered
by the fireflies' crooked street;

winter lamps do not show
where the sidewalk is lost,
nor can these tongues of snow
speak for the Holy Ghost;

the self-increasing silence
of words dropped from a roof
points along iron railings,
direction, if not proof.

But best is this night surf
with slow scriptures of sand,
that sends, not quite a seraph,
but a late cormorant,

whose fading cry propels
through phosphorescent shoal
what, in my childhood gospels,
used to be called the Soul.

Derek Walcott, *The Arkansas Testament*

and in all of the many other speeches in the Acts of the Apostles the use of passages and references from the Hebrew Scriptures to explain the person and work of Jesus.

Pentecost is celebrated as an important Christian feast. On this day, Christians from the different liturgical traditions (Roman Catholic, Anglican, Orthodox, and others) celebrate the coming of the Holy Spirit and the beginning of the Christian community, known as the church. In some English-speaking countries, the day is called Whitsunday ("white Sunday") because the people who were baptized on the vigil of this feast wore white garments. The feast is celebrated fifty days after Easter.

Healing

According to Acts, soon after the Pentecost experience, Peter and the other disciples began healing the sick and preaching courageously about Jesus. Acts 3 describes how Peter and John cured a man who had been born lame:

And a man lame from birth was being carried in. People would lay him daily at the gate of the temple called the Beautiful Gate so that he could ask for alms from those entering the temple. When he saw Peter and John about to go into the temple, he asked them for alms. Peter looked intently at him, as did John, and said, "Look at us." And he fixed his attention on them, expecting to receive something from them. But Peter said, "I have no silver or gold, but what I have I give you; in the name of Jesus Christ of Nazareth, stand up and walk." And he took him by the right hand and raised him up; and immediately his feet and ankles were made strong. Jumping up, he stood and began to walk, and he entered the temple with them, walking and leaping and praising God.

Acts 3:2–8

In response to the people's amazement, Peter gave another speech, explaining that this miracle was attributable to the name of Jesus. There are many references to Jesus' name throughout Acts. This use of a powerful name harks back to Hebrew Scriptures. Just as the name of God was revealed to the Hebrews in the Hebrew Scriptures and had great power, so also in Acts the name of Jesus was a source of power for the apostles. In addition, Peter reviewed Jesus' death and resurrection and said that the prophets had foretold these events. He then invited the people to repentance. Acts notes that about 5000 people believed in Jesus as a result of this event. However, the priests and Sadducees were disturbed by the disciples' activities, and they arrested Peter and John. During the hearing, Peter made the following statement:

The sculpture in the south transept portal of the cathedral at Beauvais in France, which is called the Cathedral of Saint Peter and is dedicated to both Peter and Paul, shows the healing of the lame man.

> Rulers of the people and elders, if we are questioned today because of a good deed done to someone who was sick and are asked how this man has been healed, let it be known to all of you, and to all the people of Israel, that this man is standing before you in good health by the name of Jesus Christ of Nazareth, whom you crucified, whom God raised from the dead. This Jesus is 'the stone that was rejected by you, the builders; it has become the cornerstone.' There is salvation in no one else, for there is no other name under heaven given among mortals by which we must be saved.
>
> *Acts 4:8–12*

Luke made it a point that, after Jesus' ascension, the apostles themselves carried on the physical and spiritual healings that Jesus had done. Here are more interesting parallels with the Gospel of Luke. In Luke, Jesus healed the sick, cast out demons, and raised Jairus's daughter from the dead. In Acts, Luke portrayed the apostles as performing similar miraculous deeds such as the one just described as well as in 9:36–43, where Peter reportedly brought Tabitha back to life. One reason for this parallel may be to connect the words and actions of Jesus with life in the church. Luke may also have wanted to emphasize a major theme in Acts: The ministry of the church began with healing and preaching, just as Jesus' public ministry did.

Common Life

The end of Acts 4 describes a communal life:

> Now the whole group of those who believed were of one heart and soul, and no one claimed private ownership of any possessions, but everything they owned was held in common. . . . There was not a needy person among them, for as many as owned lands or houses sold them and brought the proceeds of what was sold. They laid it at the apostles' feet, and it was distributed to each as any had need.
>
> *Acts 4:32, 34–35*

This painting by Raphael is called *The Death of Ananias.*

A "cautionary tale" from Acts 5 illustrating the ideals of the early Christian community concerned Ananias and Sapphira, a husband and wife who were members of the Jerusalem community. Ananias sold some property and, with his wife's knowledge, presented only part of the proceeds to the Christian community, holding the rest back. Peter rebuked him, saying, "You did not lie to us but to God" *(Acts 5:4)*, and Ananias immediately dropped dead—apparently in punishment for his dishonesty. A few hours later, Sapphira came to the community and also lied about the price of the property. She, too, dropped dead.

CULTURAL
CONNECTIONS

Religious Communities

Many religious communities, Catholic, Orthodox, and Protestant, have found their inspiration in the vision of common life found in Acts. Some of these communities have profoundly influenced the history of Western civilization. Monastic orders have existed from the earliest centuries in both Eastern and Western Christianity. These communities were held together by the gospel and by a rule of life. The earliest monasteries developed in the Sinai Desert. A monk named Anthony codified one of the first rules around 313. Pachomius established another rule around 320. Basil the Great wrote a rule of life for his monks around 360.

The founder of Western monastic tradition was Benedict of Nursia (480–550). Augustine of Hippo (354–430) wrote a short rule for himself and his associates based directly on the Acts of the Apostles. It was a rule of common life but not a monastic rule as such. Down through the centuries, many religious orders of men and of women adopted Augustine's rule. In the thirteenth century, Francis of Assisi wrote a rule based almost entirely on the gospels and the early experiences of the church. His followers lived a common life and were mendicants who begged for their sustenance and depended on people's goodwill.

Today, there is a revived interest in monasticism and common life. Many Christian communities based on the descriptions in the Acts of the Apostles still exist. Other examples of this communal life include the Amish and the Mennonites.

After the incident with Ananias and Sapphira, Luke wrote how "great fear seized the whole church." The word translated "church" is the Greek word *ekklesia*, which literally means "gathering" or "assembly." In the Greek version of the Hebrew Scriptures, the Septuagint, this term applies to the people of Israel. By choosing this term to signify the body of Christian believers, the early Christians emphasized their roots in the Hebrew Scriptures and their continuity with the people of God.

Imprisonment

The apostles continued to perform healings, sometimes called "signs and wonders," in a similar fashion to healings that Jesus performed in the gospel accounts. These healings endeared them to the people. Luke writes about the reaction of the people to these miraculous events:

> Yet more than ever believers were added to the Lord, great numbers of both men and women, so that they even carried out the sick into the streets, and laid them on cots and mats, in order that Peter's shadow might fall on some of them as he came by. A great number of people would also gather from the towns around Jerusalem, bringing the sick and those tormented by unclean spirits, and they were all cured.
> *Acts 5:14–16*

This painting by Tommaso Masaccio (1401–1428) shows *Saint Peter Healing with His Shadow.*

When the high priest and the Sadducees heard of these activities, they imprisoned the apostles. But, according to the text, they were released from prison by an angel, who ordered them to continue preaching in the temple. Again, they were brought before the Sanhedrin (the Jewish council). Its members were so enraged at the obstinacy of Peter and the apostles that they wanted to have them executed. One member of the council, however, a Pharisee named Gamaliel, spoke in their defense:

> So in the present case, I tell you, keep away from these men and let them alone; because if this plan or this undertaking is of human origin, it will fail; but if it is of God, you will not be able to overthrow them—in that case you may even be found fighting against God!
> *Acts 5:38–39*

In response to Gamaliel's advice, the council released the apostles but first had them flogged and ordered them not to speak in the name of Jesus anymore. But Luke explains that:

> As they left the council, they rejoiced that they were considered worthy to suffer dishonor for the sake of the name. And every day in the temple and at home they did not cease to teach and proclaim Jesus as the Messiah.
> *Acts 5:41–42*

The sixteenth-century Spanish artist Alonso Sanchez Coello follows a tradition of presenting Stephen along with Lawrence (both deacons and martyrs) dressed in the elaborate vestments worn by deacons in the Middle Ages.

Deacons

As the church began to grow, a conflict developed between the **Hellenists** and the Hebrews (read Acts 6:1–6). The Hellenists were Greek-speaking Jews who felt that the widows among them were being given less food than the widows of the Hebrew-speaking Jewish members of the church. In response to this problem, the apostles directed the community to choose seven men who would take care of serving the physical needs of the group, thus freeing the apostles for their ministry of prayer and preaching. Among these men was Stephen, described as "a man full of faith and the Holy Spirit." The apostles prayed and laid their hands on these men. Traditionally, these men came to be called **deacons** (from the Greek word for "service"). Deacons are mentioned frequently in the letters of the New Testament. In the later development of Christianity, deacons came to be regarded as official ministers of the church. In some denominations, they are **ordained,** or formally admitted to ministry. In some Christian denominations, ordination still involves the laying on of hands, just as described in verse 6.

Acts shows Stephen performing signs and wonders and participating in debates with officials. He was brought before the council, where he was accused by false witnesses who said, "This man never stops saying things against this holy place and the law; for we have heard him say that this Jesus of Nazareth will destroy this place and will change the customs that Moses handed on to us" *(Acts 6:13–14).* As he was accused, the Sanhedrin noted, "his face was like the face of an angel" *(6:16).*

Stephen's Execution

When the high priest asked him to defend himself, Stephen gave one of the longest and most powerful speeches in Acts *(Acts 7:2–53).* This speech provides a review of the Hebrew Scriptures, for he mentioned Abraham, Joseph, Moses, Joshua, David, Solomon, and the prophets, speaking of the unfaithfulness of the Jewish people through the ages. Stephen concluded with a stinging rebuke of his accusers:

> You stiff-necked people, uncircumcised in heart and ears, you are forever opposing the Holy Spirit, just as your ancestors used to do. Which of the prophets did your ancestors not persecute? They killed those who foretold the coming of the Righteous One, and now you have become his betrayers and murderers. You are the ones that received the law as ordained by angels, and yet you have not kept it.
>
> *Acts 7:51–53*

This speech and attendant violent response need to be viewed as an early polemic against the Jews who did not accept Jesus as the messiah. Then the Acts gives an account of Stephen's death:

> With a loud shout all rushed together against him. Then they dragged him out of the city and began to stone him; and the witnesses laid their coats at the feet of a young man named Saul. While they were stoning Stephen, he prayed, "Lord Jesus, receive my spirit." Then he knelt down and cried out in a loud voice, "Lord, do not hold this sin against them." When he had said this, he died.
>
> *Acts 7:57–60*

THE BIBLE
IN Literature

A medieval English ballad imaginatively connects King Herod, the killer of the baby boys in the Gospel of Matthew, with Stephen. According to the ballad, Stephen was a server in the household of Herod at the time of Christ's birth, thus connecting him to that event. The traditional feast in the liturgical calendar honoring Stephen is celebrated on December 26, the day after Christmas. The ballad concludes with a dialogue between Stephen and Herod:

"Lacketh me neither gold ne fee
    Ne none rich weed;
There is a child in Bethlehem born
    Shall helpen us at our need."

"That is all so sooth, Stephen,
    All so sooth, I-wys,
As this capon crowé shall
    That li'th here in my dish."

That word was not so soon said,
    That word in that hall,
The capon crew *Christus natus est*
    Among the lordés all.

"Risit up, my tormenters,
    By two and all by one,
And leadit Stephen out of this town,
    And stonit him with stone.'

Tooken they Stephen
    And stoned him in the way;
And therefore is his even
    On Christe's own day.

The Oxford Book of Ballads

Stephen has been given the title of "first martyr of the Christian community." The word *martyr* means "witness." During one of the persecutions of Christians by the Roman Empire, the second-century theologian Tertullian observed, "The blood of the martyrs is the seed of the Church."

projects

Choose one or both of the projects below. You may work on your own, with a partner, or in a small group.

1. Review the first seven chapters of Acts and survey how many references there are to the Hebrew Scriptures. Create a short report or hold a discussion on what all these references tell the reader about this new Christian community.

2. Research some contemporary communities (for example, Bruderhof, Focolare, or Opus Dei) practicing a form of common life based on the Acts of the Apostles. Create a presentation of what daily life in one of these communities is like. What impact do these communities have on society?

KEY BIBLICAL TEXTS

- Acts 8–12

DISCOVER

- How the new community spread throughout Judea and Samaria
- How Christianity opened itself to welcoming Gentiles
- Herod's persecution of the Christian community

GET TO KNOW

- Philip, Simon Magus, the Ethiopian eunuch, Ananias, Saul (Paul), Cornelius, Barnabas, King Herod

CONSIDER

- How do movements today grow and spread?

The Church Grows

At first glance, you might see this second section of Acts as an unrelated group of narratives connecting the beginnings of the church in Jerusalem (Chapters 1–7) and the missionary journeys of Paul (Chapters 13–18). This section, however, explains how the Christian movement grows from being simply a **sect** of Judaism to being a distinct faith for both Jews and Gentiles (non-Jews). Likewise, the chapters here document the beginning of Christianity's geographical expansion. (All quotations in this chapter are from the NRSV.)

The centerpiece of this section is the conversion of Paul. He would become "the apostle to the Gentiles." His letters, moreover, form most of the rest of the New Testament.

Scattered Jewish Christians

The spread of those following Jesus started with a scattering of Jewish Christians as a result of rejection and persecution. Many followers were dispersed in the regions of Judea and Samaria.

This fifteenth-century painting by Filippino Lippi depicts two aspects of Peter's life: the dispute with Simon the magician from Acts and Peter's crucifixion.

These regions were predominantly Gentile in population. But the followers saw this as another opportunity to spread the good news of Jesus.

Philip, the first character in this section of Acts, centers his ministry in Samaria. You have already learned about the Samaritans and their differences with the Jews—both their worship on Mount Gerazim rather than in Jerusalem and their different canon of scripture. According to Acts, Jesus had specifically mentioned Samaria in his final words to his disciples. Chapter 8 of Acts recounts his works among the Samaritans.

When the church in Jerusalem heard of Samaritan conversions, it sent Peter and John to visit Philip. Because Philip had been baptizing in the name of Jesus only, the Jerusalem leaders laid hands on the converts to convey to them the gift of the Holy Spirit.

The first major convert won by Philip was Simon the magician. Along with his neighbors, he was baptized by Philip and indeed traveled with him, witnessing his healings. When he saw how Peter and John conveyed the gift of the Holy Spirit by the laying on of hands, he wanted to have this gift for himself and even offered the apostles money to pay for it. But Peter rebuked him: "May your silver perish with you, because you thought you could obtain God's gift with money!" The lesson was simply that the Holy Spirit was not for sale.

The Ethiopian Eunuch

The next major conversion story in this second section of Acts concerns the Ethiopian **eunuch.** A eunuch is a man who has been castrated and therefore is incapable of sexual relations. Conquering armies often castrated their prisoners of war for much the same reason male animals are castrated. The captors could make use of the prisoner's strength and abilities without concern that the prisoner would have sexual relations or would procreate. A eunuch could be trusted with female members of the court.

The Ethiopian eunuch was a very high official in the court of Candace, an Ethiopian queen, for the text remarks he was "in charge of her entire treasury" (Acts 8:27). He may well have been the equivalent of today's U.S. Secretary of the Treasury. The eunuch was most likely a Jew or Jewish convert because he had come to Jerusalem to worship.

The eunuch was reading from the "suffering servant" songs of Isaiah. Philip, in explaining these verses, interpreted them as pointing to the suffering of Jesus. The eunuch requested immediate baptism, and Philip baptized him in some water that they passed on the road. Among other things, this incident shows how, from very early on, Christianity was not confined to one geographical place or culture but spread to the entire world of the time.

Though today Christianity is often considered a Western religion, the New Testament shows how deep its origins are in the Middle East and that among the earliest converts was an African. The Ethiopian Church never died out. In its ancient churches, the worship has not changed in two millennia. Egypt likewise has maintained a Christian church. Africa has had an indigenous Christianity from the first century.

Paul

By Chapter 8, Acts, with some exceptions, becomes a narrative about Paul and his missionary journeys to spread the gospel throughout the Roman Empire. Saul of Tarsus was a Jew—a Pharisee. He was a member of a party in Judaism that was very much concerned with fidelity to Jewish law. Saul was traveling to the city of Damascus. According to the account, he was going to arrest the Christians there and bring them bound to Jerusalem. But on his way, he had a

INTO EVERYDAY *language*

We trace the origin of the English word *simony* to the story of Simon the magician in Acts. *Webster's* defines this term as "the buying or selling of sacred or spiritual things, as sacraments or benefices." As the definition implies, this term came to be applied to any selling of sacred things, such as church offices or spiritual favors.

This twentieth-century wooden crucifix, depicting a black Christ, is from Nigeria.

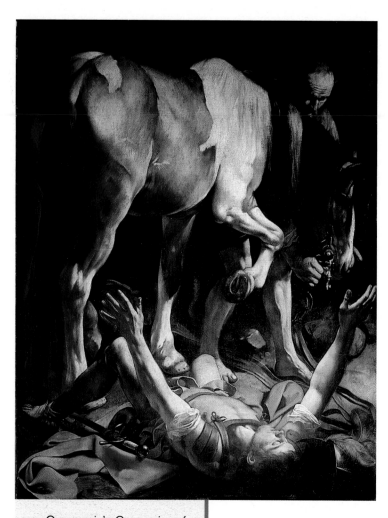

Caravaggio's *Conversion of Saint Paul*, one of the most famous depictions of this event in Western art, emphasizes the dramatic event through the use of light and shadow.

powerful and unusual experience that brought about a very sudden change of heart, or **conversion:**

> Now as he was going along and approaching Damascus, suddenly a light from heaven flashed around him. He fell to the ground and heard a voice saying to him, "Saul, Saul, why do you persecute me?" He asked, "Who are you, Lord?" The reply came, "I am Jesus, whom you are persecuting. But get up and enter the city, and you will be told what you are to do." The men who were traveling with him stood speechless because they heard the voice but saw no one.
>
> *Acts 9:3–7*

When Saul was able to get up from the ground, he discovered that he was blind, and he remained blind for three days. During that time, he didn't eat or drink.

According to the account, God called on a Christian in Damascus named Ananias and directed him to go to Saul. Ananias was reluctant, but the Lord said to him:

> Go, for he is an instrument whom I have chosen to bring my name before Gentiles and kings and before the people of Israel; I myself will show him how much he must suffer for the sake of my name.
>
> *Acts 9:15–16*

When Ananias came to Saul, he laid his hands on Saul, "'Brother Saul, the Lord Jesus, who appeared to you on your way here, has sent me so that you may regain your sight and be filled with the Holy Spirit.' And immediately something like scales fell from his eyes, and his sight was restored" *(Acts 9:17–18)*.

Ananias baptized Saul, who afterward ate and grew strong once again. He immediately began to preach to the Jews and aroused much suspicion and anger. Eventually, Saul had to sneak out of town. Later in Acts, he would be called by the Latin name Paul.

The Conversion of Cornelius

Chapter 10 marks a real turning point in Acts. Here the question of whether Gentiles could become Christians is faced head-on. The chapter begins by recounting a vision of a man named Cornelius. Cornelius was a Roman centurion, or man in charge of 100 men of the occupying Roman army. Thus, he was both a Gentile and a hated part of the occupation. But the text notes that "He was a devout man who feared God with all his household; he gave alms generously to the people and prayed constantly to God." One afternoon, Cornelius had a vision of an angel, who told him to send men to Peter in Joppa, and Cornelius immediately complied.

The next day, Acts explains that Peter had a vision, too:

IN YOUR *journal*

Peter was distressed because Simon the magician tried to purchase the gifts of God with money. What is an example of something else which is valuable but which cannot be bought?

He saw the heaven opened and something like a large sheet coming down, being lowered to the ground by its four corners. In it were all kinds of four-footed creatures and reptiles and birds of the air. Then he heard a voice saying, "Get up, Peter; kill and eat." But Peter said, "By no means, Lord; for I have never eaten anything that is profane or unclean." The voice said to him again, a second time, "What God has made clean, you must not call profane." This happened three times, and the thing was suddenly taken up to heaven.

Acts 10:11–16

This portrayal of Peter's vision is by nineteenth-century English artist Margaret Gere.

Remember that Jewish laws of kashrut (kosher) made a distinction between animals that may be eaten (clean) and animals that are unsuitable for eating (unclean).

Though Peter himself was not sure what this vision meant, very soon the men sent by Cornelius arrived, and together they traveled to the home of Cornelius. Cornelius at first attempted to worship Peter, but Peter stopped him and explained that God had sent him to stay with Cornelius, even though he was a Gentile: "God has shown me that I should not call anyone profane or unclean" *(Acts 10:28)*.

At this point, Peter delivered another one of those speeches so central to the literary architecture of Acts. Before preaching about Jesus to the group, Peter noted, "I truly understand that God shows no partiality, but in every nation anyone who fears him and does what is right is acceptable to him" *(Acts 10:34–35)*. As if in answer to these words, immediately following the speech of Peter, the Holy Spirit according to the text came upon the Gentiles who, like the apostles at Pentecost, spoke in tongues as a manifestation of the Holy Spirit. Peter then baptized them.

The chapter shows in literary form and metaphor that the new way was open to Gentiles. Not only were non-Jews to be welcomed as followers of Christ, but also even the hated Roman soldiers were to be welcomed.

Controversy in Jerusalem

When Peter arrived back in Jerusalem, he encountered severe opposition. "Now the apostles and the believers who were in Judea heard that the Gentiles had also accepted the word of God. So when Peter went up to Jerusalem, the circumcised believers criticized him" *(Acts 11:1–2)*. But Peter explained to them in great detail his vision and his experiences with the household of Cornelius. He ended his speech with this exhortation:

The Holy Spirit fell upon them just as it had upon us at the beginning. And I remembered the word of the Lord, how he had said, 'John baptized with water, but you will be baptized with the Holy Spirit.' If then God gave them the same gift that he gave us when we believed in the Lord Jesus Christ, who was I that I could hinder God?

Acts 11:15–17

These words of Peter convinced the circumcised Christians, who said, "Then God has given even to the Gentiles the repentance that leads to life" *(Acts 11:18)*.

INTO EVERYDAY *language*

An interesting detail emerging from this episode about the founding of the church in Antioch is cited in Acts 11:26. "It was in Antioch that the disciples were first called Christians." Whereas earlier in the Book of Acts, the followers of Jesus were called "disciples" or "followers of the way," here they are given the name that would come to distinguish them from their Jewish origins.

CHAPTER 30

KEY BIBLICAL TEXTS

■ Acts 13–28

DISCOVER

■ How the journeys of Paul began to establish Christianity in the Middle East

■ Some of the important issues in the new community—especially the issue of circumcision

■ How the new community began to distinguish itself from Judaism

GET TO KNOW

■ Silas, Timothy, Lydia, Demetrius the silversmith, King Agrippa

CONSIDER

■ Have you ever taken a long journey? If you were telling someone about the trip, what details would you include?

The Journeys of Paul

Accounts of Paul's journeys through Asia Minor (Turkey) and Greece comprise the last part of the Book of Acts. They were anything but easy; the journeys were filled with controversy and imprisonment, riots and near riots. Paul undertook harrowing sea journeys and endured shipwreck. He was put under house arrest in Rome.

After his experience on the road to Damascus, his time alone, and his early preaching, Paul found himself in a position of leadership in the new movement. He was anxious to spread the story of Jesus "to the ends of the earth." And, in so doing, he would fulfill the mandate given by Jesus in the first chapter of Acts. Also, at a council in Jerusalem the Christian community would settle how to integrate the many non-Jewish converts into the church.

The First Journey

This final section of Acts begins with an account of the first of three missionary voyages, during which Paul and various companions seek to spread the gospel throughout the Roman Empire. The setting for the beginning of this section is Antioch, where the prophets and teachers who lead the church were worshipping and fasting (all quotations in this chapter are from the NRSV):

The Holy Spirit said, "Set apart for me Barnabas and Saul for the work to which I have called them." Then after fasting and praying they laid their hands on them and sent them off.

Acts 13:2–3

Missionary Journeys
— First Missionary Journey
— Second Missionary Journey
— Third Missionary Journey

Use this map to guide you through Paul's three journeys.

CULTURAL
CONNECTIONS

*M*issions in California

Missionary journeys have a long tradition through the ages and particular relevance to the early history of what was to become the state of California through the establishment of a chain of twenty-one missions along California's *El Camino Real* ("the Royal Highway"), representing the first arrival of non–Native Americans to California.

The man who founded the first mission in San Diego in what is now the state of California in July 1769 was Father Junipero Serra (1713–1784). Born Miguel Jose Serra on the Spanish Mediterranean island of Mallorca, Father Junipero Serra entered the service of the Catholic Church in the Order of Saint Francis of Assisi. He volunteered to serve the Franciscan missions in the New World and spent seventeen years in missionary work in north-central Mexico. When the Franciscans were asked to take over the missions from the Jesuits in Baja California, in 1767, these remote facilities became Father Serra's responsibility. In 1769, he set off on an expedition to found missions at San Diego and Monterey, to establish the Spanish right to California, and convert the natives to Christianity, probably in a way similar to what Paul had done with the Gentiles. Father Serra would spend the rest of his life in California.

The bells of California Mission San Miguel, established 1797

When Father Serra founded the first of California's missions in San Diego, he was 56 years old. Serra himself established nine missions. A total of twenty-one missions were eventually established along *El Camino Real,* from San Diego to Solano, a distance of 700 miles. On August 28, 1784, at the age of 70 and after traveling 24,000 miles, Father Junipero Serra died at Mission San Carlos Borromeo in Carmel and is buried there under the sanctuary floor.

European missionary activity in the New World, in Africa, and in Asia was often linked to the colonial outreach of the major world powers. At times, the colonialism diluted the religious motivation of the Christian missionaries. Although it is virtually impossible to use a contemporary yardstick to measure events hundreds of years ago, there is a continuing debate over both the tactics and the results of the Christian missionary efforts over the centuries.

The interior of California Mission San Juan Bautista, established 1797

What Paul and Barnabas did first in virtually every town was enter the Jewish synagogue. In the synagogue, Paul spoke after the reading of the Hebrew Scriptures. Some of Paul's sermons have been recorded in the Acts of the Apostles. Paul had a format that he used in the synagogue. He started out with what Jews would know—how God chose the people of Israel, taking them out of Egypt and into the land of Canaan as God had promised. Paul would

This tapestry is based on a design by Raphael showing Paul preaching at the Areopagus.

him on his journey; and, to avoid more controversy, he had Timothy circumcised.

In the Macedonian city of Philippi, Paul and his companions baptized a young woman named Lydia and cast out a demon from a slave girl. The girl's owners were furious, as they had made money through the demon within her, which allowed her to tell fortunes. Once again, Paul encountered trouble. He and Silas were stripped, beaten, and imprisoned by the authorities of the city. However, they were released from prison by an earthquake, and their jailer was converted. The magistrates of the city released Paul when they discovered he was a Roman citizen.

Paul and Silas then went to the town of Beroea, where the townspeople in the synagogue were "more receptive than those in Thessalonica, for they welcomed the message very eagerly and examined the scriptures every day to see whether these things were so" *(Acts 17:11–12)*.

Paul then went to Athens where, as usual, he talked with the Jews of the city in the synagogue and also spoke to passersby in the marketplace. Then he gained the attention of some philosophers of the Stoic and Epicurean schools, and they took him to the **Areopagus** to debate. The Areopagus was a low hill in Athens dedicated to the Greek god of war, Ares, known as Mars to the Romans. The hill was just under the Acropolis, and the word also referred to a council of advisors who met on the hill. The Areopagus served as a sort of judicial council in ancient Greece.

Paul's debate with the philosophers at the Areopagus is one of the most famous scenes in the Book of Acts. The philosophers did not understand what Paul meant. They asked him to explain himself, setting the stage for his famous speech at the Areopagus *(Acts 17:22–31)*. In his speech, Paul shared the gospel with the Greeks using their own culture and authors. For example, Paul said that their altar inscription "to an unknown god" actually referred to his own god, and he explained how God created all things. Paul also quoted Greek thinkers *(Acts 17:28)* to explain the characteristics of God. Finally, he called the Greeks to forsake their gods and worship the true God *(Acts 17:30–31)*.

Some of the philosophers ridiculed Paul. Others joined with him, including a woman named Damaris and a man named Dionysius the Areopagite. Paul's speech at the Areopagus set a pattern followed in later Christian history; he did not entirely reject the local culture but made use of it to explain the teachings of Christianity.

After leaving Athens, Paul went to Corinth, where Silas and Timothy soon joined him. He stayed in Corinth for a year and a half, after which he was put on trial for his teachings. The proconsul Gallio, however, released him, and he went on to Syria. After a brief stop in Ephesus, he returned to Jerusalem.

The Third Journey

Next, Acts gives an account of a third journey by Paul. He left Antioch for Galatia and Phrygia and came again to Ephesus, where he remained for two years. Though he began his ministry among the Jewish population, he

L ok It Up

Read these three accounts:

- The conversion of Lydia—
  Acts 16:14–15
- The slave girl—Acts 16:16–24
- The jailer—Acts 16:27–34

Discuss what literary purpose is served by the juxtaposition of these three narratives.

IN YOUR
journal

In his speech at the Areopagus, we see Paul working to convince the Greek philosophers of the truth of the gospel. Have you ever tried to win someone over to your point of view? How did you accomplish this? Did you use any of Paul's techniques?

encountered rejection, so he preached in a public lecture hall. The text remarks that "God did extraordinary miracles through Paul, so that when the handkerchiefs or aprons that had touched his skin were brought to the sick, their diseases left them, and the evil spirits came out of them" *(Acts 19:11–12)*.

About this time, a controversy arose in Ephesus, led by a silversmith named Demetrius. He made his living making shrines to the Greek goddess Artemis. He rallied other artisans against the Christians, saying they were bad for business. After a near riot, Paul left to visit Macedonia and Greece. Then he traveled again through Macedonia, then to Troas, where, according to Acts, he raised the dead boy Eutychus, who fell from a window after he drifted off to sleep during a lengthy late-night talk by Paul. Paul then traveled back toward Jerusalem. When he passed Ephesus, he again met with the Ephesians and gave a long farewell speech *(Acts 20:18–35)*. He predicted that he would suffer imprisonment, persecution, and death, and he predicted that their own faith would face challenges, too.

Though he intended to return to Jerusalem, Paul was warned not to go there yet, so he traveled to Caesarea instead. He and his companions were visited by a prophet from Jerusalem, who predicted that Paul would be bound and handed over to the Gentiles if he should go there. But Paul responded, "I am ready not only to be bound but even to die in Jerusalem for the name of the Lord Jesus" *(Acts 21:13)*. He and his followers then went to Jerusalem, concluding this third missionary journey.

Paul's Arrest

After he greeted James and the Christians in Jerusalem, Paul was warned of opposition against him among the Jews, who said he was teaching against observance of the law. Paul went through a ritual of purification to show his loyalty to Judaism. Still, Jews from Asia stirred up public sentiment against Paul. They even dragged him out of the temple and tried to kill him. When tribunes took Paul into custody, he asked to address the crowd, and he did so in Hebrew.

This painting by the late medieval artist Giotto di Bondone depicts the martyrdom of Paul.

He defended his Jewish heritage and gave an account of his conversion to the way. Nevertheless, the crowd became violent, and the soldiers took Paul away to be flogged. When they discovered he was a Roman citizen, however, they released him and sent him to the chief priests and the Jewish council. Again, his speech to them aroused great controversy and agitation. In the night, he had a vision of Jesus, who said, "Keep up your courage! For just as you have testified for me in Jerusalem, so you must bear witness also in Rome" *(Acts 23:11)*.

When the tribune learned of a plot of the Jews to kill Paul, he sent him to Caesarea to be tried before the governor, Felix. Paul defended himself before Felix *(Acts 24:10–21)*. Felix kept Paul for more than two years, hoping to receive a bribe for his release. When a new governor named Festus took office, he offered to send Paul to Jerusalem for trial, but Paul requested instead to be tried by the emperor:

> I have done no wrong to the Jews, as you very well know. Now if I am in the wrong and have committed something for which I deserve to die, I am not trying to escape death; but if there is nothing to their charges against me, no one can turn me over to them. I appeal to the emperor.
>
> *Acts 25:10–11*

Before Festus sent him to Rome, King Herod arrived in Caesarea and asked to meet him. Paul made an appeal before Herod *(Acts 26:2–23)*. He even challenged the king to accept Jesus. Herod observed, "This man is doing nothing to deserve death or imprisonment. This man could have been set free if he had not appealed to the emperor" *(Acts 26:31–32)*.

To Rome in Chains

The final section of Acts centers on Paul's adventurous journey by sea to Rome. Paul and his shipmates encountered severe weather, and finally their ship was wrecked. However, through it all, the text emphasizes God's guiding providence. At a seemingly hopeless point, when the company had no more food and was in the midst of a storm, Paul encouraged them:

> I urge you now to keep up your courage, for there will be no loss of life among you, but only of the ship. For last night there stood by me an angel of the God to whom I belong and whom I worship, and he said, 'Do not be afraid, Paul; you must stand before the emperor; and indeed, God has granted safety to all those who are sailing with you.' So keep up your courage, men, for I have faith in God that it will be exactly as I have been told.
>
> *Acts 27:22–25*

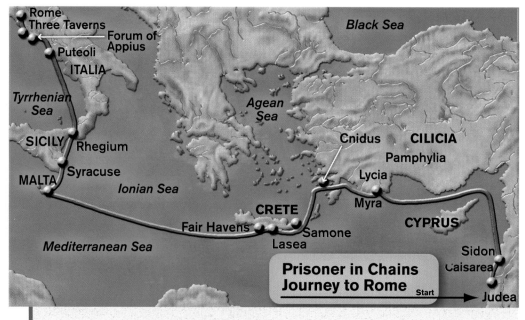

This map will help you envision Paul's final journey to Rome.

When at last they were in reach of the island of Malta, the ship crashed upon a reef, and all swam for shore. They remained in Malta for three months, and Paul took the opportunity to minister to the island's inhabitants.

Afterward, with a new ship, they went on to Rome. While there, Paul was under house arrest. The Jews of Rome visited Paul in large numbers; and, while some accepted his teaching, others flatly rejected it. In Paul's final recorded speech he cited Isaiah 6:9–10. He applied these verses to the rejection of Jesus by the Jews. "Let it be known to you then that this salvation of God has been sent to the Gentiles; they will listen" *(Acts 28:28).*

Choose one of the following projects. You can work on your own or with a partner. Share the results.

1. Get an up-to-date map of the Mediterranean region. Overlay Paul's journeys on that map. Then, create a report on current events in these places.

2. Select one of Paul's speeches. Analyze the speech's content and methodology. How would you categorize the speech? What kind of contemporary public speaking do you find comparable?

3. The accounts of Paul's journeys take him to cities that were centers of influence in the Greco-Roman world.

- Athens: The academic and cultural center
- Corinth: The commercial center
- Ephesus: The religious center
- Rome: The legal and governing center

Write a brief report showing what centers of influence a person would have to visit in the United States to garner support for some new organization or movement. Give reasons for your choices.

Unit Feature
A Death with Meaning

In the Acts of the Apostles, the young church for the first time began to grapple with the meaning of Jesus' death. In the gospels, the writers gave accounts of the events during the last week of Jesus' life, including his entry into Jerusalem, his arrest, his trial, and his crucifixion. They point out that the Roman authorities and the religious leaders in Jerusalem considered Jesus a threat to civil order.

The Gospel of Luke sows the seeds of how Jesus' death would be viewed as the church began to grow. On the road to Emmaus, Jesus appeared to two disciples. He said to them, "Oh, how foolish you are, and how slow of heart to believe all that the prophets have declared! Was it not necessary that the Messiah should suffer these things and then enter into his glory?" *(Luke 24:25–26)*.

THE VIEW OF THE EARLY CHURCH

The Acts of the Apostles began to articulate how the early followers of Jesus reflected on his death. Throughout Acts, some common themes develop:

1. Jesus' life, ministry, and death were the fulfillment of divine promises to the ancestors.
2. His death conquered death and confirmed life after death.
3. His death showed the ultimate need for judgment and justice.
4. His death confirmed the forgiveness of sins once and for all.

THREE UNDERSTANDINGS

One of the earliest understandings of the mission of Jesus did not focus solely on his death. Athanasius in the year 320 articulated this view best in his treatise on the **incarnation.** The notion was that Jesus rescued people from enslavement to sin and death first by coming to Earth and then by going into the realm of Hades, destroying it, and conquering the evil one. His was a rescue action like the Passover of the Jews, and it was described in similar terms.

Jesus died for others. Over time the term used to describe this was **substitutionary atonement.** Jesus was also seen as an example of self-sacrifice that can be imitated and followed: "No one has greater love than this, to lay down one's life for one's friends" *(John 15:13)*. In the Middle Ages, Jesus' example was described with the term **exemplary atonement.**

Atonement is a word of Middle English origin that means "reconciliation, or bringing back together." It is an important concept in both the Jewish and the Christian traditions.

All three views of the meaning of Jesus' death are part of the literature of the New Testament and in the tradition of how that literature has been interpreted. In the gospels, Jesus is seen in relationship to a new Passover. In the letters of Paul, Jesus as substitute is the primary meaning for his death and subsequent resurrection. But Jesus is also seen as the crowning example of perfect and unselfish love. "For to this you have been called, because Christ also suffered for you, leaving you an example, so that you should follow in his steps" *(1 Peter 2:21)*. Literature abounds with examples of Christ figures that rescue or stand in for others in self-sacrifice or whose selfless love saves the day and becomes an example to others.

■ On your own, try to find examples of such Christ figures in literature, film, or even music. Share what you find.

A TALE OF TWO CITIES

Perhaps the best way to understand how the death of Jesus is mirrored in literature is to experience one of the great examples of that reflection.

"It was the best of times, it was the worst of times. It was the age of wisdom; it was the age of foolishness. It was the epoch of belief; it was the epoch of incredulity. It was the season of Light; it was the season of Darkness." Those words begin one of the most popular English novels of all time.

A Tale of Two Cities by Charles Dickens (1812–1870) was written in 1859. It is the story of London and Paris at the time of the French Revolution. At the end of the book, the character Sydney Carton takes the place of a prisoner who is to be sent to the guillotine. He demonstrates what it is like to die for another person and to thereby give that person a great grace. He takes on the "crime" of another so that person could be free. He also provides comfort to the woman who is just ahead of him in line to be executed:

As The Vengeance descends from her elevation to do it, the tumbrils begin to discharge their loads. The ministers of Sainte Guillotine are robed and ready. Crash!—A head is held up, and the knitting-women who scarcely lifted their eyes to look at it a moment ago when it could think and speak, count One.

The second tumbril empties and moves on; the third comes up. Crash!—And the knitting-women, never faltering or pausing in their work, count Two.

The supposed Evrémonde [Sydney Carton standing in Evrémonde's stead] descends, and the seamstress is lifted out next after him. He has not relinquished her patient hand in getting out, but still holds it as he promised. He gently places her with her back to the crashing engine that constantly whirrs up and falls, and she looks into his face and thanks him.

"But for you, dear stranger, I should not be so composed, for I am naturally a poor little thing, faint of heart; nor should I have been able to raise my thoughts to Him who was put to death, that we might have hope and comfort here to-day. I think you were sent to me by Heaven."

"Or you to me," says Sydney Carton. "Keep your eyes upon me, dear child, and mind no other object."

"I mind nothing while I hold your hand. I shall mind nothing when I let it go, if they are rapid."

"They will be rapid. Fear not!" . . .

"Do you think:" the uncomplaining eyes in which there is so much endurance, fill with tears, and the lips part a little more and tremble: "that it will seem long to me, while I wait for her in the better land where I trust both you and I will be mercifully sheltered?"

"It cannot be, my child; there is no Time there, and no trouble there."

"You comfort me so much! I am so ignorant. Am I to kiss you now? Is the moment come?"

"Yes."

She kisses his lips; he kisses hers; they solemnly bless each other. The spare hand does not tremble as he releases it; nothing worse than a sweet, bright constancy is in the patient face. She goes next before him—is gone; the knitting-women count Twenty-Two.

"I am the Resurrection and the Life, saith the Lord: he that believeth in me, though he were dead, yet shall he live: and whosoever liveth and believeth in me shall never die."

The murmuring of many voices, the upturning of many faces, the pressing on of many footsteps in the outskirts of the crowd, so that it swells forward in a mass, like one great heave of water, all flashes away. Twenty-Three.

They said of him, about the city that night, that it was the peacefullest man's face ever beheld there. Many added that he looked sublime and prophetic.

One of the most remarkable sufferers by the same axe—a woman—had asked at the foot of the same scaffold, not long before, to be allowed to write down the thoughts that were inspiring her. If he had given an utterance to his, and they were prophetic, they would have been these:

"I see Barsad, and Cly, Defarge, The Vengeance, the Juryman, the Judge, long ranks of the new oppressors who have risen on the destruction of the old, perishing by this retributive instrument, before it shall cease out of its present use. I see a beautiful city and a brilliant people rising from this abyss, and, in their struggles to be truly free, in their triumphs and defeats, through long years to come, I see the evil of this time and of the previous time of which this is the natural birth, gradually making expiation for itself and wearing out.

"I see the lives for which I lay down my life, peaceful, useful, prosperous and happy, in that England which I shall see no more. I see Her with a child upon her bosom, who bears my name. I see her father, aged and bent, but otherwise restored, and faithful to all men in his healing office, and at peace. I see the good old man, so long their friend, in ten years' time enriching them with all he has, and passing tranquilly to his reward.

"I see that I hold a sanctuary in their hearts, and in the hearts of their descendants, generations hence. I see her, an old woman, weeping for me on the anniversary of this day. I see her and her husband, their course done, lying side by side in their last earthly bed, and I know that each was not more honoured and held sacred in the other's soul, than I was in the souls of both.

"I see that child who lay upon her bosom and who bore my name, a man winning his way up in that path of life which once was mine. I see him winning it so well, that my name is made illustrious there by the light of his. I see the blots I threw upon it, faded away. I see him, foremost of just judges and honored men, bringing a boy of my name, with a forehead that I know and golden hair, to this place—then fair to look upon, with not a trace of this day's disfigurement—and I hear him tell the child my story, with a tender and a faltering voice.

"It is a far, far better thing that I do, than I have ever done; it is a far, far better rest that I go to than I have ever known."

A Tale of Two Cities has been made into film many times. The definitive movie version and perhaps one of the most memorable recitations of that last line is the 1935 release. It starred Ronald Colman as Sydney Carton, and there is never a dull moment. Colman was one of the finest actors of his age. In fact, you can hear the line as Colman said it if you go to http://www.moviewavs.com/Movies/Tale_Of_Two_Cities.shtml.

The Letters of Paul

Now I appeal to you, brothers and sisters, . . . that all of you be in agreement and there be no divisions among you, but that you be united in the same mind and the same purpose.

1 Corinthians 1:10 [NRSV]

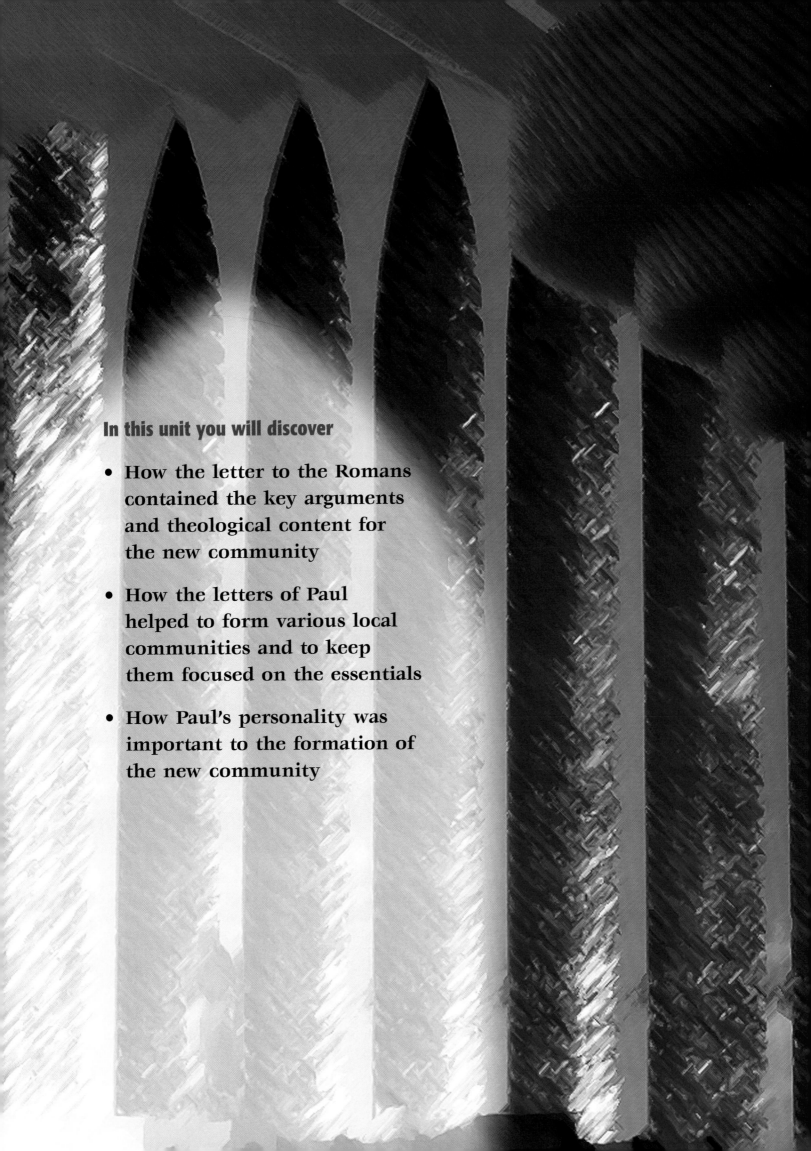

In this unit you will discover

- How the letter to the Romans contained the key arguments and theological content for the new community

- How the letters of Paul helped to form various local communities and to keep them focused on the essentials

- How Paul's personality was important to the formation of the new community

KEY BIBLICAL TEXTS

- Letter to the Romans

DISCOVER

- The rhetorical form of ancient letters
- Why this letter was one of the most influential ancient letters

CONSIDER

- What are some examples of things, persons, or ideas you have faith in?

Grace and Faith
Letter to the Romans

Twenty-one of the twenty-seven books of the New Testament have the form of a letter, and fourteen of these letters have traditionally been viewed as having been written by Paul. There are two types of letters by Paul, letters to churches and letters to individuals. The letters are arranged in the canon of the New Testament according to their type and length. Letters to churches come first, followed by letters to individuals. And each type is arranged from longest to shortest. Romans, being the longest letter to a church, is placed first.

Of all of the letters in the New Testament, the letter to the Romans is considered by Christians to be the pivotal one. It has had the greatest impact on Christianity and Western civilization, generating reforms and revivals that changed world history and Christianity. In many ways, this is the most complete and fully developed letter and exposition of Paul's understanding of what it means to be a follower of Jesus. It is at the heart of Christian belief.

Scholars believe that Paul wrote this letter around the spring of the year 57 while on his third missionary journey. Because Paul had not yet visited the Roman Christian community, the letter also served to introduce both Paul and his message.

First-Century Letters and Rhetoric

In Romans, Paul incorporated the basic literary form and style of ancient rhetoric to present his message and make it persuasive. The letter to the Romans is Paul's most highly developed letter in terms of form and argument.

In ancient times, rhetoric was a highly prized form of communication. Rhetoric is defined as "the art or science of using words effectively in speaking or writing." Rhetoric as a form emerged early on in the Greek city-states and eventually permeated the Greco-Roman world, including its system of education and public discourse. Rhetoric was a separate subject studied in schools and universities and occupied a central place in education until relatively recent times. The overall goals of rhetoric as an academic subject were to train students to understand how language works and to help them become proficient in the effective use of language in speaking and writing. Students of rhetoric analyzed the speeches and writings of the best orators and writers.

In this chapter, you are going to analyze Paul's letter to the Romans by following its six rhetorical parts. You will be able to judge the effectiveness of Paul's writing and see why his complex and compelling arguments had so much impact when he wrote them and continued to have impact through the ages. (All the references in this chapter are from the NRSV.) Here are the six parts you will analyze:

THE BIBLE
AND **History**

CHRISTIANS IN ROME

The Roman writer Suetonius (75–160) reported that Emperor Claudius expelled the Jews from Rome (about the year 49) because of riots instigated by Chrestus, which may be a corruption of the Latin *Christus*. These disturbances in the Jewish community may have been the conflict between the Jews and those who had come to accept Jesus as the messiah. Although there is no evidence that this expulsion was allowed to lapse after the emperor's death in 54, it does appear that Jewish Christians did return to Rome, where non-Jewish Christians, called Gentiles, had remained. Tensions would have developed, which Paul appeared to address. Paul presented the theological basis on which these groups with different experiences could live in mutual love and acceptance.

This painting by French painter Hubert Robert (1733–1808) depicts the burning of Rome in 64. The Emperor Nero blamed the fire on the Christian community and began a persecution of the Christians.

1. **INTRODUCTION:** Seeking to gain the attention and goodwill of the audience. In the greeting, Paul *(Romans 1:1–7)* sought the goodwill of the audience by thanking God for their faith, which was proclaimed worldwide, and by expressing his strong desire to see them.
2. **NARRATION:** Providing facts and background information. Paul presented a brief narration about himself and about Jesus as the son of God.
3. **THESIS:** Stating and explaining the premise or premises to be proved. Paul stated that the gospel of Jesus was the power of God unto salvation for all who believe *(Romans 1:16–17)*.
4. **PROOF:** Positively stating the case for the theses.
   a. The need for redemption *(1:18–3:20)*
   b. Justification by faith *(3:21–4:25)*
   c. Freedom *(5:1–8:39)*
   d. God's righteousness *(9:1–11:35)*
   e. Christian behavior *(12:1–15:13)*
5. **REFUTATION OF OPPOSING VIEWS:** Neutralizing contrary views. Paul in various places raised what he believed were objections to or false conclusions drawn from his position and refuted them. This technique is called **diatribe.**
6. **EPILOGUE/PERORATION:** Summarizing the argument and seeking to move the emotions of the audience to take action or make a commitment *(Romans 15:14–32)*.

Introduction and Narration

Unlike modern letters, which begin with a salutation to the person to whom the letter is addressed, ancient letters began with the name of the person writing the letter, in this case the apostle Paul. This is followed by a brief self-description:

Several times in the letter to the Romans, Paul uses the term _stumbling block_ (for example, _Romans 9:32–33, 11:9_ [quoting David], and _14:13_). A stumbling block has come to mean an obstacle that can lead to a good person's downfall, literally or figuratively.

> Paul, a servant of Jesus Christ, called to be an apostle, set apart for the Gospel of God, which he promised beforehand through his prophets in the holy scriptures, the gospel concerning his Son, who was descended from David according to the flesh and was declared to be the Son of God with power according to the spirit of holiness by resurrection from the dead, Jesus Christ our Lord, through whom we have received grace and apostleship to bring about the obedience of faith among all the Gentiles for the sake of his name, including yourselves who are called to belong to Jesus Christ.
>
> _Romans 1:1–6_

In this description, Paul used the word **apostle,** which means someone who is commissioned, or sent. In the gospels, Jesus spoke of being sent into the world by God the Father. Paul was invoking both the position to which he was called as well as the message that he believed he was called to give to all, including those in Rome to whom he addressed this letter. Paul addressed the letter "To God's beloved in Rome, who are called to be saints." In the New Testament, the word _saint_ means "a believer."

Thesis

After a prayer of thanksgiving that finished the narration, Paul stated the thesis of the letter in verses 16 and 17 of the first chapter:

> For I am not ashamed of the gospel; it is the power of God for salvation to everyone who has faith, to the Jew first and also to the Greek. For in it the righteousness of God is revealed through faith for faith; as it is written, "The one who is righteous will live by faith."
>
> _Romans 1:16–17_

This passage summarized the major thesis of this long and detailed letter. In this statement, Paul indicated that everyone who had faith would be considered righteous by God and should receive **salvation.** This salvation was not for Jews only, but was also available to Gentiles (non-Jews). By means of rhetorical technique, Paul presented his arguments to support this thesis as well as refuting opposing arguments.

Proof

There are five parts to Paul's argument:

1. _The Need for Redemption (1:18–3:20)_   Paul surveyed the spiritual condition of the people. Paul stated that God's wrath delivers rebellious people to the ruinous consequences of their own actions. All creation is in need of redemption:

> For the wrath of God is revealed from heaven against all ungodliness and wickedness of those who by their wickedness suppress the truth. For what can be known about God is plain to them, because God has shown it to them. Ever since the creation of the world his eternal power and divine nature, invisible though they are, have been understood and seen through the things he has made. So they are without excuse.
>
> _Romans 1:18–20_

Philosophers in the Western tradition would refer to this idea of knowing God's will through creation as the **natural law.**

Paul went on to explain that even the Jews, to whom the law of God was revealed through the Hebrew Scriptures, were sinners. So all were in need of redemption: "all, both Jews and Greeks, are under the power of sin" _(Romans 3:9)._

CULTURAL
CONNECTIONS
*A*merican History

This eighteenth-century engraving shows Jonathan Edwards when he was serving as president of the College of New Jersey, which would become Princeton University.

The period in American colonial history known as the **Great Awakening** shows the influence of the thought of the letter to the Romans. This movement consisted of a series of religious revivals that spread throughout the colonies between the 1720s and 1740s. The movement grew in religious groups who found their roots in the teaching of the French Protestant reformer John Calvin. The preachers involved in the movement emphasized the negative influence of "the law" for sinners and the tremendous grace of God, which is wholly undeserved and leads to "new birth" through faith in Jesus.

One outstanding figure of the Great Awakening was the great Puritan theologian Jonathan Edwards (1703–1758), a Congregational minister from Northampton, Massachusetts. Edwards emphasized the doctrine of justification by faith and sought to help his congregations discern the works of God's spirit. One of his most famous sermons is called "Sinners in the Hands of an Angry God." Though his works may seem stern to contemporary readers, they were informed with a sense of God's tremendous love and glory.

The Great Awakening was a reaction to the European Enlightenment, which emphasized the importance of human reason and science. Several universities were established as a result of the Great Awakening, including Brown, Rutgers, and Dartmouth.

2. *Justification by Faith (3:21–4:25)*   Paul showed how one is justified. Paul discussed this process of justification in Chapter 3:

> But now, apart from law, the righteousness of God has been disclosed, and is attested by the law and the prophets, the righteousness of God through faith in Jesus Christ for all who believe. For there is no distinction, since all have sinned and fall short of the glory of God; they are now justified by his grace as a gift, through the redemption that is in Christ Jesus, whom God put forward as a sacrifice of atonement by his blood, effective through faith. He did this to show his righteousness, because in his divine forbearance he had passed over the sins previously committed; it was to prove at the present time that he himself is righteous and that he justifies the one who has faith in Jesus.
>
> *Romans 3:21–26*

For Paul, Jesus' life was a sacrifice that made up for (atoned for) the sins of human beings. By virtue of that sacrifice, people who have faith in Jesus became justified ("viewed as just") in the eyes of God. Justification is a legal concept. Paul's argument was in essence that the sinner's situation is parallel to a criminal who comes before a judge and, because of his faith in Jesus, is declared to be just by the judge in spite of his previous crime because Jesus has already paid for that crime. Another important point in the passage is in the first few words: "apart from law." In Paul's line of argument, this process of justification didn't have anything to do with the Jewish law. Thus, a Jew would not be justified by observing the law but by faith in God. Moreover, according to Paul, a Gentile would also be justified by faith in Jesus.

This fifteenth-century Russian icon depicts Abraham, Sarah, and their mysterious visitors.

In Chapter 4, Paul explained his theory of justification by drawing on the example of Abraham. Paul began by analyzing how Abraham came to be considered just in the eyes of God, noting that it was not due to any of his works or even to his circumcision, but because of his faith. Remember that circumcision came to be seen as a sign of the covenant of the Jews with God. Paul drew a parallel between Abraham's justification and that of people of his own day. They were made just, not by observing the law (if they were Jews), and not by performing good actions (if they were Gentiles), but by their faith in Christ and his saving death *(Romans 4:9–24).*

3. *Freedom (5:1—8:39)*   Paul demonstrated the results of the justification. In Chapter 5 the first result, according to Paul, was that it provided peace with God, access to grace, and the hope of sharing glory with God. Paul pointed not to a subjective peace of mind but to a new relationship with God. Paul went on to explain how his views on sin and justification could be applied not just to Jews but to everyone. Paul drew a parallel between Adam and Christ:

> Therefore just as one man's trespass led to condemnation for all, so one man's act of righteousness leads to justification and life for all. For just as by the one man's disobedience the many were made sinners, so by the one man's obedience the many will be made righteous.
> *Romans 5:18–19*

Paul interpreted Adam's sin as leading to condemnation, not just for himself, but for all human beings. This interpretation was refined in Western Christian thought as the doctrine of original sin.

4. *God's Righteousness (9:1—11:35)*   Paul argued that God's righteousness would save Israel. He began with the role that Jews were to play in salvation. He noted the importance of the people of Israel. In so doing, Paul also made one of the clearest statements in the New Testament of the belief in the divinity of the messiah:

> They are Israelites, and to them belong the adoption, the glory, the covenants, the giving of the law, the worship, and the promises; to them belong the patriarchs, and from them, according to the flesh, comes the Messiah, who is over all, God blessed forever. Amen.
> *Romans 9:4–5*

Why, then, according to Paul's line of reasoning, did God choose Gentiles to be his people? Paul invoked an image from the Hebrew Scriptures, recalling how God chose Rebecca's son Jacob over Esau, even before the children were born. He also noted that historically only a remnant had been chosen by God. "So too at the present time there is a remnant, chosen by grace. But if it is by grace, it is no longer on the basis of works, otherwise grace would no longer be grace" *(Romans 11:5–6).* Paul saw the rejection of Jesus by many Jews to be part of God's providential plan; but in the end, he seemed to say, they, too, would be offered salvation. Indeed, in Chapter 10, he noted:

> If you confess with your lips that Jesus is Lord and believe in your heart that God raised him from the dead, you will be saved. For one believes with the heart and so is justified, and one confesses with the mouth and so is saved. The scripture says, "No one who believes in him will be put to shame." For there is no distinction between Jew and Greek; the same Lord is Lord of all and is generous to all who call on him. For, "Everyone who calls on the name of the Lord shall be saved."
> *Romans 10:9–13*

An interesting symbol, which Paul used to describe the relationship between Israel and the Gentiles, is that of the olive tree. He used this symbol as a warning to the Gentiles not to take their own salvation too lightly. He saw God's chosen people as an olive tree. Israel was a cultivated olive tree. But some branches were cut off, and branches from a wild olive tree (the Gentiles) were grafted in. Paul warned the Gentiles, however, that they needed to be faithful to remain part of the tree *(Romans 11:22–24)*.

Paul's teaching of universal sin and justification by faith has had tremendous impact on both the early development of Christianity and also on its reforms and counter-reforms. Varying interpretations of this teaching became a source of contention and division within Christianity. And it is the key issue in dialog between Catholics and Protestants to this very day.

This painting of an olive grove is by the American Impressionist artist John Singer Sargent.

5. *Christian Behavior (12:1—15:13)* Paul emphasized that good behavior still had great importance. Perhaps he did this so the Christians would remember that even though they were justified by their faith, they still had to behave in a manner befitting their calling. One interesting point here is the way he spoke of the Roman authorities. He encouraged obedience to the authorities, paying taxes, and so on. Also in this section are references to a judgment at the end of the world: "Why do you pass judgment on your brother or sister? Or you, why do you despise your brother or sister? For we will all stand before the judgment seat of God" *(Romans 14:10)*. Likewise, in the final chapter, Paul wrote, "The God of peace will shortly crush Satan under your feet" *(Romans 16:20)*.

Refutation of Opposing Views

Throughout the letter, Paul used the technique of diatribe—that is, refuting the opposing view by stating contrary questions and answering them. At various points, Paul mentioned either objections to or false conclusions drawn from his positions and then refuted them, usually by quoting from Scriptures. For example, at the end of Chapter 3 and the beginning of Chapter 4, Paul asked several questions, which he immediately answered:

> Do we then overthrow the law by this faith? By no means! On the contrary, we uphold the law. What then are we to say was gained by Abraham, our ancestor according to the flesh? For if Abraham was justified by works, he has something to boast about, but not before God. For what does the scripture say? "Abraham believed God, and it was reckoned to him as righteousness." Now to one who works, wages are not reckoned as a gift, but as something due. But to one who without works trusts him who justifies the ungodly, such faith is reckoned as righteousness.
>
> *Romans 3:31, 4:1–5*

Paul started Chapter 9 with the premise that Israelites received God's covenant in the giving of the law and in God's promises. Paul then refuted the notion that all Abraham's children are his true descendants: "It is not the children of the flesh who are the children of God" *(Romans 9:8)*. Paul then used several quotations from Hebrew Scriptures regarding Rebecca and Moses to buttress his argument. He concluded, "It depends not on human will or exertion, but on God who shows mercy. . . . So then he has mercy on whomever he chooses, and he hardens the heart of whomever he chooses" *(Romans 9:16, 18)*.

Look It Up

There are a number of other examples of Paul's refutation techniques throughout Romans:

- 3:1–9
- 6:1–3, 15–16
- 7:7, 13–14
- 9:14–16
- 11:1–3, 11

Read one or two of these examples and compare them to the ones given in the text to the left.

THE BIBLE

IN Literature

The concept of **original sin,** which later theologians developed from Paul's reflections, has also been grist for the literary mill. One example of a literary discussion of original sin is found in the works of the nineteenth-century American author Nathaniel Hawthorne. In the short story "The Birthmark," Hawthorne tells of a young scientist, Aylmer, and his beautiful wife, Georgiana, who is nearly perfect except for a tiny birthmark on her cheek:

This is a portrait of the young Nathaniel Hawthorne by the American artist Charles Osgood (1809–1890).

In the centre of Georgiana's left cheek there was a singular mark, deeply interwoven, as it were, with the texture and substance of her face. In the usual state of her complexion—a healthy though delicate bloom—the mark wore a tint of deeper crimson, which imperfectly defined its shape amid the surrounding rosiness. When she blushed it gradually became more indistinct, and finally vanished amid the triumphant rush of blood that bathed the whole cheek with its brilliant glow. But if any shifting motion caused her to turn pale there was the mark again, a crimson stain upon the snow, in what Aylmer sometimes deemed an almost fearful distinctness. Its shape bore not a little similarity to the human hand, though of the smallest pygmy size.

Elsewhere in the story, Aylmer's ponderings on the birthmark make even more obvious that he connects it to the traditional doctrine of original sin:

Seeing her otherwise so perfect, he found this one defect grow more and more intolerable with every moment of their united lives. It was the fatal flaw of humanity which Nature, in one shape or another, stamps ineffaceably on all her productions, either to imply that they are temporary and finite, or that their perfection must be wrought by toil and pain. The crimson hand expressed the ineludible gripe in which mortality clutches the highest and purest of earthly

mould, degrading them into kindred with the lowest, and even with the very brutes, like whom their visible frames return to dust. In this manner, selecting it as the symbol of his wife's liability to sin, sorrow, decay, and death, Aylmer's somber imagination was not long in rendering the birthmark a frightful object, causing him more trouble and horror than ever Georgiana's beauty, whether of soul or sense, had given him delight.

Aylmer expresses his feelings about the birthmark to his young wife, who, unhappy with his dissatisfaction with her appearance, agrees to his suggestion of conducting scientific experiments to remove the mark and thus make her perfect. His ultimate solution, a potion that he concocts and she drinks, causes the mark to fade but also brings about Georgiana's death:

The fatal hand had grappled with the mystery of life, and was the bond by which an angelic spirit kept itself in union with a mortal frame. As the last crimson tint of the birthmark—that sole token of human imperfection—faded from her cheek, the parting breath of the now perfect woman passed into the atmosphere, and her soul, lingering a moment near her husband, took its heavenward flight. Then a hoarse, chuckling laugh was heard again! Thus ever does the gross fatality of earth exult in its invariable triumph over the immortal essence which, in this dim sphere of half development, demands the completeness of a higher state. Yet, had Aylmer reached a profounder wisdom, he need not thus have flung away the happiness which would have woven his mortal life of the selfsame texture with the celestial. The momentary circumstance was too strong for him; he failed to look beyond the shadowy scope of time, and, living once for all in eternity, to find the perfect future in the present.

The Complete Works of Nathaniel Hawthorne
(Modern Library, 1965)

A Note on Hope

Hope plays a prominent role in the letter to the Romans. There are two key passages in this letter that should be highlighted. In the first passage, the Christian believer is justified through faith and has peace. At the same time, the follower of Jesus is able to boast in the hope of sharing glory with God. No only that, the follower of Jesus is able to boast in suffering, which leads to endurance, which leads to character, which leads to hope:

Therefore, since we are justified by faith, we have peace with
God through our Lord Jesus Christ, through whom we have
obtained access to this grace in which we stand; and we boast
in our hope of sharing the glory of God. And not only that, but
we also boast in our sufferings, knowing that suffering
produces endurance, and endurance produces character, and
character produces hope, and hope does not disappoint us,
because God's love has been poured into our hearts through the
Holy Spirit that has been given to us.

Romans 5:1–5

The second passage is a prayer about hope that asks that God's hope fill
the listeners, in this case the community in Rome, with joy and peace in
believing so that they may be satisfied with hope by the power of the Holy
Spirit *(Romans 15:13)*.

Epilogue

At the end of Chapter 15, Paul polished his arguments with personal witness
and an affirmation of his right to instruct the Romans. He also made a promise
to visit the church in Rome. He appealed to them to pray on his behalf that he
be rescued from the unbelievers in Judea.

Chapter 16 makes very interesting reading, because it seems to be very
personal and even contemporary. It also provides a veritable cast of characters
of the early church. Paul made quite a passionate recommendation for the
deacon Phoebe, so that she would be welcomed in Rome. He went on to add a
whole list of people for the Romans to greet, and he encouraged them all to
greet one another with a holy kiss.

This letter, filled as it is with powerful arguments that have been debated
for centuries, ends with Paul's outburst of praise to "the only wise God, through
Jesus Christ, to whom be the glory forever! Amen!" *(Romans 16:27)*.

Choose one or both of these projects to reinforce what you have learned:

1. Use the six-part rhetorical outline of the letter to
the Romans to write a letter of your own to an
individual or a group. In the letter, try to be
compelling and convincing about some cause
that you hold dear.

2. Choose a short story or a selection from a novel
by Nathaniel Hawthorne (for example, *Mosses
from an Old Manse, Twice Told Tales, The House
of Seven Gables,* or *The Scarlet Letter*). Try to
discover some of the elements from the letter to
the Romans that might be hidden there. Share
what you discover.

KEY BIBLICAL TEXTS

- 1 Corinthians, 2 Corinthians, Galatians, Ephesians

- One of the most frequently quoted descriptions of love of all time
- A declaration of liberty

DISCOVER

- More issues that were hotly discussed in the early Christian community

CONSIDER

- Has a letter or e-mail you have written ever helped to solve a problem or heal a relationship?

The Power of Love
1 and 2 Corinthians, Galatians, Ephesians

For centuries, people have found superb guidelines for life in the letters to the Corinthians, the Galatians, and the Ephesians. And so, these letters have remained relevant over the years. First and Second Corinthians, Galatians, and Ephesians are public letters addressed by Paul to the Christian churches he founded at Corinth in Greece and at Galatia and Ephesus—Greek cities that are now part of Turkey.

Corinth was an urban community with a particularly important location. It was a few miles south of the isthmus between the Greek mainland and the Peloponnesus—the mountainous southern peninsula of Greece. It was also a main port on the sea route between Italy and Asia. Thus, it was a very busy, wealthy commercial and cultural city. By the time of Paul, Corinth had become the capital of the Roman province and was home to an estimated 250,000 freeborn people and as many as 400,000 slaves.

Corinth was a microcosm of first-century religious life. There were pagan cults of every kind with at least twelve temples, including those to Apollo, Athena, Poseidon, Hera, and Zeus. The city also had a Jewish synagogue. The city was especially known for its worship of Aphrodite, the goddess of love, whose followers practiced prostitution in the name of religion. Throughout the Roman world, the mention of Corinth elicited images of sexual promiscuity. It is to this city that Paul wrote his definition of love.

In this worldly environment, Paul planted a new church, probably during his second missionary journey. The problems of the young community reflected its surroundings.

Philippi
Neapolis
Thessalonica
MACEDONIA
Troas
Assos
Aegean Sea
ASIA
Nicopolis
Lechaeum
Thebes
Athens
Smyrna
Olympia
ARCHAIA
Sparta
Corinth
Cenchreae
Ephesus
Mediterranean Sea

This map shows the location of the churches to which Paul wrote as well as other important cities.

First Corinthians

First Corinthians can be divided into two parts. Part I (Chapters 1–6) consists of Paul's response to reports from Chloe's people. Chloe was a woman whose friends, servants, or householders reported to Paul about the problems in the Corinthian church. This half of the letter deals with a variety of problems in the young church: disunity, sexual immorality, and lawsuits among the faithful. The second half of the letter (Chapters 7–16) answers questions and concerns raised in a letter to Paul from members of the Corinthian church. It concerns matters of marriage, whether or not to eat meat sacrificed to idols, worship, spiritual gifts, and the resurrection of the body. (All the references in this chapter are from the NRSV.)

In First Corinthians, Paul gave the Corinthians a practical course on how to be Christians in an often hostile environment. This letter contains some of Paul's most famous writings, including the image of the church as the body of Christ (Chapter 12), the chapter on love (Chapter 13), and the teaching on resurrection (Chapter 15).

Marriage and Divorce

In first-century Corinth, a seaport, adult sexual relationships were very loose, and prostitution was common. Paul reacted: "Do you not know that your bodies are members of Christ? Should I therefore take the members of Christ and make them members of a prostitute? Never! Do you not know that whoever is united to a prostitute becomes one body with her? For it is said, 'The two shall be one flesh'" *(1 Corinthians 6:15–16)*.

It was in this culture that Paul called for a major shift in how people behaved. Paul called for each man to have his own wife and each woman her own husband: "The husband should give to his wife her conjugal rights, and likewise the wife to her husband" *(1 Corinthians 7:3)*.

Paul wrote to the unmarried members of the Corinthian congregation, including widows. He advised them that they should remain unmarried as he had *(1 Corinthians 7:8)*. However, if they couldn't remain chaste, then they should marry *(1 Corinthians 7:9)*.

Then, Paul addressed the rest of the congregation, those followers of Jesus who were married to unbelieving partners. Paul worked from the assumption that divorce was contrary to the teachings of Jesus *(1 Corinthians 7:10–11)*. Yet, he recognized that the involvement of an unbelieving partner in a marriage created a different set of circumstances. As long as the unbelieving partner agreed, the couple might remain together. However, if the unbelieving partner left, the believing person was no longer bound to the marriage.

The Lord's Supper

In Chapter 11 of 1 Corinthians, Paul gives his teaching on the celebration of communion:

> For I received from the Lord what I also handed on to you, that the Lord Jesus on the night when he was betrayed took a loaf of bread, and when he had given thanks, he broke it and said, "This is my body that is for you. Do this in remembrance of me." In the same way he took the cup also, after supper, saying, "This cup is the new covenant in my blood. Do this, as often as you drink it, in remembrance of me." For as often as you eat this bread and drink the cup, you proclaim the Lord's death until he comes.
>
> *1 Corinthians 11:23–26*

THE BIBLE
AND Music

BEETHOVEN'S MISSA SOLEMNIS

The Eucharist was the inspiration for Ludwig van Beethoven's *Missa Solemnis,* a massive, complex, and dramatic work. The *Missa* is not a work to soothe the ears or the spirit. One gets the impression from it that Beethoven tried to seize every word in the text and shake out every ounce of its meaning. To this day and in this sense, the *Missa Solemnis* is one of the most powerful settings of the mass ever composed. Beethoven had plans to write several more masses, including a requiem, but these plans were never realized.

Beethoven died on March 26, 1827, during a violent storm. Shortly before, he had reluctantly received last rites. Legend has it that after a flash of lightning and a clap of thunder, the expiring man lifted his fist and shook it at the elements.

This third-century fresco from the Catacombs of San Calixto in Rome shows a eucharistic banquet.

This section of 1 Corinthians delineates the Christian ritual of commemorating Jesus' Last Supper. This ritual is also called the **Eucharist,** from the Greek word for "giving thanks." The Roman Catholic Mass, the Eastern Orthodox Divine Liturgy, Anglican and Lutheran communion services, and the Protestant celebrations of the Lord's Supper all reflect the actions and words found in 1 Corinthians.

The Greatest Gift

Chapter 13 of 1 Corinthians contains one of the best-known passages in the New Testament. The chapter is Paul's lesson on spiritual gifts. It is best for the words to speak for themselves:

If I speak in the tongues of mortals and of angels, but do not have love, I am a noisy gong or a clanging cymbal. And if I have prophetic powers, and understand all mysteries and all knowledge, and if I have all faith, so as to remove mountains, but do not have love, I am nothing. If I give away all my possessions, and if I hand over my body so that I may boast, but do not have love, I gain nothing.

Love is patient; love is kind; love is not envious or boastful or arrogant or rude. It does not insist on its own way; it is not irritable or resentful; it does not rejoice in wrongdoing, but rejoices in the truth. It bears all things, believes all things, hopes all things, endures all things.

Love never ends. But for prophecies, they will come to an end; as for tongues, they will cease; as for knowledge, it will come to an end. . . . And now faith, hope, and love abide, these three; and the greatest of these is love.

1 Corinthians 13:1–8, 13

THE BIBLE
AS **Literature**

STRUCTURE OF PAUL'S ODE TO LOVE

Hebrew Scriptures use a form of writing that may help explain the focus of Paul in this passage. It is a chiasm or inverse parallelism, a literary device used to guide the listener or reader. In the case of Paul's ode to love, the inverse parallelism has at its center the issues at hand in the Corinthian community: the resentment, the irritability, and the rejoicing in the wrong. The layers around that center bring out the positive aspects of love and the nature of spiritual gifts:

A   Spiritual gifts *(Chapter 12)*
B   Love and the spiritual gifts *(13:1–3)*
C   Positive definition of love: Love is patient; love is kind *(13:4)*
D   Negative definition of love: Love is not irritable or resentful *(13:5, 6a)*
C' Positive definition of love: Love bears all things *(13:6b, 7)*
B' Love and the spiritual gifts *(13:8–13)*
A' Spiritual gifts *(14:1–25)*

These poetic words are among the most beautiful and well known of any Paul wrote. They often are read at marriage ceremonies.

Resurrection

First Corinthians contains the earliest formal teaching on the resurrection of Jesus and its centrality to the Christian faith:

> For I handed on to you as of first importance what I in turn had received: that Christ died for our sins in accordance with the scriptures, and that he was buried, and that he was raised on the third day in accordance with the scriptures, and that he appeared to Cephas, then to the twelve. Then he appeared to more than five hundred brothers and sisters at one time, most of whom are still alive, though some have died. Then he appeared to James, then to all the apostles. Last of all, as to one untimely born, he appeared also to me. For I am the least of the apostles, unfit to be called an apostle, because I persecuted the church of God. . . .
> If there is no resurrection of the dead, then Christ has not been raised: and if Christ has not been raised, then our proclamation has been in vain and our faith has been in vain.
> *1 Corinthians 15:3–9, 13*

Second Corinthians

Paul's relationship with the people of Corinth fell apart during the time between the writing of 1 Corinthians and the second letter. He wrote it with quite a bit of distress and anguish. Because so much of this letter answered the concerns, words, and feelings of others that are not recorded here, it can be a very difficult bit of writing to follow. Nonetheless, it revealed a lot about Paul and the passion he felt for the churches he had started.

INTO EVERYDAY *language*

There are several phrases in 2 Corinthians that have found their way into common speech. Most of them are found in William Tyndale's translation or in the King James Version.

A stern and assertive person is often said not to s*uffer fools gladly* (*2 Corinthians 11:19*). A nagging problem that won't go away is referred to as a *thorn in the flesh* (*2 Corinthians 12:7*). A common disclaimer about human weakness is to describe the body as an *earthen vessel* or a *vessel of clay* (*2 Corinthians 4:7*). See if a quick reading of the letter can lead you to any other such phrases.

THE BIBLE

IN History

THE SECOND GREAT AWAKENING AND SOCIAL ACTIVISM

The nineteenth century in America saw a Second Great Awakening—a biblically based response to the Enlightenment's aloof deity. Religious expression in the Second Great Awakening was warm and highly emotional. People participated in boisterous celebrations at religious camp meetings and became increasingly involved in groups dedicated to social activism.

Among the outcomes of activism was the bringing to America of two organizations begun in England. William Booth, an itinerant preacher, founded the Salvation Army in 1865 to serve the desperate—thieves, prostitutes, and drunkards—in East London. The Salvation Army came to America in 1880 and today helps over 33 million people with basic services like food, shelter, and disaster relief.

The YMCA was founded in London in 1844 by George Williams to address the unhealthy social conditions in cities as a result of the Industrial Revolution. The conditions worsened as rural men needing jobs came to the cities, and the influx led to the squalid slums described by Charles Dickens in novels such as *Oliver Twist*. The YMCA came to America in 1851 when the first facility was established in Boston. Today, the YMCA has become one of the largest not-for-profit community service organizations. It serves approximately 18 million men, women, and children every year.

Other examples of social activism which became popular were the Temperance Movement to eliminate the drinking of alcohol, the Sunday School Movement to spread literacy, and the Abolition Movement to rid the nation of slavery.

Ephesians

The letter to the Ephesians has two main sections: 1:3–3:21, which focuses on God's plan of unity as embodied in the church; and 4:1—6:23, which focuses on ethical rules for church members.

The Mystery of Unity

The first section of Ephesians mentions again and again a "mystery" (for example, *Ephesians 1:9, 3:3, 3:4, 3:5,* and *3:9*). But what was this mystery? Paul answered this question in Ephesians 3:5: "In former generations this mystery was not made known to humankind, as it has now been revealed to his holy apostles and prophets by the Spirit: that is, the Gentiles have become fellow heirs, members of the same body, and sharers in the promise in Christ Jesus through the gospel." This mystery of unity between Jews and Gentiles was expressed in the church, which was made up of both. Unity was expressed at the heart of the church:

> There is one body and one Spirit, just as you were called to the one hope of your calling, one Lord, one faith, one baptism, one God and Father of all, who is above all and through all and in all.
> *Ephesians 4:4-6*

Indeed, the letter to the Ephesians is very much concerned with **church.** In other letters of Paul, he usually wrote about the local community of believers in Rome or Corinth or Galatia. In Ephesians, the concept of "church" includes a universal body of believers. The church in this letter is described as "the household of God" *(2:19),* a "holy temple" *(2:20-22),* and, as in 1 Corinthians, the "body of Christ" *(4:11-16).* Later in the letter, the relationship between the church and Christ was compared to the relationship between a husband and wife *(5:22–23)*. These images from Ephesians have shaped the Christian church's self-image for centuries.

According to the letter, members of the church have received gifts that enable them to minister to one another and so promote unity and maturity; some people were apostles, some prophets, some evangelists, some pastors, and some teachers. Paul told the Ephesians that the unity of the church was under the headship of Jesus, who united all things in heaven and on Earth.

The Armor of God

From early on, the letter to the Ephesians draws attention to the unseen world. These were not battles among humans but against the spiritual forces of evil.

In the final chapter, Paul used an extended metaphor to prepare the Ephesians for the battle against evil. The readers were very familiar with the armor worn by the Roman army when they went into battle. Paul's metaphor translated that physical armor into spiritual armor:

> Therefore take up the whole armor of God, so that you may be able to withstand on that evil day, and having done everything, to stand firm. Stand therefore, and fasten the belt of truth around your waist, and put on the breastplate of righteousness. As shoes for your feet put on whatever will make you ready to proclaim the gospel of peace. With all of these, take the shield of faith, with which you will be able to quench all the flaming arrows of the evil one. Take the helmet of salvation, and the sword of the Spirit, which is the word of God.
>
> *Ephesians 6:13–17*

In this illustration by nineteenth-century painter James Jacques Tissot, a Roman centurion is wearing the armor described by Paul.

Summary

The four letters in this chapter provide interesting and diverse reading. They give a glimpse of the various aspects of Paul's personality and show some of the very human problems in the early Christian community. They also carry within them seeds, the fruit of which has been harvested on the pages of literature, in the governing of nations, and in the human struggle to be valiant, good, and true.

projects

Choose a project to find evidence in contemporary society of the concerns that Paul had for the three churches:

1. Choose one of these four letters to read in its entirety. Then do a news search for some current reflection of the issues raised in the letter. Make a report on what you discover.

2. Many television shows and films aimed at young people have spiritual or otherworldly themes about the struggle of good against evil. Watch one of these shows. How is what you see like what Paul describes? How is it different? How do shows such as these reflect what young people are thinking and feeling today?

KEY BIBLICAL TEXTS

- Philippians, Colossians, 1 Thessalonians, 2 Thessalonians

DISCOVER

- That Paul wrote a joyful letter while waiting for execution
- A valuable lesson on perseverance
- An early view of the last judgment and the second coming of Jesus

GET TO KNOW

- Epaphroditus, Euodia, Syntyche, Silas (Silvanus), Timothy

CONSIDER

- How do you learn to live in a family?

The Christian Community
Philippians, Colossians, 1 Thessalonians, 2 Thessalonians

The letters to the Philippians, Colossians, and Thessalonians all provided the young churches Paul founded with specific guidance on how to live as Christians in a community. The focus of Philippians was on living together with joy, not getting diverted by the day-to-day, and the need for reconciliation. Paul's letter to the Colossians addressed false teachings and then set out guidelines for living a good life. His letter to the Thessalonians dealt with the end times and Last Judgment.

These letters were highly personal yet public letters that were read aloud in the church that first received them and then circulated to surrounding churches. In these letters, Paul responded to questions posed by the churches, and the letters provide some insight into the issues of concern in the first century. Some of these issues have proven timeless.

Philippians

The terms *joy* and *rejoice* occur sixteen times in Paul's letter to the Philippians. What makes the joy theme remarkable is that Paul is believed to have been writing from prison in Rome while awaiting execution. But far from being gloomy, Paul seemed exhilarated by his prison experience, and this exhilaration filled the letter to the Philippians.

The church at Philippi was the first church founded by Paul in Europe. The founding of the community at Philippi is discussed in Acts 16:11–40. Philippians is one of Paul's most personal letters. He obviously was very fond of this community. For instance, he spoke about Epaphroditus, a man whom the Philippians had sent to Paul in prison as a messenger and a gift-

Rembrandt's *Paul in Prison* uses dramatic lighting to emphasize that Paul was not overcome by his seemingly desperate situation.

THE BIBLE

IN **History**

THE GREAT SCHISM OF 1054

Constantinople's sixth-century Church of Holy Wisdom (in Greek, Hagia Sophia) became a mosque after the fall of Constantinople in the fifteenth century and is now a museum in modern-day Istanbul.

The New Testament letters often show conflicts within and between church communities. Although the new Christian community grew up in North Africa and the Middle East, it eventually spread to Rome and the West while also maintaining a strong central presence in Constantinople (now Istanbul in Turkey).

Over the years, the church of Rome began to assume preeminence over the rest of Christianity, but not necessarily with the acknowledgment or cooperation of the Eastern churches. Eventually, differences coupled with questions of the authority of the pope hit the breaking point when papal envoys excommunicated the Patriarch of Constantinople, Michael Cerularius, in 1054. Patriarch Michael, in turn, excommunicated the envoys and the pope. These events began the Great Schism that split the Western church from the Eastern church—a division that continues to this day.

Although there are no major differences between Roman Catholicism and Eastern Orthodox beliefs, one major difference that does separate the two traditions is the understanding of another theme common in the New Testament letters: the use of authority. A major step toward restoring unity between the East and West was taken in 1965 when then Patriarch Athenagoras of the Greek Orthodox Church and Pope Paul VI rescinded the excommunications that had been in effect for over a thousand years.

bearer. Epaphroditus became sick while he was with Paul, and Paul was very careful to reassure the Philippians about their brother's renewed health.

Paul began his letter by assuring the church in Philippi that he was well, and indeed that his imprisonment was bringing about conversions. Paul strongly emphasized his concern for the unity of the church: "Be of the same mind, having the same love, being in full accord and of one mind. Do nothing from selfish ambition or conceit, but in humility regard others as better than yourselves" *(Philippians 2:2–3)*. (All the references in this chapter are from the NRSV.)

Divine Humility

To support his discussion of unity through humility, Paul wrote what came to be one of the most familiar passages from his letter to the Philippians. This passage may also have been sung as a hymn in the early church:

> Let the same mind be in you that was in Christ Jesus,
> who, though he was in the form of God,
>> did not regard equality with God
>> as something to be exploited,
> but emptied himself,
>> taking the form of a slave,
>> being born in human likeness.
> And being found in human form,
>> he humbled himself
>> and became obedient to the
>>> point of death—
> even death on a cross.

INTO EVERYDAY *language*

Everybody knows what a *busybody* is (and nobody appreciates one). William Tyndale coined the word *busybody* in his translation of 2 Thessalonians. The word stuck and is now part of our everyday vocabulary.

Therefore God also highly exalted him
and gave him the name
that is above every name,
so that at the name of Jesus
every knee should bend,
in heaven and on earth and
under the earth,
and every tongue should confess
that Jesus Christ is Lord,
to the glory of God the Father.

Philippians 2:5–11

This poem describes the humility of Jesus by saying that he "emptied himself." This term, which in the original Greek is *kenosis* (emptying), has been interpreted by Christians as describing Jesus, whom they thought to be God, humbling himself to become a human being.

At the end of Chapter 3, Paul used the metaphor of a footrace to describe the need for perseverance:

Not that I have already obtained this or have already reached the goal; but I press on to make it my own, because Christ Jesus has made me his own. Beloved, I do not consider that I have made it my own; but this one thing I do: forgetting what lies behind and straining forward to what lies ahead, I press on toward the goal for the prize of the heavenly call of God in Christ Jesus.

Philippians 3:12–14

Paul used the Philippians' pride in their Roman citizenship to remind them of what he considered the only citizenship that mattered; to him, the only homeland was not an earthly kingdom at all. Paul did his reminding with stinging words for the religion of Rome:

THE BIBLE

IN **Literature**

Silence, A NOVEL BY SHUSAKU ENDO

The Japanese novelist Shusaku Endo in 1980.

The literary theme of *kenosis,* or emptying oneself, has been an important one throughout history. A contemporary example of a literary work embodying the theme of kenosis is the novel *Silence* by the Catholic Japanese author Shusaku Endo (1923–1996). The novel is about seventeenth-century Portuguese missionaries who came to Japan to spread their faith in an era when Christianity was outlawed. The priest Sebastian Rodrigues—the main character—is caught by the Japanese authorities. If he will trample on an image of Jesus, the Japanese Christians who are being tortured and killed before him will be spared. The priest is in an agony of indecision, and then hears the voice of Jesus speaking from the image: "Trample! Trample! I more than anyone know of the pain in your foot. Trample! It was to be trampled on by men that I was born into this world. It was to share men's pain that I carried my cross." The priest then puts his foot on the image.

This passage expresses the *kenosis* of Jesus, who, according to Christian belief, "emptied himself" of glory to rescue human beings. But the text also seems to say that the priest, even though his action of stepping on the image showed a betrayal of his faith and the church, also experienced *kenosis.* For the love of the Christians who were being tortured and killed, he emptied himself of his own ideals as a missionary and a Christian. Though Rodrigues was expelled from the church for his actions, Endo implies that his actions showed a new appreciation of just how much Jesus emptied himself.

> For many live as enemies of the cross of Christ; I have often told you of them, and now I tell you even with tears. Their end is destruction; their god is the belly; and their glory is in their shame; their minds are set on earthly things. But our citizenship is in heaven, and it is from there that we are expecting a Savior, the Lord Jesus Christ.
>
> *Philippians 3:18–20*

A Context for Rejoicing

In the final chapter, Paul presented his advice about life in terms of joy, the hallmark virtue of this letter:

> Rejoice in the Lord always; again I will say, Rejoice. Let your gentleness be known to everyone. The Lord is near. Do not worry about anything, but in everything by prayer and supplication with thanksgiving let your requests be made known to God. And the peace of God, which surpasses all understanding, will guard your hearts and your minds in Christ Jesus.
>
> *Philippians 4:4–7*

Colossians

The letter to the Colossians was written to address a controversy in a Gentile congregation in the town of Colossae, a town about 100 miles east of Ephesus in Asia Minor. Paul had not visited the church at Colossae *(Colossians 2:1)* but was apparently in prison *(Colossians 4:10)* in Rome when he wrote the letter.

Controversy

In his letter, Paul warned the Colossians against the false teachings of people whom he did not clearly identify. Roman and Greek **cults** and **mystery religions** were prevalent in the area; Paul argued that these offered "philosophy and empty deceit" *(Colossians 2:8)*. It seems that the church in Collosae had taken from the cults a combination of ritual practice and belief in intermediate spirits. Such mixing of different religions and practices was quite common at the time, but this letter emphasized that this would not do for Christians. The practice of mixing "pagan" elements with the gospel had to stop. Paul insisted that Jesus was the only mediator and redeemer. The opposition seemed to be urging asceticism, observances of special holy times, and worship of celestial powers as means of gaining wisdom and access to God. Paul gave the Colossians a list of do's and don'ts. The letter called for steadfastness, endurance, and behavior appropriate to the church members' calling.

Lordship

The hymn in Colossians provides much of the scriptural basis for the traditional Christian understanding of Jesus:

> He is the image of the invisible God, the firstborn of all creation; for in him all things in heaven and on earth were created, things visible and invisible, whether thrones or dominions or rulers or powers—all things have been created through him and for him. He himself is before all things, and in him all things hold together. He is the head of the body, the church; he is the beginning, the firstborn from the dead, so that he might come to have first place in everything. For in him all the fullness of God was pleased to dwell, and through him God was pleased to reconcile to himself all things, whether on earth or in heaven, by making peace through the blood of his cross.
>
> *Colossians 1:15–20*

This icon from the Monastery of St. Catherine on Mt. Sinai, Egypt, is called *Christ Pantocrator* (the Greek word for "all-powerful").

Now concerning the times and the seasons, brothers and sisters, you do not need to have anything written to you. For you yourselves know very well that the day of the Lord will come like a thief in the night. When they say, "There is peace and security," then sudden destruction will come upon them, as labor pains upon a pregnant woman, and there will be no escape! . . . So then let us not fall asleep as others do, but let us keep awake and be sober.

1 Thessalonians 5:1-3, 6

Paul closed the letter with a long, specific set of moral instructions for the community:

Be at peace among yourselves. And we urge you, beloved, to admonish the idlers, encourage the fainthearted, help the weak, be patient with all of them. See that none of you repays evil for evil, but always seek to do good to one another and to all. Rejoice always, pray without ceasing, give thanks in all circumstances; for this is the will of God in Christ Jesus for you. Do not quench the Spirit. Do not despise the words of prophets, but test everything; hold fast to what is good; abstain from every form of evil.

1 Thessalonians 5:13-22

Second Thessalonians

It seems that Paul wrote his second letter to the church at Thessalonica shortly after writing the first one. He wanted to correct the strong impression he made in the earlier letter that the "day of the Lord" was coming very, very soon. This impression left the Thessalonians sitting back waiting for a second coming and neglecting the rhythms of daily life. In his second letter, Paul gave the exact opposite direction. He set up a number of conditions that had to be fulfilled before the end time:

For it is indeed just of God to repay with affliction those who afflict you, and to give relief to the afflicted as well as to us, when the Lord Jesus is revealed from heaven with his mighty angels in flaming fire, inflicting vengeance on those who do not know God and on those who do not obey the gospel of our Lord Jesus. These will suffer the punishment of eternal destruction, separated from the presence of the Lord and from the glory of his might, when he comes to be glorified by his saints and to be marveled at on that day among all who have believed, because our testimony to you was believed.

2 Thessalonians 1:6-10

The ruins of the *agora*, or marketplace, at Philippi.

Final Judgment

The idea of the last judgment became a central belief in Christianity. Second Thessalonians emphasizes that the day of God had not yet come, apparently to correct false teachings in the Thessalonian church. Drawing on **apocalyptic** traditions (those regarding the end times) from the Hebrew Scriptures, such as the Book of Daniel, Paul said that first a "man of lawlessness" must come. Paul said of this person, "He opposes and exalts himself above every so-called god or object or worship, so that he takes his seat in the temple of God, declaring himself to be God" *(2 Thessalonians 2:4).* This verse echoed parts of the Book of Daniel (for example, 9:20–27 and 11:31). Paul went on to link the work of this "man of lawlessness" with Satan:

> The coming of the lawless one is apparent in the working of Satan, who uses all power, signs, lying wonders, and every kind of wicked deception for those who are perishing, because they refused to love the truth and so be saved. For this reason God sends them a powerful delusion, leading them to believe what is false, so that all who have not believed the truth but took pleasure in unrighteousness will be condemned.
>
> *2 Thessalonians 2:9–12*

Keep Working

In the final chapter of 2 Thessalonians, Paul encouraged the Christians of that city to continue with their everyday lives, working hard as he did. In a famous passage, he noted:

> Anyone unwilling to work should not eat. For we hear that some of you are living in idleness, mere busybodies, not doing any work. Now such persons we command and exhort in the Lord Jesus Christ to do their work quietly and to earn their own living. Brothers and sisters, do not be weary in doing what is right.
>
> *2 Thessalonians 3:10–13*

Summary

Philippians, Colossians, and 1 and 2 Thessalonians deal with different topics and circumstances and have different tones. Nevertheless, in all of these letters, Paul instructed the young churches on how to be Christians and work out faith in practical ways. Many images and phrases from these letters have passed into Western culture and have been used at times in contradictory ways, both to promote liberty and to limit it. And the view of the end times embodied in 1 and 2 Thessalonians has profoundly shaped a particular view of human history.

projects

Choose one of these projects to express what you have learned in this chapter:

1. Write a short story to describe the behavior of two groups of young people. The first group is left at home and is told by their parents that they will be back in *exactly* two hours. The second group has no idea when their parents will come home. How will they act? What will happen? Compare your story with 1 and 2 Thessalonians.

2. Do some archaeological research. Find out about first-century Philippi, or Colossae, or Thessalonica. What was life like? Commerce? Law? Share what you discover.

KEY BIBLICAL TEXTS

■ 1 and 2 Timothy, Philemon

DISCOVER

■ How letters were used to establish order in the early church

GET TO KNOW

■ Timothy, Lois, Eunice, Philemon, Onesimus

CONSIDER

■ How much do you use written communication to share your thoughts and feelings with friends?

Social Order
1 and 2 Timothy and Philemon

Paul's letters to Timothy and Philemon were written to individuals rather than to churches. First and Second Timothy are called "pastoral letters" because they discuss matters of concern to the pastor of a church—fidelity and order. The letters to Timothy were highly personal, addressed to one of Paul's closest coworkers. Timothy was called "my loyal child in the faith" and "my beloved child." Timothy had been very active in the work of the Thessalonian and Corinthian churches. The letter to Philemon dealt with a runaway slave, Onesimus, who had served Paul and been converted by him.

First Timothy

During his last journey, Paul instructed Timothy to care for the community at Ephesus, the gateway between Greece and the Middle East. Paul went on to Macedonia. When Paul realized that he might not return to Ephesus in the near future, he wrote the first letter to Timothy to review the instructions he had given Timothy to refute false teachings, to supervise the affairs of the growing community, and to appoint qualified church leaders.

Belief

Paul began with concerns over what he saw as false teachings:

I urge you, as I did when I was on my way to Macedonia, to remain in Ephesus so that you may instruct certain people not to teach any different doctrine, and not to occupy themselves with myths and endless genealogies that promote speculations rather than the divine training that is known by faith.
1 Timothy 1:3–4

James Sant's painting *The Infant Timothy Unfolding the Scriptures* illustrates Paul's words about Timothy's knowledge of the sacred writings.

Church Structure

In 1 Timothy, Paul referred to several church offices. Paul mentioned these roles as part of his discussion of order in the Christian community. He first of all discussed **bishops.** This term, from the Greek word *episcopos,* means "overseer" or "guardian." The bishop seems to have been a person in a position of authority over the church. Paul gave the following advice to bishops:

> The saying is sure: whoever aspires to the office of bishop desires a noble task. Now a bishop must be above reproach, married only once, temperate, sensible, respectable, hospitable, an apt teacher, not a drunkard, not violent but gentle, not quarrelsome, and not a lover of money. He must manage his own household well, keeping his children submissive and respectful in every way—for if someone does not know how to manage his own household, how can he take care of God's church? He must not be a recent convert, or he may be puffed up with conceit and fall into the condemnation of the devil. Moreover, he must be well thought of by outsiders, so that he may not fall into disgrace and the snare of the devil.
>
> *1 Timothy 3:1–7*

For several hundred years after the writing of this letter, the role of bishop would develop, and the bishop became the primary authority over a region of Christian churches. The office of bishop is found today in a number of Christian denominations.

Paul also offered advice about a group called elders. The word is translated from the Greek word *presbyteros.* From that word also comes the English word *priest* and the denomination name *Presbyterian.* At the time, the title seemed almost interchangeable with that of bishop. Paul wanted the elders to receive respect and honor from the community:

> Let the elders who rule well be considered worthy of double honor, especially those who labor in preaching and teaching; for the scripture says, "You shall not muzzle an ox while it is treading out the grain," and, "The laborer deserves to be paid." Never accept any accusation against an elder except on the evidence of two or three witnesses. As for those who persist in sin, rebuke them in the presence of all, so that the rest also may stand in fear.
>
> *1 Timothy 5:17–20*

Finally, Paul also mentioned the office of deacon. Recall that this order was established in Acts. The deacons handled the finances of the early church, and they provided services to widows, orphans, and others in need. Paul gave them this advice:

> Deacons likewise must be serious, not double-tongued, not indulging in much wine, not greedy for money; they must hold fast to the mystery of the faith with a clear conscience. And let them first be tested; then, if they prove themselves blameless, let them serve as deacons.
>
> *1 Timothy 3:8–10*

Women

Another feature of 1 Timothy is its discussion of the role of women, part of its discussion of community relations. Paul's words about women in 1 Timothy are a source of great discomfort. And they have been used to subjugate women. Some see in Paul a view of women—as subservient and of lower status—that is not supported by the gospel accounts:

INTO EVERYDAY *language*

Paul quoted Deuteronomy 24:15 to convince Timothy that the elders should receive a just wage. You will see the language of this on the business pages, in union negotiations, or when someone is trying to get a raise. When the allusions are made, they are usually framed as: *"Don't muzzle the ox that treads out the grain,"* or *"A laborer is worthy of the hire."*

THE BIBLE
IN **History**

THE HISTORY OF ROMAN SLAVERY

It is important to review the role of slavery in the Roman Empire. That society had very clear divisions. Roman citizens, approximately 20 percent of the population, had the most privileges, among them that they could never be beaten, and they always had the right to appeal to the emperor. Non-Romans had fewer rights than citizens, and women had fewer rights than men. And at the bottom were the slaves, whose duties ranged from hard labor, to working in the home, to administering estates.

Americans tend to think of slavery in terms of the Africans who were captured and brought to America, and the descendents of those slaves who were held in bondage, primarily in the American South. The slavery of the Roman Empire was more complicated. Some slaves became slaves when they were taken prisoner in wars. Others might have been kidnapped to be slaves. Many people became slaves when they had too much debt and were forced to sell themselves into slavery to satisfy it. And some were born to slaves. As indicated above, some people could move out of slavery by buying their freedom.

The normal penalty in ancient times for a runaway slave was severe.

The epic 1960 motion picture *Spartacus,* directed by Stanley Kubrick, is the story of a slave uprising in the year 70. It gives a vivid picture of Roman slavery. The film is worth watching to get a feel for what life was like in the Roman Empire at this time. The film also vividly shows the Roman sentence of crucifixion.

Women should dress themselves modestly and decently in suitable clothing, not with their hair braided, or with gold, pearls, or expensive clothes, but with good works, as is proper for women who profess reverence for God. Let a woman learn in silence with full submission. I permit no woman to teach or to have authority over a man; she is to keep silent. For Adam was formed first, then Eve; and Adam was not deceived, but the woman was deceived and became a transgressor. Yet she will be saved through childbearing, provided they continue in faith and love and holiness, with modesty.

1 Timothy 2:9–15

The words of Paul to Timothy often speak louder than his words to the Galatians. "There is no longer Jew or Greek, there is no longer slave or free, there is no longer male and female: for all of you are one in Christ Jesus" (*Galatians 3:28*).

Wealth

One of the final passages of 1 Timothy concerns people of wealth. While not condemning material wealth outright, in a familiar passage Paul indicated that the love of money could be poison to Christian life. Paul did, however, give an antidote to the poison:

THE BIBLE

AND **Culture**

THE GOSPEL OF WEALTH

Andrew Carnegie, the philanthropist who greatly expanded the public library system in America.

The letter to Timothy warns of the dangers of wealth. One man from the "robber baron" period of U.S. history seems to have heeded the warning. Andrew Carnegie (1835–1919) made his huge fortune providing iron and steel for the railways. He never seemed, however, to forget his humble roots in Scotland. To resolve the contradiction between creation of wealth and society's needs, he developed the notion of the "gospel of wealth." He lived up to his notion and gave away his fortune to projects to benefit society—most notably the funding of free libraries where everyone would have access to great literature and learning. His approval of the inheritance tax would surprise many contemporary billionaires.

Carnegie was born the son of a weaver in Dunfermline, Scotland. He immigrated with his family to the United States, and at age 13 he went to work as a bobbin boy in a cotton mill. At age 65, he sold the Carnegie Steel Company for $480 million, and he devoted the rest of his life to his philanthropic work. While many wealthy people have contributed to charity, Carnegie was perhaps the first to state publicly that the rich have an obligation to give away their fortunes. In 1889, he wrote *The Gospel of Wealth,* in which he asserted that all personal wealth beyond what is required for the needs of one's family ought to be regarded as a trust fund to be administered for the benefit of the community. Among the principles he developed was the premise that the wealthy person should live modestly, shunning display or extravagance. Here is a brief excerpt from Carnegie's work:

Poor and restricted are our opportunities in this life; narrow our horizon; our best work most imperfect; but rich men should be thankful for one inestimable boon. They have it in their power during their lives to busy themselves in organizing benefactions from which the masses of their fellows will derive lasting advantage, and thus dignify their own lives. The highest life is probably to be reached, not by such imitation of the life of Christ as Count Tolstoy gives us, but, while animated by Christ's spirit, by recognizing the changed conditions of this age, and adopting modes of expressing this spirit suitable to the changed conditions under which we live; still laboring for the good of our fellows, which was the essence of his life and teaching, but laboring in a different manner.

. . . the man who dies leaving behind him millions of available wealth, which was his to administer during life, will pass away "unwept, unhonored, and unsung," no matter to what uses he leaves the dross which he cannot take with him. Of such as these the public verdict will then be: "The man who dies thus rich dies disgraced."

Such in my opinion, is the true Gospel concerning Wealth, obedience to which is destined some day to solve the problem of the Rich and the Poor, and to bring "Peace on earth, among men of Good-Will."

Those who want to be rich fall into temptation and are trapped by many senseless and harmful desires that plunge people into ruin and destruction. For the love of money is a root of all kinds of evil, and in their eagerness to be rich some have wandered away from the faith and pierced themselves with many pains. But as for you, man of God, shun all this; pursue righteousness, godliness, faith, love, endurance, gentleness. Fight the good fight of faith; take hold of the eternal life, to which you were called. . . .

1 Timothy 6:9–12

This painting by the English artist Henry Le Jeune (1819–1904), *The Early Days of Timothy,* shows the young Timothy studying with his mother and grandmother.

Second Timothy

In Paul's second letter to Timothy, he summoned Timothy to his side. Timothy was presented as the ideal church leader, whose sound doctrine and morals stood in sharp contrast to the corrupt lives and words of the false teachers. The example of Paul's endurance in the face of suffering was used to encourage Timothy to similar endurance. Second Timothy was apparently written to Timothy when Paul was in prison in Rome awaiting death. It was a letter of guidance to Timothy in his ministry, encouraging him to persevere. The letter had a very personal tone. For example, the first chapter mentioned Timothy's childhood. (His grandmother, Lois, and his mother, Eunice, raised him.) Paul reminded Timothy to "rekindle the gift of God that is within you through the laying on of my hands" *(2 Timothy 1:6)*.

End Times

As in many of Paul's letters, he was concerned in 2 Timothy with the end times. In the first chapter, he mentioned the final day twice, calling it "that day" *(2 Timothy 1:12, 18)*. In Chapter 3, he provided a list of signs that would accompany the last days:

> You must understand this, that in the last days distressing times will come. For people will be lovers of themselves, lovers of money, boasters, arrogant, abusive, disobedient to their parents, ungrateful, unholy, inhuman, implacable, slanderers, profligates, brutes, haters of good, treacherous, reckless, swollen with conceit, lovers of pleasure rather than lovers of God, holding to the outward form of godliness but denying its power. Avoid them!
>
> *2 Timothy 3:1–5*

Paul again mentioned the end times in Chapter 4, where he made reference to the Last Judgment and Jesus' second coming *(2 Timothy 4:1)*. Here again, he gave another sign associated with the end times:

CULTURAL
CONNECTIONS

*A*bolition

The Man Who Abolished British Slavery: William Wilberforce (1759–1833)

William Wilberforce

While taking a holiday on the European continent, William Wilberforce began reading a book, *The Rise and Progress of Religion in the Soul*. From this book he began his spiritual journey with an intellectual assent to the Bible, followed by a deep inner conviction. He knew that his new commitment might cost him friends and influence, but he was determined to stand for what he now believed. His old friend John Newton persuaded him that his political life could be used for the service of God. He began to be concerned to reform the morals of the social elite. He wrote a book calling on the upper classes to regain true Christian values in their lives. The book sold widely for over forty years.

His greatest political efforts were for those caught in the vice of slavery. British ships were carrying slaves from Africa to the West Indies as goods to be bought and sold. Wilberforce began his campaign to abolish the slave trade in 1789. After eighteen years of effort during which Wilberforce was demonized and ostracized by his fellow Christians, he saw British slave trade abolished.

Following this victory, Wilberforce began to work for the abolition of slavery itself. Three days before he died in 1833, he heard that the House of Commons had passed the law that emancipated all the slaves in Britain's colonies. Thirty years after Wilberforce's death, Lincoln wrote the Emancipation Proclamation to free the slaves in the United States.

Wilberforce, at his death, was honored by the nation in being buried at Westminster Abbey and having a statue erected in his memory.

For the time is coming when people will not put up with sound doctrine, but having itching ears, they will accumulate for themselves teachers to suit their own desires, and will turn away from listening to the truth and wander away to myths. As for you, always be sober, endure suffering, do the work of an evangelist, carry out your ministry fully.

2 Timothy 4:3–5

Advice

The most memorable aspect of 2 Timothy is the advice Paul gave to Timothy. For example, in Chapter 2, he used three images to describe a minister of the gospel: a soldier, an athlete, and a farmer. Paul also included a list of virtues that Timothy should strive to practice:

Shun youthful passions and pursue righteousness, faith, love, and peace, along with those who call on the Lord from a pure heart. Have nothing to do with stupid and senseless controversies; you know that they breed quarrels. And the Lord's servant must not be quarrelsome but kindly to everyone, an apt teacher, patient, correcting opponents with gentleness.

2 Timothy 2:22–25

Paul concluded the letter with a farewell message in which he again mentioned the last day. These are thought to be among Paul's last recorded words:

As for me, I am already being poured out as a libation, and the time of my departure has come. I have fought the good fight, I have finished the race, I have kept the faith. From now on there is reserved for me the crown of righteousness, which the Lord, the righteous judge, will give me on that day, and not only to me but also to all who have longed for his appearing.

2 Timothy 4:6–8

Philemon's Problem

This shortest letter of Paul (only 335 words in Greek) is an interesting peek at his life and times. The letter concerns a slave named Onesimus who apparently escaped from his owner, Philemon, perhaps stealing some things at the same time. Philemon was a Christian and seems to have been a prominent member of his community. Indeed, his home served as a **house church** where the Christian community met for worship and fellowship.

After Onesimus escaped, somehow he came in contact with the Christian community and Paul, who at the time of writing this letter was in prison. Under Paul's influence, Onesimus was converted to Christianity. Thus, Paul referred to him as follows: "I am appealing to you for my child, Onesimus, whose father I have become during my imprisonment. Formerly he was

THE BIBLE
IN **Literature**

This portrait of Harriet Beecher Stowe was taken around the time of the publication of *Uncle Tom's Cabin*.

One example of a work of American literature influenced by the Bible and its message is the nineteenth-century novel *Uncle Tom's Cabin*. This antislavery work by Harriet Beecher Stowe plays out within its pages the controversies in the Christian community about the issue of slavery. It is the story of two slaves who belonged to a man in Kentucky. The owner, in financial hardship, had to hand them over to a slave trader. The novel refers to Paul's letter to Philemon. In the passage below, the speaker, Mr. Wilson, is a slave owner, and he is speaking to an escaped slave, George:

"Why, to see you, as it were, setting yourself in opposition to the laws of your country."

"*My* country!" said George, with a strong and bitter emphasis; "what country have I, but the grave,—and I wish to God that I was laid there!"

"Why, George, no—no—it won't do; this way of talking is wicked—unscriptural. George, you've got a hard master—in fact, he is—well, he conducts himself reprehensibly—I can't pretend to defend him. But you know how the angel commanded Hagar to return to her mistress, and submit herself under her hand; and the apostle sent back Onesimus to his master."

"Don't quote Bible at me that way, Mr. Wilson," said George, with a flashing eye, "don't! for my wife is a Christian, and I mean to be, if ever I get to where I can; but to quote Bible to a fellow in my circumstances, is enough to make him give it up altogether. I appeal to God Almighty;—I'm willing to go with the case to Him, and ask Him if I do wrong to seek my freedom."

"These feelings are quite natural, George," said the good-natured man, blowing his nose. "Yes, they're natural, but it is my duty not to encourage 'em in you. Yes, my boy, I'm sorry for you, now; it's a bad case—very bad; but the apostle says, 'Let everyone abide in the condition in which he is called.' We must all submit to the indications of Providence, George,—don't you see?"

George stood with his head drawn back, his arms folded tightly over his broad breast, and a bitter smile curling his lips.

"I wonder, Mr. Wilson, if the Indians should come and take you a prisoner away from your wife and children, and want to keep you all your life hoeing corn for them, if you'd think it your duty to abide in the condition in which you were called. I rather think that you'd think the first stray horse you could find an indication of Providence—shouldn't you?"

useless to you, but now he is indeed useful both to you and to me. I am sending him, that is, my own heart, back to you" *(Philemon 10–12).*

Paul wrote to show how Jesus affects relationships—because Onesimus had become a Christian, the two men were now brothers in Christ. While Paul did not address the institution of slavery, he expected Philemon to accept Onesimus without penalty and volunteered to pay for anything that Onesimus may have owed. There is an indication that Paul hoped Philemon would send Onesimus back to assist Paul.

Paul did not make his argument based on force but rather appealed to Philemon's sense of honor. Paul noted that Onesimus was now "useful" to Philemon, a play on the word *Onesimus,* which means "useful." Paul tried to motivate Philemon to action by noting how Philemon could gain advantage from accepting Paul's argument. Paul again made his case based on Philemon's need to maintain or augment his honor. Paul noted that he too was doing a selfless, honorable act by returning Onesimus, acting, in a sense, as a model for Philemon:

> I wanted to keep him with me, so that he might be of service to me in your place during my imprisonment for the gospel; but I preferred to do nothing without your consent, in order that your good deed might be voluntary and not something forced. Perhaps this is the reason he was separated from you for a while, so that you might have him back forever, no longer as a slave but more than a slave, a beloved brother—especially to me but how much more to you, both in the flesh and in the Lord.
>
> *Philemon 13–16*

Paul expanded his argument by stating that he would compensate Philemon for any losses incurred and reminding him that Philemon owed his life to Paul:

> So if you consider me your partner, welcome him as you would welcome me. If he has wronged you in any way, or owes you anything, charge that to my account. I, Paul, am writing this with my own hand: I will repay it. I say nothing about your owing me even your own self. Yes, brother, let me have this benefit from you in the Lord! Refresh my heart in Christ.
>
> *Philemon 17–20*

projects

Choose one or both of these projects to apply what you learned about the social order in this chapter:

1.   Make a list of the qualifications of bishops and deacons in 1 Timothy. Then make a list of qualifications that you think are important for those in authority today. How many are the same? How many are different? Be prepared to explain your choices.

2.   Research the abolitionist movements in Great Britain and in the United States. How did the Bible influence the activists on both sides of the movement? How was the Bible used in the movements to abolish slavery? Report on your findings.

Unit Feature
Augustine

INTRODUCTION

Augustine (354–430), one of the great writers of the early church and one of the great thinkers of all time, spent considerable energy in interpreting Genesis and further developing the thoughts of the apostle Paul. The result was his two masterpieces of Western literature, *Confessions* and *The City of God.*

The Greek church has produced many great thinkers and writers, perhaps the greatest of whom was John Chrysostom. Augustine, however, wrote in Latin, and his writing had a great influence on Western thought. Augustine, who became Bishop of Hippo in northern Africa, drew everything around him into a synthesis that articulated the main beliefs of the Christian church. It was in the Scriptures that Augustine found the focus of religious authority.

One great theme in the works of Augustine was the utter need of humanity for God and God's abundant grace. Augustine was passionate about the sovereign God of grace and the sovereign grace of God. Grace, for Augustine, was God's freedom to act without any external necessity at all, to act in love beyond human under-standing or control, to act in creation, judgment, and redemption. According to Augustine, God gave his son freely as mediator and redeemer. God gave the Holy Spirit to all who sought it. God shaped the destiny of all creation and of human society. Grace is able to touch one's innermost heart and will. For all of his body of work, Augustine was given the title of "Doctor of Grace." The scholar Albert Outler summed it up: "Augustine is one of the very few men who simply cannot be ignored or depreciated in any estimate of Western civilization without serious distortion and impoverishment of one's historical and religious understanding."

Augustine is best known for his philosophical proof of existence, which later inspired the philosopher Descartes's proof of existence ("I think, therefore I am") and Spinoza's picture of the world in a framework of eternity. Augustine's skill was the ability to move the reader to the very soul with every word, sentence, and chapter. Like other great writers—Plato, Shakespeare, Melville, Dickens—Augustine was able to capture the most profound and uplifting along with the most horri-ble events of life, from the exalted heights of the divine to the melancholy depths of selfishness and sin.

CONFESSIONS:
THE FIRST AUTOBIOGRAPHY

Confessions is the first great autobiography of Western literature. It is also perhaps the most moving diary ever recorded of a soul's journey to grace. Written at midlife, *Confessions* stands out as being among the most per-suasive works of the hard-core hedonist-turned-priest who was to exercise a greater influence on Christian thought than any other of the Western church fathers. The work occupies an important place in Western lit-erature because of the breadth and depth of Augustine himself.

In *Confessions,* an intensely personal narrative, Augustine relates his ascent from a small town in North Africa (where he had been born to a feverishly religious mother, Monica, and a nondescript and abusive father, Patricius) to the imperial court in Milan; his passionate struggle against sexual sin, and his living with a mis-tress who had borne him a son, Deodatus (Latin for "given by God"); the premature death of his son Deodatus; his renunciation of secular ambition; and his marriage and the recovery of the faith his mother had taught him during his childhood.

Augustine's slavery to a non-Christian lifestyle long prevented him from following the call of God. This con-tinued until one day he heard a child sing, *"Tolle, lege; tolle, lege"* ("take up and read"). Taking this as a divine command to read the first passage of the Bible to meet

Augustine of Hippo, one of the fathers of Western literature.

A view of the ruins of the Christian quarter in ancient Hippo Regius. Augustine served as bishop here. The ruins are just two miles from the center of the modern city of Annaba, Algeria.

"Where there is no true religion, there are no true virtues. For what kind of mistress of the body and the vices can that mind be which is ignorant of the true God, and which, instead of being subject to His authority, is prostituted to the corrupting influences of the most vicious demons." Though the earthly city may demand strict obedience to its law, true virtue will not result because there is no religion other than true religion, which has an absolute law of justice and morality. So, the earthly city's laws are always open to abuse, ambiguous interpretation, or "progress."

Augustine does point out that the two cities share a common desire for peace. Yet they have different ways of seeking it. The earthly city seeks earthly peace and an orderly society; it strives for peace as the product of human intelligence and administrative skills. The part of the heavenly city that dwells on earth seeks earthly peace as well but only when it complements the ultimate goal of peace under God *(The City of God XIX.17).*

The City of God was written in 410, shortly after the Visigoths, led by Alaric, sacked Rome. For the people of the time, August 24, 410, was an event similar to the terrorist attacks of September 11, 2001. Barbarians, people Romans considered uncivilized, had plundered Rome, the capital of the empire.

Augustine undertook to write this book to explain what had happened. Some scholars consider this book to be a literary tombstone for Roman culture with its pursuit of earthly pleasures: "grasping for praise, open-handed with their money; honest in the pursuit of wealth, they wanted to hoard glory." Augustine contrasted his condemnation of Rome with an exaltation of Christian culture. The glory that Rome failed to attain would only be realized by citizens of the city of God, the heavenly Jerusalem foreseen in Revelation, the last book of the Bible.

The City of God is organized into twenty-two books. In the first ten books, Augustine dismantles the prevailing interpretation of the meaning of human affairs and then finds hidden just beneath the surface a second interpretation, divine in origin, full of hope for the future. Books 11 through 22 chronologically go through the Bible, starting with the goodness of creation and the fall and death and the formation of two cities: brothers at war in history (Cain/Abel; Ishmael/Isaac). Augustine then tells a history of the world and the two cities from a biblical perspective.

his eyes, he opened the book to the passage, "Let us live honorably as in the day, not in reveling and drunkenness, not in debauchery and licentiousness, not in quarreling and jealousy. Instead, put on the Lord Jesus Christ, and make no provision for the flesh, to gratify its desires" *(Romans 13:13 [NRSV]).*

To earn the eternal salvation that he sought, Augustine believed that he had to confess all his past sins in a vocal and unabashed way so that he could be among those to enter into God's eternal kingdom.

THE CITY OF GOD: A TALE OF TWO CITIES

In *The City of God,* Augustine traces two cities, the city of Cain, the earthly city, and the city of Abel. At the hands of Cain, the earth first swallowed human blood, and it was recorded that Cain then went out and built cities. Augustine was certain that all of humanity is divided into one of these cities where one is to "reign eternally with God and the other to suffer eternal punishment with the devil" *(The City of God XV.1).* These two cities exhibit two loves: The earthly city loves itself to the contempt of God, while the heavenly city loves God to the contempt of everything else. The former seeks glory from people, the latter from God, saying, "But you, O Lord, are a shield around me, my glory, and the one who lifts up my head" *(Psalm 3:3 [NRSV]).*

Besides the physical qualities that surround the life of the earthly city, Augustine wrote of stark spiritual and moral qualities that threaten people. In his words,

Other Letters

Let mutual love continue. Do not neglect to show hospitality to strangers, for by doing that some have entertained angels without knowing it. Remember those who are in prison, as though you were in prison with them. . . . Keep your lives free from the love of money, and be content with what you have.

Hebrews 13:1–3, 5 [NRSV]

In this unit you will discover

- How the early Christian
  Community interpreted the
  Hebrew Scriptures

- How the general letters gave
  advice on leading a good life

- John the Apostle's message of
  love

KEY BIBLICAL TEXTS

- Letter to the Hebrews, Genesis 14:18–20, Psalm 110:4

DISCOVER

- More about the early church's interpretation of the Hebrew Scriptures
- Why the writer of Hebrews saw Jesus as a great high priest

GET TO KNOW

- Melchizedek

CONSIDER

- How does it help to have knowledge of your ancestors?

The Fulfillment Letter to the Hebrews

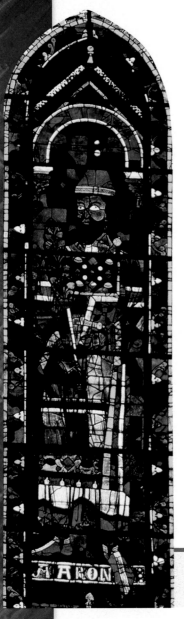

How was the early church, whose earliest followers were Jewish, to think about Jesus in the context of Hebrew Scriptures? This is the key question addressed in the letter to the Hebrews. This letter has three sections. In the first section, Jesus is revealed as the ultimate form of communication: God incarnate speaking to humankind *(Hebrews 1:1–4:13)*. Next, the letter presents Jesus as the great high priest *(Hebrews 4:14–10:39)*. Finally, biblical examples, sometimes called the "cloud of witnesses," are presented, and believers are encouraged to follow their example and live out their faith as followers of Jesus *(Hebrews 11:1–13:16)*.

Within this structure, each presentation of a new idea is followed with an exhortation to live out the implications of that idea. The whole of Hebrews is intended to inform and inspire the new church members and to encourage them to keep the faith.

Although Hebrews has always been called a letter, the only characteristic of a letter is at the end of the document. Hebrews 13:20 provides a blessing typical of the ending of New Testament letters, and the personal message and greetings of the last four verses also echo other letters:

> I appeal to you, brothers and sisters, bear with my word of exhortation, for I have written to you briefly. I want you to know that our brother Timothy has been set free; and if he comes in time, he will be with me when I see you. Greet all your leaders and all the saints. Those from Italy send you greetings. Grace be with all of you.
>
> *Hebrews 13:22–25 [NRSV]*

This stained-glass window from Chartres Cathedral in France shows Aaron, the brother of Moses. In Hebrew tradition, Aaron is seen as the first great high priest of the Israelites.

The Position of Jesus

The letter to the Hebrews opens with a brief prologue:

> Long ago God spoke to our ancestors in many and various ways
> by the prophets, but in these last days he has spoken to us by a
> Son, whom he appointed heir of all things, through whom he
> also created the worlds. He is the reflection of God's glory and
> the exact imprint of God's very being, and he sustains all
> things by his powerful word. When he had made purification
> for sins, he sat down at the right hand of the Majesty on high,
> having become as much superior to angels as the name he has
> inherited is more excellent than theirs.
>
> *Hebrews 1:1–4 [NRSV]*

After the prologue, the first main section begins by quoting seven passages from the Hebrew Scriptures: Psalm 2:7, 2 Samuel 7:14, Deuteronomy 32:43, Psalm 104:4, Psalm 45:6–7, Psalm 102:25–27, and Psalm 110:1.

These are the first of many passages and references from the Hebrew Scriptures to be found in Hebrews. These particular verses support the author's premise that Jesus is greater than the angels. These quotations and references provide an insight into how the early Christians viewed the Hebrew Scriptures and the relationship of these writings to Jesus and to Christians. Obviously, the letter sees the Hebrew Scriptures as preparing for and pointing to the coming of Jesus. The early Christians believed that Jesus was the messiah and the fulfillment of those scriptures.

The first part of the letter (the superiority of Jesus) is followed by an exhortation that is summarized in the first verse of the second chapter: "Therefore we must pay greater attention to what we have heard, so that we do not drift away from it" *(Hebrews 2:1 [NRSV])*. Here, as throughout Hebrews, the references to the Hebrew Scriptures and the teachings regarding Jesus are meant to encourage the Christians in their journey of faith, because the Hebrew Christians were apparently flagging in their faith and tending to return to ancient Jewish rituals.

Hebrews continues by describing Jesus and his role. In the author's view, Jesus became lower than the angels to taste death for all people. He was a pioneer of salvation. He took on flesh and blood to destroy evil. He came to help those descended from Abraham. The letter concludes this section by pointing ahead to the central theme of the letter:

> He had to become like his brothers and sisters in every respect,
> so that he might be a merciful and faithful high priest in the
> service of God, to make a sacrifice of atonement for the sins of
> the people. Because he himself was tested by what he suffered,
> he is able to help those who are being tested.
>
> *Hebrews 2:17–18 [NRSV]*

These verses show how the thought of Hebrews influenced the later understanding of Jesus by Christians. He was the "high priest." A **priest** is a person who mediates between God and the people. In ancient Israel, the priesthood was drawn from the tribe of Levi. The most important priestly duties were performed by the descendents of Aaron, the brother of Moses. When the temple was built, all priests served there. During the later period of the Hebrew Scriptures, the **high priest** was essentially the first among equals and came to hold much authority with the Israelite people.

The first section of Hebrews goes on to say that Jesus is greater than Moses and that Christians must beware that they do not fall away from the faith, as many people in the wilderness generation did.

Jesus as the High Priest

The theme of Jesus as the high priest is the principal one of the second section of the letter to the Hebrews, and, indeed, is perhaps the most important theme of the entire letter:

> Since, then, we have a great high priest who has passed through the heavens, Jesus, the Son of God, let us hold fast to our confession. For we do not have a high priest who is unable to sympathize with our weaknesses, but we have one who in every respect has been tested as we are, yet without sin. Let us therefore approach the throne of grace with boldness, so that we may receive mercy and find grace to help in time of need.
>
> *Hebrews 4:14–16 [NRSV]*

Jesus is compared with Melchizedek, a priest of mysterious origin in Genesis who, according to Hebrews, foreshadowed Jesus and his priestly role:

> Though he were a Son, yet learned he obedience by the things which he suffered; And being made perfect, he became the author of eternal salvation unto all them that obey him; Called of God an high priest after the order of Melchizedek.
>
> *Hebrews 5:8–10 [KJV]*

But who is Melchizedek? He is mentioned in a few verses in Genesis *(Genesis 14:18–21)* and a verse in the Psalms *(Psalm 110:4)*. He was a priest and the king of Salem at the time of Abram. The name is made up of two Hebrew words, *melek* and *zedek*. The words translate as "king of righteousness." Melchizedek was first mentioned in Genesis 14, when Abram went to visit him. Melchizedek offered Abram bread and wine and gave his blessing to Abram, who then offered him a tenth of all he had. Yet who was this priest who offered a blessing to Abram? How was this man superior to Abram, as indicated by his giving Abram a blessing and receiving a **tithe,** a tenth of Abram's possessions? Genesis does not say.

The priest-king came to be interpreted as a figure pointing to the messiah. Thus, he is mentioned again in Psalm 110, which is quoted several times in Hebrews: "The Lord has sworn and will not change his mind. 'You are a priest forever, according to the order of Melchizedek'" *(Hebrews 7:17 [NRSV])*. That is all that the Hebrew Scriptures have to say about Melchizedek, but Hebrews sees in him a foreshadowing or type of Christ.

Hebrews describes Jesus as the new high priest and greater than the priests of the old covenant:

This fifteenth-century painting by Dirck Bouts illustrates the meeting between Abraham and Melchizedek.

THE BIBLE

IN **Literature**

John Henry Newman (1801–1890), an English clergyman and scholar, wrote the following poem about Melchizedek:

John Henry Newman

> Thrice bless'd are they, who feel their loneliness;
>   To whom nor voice of friends nor pleasant scene
>   Brings that on which the sadden'd heart can lean;
> Yea, the rich earth, garb'd in her daintiest dress
> Of light and joy, doth but the more oppress,
>   Claiming responsive smiles and rapture high;
>   Till, sick at heart, beyond the veil they fly,
> Seeking His Presence, who alone can bless.
> Such, in strange days, the weapons of Heaven's grace;
> When, passing o'er the high-born Hebrew line,
> He forms the vessel of His vast design;
> Fatherless, homeless, reft of age and place,
> Sever'd from earth, and careless of its wreck,
> Born through long woe His rare Melchizedek.

For it was fitting that we should have such a high priest, holy, blameless, undefiled, separated from sinners, and exalted above the heavens. Unlike the other high priests, he has no need to offer sacrifices day after day, first for his own sins, and then for those of the people; this he did once for all when he offered himself. For the law appoints as high priests those who are subject to weakness, but the word of the oath, which came later than the law, appoints a Son who has been made perfect forever.

Hebrews 7:26-28 [NRSV]

Jesus—then seen as the perfect high priest—also participated in a new covenant, the one predicted by Jeremiah, whom the author quotes.

According to Hebrews, Jesus was not only the high priest, but he was also the ultimate sacrifice:

But when Christ came as a high priest of the good things that have come, then through the greater and prefect tent (not made with hands, that is, not of this creation), he entered once for all into the Holy Place, not with the blood of goats and calves, but with his own blood, thus obtaining eternal redemption. For if the blood of goats and bulls, with the sprinkling of the ashes of a heifer, sanctifies those who have been defiled so that their flesh is purified, how much more will the blood of Christ, who through the eternal Spirit offered himself without blemish to God, purify our conscience from dead works to worship the living God!

Hebrews 9:11-14 [NRSV]

This passage, for Christians, is a confirmation of their view that Jesus, in celebrating the Jewish Passover meal with his disciples as the Last Supper, was not only celebrating the historic protection provided by God for those who killed the lamb and spread the blood on their doorsteps so that the angel of death would pass by. Jesus was also celebrating becoming himself the lamb that would have been sacrificed on Passover. After Jesus' sacrifice, there is no need for further sacrifices, for, as Hebrews notes, "Where there is forgiveness of these, there is no longer any offering for sin" *(Hebrews 10:18 [NRSV]).*

Using the image of the tabernacle, the author encouraged the Christians to have confidence:

> Therefore, my friends, since we have confidence to enter the sanctuary by the blood of Jesus, by the new and living way that he opened for us through the curtain (that is, through his flesh), and since we have a great priest over the house of God, let us approach with a true heart in full assurance of faith, with our hearts sprinkled clean from an evil conscience and our bodies washed with pure water. Let us hold fast to the confession of our hope without wavering, for he who has promised is faithful. And let us consider how to provoke one another to love and good deeds, not neglecting to meet together, as is the habit of some, but encouraging one another, and all the more as you see the Day approaching.
>
> *Hebrews 10:19–25 [NRSV]*

After this encouraging word, however, Christians are warned not to fall into sin. In that case, Jesus' sacrifice would lead to judgment:

> How much worse punishment do you think will be deserved by those who have spurned the Son of God, profaned the blood of the covenant by which they were sanctified, and outraged the Spirit of grace? For we know the one who said, "Vengeance is mine, I will repay." And again, "The Lord will judge his people." It is a fearful thing to fall into the hands of the living God.
>
> *Hebrews 10:29–31 [NRSV]*

INTO EVERYDAY *language*

In the early translation of the Bible into English, William Tyndale coined the word *scapegoat* (used both in Leviticus and here in Hebrews) for the goat that escaped on the Day of Atonement. The term has come to mean one who is blamed for someone else's faults. Can you think of an example of a "scapegoat" in history or in current events?

A Cloud of Witnesses

The final section of Hebrews begins with a familiar definition of faith. Indeed, this definition is one of the best-known verses of the entire Bible:

> Now faith is the substance of things hoped for, the evidence of things not seen.
>
> *Hebrews 11:1 [KJV]*

Following this definition of faith, there is in Chapter 11 a list of heroes from the Hebrew Scriptures who expressed faith and who therefore serve as models for Christian faith.

Several interesting points are made in this passage. First, "without faith, it is impossible to please God, because whoever would approach him must believe that he exists and that he rewards those who seek him" *(Hebrews 11:6 [NRSV]).* Second, faith often involves a forward-looking aspect. Abraham, for example, looked "forward to the city that has foundations, whose architect and builder is God" *(Hebrews 11:10 [NRSV]):*

> All of these died in faith without having received the promises, but from a distance they saw and greeted them. They confessed that they were strangers and foreigners on the earth, for people who speak in this way make it clear that they are seeking a homeland.
>
> *Hebrews 11:13–14 [NRSV])*

THE BIBLE

IN Literature

NOAH WEBSTER AND HIS DICTIONARY

Noah Webster is famous as the writer of the first American dictionary, and his name is still associated with dictionaries in use today. In his 1828 *American Dictionary of the English Language,* Webster quoted Bible verses after the definition to illustrate the usage of many words. Under the definition of the word "faith," for example, he cites Hebrews 11:6, a verse from the chapter dealing with faith: "Without faith it is impossible to please God."

Webster (1758–1843), who also translated the Bible, was a teacher who wanted to implement a distinctly American form of education. Thus, he wrote *The American Spelling Book* (1783), as well as a grammar (1784) and a reader (1785). These three books were known as *A Grammatical Institute of the English Language.* His work is responsible for the differences in American and British spelling (for example, *color* versus *colour*).

He worked on his *American Dictionary* for twenty-two years, traveling to France and England for research and becoming acquainted with twenty languages in the process. The dictionary is filled with biblical references such as the one from Hebrews. For example, the definition of faith also includes references to Romans 5 and 10 and 2 Corinthians 5.

After Webster's death, George and Charles Merriam acquired the rights to his dictionary, giving rise to the Merriam-Webster dictionaries.

This engraving of Noah Webster by Frederick W. Halpin was done around 1850.

This section concludes with a typical exhortation to faith and endurance:

> Wherefore seeing we also are compassed about with so great a cloud of witnesses, let us lay aside every weight, and the sin which doth so easily beset us, and let us run with patience the race that is set before us, looking unto Jesus the author and finisher of our faith; who for the joy that was set before him endured the cross, despising the shame, and is set down at the right hand of the throne of God. For consider him that endured such contradiction of sinners against himself, lest ye be wearied and faint in your minds.
>
> *Hebrews 12:1–3 [KJV]*

This final section of the letter to the Hebrews encourages the faith of Christians by comparing the trials sent to Christians to the discipline children receive from their parents:

> Endure trials for the sake of discipline. God is treating you as children; for what child is there whom a parent does not discipline? If you do not have that discipline in which all children share, then you are illegitimate and not his children. Moreover, we had human parents to discipline us, and we respected them. Should we not be even more willing to be subject to the Father of spirits and live? For they disciplined us for a short time as seemed best to them, but he disciplines us for our good, in order that we may share his holiness. Now, discipline always seems painful rather than pleasant at the time, but later it yields the peaceful fruit of righteousness to those who have been trained by it.
>
> *Hebrews 12:7–11 [NRSV]*

CHAPTER 36

KEY BIBLICAL TEXTS

- Letter of James; 1 and 2 Peter; 1 John

DISCOVER

- Advice on living a good life
- Suggestions on how to deal with suffering
- The power and value of love

CONSIDER

- How is a letter you write to an individual different from a letter you might write to a group?

General Letters
James, Peter, and John

The final set of letters in the New Testament, those of James, Peter, John, and Jude, are sometimes called the "general" or "catholic" letters. The term *catholic* comes from the Greek word *katholicos,* which means "universal." These letters, rather than being addressed to individuals, were for the most part addressed to the church as a whole. In this chapter you will get an overview of James, the two letters of Peter, and 1 John.

James: The Way to Live Life

The identity of James, the author of the first of the general letters, is a source of some confusion, as there are a number of people named James in the New Testament: James the son of Zebedee

(known as "James the Greater"); James the son of Alphaeus; James the brother of Jesus; James, son of Mary, brother of Joseph; and James the brother of Jude. Most Christians attribute this letter to James the brother of Jesus, a leader of the Jerusalem church, who is mentioned in Mark 6:3, Matthew 13:55, 1 Corinthians 15:7, Galatians 1:19 and 2:9, and Acts 12:17, 15:13–21, and 21:18.

James addressed "the twelve tribes in dispersion" *(James 1:1).* This way of addressing the Christians shows that many of them saw themselves as part of the Diaspora, as Jews in exile. Other than this opening, the document has no further characteristics of a letter.

The letter of James is a thematic and practical document, showing a passionate

Rahab and the Emissaries of Joshua. Italian school. 17th century.

concern for the role of faith in the everyday circumstances of life. James challenged believers to control their tongues. Rather than debate the meaning of various teachings, James called on followers of Jesus to treat the poor and the rich with equal respect. James called for purity and faithfulness in all areas of life.

After the address and greeting in this letter, James outlined six themes of a believer: Testing produces joy, prayer produces wisdom, wealth is transient, sin results in death, God gives perfect gifts, and the obedient care for the oppressed.

Within these themes are specific instructions such as "You must understand this, my beloved: let everyone be quick to listen, slow to speak, slow to anger; for your anger does not produce God's righteousness" (James 1:19 [NRSV]). This section concludes by stating that "Religion that is pure and undefiled before God, the Father, is this: to care for orphans and widows in their distress, and to keep oneself unstained by the world" (James 1:27 [NRSV]).

In Chapter 2 James forbade the favoritism generally shown to the wealthy. He saw love of neighbor as the essence of the law. One could not despise or dishonor another person by showing favoritism and still please God.

James was apparently confronting a situation in which people in the church were professing faith in Jesus but felt no need for moral purity or ethical living. Faith alone was regarded as essential, while works were unnecessary. While not addressing how one comes to faith, James did show concern that followers of Jesus had become complacent about living faithfully. James said, "Has not God chosen the poor in the world to be rich in faith and to be heirs of the kingdom that he has promised to those who love him?" (James 2:5 [NRSV]).

James then moved to the most controversial part of his letter: the discussion of faith and works. After citing the royal law ("You shall love your neighbor as yourself"), James went on to promote what he called the "law of liberty," and discussed the ideas of faith and works:

> What doth it profit, my brethren, though a man say he hath faith, and have not works? Can faith save him? If a brother or sister be naked, and destitute of daily food, and one of you say unto them, Depart in peace, be ye warmed and filled; notwithstanding ye give them not those things which are needful to the body; what doth it profit? Even so faith, if it hath not works, is dead, being alone.
>
> *James 2:14–17 [KJV]*

James continued this subject by discussing Abraham as a model of faith: "Was not our ancestor Abraham justified by works when he offered his son Isaac on the altar?" (James 2:21 [NRSV]). He went on to say that it was Abraham's faith, made active by his works, which justified him in God's sight: "You see that a person is justified by works and not by faith alone" (James 2:24 [NRSV]). He then offered the example of Rahab the prostitute from the book of Joshua as another instance of works that brought justification.

Because of this emphasis, the reformer Martin Luther saw much of the letter of James as defective and in direct contrast with the letter to the Romans and justification by faith alone. In fact, Luther declared James—along with the gospel of Luke, the letter to the Hebrews, and Revelation—to be a "canon within the canon."

Chapter 3 is concerned with controlling one's speech and recognizing the true wisdom of God. James warned of three dangers to the communities of faith: dissension, presumption, and inappropriate use of wealth. James referred to the tongue as "a restless evil, full of deadly poison" (James 3:8 [NRSV]).

The final section, Chapter 4 and Chapter 5, has a strong **eschatological** tone. This word is based on the Greek term *eschaton,* meaning "end." Thus, these chapters deal with the end times. James cautioned that no one knows what tomorrow holds, that the coming of the Lord is soon, and that the Lord will judge human beings. James used the figure of Job in the Hebrew Scriptures as a model of patience and endurance in waiting for the end.

A final influential section of the letter of James is in the last verses: "Are any among you sick? They should call for the elders of the church and have them pray over them, anointing them with oil in the name of the Lord" (James 5:14 [NRSV]). Some churches, such as the Roman Catholic and Eastern Orthodox churches, point to this verse as the origin of the sacrament of anointing of the sick.

James concluded with an exhortation to prayer, noting that the prayer of the ordinary person is powerful when God makes it effective.

THE BIBLE
IN Literature

The Screwtape Letters

Clive Staples Lewis (1898–1963) was one of the literary lights of the twentieth century. He was a close friend of J. R. R. Tolkien, who wrote *The Lord of the Rings.* As a fellow and tutor in English literature at Oxford University and then as Chair of Medieval and Renaissance English at Cambridge University, Lewis wrote literary criticism and more than thirty books, including children's literature as well as books on theology that brought him an international following. Among his most popular books are *The Chronicles of Narnia.*

Below is the first of thirty-one letters from Screwtape to his nephew Wormwood in Lewis's *The Screwtape Letters.* In this witty, popular book, Lewis portrays Satan, who, along with his team of cohorts, is looking for opportunities to derail the faithful. The image of Satan in this book is reminiscent of 1 Peter: "Your enemy the devil prowls around like a roaring lion looking for someone to devour" *(1 Peter 5:8).*

In this book Lewis presents the correspondence of the worldly-wise Screwtape, a highly placed assistant to "Our Father Below" (Satan), to his nephew Wormwood, a novice demon in charge of securing the damnation of an ordinary man:

C. S. Lewis, circa 1945.

My dear Wormwood,

I note what you say about guiding your patient's reading and taking care that he sees a good deal of his materialist friend. But are you not being a trifle naive? It sounds as if you supposed that argument was the way to keep him out of the Enemy's clutches. That might have been so if he had lived a few centuries earlier. At that time the humans still knew pretty well when a thing was proved and when it was not; and if it was proved they really believed it. They still connected thinking with doing and were prepared to alter their way of life as the result of a chain of reasoning. But what with the weekly press and other such weapons, we have largely altered that. Your man has been accustomed, ever since he was a boy, to having a dozen incompatible philosophies dancing about together inside his head. He doesn't think of doctrines as primarily "true" or "false," but as "academic" or "practical," "outworn" or "contemporary," "conventional" or "ruthless." Jargon, not argument, is your best ally in keeping him from the Church. . . .

You begin to see the point? Thanks to processes which we set at work in them centuries ago, they find it all but impossible to believe in the unfamiliar while the familiar is before their eyes. Keep pressing home on him the ordinariness of things. Above all, do not attempt to use science (I mean, the real sciences) as a defense against Christianity. They will positively encourage him to think about realities he can't touch and see. There have been sad cases among the modern physicists. If he must dabble in science, keep him on economics and sociology; don't let him get away from that invaluable "real life." But the best of all is to let him read no science but to give him a grand general idea that he knows it all and that everything he happens to have picked up in casual talk and reading is "the results of modern investigation." Do remember you are there to fuddle him. From the way some of you young fiends talk, anyone would suppose it was our job to teach!

Your affectionate uncle,

Screwtape

First Peter: A Letter to Suffering Christians

The First Letter of Peter addressed the social tensions and suffering reflected in the conversions of non-Jews in the Roman world to Christianity, which by the time of this letter had become a despised, foreign religion. Roman society feared that foreign religions would threaten the patriarchal relationship and allow women to misbehave. Romans expected that foreign religions would cause immorality, disrupt the household structure, and be hostile to the state. First Peter addressed the converts, urging them to imitate Jesus by doing good and not retaliating against those who slander them.

Traditionally, Christians have believed that the apostle Peter wrote this letter just before the year 64, when tradition holds that Peter was executed in the persecution of the Christians by the Roman Emperor Nero.

First Peter emphasized that those converted were to imitate Jesus by, among other things, doing good and not retaliating against those who slander their community. One of the most familiar phrases in First Peter is, "Do not repay evil for evil or abuse for abuse, but on the contrary, repay with a blessing. It is for that you were called—so that you might inherit a blessing" *(1 Peter 3:9 [NRSV])*. This statement reflected Peter's sentiment on how the early Christians were to react to their persecutors.

The First Letter of Peter is structured very much like the letters of Paul, with a greeting, thanksgiving, body, exhortation, and closing. It has three main divisions: first, Peter discussed the calling of Christians; second, he discussed the duties of Christians; and third, he discussed the meaning of suffering. He seemed to be addressing Gentile Christians (see 1 Peter 1:14, 18 and 2:9–10). The audience of the letter seemed to be facing difficulties and perhaps even persecution.

In the first section of the letter, Peter described the faith and calling of Christians with a number of images that have become famous. He described Christian faith as "more precious than gold that, though perishable, is tested by fire" *(1 Peter 1:7 [NRSV])*. He described Christians as newborn babies *(1 Peter 2:2–3)* and as living stones: "Like living stones, let yourselves be built into a spiritual house, to be a holy priesthood, to offer spiritual sacrifices acceptable to God through Jesus Christ" *(1 Peter 2:5 [NRSV])*. He then noted that "you are a chosen race, a royal priesthood, a holy nation, God's own people" *(1 Peter 2:9 [NRSV])*.

This fresco by Michelangelo depicts the martyrdom of Peter. Tradition has it that Peter requested to be crucified upside down because he didn't feel worthy to die in exactly the same way as Jesus.

THE BIBLE
IN Literature

Jesus' descent into hell (also called the "harrowing of hell") is portrayed in Dante's great medieval epic poem, *The Divine Comedy*. In the first part of the poem, which is called "Inferno" (or "Hell"), the character Dante the Pilgrim, who is traveling through hell on his way to heaven, encounters the place where the souls of the just live. He meets the soul of the ancient Roman poet Virgil, who lived just before the time of Jesus, and Virgil described Jesus' visit to hell:

> I had but newly come into this realm
> When One descended, crowned in victory,
> To take away the souls of Adam, Abel,
> Noah, and Moses, giver of the Law,
> Who served the Lord with such obedience;
> Abraham the patriarch, King David;
> Israel, together with his father,
> His children, and Rachel, whom he would wed
> Despite great obstacles; and many more,
> And brought them all to Heaven, blessing them.
> Before that time no soul was saved from Hell.
>
> *Inferno,* canto IV

This fifteenth-century painting by the Italian artist Fra Angelico portrays Christ's visit to limbo to free the souls of the just.

The next section of the letter is a household code, with specific exhortations for slaves, wives, husbands, and all Christians. A key characteristic of this section on Christian behavior is the idea that Christians must accept suffering as Jesus did. For example, Peter said this:

> For to this you have been called, because Christ also suffered for you, leaving you an example, so that you should follow in his steps. . . . When he was abused, he did not return abuse; when he suffered, he did not threaten; but he entrusted himself to the one who judges justly. . . . by his wounds you have been healed.
>
> *1 Peter 2:21, 23, 24 [NRSV]*

Among the more interesting verses in 1 Peter are those that describe what happened to Jesus after his death:

> He was put to death in the flesh, but made alive in the spirit, in which also he went and made a proclamation to the spirits in prison, who in former times did not obey, when God waited patiently in the days of Noah, during the building of the ark, in which a few, that is, eight persons, were saved through water. And baptism, which this prefigured, now saves you.
>
> *1 Peter 3:18–21 [NRSV]*

This passage is noteworthy for several reasons. First of all, it refers to baptism, seeing Noah's ark as a prefiguring of Christian baptism, which came to be a rite of initiation into Christianity. But this passage is also notable for mentioning Jesus' visit to the "spirits in prison." Peter referred to this event again in the following chapter: "For this is the reason the gospel was proclaimed even to the dead, so that, though they had been judged in the flesh as everyone is judged, they might live in the spirit as God does" *(1 Peter 4:6 [NRSV])*. This passage is a key to the early understanding that Jesus' mission was to rescue people from sin and from death and to give eternal life to those righteous ones who had died and were waiting in the netherworld.

The final section of 1 Peter encourages the readers who are undergoing suffering, using the image of a lion to describe Satan:

> Discipline yourselves, keep alert. Like a roaring lion your adversary the devil prowls around, looking for someone to devour. Resist him, steadfast in your faith, for you know that your brothers and sisters in all the world are undergoing the same kinds of suffering.
>
> *1 Peter 5:8–9 [NRSV]*

Second Peter: A Message of Hope

In his second letter, Peter defended his teaching against critics, who probably wanted to free the message of Jesus from the features that were embarrassing to the church. Christian moral strictness made life difficult for Christians in the more permissive society. The Christian hope that Jesus would come to judge the world and to establish a new world of righteousness was also alien to prevailing views. Peter insisted that Christian hope was essential to the gospel and provided a motive for righteous living.

The three parts of Second Peter are: (1) an exhortation to virtue *(2 Peter 1:1–21);* (2) a condemnation of false teaching *(2 Peter 2:1–22);* and (3) a defense of the second coming of Jesus at the end of the world and an encouragement to watchfulness in view of Jesus' certain return.

In the first chapter, Peter encouraged conduct such as goodness, knowledge, self-control, endurance, godliness, affection, and love. In the second chapter, he focused on false teachers who apparently had been denying the second coming of Jesus. Peter affirmed the second coming and noted that, just as the angels underwent judgment, so would human beings. Thus, he here referred to a belief in the "fall of the angels." Traditionally, this scriptural passage has been interpreted as referring to a choice made by some of the angels to turn away from God. These "fallen" angels are called "devils" or "demons" in the Christian Scripture and tradition.

In this second letter, Peter was very critical of the false teachers, comparing them to Balaam in the Book of Numbers, who was rebuked by a donkey (see Numbers 22:21–35), and he quoted Proverbs 26:11 to describe them. In Chapter 3, he specifically pointed out the error of denying the second coming of Jesus simply because it has not happened yet:

> But do not ignore this one fact, beloved, that with the Lord one day is like a thousand years and a thousand years are like one day. The Lord is not slow about his promise, as some think of slowness, but is patient with you, not wanting any to perish, but all to come to repentance. But the day of the Lord will come like a thief, and then the heavens will pass away with a loud noise, and the elements will be dissolved with fire, and the earth and everything that is done on it will be disclosed.
>
> *2 Peter 3:8–10 [NRSV]*

This engraving by the nineteenth-century French artist Gustave Doré illustrates the fall of the angels, as mentioned in 2 Peter.

St. John on Patmos by Hieronymus Bosch. Traditionally, John was believed to be the author of the Gospel of John, the Book of Revelation, and all three letters of John.

First John: Joy and God's Love

The beginning of 1 John has a prologue that echoes the prologue of John's gospel:

> We declare to you what was from the beginning, what we have heard, what we have seen with our eyes, what we have looked at and touched with our hands, concerning the word of life—this life was revealed, and we have seen it and testify to it, and declare to you the eternal life that was with the Father and was revealed to us—we declare to you what we have seen and heard so that you also may have fellowship with us; and truly our fellowship is with the Father and with his Son Jesus Christ. We are writing these things so that our joy may be complete.
>
> *1 John 1:1–4 [NRSV]*

The similarities of the first four verses of First John with the prologue to the Gospel of John *(John 1:1–18)* are striking. The differences are striking as well. In First John there is a stronger emphasis on the eyewitness testimony to the real humanity of Jesus—"what we have seen with our eyes, what we have looked at and touched with our hands." This focus on the eyewitness suggests that false teachers were influencing the community, and John was calling the listeners back to their roots, to the apostolic eyewitness of Jesus and the word they first heard. John appeared to be emphasizing the participation of the believer with the experience of hearing, seeing, and touching the incarnate God.

This document lacks many of the formal characteristics of a letter (salutation, greeting, and the like) but nevertheless seems to be addressed to a group of people. The words of the prologue show a concern for affirming the humanity of Jesus; this letter deals with a false teaching that seemed to deny Jesus' humanity.

Each person, according to John, belonged either to darkness or light. There was no in-between. Darkness was marked by sin, falsehood, hate, and death. Life was characterized by righteousness, truth, love, and life. Those who walked in light were cleansed from sins and kept the commandments of God. The world was to be shunned as a world of darkness.

God's righteousness dominates the first half of the First Letter of John. God's love dominates the second half. There are three Greek words for love: *philos,* or familial love; *eros,* or romantic and passionate love; and *agape,* or selfless love. John chose this last word when he made his admonition that "we should love one another" *(1 John 3:23).*

In this short letter, the word *love* is used forty-three times. In this section alone, it is used thirty-two times. The statement "God is love" is a description, according to John, of God's essence, in much the same way that God was earlier described as "light." First John also makes the point that to show love for an invisible God, one has to respond by reaching out in love to others who are visible:

> Beloved, let us love one another, because love is from God; everyone who loves is born of God and knows God. Whoever does not love does not know God, for God is love. God's love was revealed among us in this way: God sent his only Son into the world so that we might live through him. In this is love, not that we loved God but that he loved us and sent his Son to be the atoning sacrifice for our sins. Beloved, since God loved us so much, we also ought to love one another. No one has ever seen God; if we love one another, God lives in us, and his love is perfected in us.
>
> *1 John 4:7–12 [NRSV]*

INTO EVERYDAY
language

John made a distinction between sin that was and was not mortal *(1 John 5:14–17).* By "mortal," he meant sin that kills the life of the soul. The words come into everyday language to explain something really wrong (but not necessarily sinful). For example, it is common to hear something like "It would be a *mortal sin* not to give Sheila an A in chemistry."

projects

Choose one of the following projects. Report on your findings.

1. The author of 1 Peter seemed to be familiar with the traditions that shaped the gospel of Matthew. Discover some similarities between the letter and the gospel.

2. Compare Peter's household code with those found in Ephesians 5:21–6:9 and Colossians 3:18–4:1.

3. Compare the descriptions of love in 1 John with the notions of romantic love in literature or films.

Unit Feature

The Legacy of the Reformation

One of the pivotal moments of the history of Western civilization was the Reformation of the sixteenth century. Martin Luther, John Calvin, and other reformers developed ideas based largely on the New Testament, and these ideas eventually led them to break away from the Roman Catholic Church. This was the origin of Protestantism, one of the three major branches of Christianity (the other two being Roman Catholicism and Eastern Orthodoxy). The Christian groups formed as a result of the Reformation had a tremendous influence not only on European history but also on the early culture of the United States.

was solved by faith alone. Further, Luther believed that God revealed himself to human beings not through Church doctrines, but by Scripture alone.

Luther wrote down many of his beliefs in a document called the Ninety-Five Theses and nailed it to the church door in Wittenberg, Germany. The church door was like a bulletin board for the community. As a result of this action, which occurred on October 31, 1517, the Reformation began. The church that grew out of his teachings was later called the Lutheran Church, and Luther's thought inspired many other Reformation theologians.

This portrait of Martin Luther is by the artist Lucas Cranach the Elder.

THE POWER AND THE GLORY OF GOD

Another great reformer of the sixteenth century was the French theologian John Calvin (1509–1564). Calvin shared many of Martin Luther's ideas, such as justification by faith and the importance of Scripture. But even more than Luther, he emphasized God's immense power and glory. The notion of grace (God's gift of spiritual life to the soul) was extremely important to Calvin, and he taught the doctrine of predestination (that God, having foreknowledge of all events, infallibly guides those who are worthy of salvation). More than Luther, Calvin saw a positive role for law in this world, and he was very influential in forming a self-governing Protestant community in the city of Geneva, Switzerland. Groups that developed from the Calvinist tradition include the Reformed, Presbyterian, and Congregationalist churches.

FAITH AND SCRIPTURE ALONE

Martin Luther (1483–1546) is the person whom most people consider to be the founder of Protestantism. Luther was a German Catholic who entered the Augustinian order of priests. He received his doctoral degree in theology and became a theology professor. But he was very distressed at the state of the Catholic Church, particularly its teachings on sin and penance. At this time the Church taught that the punishment for the sins of both living and dead people could be removed by an "indulgence" of the Church. During Luther's lifetime, there was much abuse of these indulgences, and they were even being sold for money.

Luther did not believe that the Church had this power. Indeed, he felt that there were no actions or works that would make a person just in God's eyes. When Luther began to translate the letter to the Romans into German, he became struck by verses 1:16–17. Luther ultimately concluded that the problem of sin

The Venetian Renaissance artist Titian painted this portrait of John Calvin.

THE REFORMATION IN ENGLAND

Another phase of the Reformation occurred in England, but at first the English Reformation was more political than religious. Henry VIII, the English king, wanted to have a son, but his wife, Catherine of Aragon, had borne him only one surviving child, a girl. Henry wanted the Pope to grant him an annulment (a decree that his marriage with Catherine was not valid) so that he could marry a woman named Anne Boleyn. The Pope refused, so Henry declared himself to be the head of the Church in England, divorced Catherine, and married Anne. This action separated the Church in England from the Roman Church.

Eventually, the Church of England (or "Anglican Church") came to be very deeply influenced by the theology of the reformers. For example, one group that developed within the English Church was the Puritans. They were called Puritans because they wanted to purify the Church of trappings and rituals they saw as idolatry. Churches that developed from the English branch of the Reformation are the Anglican, Episcopal, and Methodist churches.

King Henry VIII, shown in this portrait by Hans Holbein the Younger, was named "Defender of the Faith" by the Pope before he broke from Roman Catholicism and declared himself head of the Church in England.

RADICAL REFORMATION

A last major branch of the Reformation is called the Radical Reformation. The members of this group were at first known as *Anabaptists* (which literally means that they "baptized again"). They were opposed to baptizing infants and children, believing that only adult believers should be baptized. The Anabaptists were also pacifists, refusing to serve in war. They believed in a strict separation of church and state. Groups that

This Amish buggy was photographed in Lancaster County, Pennsylvania. The Amish are part of the Anabaptist tradition.

developed from this branch of the Reformation include the Mennonites, the Hutterites, the Amish, and the Quakers.

THE HERITAGE OF THE REFORMATION

Historically, the Protestant denominations were very much part of the founding of the American republic. Puritan thought influenced the settlers of the Jamestown colony in Virginia in 1607. The Christians who traveled to America on the *Mayflower* in 1620 were Puritans who had originally come from England, then sought refuge in Holland; they founded the Plymouth Colony. The Massachusetts Bay Colony was founded as a Puritan community in the seventeenth century. The Connecticut and New Haven Colonies were also founded by Puritans, as was Rhode Island. Even Maryland, which was founded as a haven for Roman Catholics, had a Protestant influence, as, indeed, did all of the original colonies. William Penn founded Pennsylvania as a Quaker colony.

Culturally, an enormous influence of the Reformation was in the translation of the Bible into the language of the people. Great Protestant writers also influenced the world of literature. Among the great Protestant literary figures, John Milton ranks highly. One example of a great artist in the Protestant tradition who is among the greatest painters of Western civilization is Rembrandt, a member of the Dutch Reformed Church. In the realm of music, perhaps the greatest Protestant composer is Johann Sebastian Bach, a Lutheran.

The Reformation also influenced social and economic systems. Some scholars believe that the thought of John Calvin influenced the development of the economic system called capitalism, and the Protestant movement in general strengthened the development of individual nation-states.

The Reformation also inspired renewal within the Roman Catholic community. The Roman Church worked to get back to its roots in Scripture and tradition. The Catholic Church is known for its worldwide good works, hospitals, and educational institutions.

UNIT THIRTEEN

Revelation

The first angel blew his trumpet, and there came hail and fire, mixed with blood, and they were hurled to the earth; and a third of the earth was burned up, and a third of the trees were burned up, and all green grass was burned up.

Revelation 8:7 [NRSV]

In this unit you will discover

- A New Testament example of apocalyptic literature

- That this type of literature is written in a form of code to give comfort to people in crisis or under persecution

- A message of hope hidden within visions

KEY BIBLICAL TEXTS

- Revelation 1:1–3:22

GET TO KNOW

- John, Domitian

DISCOVER

- The purpose of the Book of Revelation
- The nature of apocalyptic literature
- The messages to the seven churches in Asia Minor

CONSIDER

- Why do people need encouragement when they're suffering?

Crisis and Persecution

Visions, angels, dragons, beasts, great earthquakes, war, and victory—the Book of Revelation has fired the imagination of writers, artists, and ordinary people for centuries. But how is one to understand its often-confusing symbols, numbers, and images? It is possible to look at Revelation as a series of three one-act plays:

- The first play is composed of a group of letters to seven existing churches in what is now western Turkey *(1:1–3:22)*.
- The second play consists of a scene in the heavenly throne room and the conflict between the dragon, representing evil, and the Lamb of God, a symbol for Jesus *(4:1–20:15)*.
- The third play is a vision of a New Jerusalem and of eternal life with God *(21:1–22:21)*.

The Book of Revelation is sometimes called the Apocalypse. That word comes from its title in Greek (the language in which the book was originally written). The word *apocalypsis* means "unveiling," or "revelation."

Suffering and Execution

By the time Revelation was written, many Christians had died for their faith. These martyrs included leaders of the community such as Peter and Paul. The writing of Revelation is commonly placed during the time of the Emperor Domitian (81–96). Domitian, like other Roman emperors, wanted the people in the Roman Empire to call him "Lord and God" and to treat him as one of the many Roman deities. This caused a problem for the Christians in the empire. Because they believed that there was only one God, they could not and would not worship the emperor. The Christians were already unpopular in the empire because they avoided public functions where people ate meat that had been sacrificed to Roman idols. This made them stand out, and some Romans saw the Christians as disloyal. They were

This first-century coin features a profile of the Emperor Domitian, who was worshiped as "Lord and God" by his Roman subjects.

often called atheists because they refused to worship the Roman gods. When the Christians refused to worship the emperor, some of them were punished by being put in prison or by being tortured. Some were even executed.

The late first century, when Revelation was written, was a time of suffering and persecution for the Christians. Many of them were tempted to abandon their faith rather than face persecution. Revelation was written as a message of hope that revealed the meaning and value of the suffering and helped the Christians understand what was coming next. Justice would prevail, good would triumph, and evil would be punished. It encouraged them and helped them keep their Christian faith in spite of persecution.

Because Revelation was written at a time of persecution, it was written using a great deal of symbolism that was meant to hide its meaning from civil authorities. As a result, without considerable biblical knowledge based on a thorough understanding of Hebrew Scriptures, it can be very confusing reading.

Revelation as a Letter

The opening words of the book set its context as visionary writing: "The revelation of Jesus Christ, which God gave him to show his servants what must soon take place; he made known by sending his angel to his servant John, who testified to the word of God and to the testimony of Jesus Christ, even to all that he saw" *(Revelation 1:1–2 [NRSV]).*

Though Revelation is an example of apocalyptic literature, it also shares characteristics with other biblical literary forms, such as prophecy and narrative. The entire document is cast in the form of a letter from the author, John, to the seven churches in Asia Minor:

> I, John, your brother who share with you in Jesus the persecution and the kingdom and the patient endurance, was on the island called Patmos because of the word of God and the testimony of Jesus. I was in the spirit on the Lord's day, and I heard behind me a loud voice like a trumpet saying, "Write in a book what you see and send it to the seven churches, to Ephesus, to Smyrna, to Pergamum, to Thyatira, to Sardis, to Philadelphia, and to Laodicea."
>
> *Revelation 1:9–11 [NRSV]*

According to the text, the Book of the Revelation was written on the isle of Patmos, a small volcanic island in the Aegean Sea off the coast of Turkey, near the town of Ephesus. John had been exiled from Ephesus to Patmos, where he was in effect a prisoner.

The visions in the Book of Revelation reflect the scenery the author saw around him. Patmos is an island about ten miles long and about six miles across with a coastline of thirty-seven miles. The highest point is Hagios Elias (Mount St. Elias), rising to over 1050 feet. About halfway up the mountain is the cave where tradition suggests that John wrote Revelation.

After the opening quoted above, John then gave more details about his vision:

> Then I turned to see whose voice it was that spoke to me, and on turning I saw seven golden lampstands, and in the midst of the lampstands I saw one like the Son of Man, clothed with a long robe and with a golden sash across his chest. His head and his hair were white as white wool, white as snow; his eyes were like a flame of fire, his feet were like burnished bronze, refined as in a furnace, and his voice was like the sound of many waters. In his right hand he held seven stars, and from his mouth came a sharp, two-edged sword, and his face was like the sun shining with full force.
>
> *Revelation 1:12–16 [NRSV]*

THE BIBLE

AS **Literature**

APOCALYPTIC LITERATURE

The historical setting explains some of the signs, symbols, images, and numbers that fill the Book of Revelation. Most of the mysterious content of Revelation would have been difficult for the Romans to understand. Thus, it was a kind of "code." But how could the Christians understand the code if the Romans could not? First-century Christians were very familiar with the literary form of Revelation—a form called apocalyptic literature.

Apocalyptic Literature in the Bible
Hebrew Scriptures
Isaiah 24–27
Ezekiel 38–39
The Book of Daniel
Joel 2
Zechariah 9–14

New Testament
Mark 13, Matthew 24, Luke 12
1 Corinthians 15
2 Thessalonians 2
The Book of Revelation

As the list shows, there are a number of examples of apocalyptic literature in both the Hebrew Scriptures and the New Testament. The clearest example of apocalyptic literature in the Hebrew Scriptures is Daniel, and the clearest example of apocalyptic literature in the New Testament is the Book of Revelation.

The vision of "the Son of Man" in Chapter 1 is very similar to the vision in Chapter 7 of the Book of Daniel: "I saw one like a human being coming with the clouds of heaven" *(Daniel 7:13 [NRSV])*. The readers of Revelation would have been familiar with the Book of Daniel.

All apocalyptic literature follows a pattern:

- It is addressed to communities undergoing some kind of suffering or difficulty.
- It reassures the community that the evil force in control of their life will be destroyed and a new era will begin.
- First, however, the suffering may become extreme.

"Sign" Language

In many ways, this first vision of Revelation is a very typical apocalyptic vision. It shows how John used terms, symbols, and numbers that—although quite mysterious to contemporary readers—had meaning for his audience. For example, the term *Son of Man,* while unfamiliar to contemporary readers, was a familiar term to the first-century audience of Revelation. This term was also used in the Book of Daniel to designate a future messiah-like figure, and Jesus in the gospel accounts often referred to himself as "the Son of Man." Another example is the use of the number seven. Seven recurs fifty-seven times in the Book of Revelation. The number seven was central in the Hebrew Bible—seven days of creation, seven festivals, seven phases for the building of the tabernacle. Seven symbolizes a divine pattern of events.

John identified the Son of Man figure, and he also interpreted some of the imagery: "Do not be afraid; I am the first and the last, and the living one. I was dead, and see, I am alive forever and ever; and I have the keys of Death and of Hades" *(Revelation 1:17–18 [NRSV])*. Saying he was the "first and the last" echoes an earlier verse where John quoted God saying, "I am the Alpha and the Omega" *(Revelation 1:8 [NRSV])*. Alpha and omega are the first and last letters of the Greek alphabet. The author sought to demonstrate that he was writing about the Jesus revealed in the gospels. He went on to say that the seven stars represented the angels of the seven churches of Asia Minor, and the lampstands represented the churches themselves.

Revelation then presents a series of letters to seven churches. These churches were located in seven cities about fifty miles apart. The cities were postal centers for their respective geographic regions. Apparently, the entire Book of Revelation, including all seven letters, was sent to each church. Six of the seven cities still exist.

The letters to the seven churches are more like the decrees or edicts of the Persian kings and Roman emperors than like letters. Here is a brief outline of that literary form:

1. The recipient is named: "To the angel of the church in . . ." (Note: the "angel" may have been the church elder there.)
2. A command to write is expressed.
3. The writer and titles are designated, in words like "thus says" or "these are the words of." The titles used have some application to the church being addressed in the letter.

THE BIBLE
IN **History**

Ever since the writing of the Book of Revelation, Patmos has been revered as a holy place by all of Christendom. In 1088, the monk Christodoulos Latrenus petitioned the Byzantine Emperor Alexius I, who granted him the whole island, where he founded a monastery in honor of John. This fortified monastery is at the top of the mountain. Inside the monastery is a museum that over the years has preserved valuable relics, including silver- and gold-embroidered vestments and a rich collection of icons, making up a collection of ecclesiastical art from the eleventh to the eighteenth centuries. A library contains over 1000 parchments and 1000 ancient books.

In 1981 the Greek Parliament passed a special law designating Patmos as a "sacred island." It is a part of the Ecumenical Patriarchate of Constantinople, which organized a celebration in 1988 to commemorate the 900th anniversary of the founding of the Monastery of St. John and, in 1995, commemorated the 1900th anniversary of the writing of the Book of the Revelation.

A view of the Isle of Patmos. Behind the fortress-like walls is the Monastery of Saint John.

4. A commendation is given in the form of some acknowledgment of the value of the community, usually following the words "I know your deeds . . ." (except for Laodicea and Pergamum).

5. An admonition and exhortation are expressed. There is a rebuke, if applicable (except in the cases of Smyrna and Philadelphia), and a charge to repent or a warning.

6. A proclamation formula is given, usually as a call to hear—"He who has an ear, let him hear what the Spirit says to the churches."

7. A victory and reward formula is used. Victory consists of a promise. The phrase, "To him who overcomes," is followed by a reference to a reward. The rewards follow a biblical order. For example, being able to eat from "the tree of life" refers to the garden of Eden in Genesis, and being saved from the "second death" refers to the disobedience of Adam and Eve.

The Seven Churches

Here is a brief guide to the letters to the seven churches:

1. *Ephesus—First Love (2:1-7):* Ephesus was the port city that acted as the gateway to Asia Minor from Europe. The harvesting of trees for firewood had caused great erosion in and around Ephesus, and the central city was no longer habitable. The Christian community there had changed as well, having lost its initial passion and enthusiasm. The letter challenges the community to repent and return to their "first love." Their reward would be to eat from the tree of life.

2. *Smyrna—Persecution (2:8-11):* Smyrna was a port city at the site of what is today Izmir, Turkey—a thriving seaport and industrial city of over two million people. The community in Smyrna had suffered poverty and affliction, and

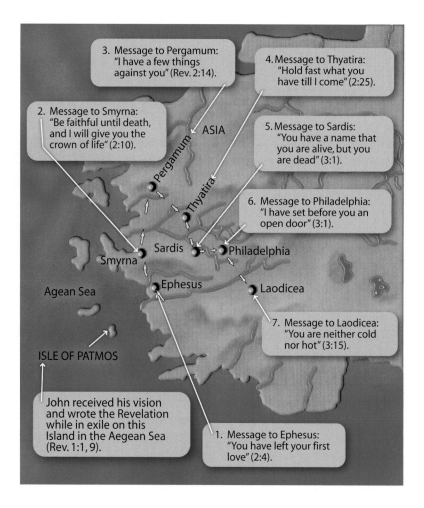

3. Message to Pergamum: "I have a few things against you" (Rev. 2:14).

4. Message to Thyatira: "Hold fast what you have till I come" (2:25).

2. Message to Smyrna: "Be faithful until death, and I will give you the crown of life" (2:10).

ASIA

5. Message to Sardis: "You have a name that you are alive, but you are dead" (3:1).

Pergamum

Thyatira

6. Message to Philadelphia: "I have set before you an open door" (3:1).

Sardis   Philadelphia

Smyrna

Ephesus

Agean Sea

Laodicea

7. Message to Laodicea: "You are neither cold nor hot" (3:15).

ISLE OF PATMOS

John received his vision and wrote the Revelation while in exile on this Island in the Aegean Sea (Rev. 1:1, 9).

1. Message to Ephesus: "You have left your first love" (2:4).

The seven churches, the most important in Asia Minor, formed a postal circuit.

The ruins of an ancient temple in Smyrna, now the modern Turkish city of Izmir.

A view of the ruins of the Roman amphitheater in Pergamum.

more suffering was presumably coming their way. They would, however, remain faithful. Their reward would be the crown of life and avoidance of the second death.

3. *Pergamum—Adversity (2:12–17):* The city of Pergamum was a place of emperor worship and was noted for idolatry. Pergamum was an administrative center for the Roman province. Its impressive acropolis made it appear impregnable. There are a number of references to the Hebrew Scriptures in this letter. The community was holding fast in unfriendly circumstances. Its reward would be hidden manna (recalling the food given to the wandering Israelites in the Book of Exodus).

4. *Thyatira—Endurance (2:18–28):* This city had a low, small acropolis in a beautiful valley between two gently rolling hills. In this serene setting, there was great temptation to fall into sexual license and to eat food sacrificed to idols. The community there showed love, faith, service, and endurance. Their reward for avoiding the pitfalls around them would be authority over the nations and the morning star. Note that the images of the iron rod and the shattered pottery in verse 27 echo Psalm 2:8–9 and are typical images from the Hebrew Scriptures describing the age of the messiah.

5. *Sardis—Repent (3:1–6):* Looked at from the north in the open plain, Sardis seemed to be another imposing city. However, the reality was quite the opposite. The city was often invaded and conquered. The community in Sardis was not doing well at all. They may have had a reputation of being alive; but, according to the letter, they were dead.

CULTURAL
CONNECTIONS

Letters from Prison

Dietrich Bonhoeffer (1906–1945)

Dietrich Bonhoeffer in a Nazi prison, circa 1943.

Letters composed in prison may be deeply touching, sometimes with a message of hope, grace, and courage for us all. Dietrich Bonhoeffer wrote from a German prison cell while awaiting execution by the Nazis toward the end of World War II. Bonhoeffer, a Lutheran pastor, had become concerned in 1933 when Hitler came to power as Chancellor of Germany and began implementing euthanasia laws, legalizing the elimination of "useless lives." While many of his fellow pastors had given in and even acquiesced for the most part, Bonhoeffer began to organize opposition, setting up clandestine seminaries where pastors would be trained to preach and uphold biblical teachings.

Bonhoeffer left Germany for a while and was in New York in 1939, where he was strongly urged to stay. But his desire was to return. He wrote, "I must live through this difficult period of our national history with the Christian people of Germany. I shall have no right to participate in the reconstruction of Christian life in Germany after the war if I do not share the trials of this time with my people." Elsewhere he said, "Christians in Germany will face the terrible alternatives of either willing the defeat of their nation in order that Christian civilization may survive or willing the victory of their nation and thereby destroying our civilization." With that, he returned to Germany. He was later arrested and imprisoned for involvement in an assassination attempt on Adolph Hitler.

Letters and Papers from Prison gathers some of the sermons, poems, and letters Bonhoeffer wrote while awaiting his fate. On July 18, 1944, he sent these reflections to his friend and fellow pastor Eberhard Bethge:

> I wonder how many of our letters have been destroyed in the raids on Munich? . . . As Jesus asked in Gethsemane, "Could ye not watch with me one hour?" That is the exact opposite of what the religious man expects from God. Man is challenged to participate in the sufferings of God at the hands of a godless world.
>
> He must therefore plunge himself into the life of a godless world, without attempting to gloss over its ungodliness with a veneer of religion or try to transfigure it. He must live a "worldly" life and so participate in the suffering of God. He may live a worldly life as one emancipated from all false religions and obligations. To be a Christian does not mean to be religious in a particular way, to cultivate some particular form of asceticism (as a sinner, a penitent, or a saint), but to be a man. It is not some religious act that makes a Christian what he is, but participation in the suffering of God in the life of the world.

On April 9, 1945, Bonhoeffer was hanged at Flossenberg concentration camp, just days before it was liberated by the Allies.

IN YOUR
journal

Compose a letter to a friend in trouble. How would you address the trouble? How would you give consolation and hope to your friend?

The members were encouraged to remember, obey, and repent. There was some acknowledgment that the ones who "have not soiled their clothes" would be rewarded. The reward for repentance and for persevering would be white robes and names recorded in the book of life.

6. *Philadelphia—The Key (3:7-13):* In ancient times, Philadelphia was known to the whole world as a city of earthquakes, and most of the citizens lived outside what was really quite a small town. There is a description of strong conflict between the Christian community and the Jewish community. The Christian community had patient endurance, and their reward would be to become a symbolic pillar in the temple (which had already been destroyed)

and to have the name of God written on them. There is also a mention of the New Jerusalem—a concept that would be more fully developed later in the Book of Revelation.

7. ***Laodicea—Lukewarm (3:14-22):*** Laodicea is located next to Permukule, a spa where people came to enjoy their final days. The citizens of Laodicea were wealthy and pampered. The community there received a very harsh message condemning them for being lukewarm. Their riches and comfort, according to the letter, left them wretched, pitiable, poor, blind, and naked. If they answered the call to reform and repent, their reward would be a place on the throne. This letter contains a well-known line, "Behold, I stand at the door, and knock: if any man hear my voice, and open the door, I will come in to him, and will sup with him, and he with me" *(Revelation 3:20 [KJV])*. This line has inspired many paintings of Jesus knocking on a door.

William Holman Hunt along with Dante Gabriel Rossetti and John Everett Millais founded the Pre-Raphaelite Brotherhood—a school of art grounded in realism and meticulous detail. His painting *Light of the World* captures the image from the letter to the church in Laodicea.

projects

Choose one or both of the projects. You can work alone or with a partner.

1. Pliny the Younger, who was governor of Pontus in what is now Turkey in the early second century, wrote letters to the Emperor Trajan concerning the crisis the Christians were causing. Use the Internet to find Pliny's famous letter to Trajan and Trajan's reply. Report your findings to the class.

2. Find out more about the seven ancient and modern cities that received the letters. Make an audiovisual report of what you discover.

KEY BIBLICAL TEXTS

- Revelation 4:1–5:14; 12:1–13:18; 17:1–20:5

DISCOVER

- Some of the most intriguing passages in all apocalyptic literature
- How difficult it is to interpret the symbolism of Revelation
- The image of the four horsemen and how they symbolize disaster

GET TO KNOW

- The Woman Clothed with the Sun; Michael; the Woman on the Scarlet Beast

CONSIDER

- What are some symbols you use in everyday life?

A Great Battle

The second part of the Book of Revelation (Chapters 4 through 20) provides a riot of images, creatures, battles, and symbols. All of them have inspired writers, composers, artists, and filmmakers. If many of the images seem vaguely familiar, it is probably because you have encountered them in novels or short stories, in films, or on television. The visions described in this section of Revelation have nourished many other visions of the future, ranging from sheer fancy to profound reflection.

The Throne Room of Heaven

John introduced this section of the book with his vision of heaven:

> At once I was in the spirit, and there in heaven stood a throne, with one seated on the throne! And the one seated there looks like jasper and carnelian, and around the throne is a rainbow that looks like an emerald. Around the throne are twenty-four thrones, and seated on the thrones are twenty-four elders, dressed in white robes, with golden crowns on their heads. Coming from the throne are flashes of lightning, and rumblings and peals of thunder, and in front of the throne burn seven flaming torches, which are the seven spirits of God; and in front of the throne there is something like a sea of glass, like crystal.
> *Revelation 4:2–6 [NRSV]*

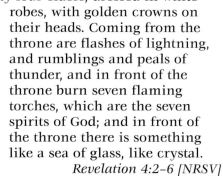

This fourteenth-century tapestry by Nicolas Bataille shows images from Chapters 4 through 22 of Revelation.

the sea gave up the dead that were in it, Death and Hades gave up the dead that were in them, and all were judged according to what they had done. Then Death and Hades were thrown into the lake of fire. This is the second death, the lake of fire; and anyone whose name was not found written in the book of life was thrown into the lake of fire.

Revelation 20:12–15 [NRSV]

Interpretation

Symbolic writing is never easy to understand. It forces the reader to work at the meaning of the symbols, to interpret them, and finally to integrate them into an understanding of the writing itself. Over the centuries there have been numerous attempts to apply these three steps to Revelation. The attempts boil down to four basic approaches:

Past history	The events of Revelation were all fulfilled in the first century.
Symbolic history	Revelation concerned first-century Christians but has symbolic value for other centuries as well.
Continuous history	Revelation predicted specific events in church history.
Future history	Revelation 4–22 described events that will happen in the future.

Each approach has some merit. Perhaps the most common approach is a combination of the first two. The events that were happening at the time Revelation was written were described in "coded," or symbolic, terms. Those events are now all in the past. The symbols, however, even though they may have lost some of their immediate meaning, can still be used to help readers understand and cope with events in today's world.

Choose one of these projects to better understand apocalyptic literature in general and Revelation in particular:

1.   Research the effect Revelation has had on contemporary popular culture. Investigate novels—fantasy or science fiction. View a film or a DVD of a television series that explores the themes of Revelation. Report your findings to the class.

2.   Use the library or the Internet to collect artistic interpretations of images in Revelation—the seven seals, the bowls, the trumpets, and the like. Make a visual presentation to the class. Be sure you can make the link to Revelation.

KEY BIBLICAL TEXTS

- Revelation 21:1–22:21; Ezekiel 40–48

DISCOVER

- How Revelation mirrors Genesis in a story of a new creation
- Different views of a New Jerusalem
- The influence of Revelation on art, literature, and popular culture

GET TO KNOW

- The Bride of the Lamb, the New Jerusalem

CONSIDER

- What are your deepest hopes for the future? How do these hopes sustain you in the present?

A New Jerusalem

The final two chapters of the Book of Revelation, John's vision of "a new heaven and a new earth," are not so much about the end of time as beyond the very concept of time. In these chapters, John shared his vision of the New Jerusalem (the new creation) and then drew to a close the letter that frames the Book of Revelation. These chapters provided comfort to the suffering first-century readers, as well as to believers through the ages:

> And I saw a new heaven and a new earth: for the first heaven and the first earth were passed away; and there was no more sea. And I John saw the holy city, new Jerusalem, coming down from God out of heaven, prepared as a bride adorned for her husband.
> *Revelation 21:1-2 [KJV]*

This is followed by an echo of both Genesis and Isaiah 66:22–23: "And the one who was seated on the throne said, 'See, I am making all things new'" (*Revelation 21:5 [NRSV]*). Just as God in the Genesis account created the heavens and the earth and in Isaiah made them new, here God re-creates them. The symbol of this new creation, the "New Jerusalem," is that of a bride. Using bridal imagery to describe the relationship of God and his creation is nothing new in scripture. In the Hebrew Scriptures there are many examples of this imagery, including the Book of Hosea and the Song of Solomon.

The bridal imagery is continued in a second vision: "Then one of the seven angels who had the seven bowls full of the seven last plagues came and said to me, 'Come, I will show you the bride, the wife of the Lamb'" (*Revelation 21:9 [NRSV]*).

Three Views of the New Jerusalem

Revelation provides not one description of the New Jerusalem, but three. First of all, it is described from an external perspective:

Altarpiece of St. John the Baptist and St. John the Evangelist. Right wing: *Apocalyptic Vision of Saint John the Evangelist.*

And in the spirit he carried me away to a great, high mountain and showed me the holy city Jerusalem coming down out of heaven from God. It has the glory of God and a radiance like a very rare jewel, like jasper, clear as crystal. It has a great, high wall with twelve gates, and at the gates twelve angels, and on the gates are inscribed the names of the twelve tribes of the Israelites; on the east three gates, on the north three gates, on the south three gates, and on the west three gates. And the wall of the city has twelve foundations, and on them are the twelve names of the twelve apostles of the Lamb.
Revelation 21:10-14 [NRSV]

A section of *The Apocalypse of Angers* tapestry by Nicolas Bataille illustrates the image of a New Jerusalem.

Here John was explicit in his symbolism of the twelve gates representing the twelve tribes of Israel and the twelve foundations representing the twelve apostles. In this combination of images he drew on the imagery of the Hebrew Scriptures and put it in a distinctive new light.

Also clarified in this section is the identity of the bride: the New Jerusalem. Just as the whore of Chapter 17 was a symbol of Babylon (the human city), so the bride is the symbol of the New Jerusalem (the divine city).

John went on to describe, in great detail, a second view of the city, this time in terms of its enormous dimensions. The city was fifteen hundred miles long and wide, and its shape was a perfect cube. Interestingly, this is the shape prescribed for the holy of holies in the Exodus account of the tent of meeting and later the temple. (Recall that the holy of holies is the place in the temple where the Israelites believed the presence of God dwelt.) This description is also reminiscent of Ezekiel's measuring of the temple area *(Ezekiel 40–41)*.

John next described in great detail the materials of which the city was built: gemstones, gold, and pearls. What sets this description apart from Ezekiel's, however, is that there was no temple in this city:

I saw no temple in the city, for its temple is the Lord God the Almighty and the Lamb. And the city has no need of sun or moon to shine on it, for the glory of God is its light, and its lamp is the Lamb. The nations will walk by its light, and the kings of the earth will bring their glory into it. Its gates will never be shut by day—and there will be no night there. People will bring into it the glory and the honor of the nations. But nothing unclean will enter it, nor anyone who practices abomination or falsehood, but only those who are written in the Lamb's book of life.
Revelation 21:22-27 [NRSV]

In his third and final vision in this last section of the book, John shifted from the imagery of the city to the imagery of a garden:

Then the angel showed me the river of the water of life, bright as crystal, flowing from the throne of God and of the Lamb through the middle of the street of the city. On either side of the river is the tree of life with its twelve kinds of fruit, producing its fruit each month; and the leaves of the tree are for the healing of the nations. Nothing accursed will be found there any more.
Revelation 22:1-3 [NRSV]

Taddeo Gaddi's *Tree of Life* applies the imagery of Genesis and the Book of Revelation to Jesus' death on a "tree."

With its images of the river and the tree of life, this vision mirrors the garden of Eden in Genesis 2 and 3. But, unlike the Genesis account, there was no serpent, there was no rebellion against God, and there was no darkness of night in this new garden. The tree of life was the centerpiece, and the description of it was amplified from the Genesis narrative.

John also described those who dwelt in the city: "The throne of God and of the Lamb will be in it, and his servants will worship him; they will see his face, and his name will be on their foreheads" *(Revelation 20:3–4 [NRSV])*. Here again is the imagery of a mark on the forehead, just as those who followed the beast had a mark to signify their allegiance (see Revelation 14:9 and 19:20).

The last verse of this section provides an epilogue for the entire Book of Revelation:

> These words are trustworthy and true, for the Lord, the God of the spirits of the prophets, has sent his angel to show his servants what must soon take place. See, I am coming soon! Blessed is the one who keeps the words of the prophecy of this book.
>
> *Revelation 22:6–7 [NRSV]*

Important elements in these final verses are the urgent statements on the part of the author and the church, calling upon Jesus to come and initiate the new kingdom:

> The Spirit and the bride say, "Come."
> And let everyone who hears say, "Come."
> Let anyone who wishes take the water of life as a gift.
>
> *Revelation 22:17 [NRSV]*

The second-to-last verse in the book contains one of the earliest Christian liturgical acclamations. It is a translation of the Aramaic **maranatha,** "Amen. Come, Lord Jesus!" *(Revelation 22:20b [NRSV]).*

Important Themes

These last chapters echo some important themes from both the Hebrew Scriptures and the New Testament. The theme of the new creation recalls the first chapters of Genesis. Also, there is an emphasis on a "new Israel." Israel is, throughout the Hebrew Scriptures and the New Testament, the image of the people of God. Revelation's images of the New Jerusalem contain a vision for a new Israel.

There is also the image of the temple. However, just as there is a new creation and a new Israel, so there is a new temple: God. Along with this new understanding of the human relationship with God, which will involve no new sacrifices to mediate between God and human beings, comes the bridal imagery. The intimate relationship of marriage is used to describe the relationship between God and the people—just as it had been used before in both the Hebrew Scriptures and the New Testament.

The Book of Revelation also embodies and reflects the message of the New Testament in several ways. Apocalyptic themes occur in the New Testament as early as the teaching of Jesus in the gospels. The Book of Revelation expands on these apocalyptic expectations. Revelation interprets further the death and resurrection of Jesus and his very identity, calling him the Lamb of God and

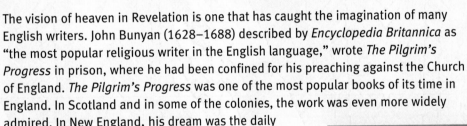

THE BIBLE
IN **Literature**

INSPIRED BY REVELATION

John Bunyan

T. S. Eliot

Archibald MacLeish

The vision of heaven in Revelation is one that has caught the imagination of many English writers. John Bunyan (1628–1688) described by *Encyclopedia Britannica* as "the most popular religious writer in the English language," wrote *The Pilgrim's Progress* in prison, where he had been confined for his preaching against the Church of England. *The Pilgrim's Progress* was one of the most popular books of its time in England. In Scotland and in some of the colonies, the work was even more widely admired. In New England, his dream was the daily subject of the conversation of thousands. He had numerous admirers in Holland and among the Protestant Huguenots of France. Most scholars acknowledge that *The Pilgrim's Progress* is the most successful allegory ever written. It is the one of the most commonly translated books by Protestant missionaries, and it is read in many languages.

In the nineteenth century, British Romantic poets William Wordsworth and Percy Bysshe Shelley embodied imagery from the Book of Revelation in their works (as in Wordsworth's *The Prelude* and Shelley's "Ode to the West Wind"). Early twentieth-century poetry was influenced by the horrors of World War I, which led some poets to apocalyptic images and expectations. For example, in William Butler Yeats, one can see apocalyptic imagery in individual poems such as "The Second Coming" and in his work called "A Vision." T. S. Eliot (1888–1965), in poems such as "The Hollow Men" and "The Wasteland," also drew on images similar to those in the Book of Revelation, as did American poet Archibald MacLeish (1892–1982) in his poem "The End of the World."

The title of this painting on the ceiling of the Church of St. Michael in Hildesheim, Germany, is *Jesus Christ as Pantocrator.* It shows Jesus as "ruler of all."

attributing to him divine characteristics. Finally, there is the concept of the church, discussed in detail in the letters of Paul, in its heavenly form as the New Jerusalem.

The final verse of Revelation recalls again the structure of the book: Just as the beginning was similar to other New Testament letters, so this closing verse echoes the closings of Paul's letters: "The grace of the Lord Jesus be with all the saints. Amen."

THE BIBLE
IN Literature

Charlotte Brontë, who wrote the novel *Jane Eyre,* published in 1847, was the daughter of a clergyman in Victorian England, a time when the head of the household usually read the Bible aloud while everyone else gathered around to listen; even homes where no one could read displayed the Bible prominently. Biblical allusions are everywhere in Brontë's novel. According to Catherine Brown Tkacz, *Jane Eyre* contains 176 spiritual allusions, at least eighty-one quotations and paraphrases from twenty-three books of Hebrew Scriptures and ninety-five from fifteen books of the New Testament. Brontë ends her novel with a description of the life of the secondary character whose given name is actually St. John, who becomes a missionary, instead of the heroine Jane. While St. John does not receive what readers might see as a happy ending for him, he receives the ending he wanted for himself, to be accepted into the arms of the Lord. The last line of the novel borrows the last lines of the Book of Revelation:

No fear of death will darken St. John's last hour: his mind will be unclouded; his heart will be undaunted; his hope will be sure; his faith steadfast. His own words are a pledge of this: "My master," he says, "has forewarned me. Daily he announces more distinctly—'Surely I come quickly!' and hourly I more eagerly respond—'Amen'; even so come, Lord Jesus!"

Charlotte Brontë

Revelation and Western Culture

Revelation has had a profound influence on Western culture—on literature, art, music, and even on popular culture. John's apocalyptic visions have shaped perceptions throughout the ages, especially in times of conflict or catastrophe—natural disasters, plagues, social strife, war. The Western understanding of the movement from suffering to redemption and the notion of an end time have been influenced by the Book of Revelation.

Revelation's pervasive influence on the world of literature can be found in the poetry of the Western tradition. For example, Dante Alighieri's great fourteenth-century epic *The Divine Comedy* draws on John's visions in its descriptions of hell, purgatory, and heaven.

Revelation is among the most widely illustrated books of the Bible. In the eighth century, the Spanish monk Beatus of Liebana wrote a commentary on the Book of Revelation that was then copied and illustrated by a number of artists. This was the origin of numerous cycles of illustrations known as "Beatus" manuscripts. The early manuscripts also inspired the Trier Apocalypse (c. 800) and the Bamberg Apocalypse (c. 1000). Another famous cycle, the Gulbenkian Apocalypse, was produced in thirteenth-century England, as was the Trinity Apocalypse now in the collections of Cambridge University.

Works based on the apocalypse were of course not confined to illuminated manuscripts. Church murals and altarpieces were also produced, as well as tapestries such as the Angers Tapestry woven in the fourteenth century by Nicolas Bataille. The exteriors of the great medieval cathedrals of Western Europe also incorporated much imagery from the Book of Revelation, particularly on their exterior doorways.

When the printing press was invented, woodcuts began to be produced to illustrate books. Perhaps the most famous of these are the Revelation woodcuts of Albrecht Dürer (1471–1528). Other artists who have dealt extensively with the Book of Revelation include William Blake (1757–1827), Gustave Doré (1832–1883), and Salvador Dalí (1904–1989).

The Book of Revelation has influenced music as well, beginning with the liturgical music of the church. For example, the famous chant "Dies Irae," filled with

This painting by Domenico di Michelino shows Dante reading from his epic poem, *The Divine Comedy.*

A detail of the tympanum of the south portal of Saint Pierre Abbey in Moissac, France, shows the twenty-four elders around the throne.

THE BIBLE

IN **Literature**

William Blake combined talent both in poetry and in visual art, and he illustrated many of his own poems. Much of his work was influenced by the themes and images of the Book of Revelation, though he worked those themes and images into his own personal mythological system. One example of his work, which shows the influence of Revelation, is his very large work *Jerusalem:*

> England! awake! awake! awake!
> Jerusalem thy Sister calls!
> Why wilt thou sleep the sleep of death?
> And close her from thy ancient walls.
>
> Thy hills and valleys felt her feet
> Gently upon their bosoms move:
> Thy gates beheld sweet Zion's ways:
> Then was a time of joy and love.
>
> And now the time returns again:
> Our souls exult, and London's towers
> Receive the Lamb of God to dwell
> In England's green and pleasant bowers.

From *Jerusalem* by William Blake

apocalyptic imagery, became part of the traditional Catholic funeral Mass, for which numerous composers have written settings. Also, several of Johann Sebastian Bach's cantatas have apocalyptic themes, as does Handel's famous *Messiah.* Contemporary composers whose works are based on the Book of Revelation include Gian Carlo Menotti ("Apocalypse"), Olivier Messiaen ("Quartet for the End of Time"), John Tavener ("The Apocalypse"), and Philip Wilby ("Revelation").

Contemporary popular culture also shows the influence of the Book of Revelation. Catholic novelist Michael O'Brien has written a set of apocalyptic novels. And some scholars also see apocalyptic themes in science fiction such as Ray Bradbury's *Farenheit 451;* Walter M. Miller, Jr.'s, *A Canticle for Leibowitz;* and Arthur C. Clarke's *Childhood's End.* Contemporary music also deals with these themes. For example, Rap artist Busta Rhymes deals with the imminent end of the world in his album *The Coming.* The rock group Rage Against the Machine, in albums such as *The Battle of Los Angeles,* deals with a struggle between good and evil and a coming time of tribulation. And apocalyptic themes are the stock in trade of the immensely popular "Left Behind" series of novels.

Revelation has also provided inspiration for films and television. Francis Ford Coppola saw evocations of Revelation in the Vietnam War and titled his film on the subject *Apocalypse Now.* The *Omen* series of films depicted the beast of Revelation being born into a well-to-do American family. Many television series, from the *Twilight Zone* to *Angel* to *Charmed,* have used aspects of Revelation as key plot elements.

This scene is from Francis Ford Coppola's movie *Apocalypse Now,* which interpreted the Vietnam War.

Conclusion

The Book of Revelation was written to meet the crisis needs of the early church, but its strong imagery and fantastic symbolism have profoundly influenced serious literature, music, and art for centuries. It has also provided a vocabulary for the feelings and frustrations of popular culture. It is important, however, to remember that films, novels, and paintings are not the book itself. It has a context in the canon of the Christian Scriptures, and it is within that context that it must be judged and interpreted.

projects

Choose one of the following projects to extend your knowledge of the Book of Revelation:

1. Find a copy of *The Pilgrim's Progress.* Locate some of Bunyan's writing on the Celestial City. How is his vision like that of Revelation? How does it differ? Share what you discover.

2. Search through movie listings or television schedules to find a film or show that uses apocalyptic imagery. View the film or program and report how that imagery is used. Is it used to inspire? to startle? to terrify? Report on your findings.

Unit Feature
Dante's *Purgatorio*

La Divina Commedia, or *The Divine Comedy,* by Dante Alighieri (1265–1321), uses the apocalypse genre to describe a journey through the afterlife, drawing on many of the images in the Book of the Revelation—the defeated Satan, the twenty-four elders, the four creatures, the seven lamps, the seven-headed beast, the Whore of Babylon, the rivers of Paradise, a history of the tribulation of the church that accords with the seven seals, and the exalted and glorified God of the universe at the end.

In *Purgatorio,* the second of the three parts of *The Divine Comedy,* Dante imagines purgatory as a mountain of seven stories or terraces, one for each of the seven deadly sins. Purgatory is located in a bulge pushed out of the opposite side of the earth by the crater that Satan's fall from heaven made. Its higher levels are closer to Paradise, its lower levels closer to Hell. Dante considers the deadly sins as offenses against love and groups them accordingly:

Perverted Love:	**Pride, Envy, Wrath or Anger**
Insufficient Love:	**Sloth**
Misdirected Love:	**Avarice or Greed, Gluttony, Lust**

Medieval Christianity had developed a notion that even after death many people still had to overcome the residual effects of earthly sin. This was accomplished in the state of purgatory. Souls in purgatory would eventually become fit for heaven after purging the last remnants of sin. It was on this notion that Dante built his *Purgatorio.*

THE FIRST TERRACE

Canto X to Canto XXXI describe the seven terraces of the seven deadly sins. Before he may enter purgatory, Dante's forehead is marked seven times with the letter *P* (for the Italian *peccato,* meaning "sin"). In Canto X, Dante and the Roman poet Virgil encounter the Prideful, who, beating their breasts, make their way around a ledge under a heavy weight that they carry on their backs. Dante recognizes three of his former fellow countrymen. One acknowledges that the sin of pride has ruined not only himself but his entire household. Another proclaims the empty glory of human talent. An Angel of Humility comes to remove the first *P* from Dante's forehead, and the first of the Beatitudes from the Gospel of Matthew is heard: "Blessed are the poor in spirit." As the first *P* disappears, Dante feels lighter and is able to climb the mountain with less effort.

THE SECOND TERRACE

As Dante and Virgil walk along the second terrace, they hear a disembodied voice crying out examples of generosity, the virtue that is the opposite of envy. Two of the examples are from the gospels; one is from Greek history. Dante then becomes aware of how envy is punished: The penitents are sitting side by side against a rock, reciting a prayer. They are dressed in coarse haircloth; their eyelids have been stitched shut with iron thread. Dante talks to a woman from Siena, who confesses she rejoiced in the defeat of her own townsmen in a battle. In the passage from the second to the third terrace, Dante is stunned by the light emanating from the Angel of Fraternal Love, who performs the ritual of passage with the cleansing of the second *P* and the singing of a second Beatitude, "Blessed are the merciful."

THE THIRD TERRACE

On the third terrace Dante encounters the Wrathful. The poet's first experience consists of three examples of meekness, the virtue opposite of wrath. These come in ecstatic visions: The first is the Virgin Mary questioning Jesus after he had stayed behind in the temple *(Luke 4);* the second is of a man who forgives the man who embraced his daughter; and the third is Lazarus, the first man to die and be resurrected in the Bible. As Dante emerges from the cloud of smoke that surrounds the Wrathful, the sun is about to set. The Angel of

Statue of Dante in Verona, Italy.

Meekness appears and points the way to continue the journey up the mountain. Another *P* is removed from Dante's forehead, and the poet hears another Beatitude: "Blessed are the peacemakers."

THE FOURTH TERRACE

As Dante and Virgil reach the next level, they are weak and take rest from the journey. This is the terrace of the Slothful. Night has arrived, and Virgil takes advantage of the pause to talk to Dante about the nature of love, showing that all the sins in purgatory derive from one of the three perversions of love. As Dante is about to fall asleep, a group of penitents rushes from behind. These are the Slothful. They walk fast, shouting examples of the virtue of solicitude—the opposite of sloth. Eventually, as the two poets begin their third day, the Angel of Zeal appears and washes away another *P* from Dante's forehead while they hear the Beatitude, "Blessed are they who mourn."

THE FIFTH TERRACE

On the fifth terrace, Dante and Virgil encounter the Avaricious. As they proceed through the terrace, they hear someone calling out examples of the virtue opposite to greed. The speaker denounces his descendants for their avarice. Then he explains that the penitents keep reciting examples of condemnation of greed. In leaving the fifth terrace, Dante and Virgil, along with the Roman poet Statius, who has been freed from this level, are directed by the Angel of Liberality, who removes another *P* from Dante's forehead.

THE SIXTH TERRACE

On the next level, the travelers encounter the Gluttonous. They see in the middle of the road a tree with sweet-smelling fruits and a cascade of fresh water raining down on the leaves. From the tree comes a voice shouting examples of moderation, a virtue opposite to gluttony. Dante recognizes several of the souls, including a friend who was a late repentant and dead for only five years, who tells Dante that it had been his wife's prayers that helped him advance up the mountain. As the poets come to the end of the terrace, the Angel of Temperance wipes out the sixth *P* from Dante's forehead.

THE SEVENTH TERRACE

On the last terrace, the poets encounter a wall of fire. From inside the flames, Dante hears a song and sees the souls of the Lustful. Then the poets see examples of chastity, the virtue opposite to lust. They are followed by examples of husbands and wives who observe the laws of virtuous marriage. As the day ends, Dante is still afraid to enter the fire and go to the other side. He then encounters the Angel of Chastity, who removes the last *P* and recites the last Beatitude: "Blessed are the pure in

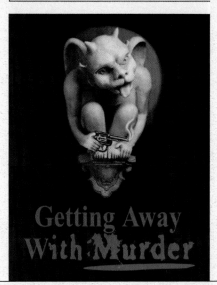

The play by Stephen Sondheim and George Furth is a comedy/mystery exploring human weakness in the context of the deadly sins.

heart." The Angel reminds Dante that he can go no farther without passing through the flames. As Dante hesitates a long time, Virgil urges him to go through, reminding him that his love Beatrice is waiting for him. Dante then enters the excruciating heat.

THE CONCLUSION

Purgatorio ends with the approach of a heavenly pageant. In imagery drawn from the Book of the Revelation, the pageant is led by seven golden candlesticks, which produce a light that extends over the following procession. Next come twenty-four elders, two by two. Behind them, four creatures form a square in which there is a chariot drawn by a griffin. To the right of the chariot are three women, to the left four women, and finally an old man alone—the author of the Book of Revelation. As the procession comes to a halt, the twenty-four elders turn toward the chariot. One of them sings: "Come, O Bride from Lebanon." A hundred singing angels appear overhead, filling the air with a rain of flowers.

The deadly sins of the seven terraces are staples of both literature and art. In the centuries after Dante, the sins provided plot lines for Chaucer's *Canterbury Tales* and, later, the inspiration for many of the paintings of Hieronymus Bosch. In the twentieth century, the seven deadly sins were the subject of a ballet and opera by Kurt Weil and Berthold Brecht in 1933; a series of books by C. S. Lewis, *The Chronicles of Narnia,* where each volume represents one of the sins; watercolors by Salvador Dalí to illustrate Dante; a 1996 play by George Furth and Stephen Sondheim, *Getting Away with Murder;* and a 2002 book by Dan Savage, *Skipping towards Gomorrah: The Seven Deadly Sins and the Pursuit of Happiness in America.*

UNIT FOURTEEN

Epilogue

For you were called to freedom, brothers and sisters; only do not use your freedom as an opportunity for self-indulgence, but through love become slaves to one another. For the whole law is summed up in a single commandment, "You shall love your neighbor as yourself."

Galatians 5:13–14 [NRSV]

In this unit you will discover

- The role the English Bible played in the development of literacy and language

- The impact the first English Bible had on the people of its time

- How that influence continues today in a legacy of both freedom and faith

LOOK BACK

■ Take a moment to page back through this textbook. Pause at each chapter and make a note of one important lesson the chapter provided.

CONSIDER

■ What is the importance for you as a student of having a basic overview of the literature of the Bible?

The Bible and Literacy
A Review

The purpose of this textbook has been to give you some very basic literacy concerning the Bible. To accomplish this, you have surveyed the Hebrew Scriptures and the New Testament. You have had a chance to read sections of the Bible, and you have seen the influence of the Bible on language, on literature, on art, on music, and on public policy and national ideals. You have met many of the people whose actions, lives, and stories make up this great literary feat. Down through the centuries, the Bible has also nourished another important component of human life—literacy.

Literacy and Freedom

Simply put, literacy is the ability to read and write. The word also carries with it the meaning of "education," or "culture." The first step toward literacy is the command of oral language. In the early days of civilization, few people knew or used written language. They learned command of

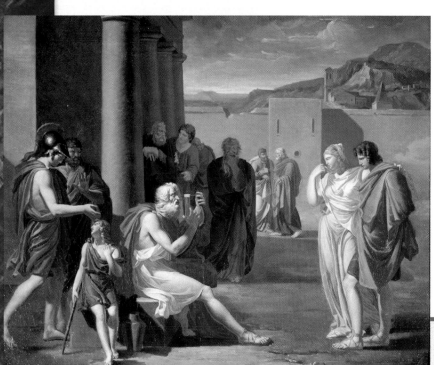

language from the storytellers. The great epics of Greek literature, Homer's *Iliad* and *Odyssey,* were told as stories, and the storytelling was a community event. It not only provided entertainment but stressed and clarified the most basic values and beliefs of the ancient Greeks.

The Bible served a similar function in the development of English, in teaching both oral and written language. The Bible provided a common narrative and vocabulary for looking at life's questions: "Who are we?" "Why are we here?" "What is our purpose?" "What are we to do?"

Homer Singing with His Lyre by Felix Boisselier.

The biblical content was contained in quite sophisticated literary forms. It was redacted, compiled, edited, and copied meticulously by hand. Although literacy may have been limited, the Bible and its contents were preserved extremely well.

Into the Middle Ages, frescoes, stained glass, and the very architecture of cathedrals told biblical accounts in visual terms. The words of the Bible were read in Latin or Greek or Hebrew for the scholars and the worshipers. Morality

A Decade of Literacy
2003 to 2012

The United Nations Educational, Scientific and Cultural Organization (UNESCO) has dedicated an entire decade to the pursuit of universal literacy. UNESCO describes its own goals as follows: "Literacy efforts have so far failed to reach the poorest and most marginalized groups, and priority attention will be given to the most disadvantaged groups, especially women and girls, ethnic and linguistic minorities, indigenous populations, migrants and refugees, disabled persons, and out-of-school children and youth. The implementation of the decade's plan of action is structured around biennial themes such as gender, poverty, health, peace, and freedom."

At the launch ceremony at U.N. headquarters in New York, Deputy Secretary-General Louise Fréchette said, "Literacy remains part of the unfinished business of the twentieth century. One of the success stories of the twenty-first century must be the extension of literacy to include all humankind. . . . When women are educated and empowered, the benefits can be seen immediately: families are healthier, they are better fed; their income, savings, and reinvestments go up. And what is true of families is true of communities, indeed, of whole countries."

Koïchiro Matsuura

UNESCO Director-General Koïchiro Matsuura also spoke at the ceremony: "Through literacy, the downtrodden can find their voice, the poor can learn how to learn, and the powerless can empower themselves. The drive for universal literacy is integrally linked to the human rights agenda. Literacy is not a universal panacea for all development problems, but as a tool of development, it is both versatile and proven. Literacy is freedom."

Laura Bush, the wife of President George W. Bush, serves as Honorary Ambassador to the United Nations for the Decade of Literacy. In her remarks at a ceremony at the New York Public Library celebrating the start of the decade, she stressed that education is "the most important long-term investment all of us make in our future." She highlighted the need to turn the ideal of universal literacy into a reality: "Advancing education is fundamental to the development of nations and of generations. These are not simply goals for the next decade; these are moral responsibilities every nation must embrace."

Mrs. Bush further announced that the United States, which recently rejoined UNESCO after an absence of eighteen years, has set aside $333 million for international primary, secondary, and college education. Of that amount, about $100 million is to be spent in Africa.

Laura Bush acting in her role as Ambassador for the Decade of Literacy.

plays, pageants, and passion plays kept the plotlines, characters, and events part of every person's intellectual treasure.

In addition to the plays, there were trained storytellers in England, as there had been in Greece. In the fourteenth century, a group know as the Lollards, trained and inspired by John Wycliffe (who had translated the Bible into English), went throughout the land engaged in the subversive activity of sharing the words of the Bible in English. The Lollards' activity gave the common people a common narrative and an oral vocabulary. And this common narrative and vocabulary left the people hungry to read the texts for themselves.

The situation in medieval England is reflected in modern African villages, where illiteracy can be the lot of over 90 percent of the population. There, hearing biblical accounts in their own language again inspires people to want to learn to read those accounts on their own. The inherent power of the words and thoughts of the Bible are such that biblical storytellers did not so much need to bring those stories to life as (so one storyteller put it) to "be sure not to kill them."

In Print

Time Magazine, in a "millennium edition" in 2000, cited Gutenberg's invention of printing with movable type as the high-water mark of the previous millennium. This breakthrough in printing put the written word into the hands of ordinary people. It is not without reason that the first book to be printed by Gutenberg was the Bible. Today the Bible remains the most widely printed and distributed book. For almost 600 years, the Bible has motivated people to want to read and has been the tool that taught them how.

In the United States, even today there are some adults who cannot read and write but want to learn. Ruth Colvin founded Literacy Volunteers of America in the 1960s. (The organization is now called Proliteracy.) Responding to a demand from churchgoing adults who had no more than a third-grade education, she developed a program to teach adults basic reading and writing skills from Bible stories that they already know orally.

A working model of Gutenberg's press.

An Impact on English

You have seen what a great impact the English translation of the Bible had on the English language. In this, the Bible has had influence beyond its religious content. Leaving out all the religious literature, sermons, and commentaries, the Bible influenced the English so greatly because it was meant to be translated. It is not the language of the Bible that is important or sacred. It is the content. And that content is for everyone—in his or her own language. In Eastern Christianity, the Bible was always translated into the language of the people. The Armenian alphabet, as well as the alphabet developed by Cyril and Methodius for the Slavs, was created precisely to translate the Bible into local languages.

The Latin version of the Bible arrived in England in the second and third centuries. In the seventh century, a musical monk named Caedmon took accounts from the Bible and put them to song in the local language. John Wycliffe was the first to

THE BIBLE

AND **Language**

Review some of the important characteristics of the early translations of the Bible into English:

1. The vocabulary of the Bible was not as large as that of some other works. For example, Shakespeare's writings used somewhere between 15,000 and 24,000 different words (estimates vary). The whole English Bible uses about 6000.

2. The translators stayed close to the simple language and structure of the original Hebrew. Hebrew is a language not of abstract terms but of concrete images. One simple sentence follows another, often beginning with a connective. In the first ten chapters of 1 Samuel, for example, there are 238 verses. One hundred and sixty of them begin with an "and"; only twenty-six verses have no connective words.

3. Descriptions are straightforward. For example, God is described in everyday terms. God is a shepherd, a husbandman threshing grain or treading a winepress. Simple metaphors make the language accessible.

4. The translators chose predominantly short, strong words. The average word in the English Bible contains but five letters. For example, in the King James Version, the Twenty-third Psalm contains 119 words. Ninety-five of them are of one syllable, and only three have three syllables. There are no longer words.

5. There are very few Latin derivatives in the translations. For example, people don't *prevaricate;* they *lie.*

6. The accounts are very direct and quite dramatic, written with an economy of words. For example, it is nearly impossible to read aloud Elijah's encounter with the priests of Queen Jezebel on Mount Carmel *(1 Kings 18:21–39)* without dramatic expression.

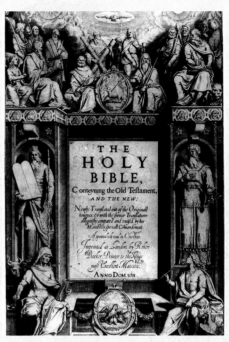

The title page from a 1772 edition of the King James Bible.

7. The translation emulates the lilt of Hebrew poetry, resulting in a rhythm in the English that makes the poetry easy to set to music.

The English essayist Joseph Addison commented on the translation of the English Bible, "If any one would judge of the beauties of poetry that are to be met within the divine writings and examine how kindly the Hebrew manners of speech mix and incorporate with the English language, after having perused the book of Psalms, let him read a literal translation of Horace or Pindar. He will find in these two last such an absurdity and confusion of style with such a comparative poverty of imagination as will make him very sensible of what I have been here advancing" (*The Spectator,* No. 405, 1712).

translate the Bible into English, in 1382. From the very beginning his focus was on opening the Bible to the average person.

Yet his passion was not greeted with great enthusiasm by some clerics and nobles. And so, in the Oxford Convocation of 1406, translating the Bible into English was outlawed in England.

Almost a century later, William Tyndale, a masterful linguist and writer, dared to make an English translation. He benefited from Gutenberg's press; and, despite laws to the contrary, the Bible was now in the hands of the "ploughboy."

John Wycliffe Reading His Translation of the Bible to John of Gaunt by Ford Maddox Brown (1821–1893).

Tyndale's reward was execution, but his legacy was an English language that had the weight and dignity and vocabulary it needed to grow into the powerful world language it has become. Less than two years after Tyndale's death, King Henry VII authorized the publication of an English translation of the Bible.

Even after more than three thousand translations of the Bible into English, the language of Tyndale prevails. For example, about 80 percent of the King James Version of the New Testament is from Tyndale. You have been learning the words and phrases from the Bible that have become standard in everyday English—such as "apple of my eye," "stranger in a strange land," or "a thorn in my side." In their book *Coined by God: Words and Phrases That First Appeared in the English Language through the Bible,* Professors Stanley Malless and Jeffrey McQuain discussed 131 words and phrases that had their origin in the translation of the Bible. These entries represent only a fraction of the English words, phrases, rhythms, patterns, and idioms that have the Bible as their source. That means they have no earlier recorded history in written or printed form.

The Impact on People

The translation of the Bible had a revolutionary impact on the common person in England. When first printed in 1526 in Europe and shipped to England, the Bible became the first widely distributed printed book in the country. By the mid-sixteenth century, it was the most frequently purchased book in England.

The translation and printing of the English Bible had several major effects on the people:

1. *Engagement in ideas:* The translation gave people greater access to ideas and a more sophisticated vocabulary to discuss them.
2. *Unification of language:* The translation did much to standardize spoken English among the speakers of many dialects.
3. *A professional language:* The translation helped move the language of law, medicine, and education from Latin to English.
4. *Codification:* The translation helped establish and stabilize the meanings of many words and phrases still used in modern English.

The Bible can inspire social action. These two teenagers have volunteered their time for Habitat for Humanity, an organization that builds and provides low-income housing.

5. *Personal reading and writing:* The translation was a boon to literacy. Average people were motivated to learn to read and to gain the freedom to express themselves in writing as well.

The popularity of the Bible grew rapidly and helped the English language to flower, to develop a richness conducive to the plays of Shakespeare, the poetry of Spencer, and the music of Handel.

A Literary Standard

Although the Bible clearly was written, compiled, and translated as a sacred text, it nevertheless sets an extraordinary literary standard. The British essayist and historian Thomas Babington Macaulay wrote of the English Bible, "In a period when the English language was imperiled there appeared the English Bible, a book which, if everything else in our language should perish, would alone suffice to show the extent of its beauty and power" (*Essay on Dryden*).

The reasons for the Bible's primacy as a literary standard are many. You have seen and examined the literary forms found in the Bible—narrative, poetry, song, chronicles, gospels, letters, and the like. Those forms were important in the original languages of the Bible—Hebrew, Aramaic, Greek, and others. When those forms were translated into English, they had an effect on English literary form.

The content of the Bible itself was important, too. The ancestor stories, the Sinai covenant, the fall of the kingdoms, the words of the prophets, the proverbs, the psalms, the suffering of Job, the apocalyptic reassurances—all dealt with the struggles, defeats, and triumphs of the human spirit. They dealt with promises and covenants—kept and broken. They dealt with colossal ideas and with household codes. And even extracted from the powerful religious context, the content of the Bible was the content of life.

Finally, as you have seen many times in your academic study of the Bible, the accounts, characters, and stories found there have provided material for writers, painters, musicians, and sculptors. The Bible has found its way into every corner of culture, so much so that it is fair to say that without a basic knowledge of the Bible, one's education is incomplete.

The painting by contemporary artist Robert Moseley entitled *But Revealed to the Babes* (a phrase from Luke 10:21) demonstrates the Bible's continuing influence.

The Bible Today

Even if the Bible did not continue to influence language, literature, and culture today, it would be important to study. But after thousands of years, the Bible still exerts its influence. What happened with the English Bible in the fifteenth and sixteenth centuries is still going on. Several factors contribute to this continuing influence:

1. *Bible distribution and ownership:* The United Bible Society, based in Reading, England, reports that the sale of Bibles approaches 500 million a year. The Christian Booksellers Association estimates the annual revenue from Bibles approaches $5 billion. In addition, organizations like the Gideons distribute Bibles at the rate of over 50 million a year. According to a survey by George Barna of the Barna Group (a marketing research firm in Ventura, California), 92 percent of American households own at least one Bible.
2. *Bible reading:* The Bible is one book that millions of people read regularly. A Gallup poll discovered that 39 percent of Americans read the Bible at least weekly, and 59 percent read it at least occasionally. According to the same survey, Americans accord the Bible a high degree of credibility. Finally, eight of ten Americans believe the Bible has wisdom that can help with "most or all" of life's problems.
3. *Weekly worship:* The Bible is alive and well within the churches and synagogues throughout the land. It is read aloud every week. The role of religion is still much respected in the United States, and religious faith guides and motivates a majority of its citizens. Over 80 percent of Americans consider their faith important to life and feel quite strongly about their beliefs. Almost 40 percent of Americans worship in a church,

synagogue, or mosque at least weekly. Although the Bible is interpreted differently by Christians and Jews and by the adherents of different Christian denominations, it is being read aloud, proclaimed, and commented on each week.

4. *Popular culture:* The Bible, its contents, and its language are all part of music, movies, and television programs with biblical themes. Endeavors like the Jesus Film Project have fostered people's desire to read the New Testament. Dr. Eugene Habecker, past president of the American Bible Society, has noted that "Our need for meaning—to find a heroic figure— shows itself in a tireless fascination with Jesus, who continues to get more media exposure than any other history maker." Christian contemporary music based on the psalms and verses from the Bible is a major industry. There are Christian radio stations, youth rallies, and other events that keep the Bible high in the country's consciousness.

summary

The Bible continues to influence language, literature, and culture. It is at the heart of the Christian and Jewish faiths, whose followers comprise one-third of the world's population and 86 percent of the population of the United States. The Bible is present in novels, in poems, in movies, on television. And, of course, its influence pervades Western culture down through the ages. In taking this course on the Bible and its influence on literature and culture, you have equipped yourself to have a greater understanding of the world in which you live, and you have positioned yourself for a full and complete education.

Unit Feature

Freedom and Faith in America

SAVE FREEDOM OF WORSHIP
EACH ACCORDING TO THE DICTATES OF HIS OWN CONSCIENCE

NORMAN ROCKWELL

BUY WAR BONDS

The Freedom of Worship, from a series of paintings on "the four freedoms" by Norman Rockwell.

The themes of freedom and faith have been entwined in America from the earliest days of European settlement. **Pluralism** became a distinctive feature of life in America—people of many faiths, races, ethnic and cultural groups, all seeking to live together in one nation and under one government. It has been said that religious liberty makes pluralism more likely; pluralism makes religious liberty more necessary.

THE 1600s

Roger Williams (1603–1683), the founder and first governor of Rhode Island, was exiled from the Massachusetts Bay Colony for his religious convictions. Chief among them was his determination to respect the religious views of those with whom he disagreed. Williams was a devout man, but his very devotion gave him a unique view of community. Williams insisted that it was against the will of God for any government to interfere in matters of faith. He pointed out that coercion in matters of faith had led to bloodshed or at least hypocrisy. People need, he contended, "soul liberty," even if they are wrong, because only a free conscience can know the truth.

King Charles II incorporated Roger Williams's concern for religions freedom into the charter for the colony of Rhode Island:

> We have therefore thought fit, and do hereby publish, grant, ordain, and declare that our royal will and pleasure is, that no person within the said colony, at any time hereafter shall be anywise molested, punished, disquieted, or called in question, for any differences in opinion in matters of religion, and do not actually disturb the civil peace of our said colony; but that all and every person and persons may, from time to time, and at all times hereafter, freely and fully have and enjoy his and their own judgments and consciences in matters of religious concernments.

THE 1700s

Freedom and faith in the eighteenth century came together in one of the founding documents of the United States. The First Amendment to the Constitution, drafted by Congress in 1789, defined five rights: freedom of religion, of speech, of the press, and of assembly and the right to petition. The first sixteen words include a provision for religious liberty and at the same time prohibit the establishment of a national religion:

> Congress shall make no law respecting an establishment of religion, or prohibiting the free exercise thereof; or abridging the freedom of speech, or of the press; or the right of people peaceably to assemble, and to petition the Government for a redress of grievances.

In 1787, Congress enacted the Northwest Ordinance. The ordinance provided the framework for the creation of three to five new states in the territory from Ohio to the Mississippi. Article 3 of that ordinance stated:

> Religion, morality, and knowledge, being necessary to good government and the happiness of mankind, schools and the means of education shall forever be encouraged.

The views of the early presidents on the relationship of faith and freedom are well summed up in George Washington's 1796 farewell address to the nation:

> Of all the dispositions and habits, which lead to political prosperity, religion and morality are indispensable supports. Whatever may be conceded to the influence of refined education on minds of peculiar structure, reason and experience both forbid us to expect that national morality can prevail in exclusion of religious principle.

THE 1800s

Alexis de Tocqueville (1805–1859) was a French aristocrat who toured the United States to observe the American people and their institutions. In his book *Democracy in America,* published in 1835 and in 1840, he noted:

> Upon my arrival in the United States, the religious aspect of the country was the first thing that struck my attention; and the longer I stayed there, the more I perceived the great political consequences resulting from this new state of things.

> Religion in America . . . must be regarded as the foremost of the political institutions of that country; for if it does not impart a taste for freedom, it facilitates the use of it. Indeed, it is in the same point of view that the inhabitants of the United States themselves look upon religious belief.

> I sought for the key to the greatness and genius of America in her harbors . . . in her fertile fields, in her boundless forests, in her rich mines and vast world commerce; in her public school systems and institutions of learning. I sought for it in her democratic Congress and her matchless Constitution. Not until I went into the churches of America and heard her pulpits flame with righteousness did I understand the secret of her genius and power.

THE 1900s

Woodrow Wilson (1856–1924) was president of the United States during World War I. In his war message to Congress in 1917, he gave this conclusion:

> To such a task we can dedicate our lives and our fortunes, everything that we are and everything that we have, with the pride of those who know that the day has come when America is privileged to spend her blood and her might for the principles that gave her birth and happiness and the peace which she has treasured. God helping her, she can do no other.

Franklin Delano Roosevelt (1882–1945) made a memorable speech to Congress on January 6, 1941, that became known as the "Four Freedoms Speech." Here is what he said about the freedom of religion:

> The second [of those four freedoms] is the freedom of every person to worship God in his own way. This nation has placed its destiny in the hands and heads and hearts of its millions of free men and women, and its faith in freedom under the guidance of God.

TODAY

In his book *Jesus in Beijing,* the journalist David Aikman tells of a lecture he attended in China in 2002. A professor from the Chinese Academy of Social Sciences had this to say to a group of American visitors about his years of study in the West:

> One of the things we were asked to look into was what accounted for the success, in fact, the pre-eminence of the West over all the world. We studied everything we could from the historical, political, economic, and cultural perspective. At first, we thought it was because you had more powerful guns than we had. Then we thought it was because you had the best political system. Next we focused on your economic system. But in the past twenty years, we have realized that the heart of your culture is your religion: Christianity. The moral foundation of social and cultural life was what made possible the emergence of capitalism and then the successful transition to democratic politics. We don't have any doubt about this.

As did Tocqueville, this scholar from another land had come to understand the power of freedom and faith in the life of the nation.

glossary

abyss (p. 29): "Formless and void" primal chaos before the creation.

Ancient of Days (p. 180): Another name for the God of Israel.

anger (p. 147): One of the seven deadly sins; unjustified hatred, rage, and violence.

apocalyptic (pp. 175, 302): Writing concerning dire prophecies of the end times but using elaborate codes to provide hope to people in distress. To those familiar with the code, the narratives and visions reveal a message of hope and transformation. From the Greek word *apocalypse*, meaning *revelation*.

Apocrypha (p. 201): Writings that are part of Jewish lore but do not appear in the Hebrew Scriptures. They were included in the Greek Septuagint and are part of the Christian tradition. They are recognized as Scriptures by the Roman Catholics and Eastern Orthodox but not by most Protestants. From a Greek word meaning "hidden." *See also* Deuterocanonical.

apology (p. 292): In the rhetorical sense, a formal justification.

apostate (p. 251): One who renounces a religious faith.

apostle (p. 282): Someone who is sent on a mission or commissioned to spread the gospel. Refers especially to Jesus' original disciples and Paul.

archangel (p. 181): A member of one of the higher orders of angels.

Areopagus (p. 272): A low hill in Athens dedicated to the Greek war god, Ares. A meeting place for the justice courts, politicians, and philosophers. Also the name of the council of advisors who met there.

ark of the covenant (p. 75): Richly decorated chest that held the stone tablets that bore the Ten Commandments.

Armageddon (p. 349): Site of the final great battle between the forces of good and evil, as described in Revelation.

ascension (p. 255): The rise of Jesus up to heaven following his resurrection.

avarice (p. 147): One of the seven deadly sins; unjust coveting or acquisition of money, property, and material goods.

beatitudes (p. 229): The declarations of blessedness made by Jesus in the Sermon on the Mount. From the Latin word for *happiness* or *blessedness*.

birthright (p. 55): An inheritance; something to which one is entitled by birth.

bishop (p. 305): A church office first mentioned by Paul in 1 Timothy. Over time, the bishop became the primary authority over a region of Christian churches. The office of bishop is found in a number of Christian denominations.

blasphemy (pp. 162, 220): Insult, contempt, or lack of reverence for God; or, claiming attributes of the deity.

canticle (p. 83): A song or chant.

cardinal virtues (p. 146): In medieval Christian thought, the four habits upon which other moral behavior hinges-prudence, justice, temperance, and fortitude.

chiasm (pp. 43, 139): A form of parallelism in Hebrew poetry, inverting the structure of a sentence or a portion of a text to form a mirror image rather than a simple echo. An example can be seen in the first and last parts of Genesis.

church (p. 294): In most of the New Testament, the local community of Christians. In Paul's letter to the Ephesians, the universal body of believers.

church councils (p. 271): Formal gatherings of church leaders from all regions to make decisions on doctrine.

commonwealth (p. 163): In the philosophy of Thomas Hobbes, a voluntary banding together of people under one ruler or one assembly for the peace and safety of all.

conversion (p. 264): A decisive, dramatic change of heart and mind.

covenant (p. 50): A formal, solemn, and binding agreement.

creed (pp. 243, 271): A brief, authorized statement of religious belief.

cult (p. 299): A small group of people with great devotion to a system of religious beliefs.

day of the Lord (p. 125): A term for God's final judgment of humankind.

deacons (p. 260): In the early church, persons chosen to help with the physical needs of a congregation. In the later development of Christianity, deacons came to be regarded as official ministers of the church. In some denominations, they are ordained. From the Greek word for "service."

deadly sins (p. 146): In medieval Christian thought, the seven vices of pride, envy, anger, lust, sloth, avarice, and gluttony.

Decalogue (p. 74): Greek term for the Ten Commandments.

Deuterocanonical (p. 201): Another word used to describe the Apocrypha; from the Greek for "second canon," because these books were accepted after the first canon of Christian Scriptures was set.

diatribe (p. 281): Rhetorical technique of raising potential false conclusions or objections to an argument and refuting them.

disciples (p. 220): The twelve who formed the inner circle of Jesus' followers; more generally, those who believe and help to spread the doctine of a teacher or leader.

dominion (p. 31): English translation of the term describing the relationship between the first humans and other living things; the Hebrew word has the gentler and more familial connotation of stewardship.

doxology (p. 230): An expression of praise to God, especially a short hymn sung as part of a worship service.

Eden (p. 31): Garden created by God as the home of the first humans.

elegy (p. 138): One of three types of psalm; a poem of personal or communal sorrow. Also called a *lament*.

envy (p. 147): One of the seven deadly sins; a refusal to acknowledge or enjoy one's gifts, while constantly yearning for more and resenting what others have.

eschatological (p. 325): Dealing with the end times; based on the Greek term *eschaton*, meaning "end."

Eucharist (p. 290): Ceremony celebrating Jesus' Last Supper; from the Greek word for "giving thanks."

eunuch (p. 263): A man who has been castrated and therefore is incapable of sexual relations.

exemplary atonement (p. 276): Term used to describe Jesus' love and self-sacrifice as an example to be imitated and followed.

exodus (p. 64): An emigration, or mass departure.

exorcism (p. 220): The driving out of evil spirits.

fulfillment citation (p. 228): The use of typology to show how an Old Testament prophecy is fulfilled in the New Testament.

fortitude (p. 147): The habit of courage in choosing what is right; one of the four cardinal virtues.

gleaning (p. 165): Gathering the stalks of grain left behind for the poor when the reapers had finished harvesting a field.

gloss (p. 230): A brief explanation or interpretation of a difficult or obscure word or expression, often in the margin or between the lines of a text.

gluttony (p. 147): One of the seven deadly sins; overindulgence in food and drink.

Gnostics (p. 208): Members of certain sects among the early Christians that taught great separation between material and spiritual things. Gnostics based these and their other beliefs on hidden or special knowledge.

Great Awakening (p. 283): The period in American colonial history that consisted of a series of religious revivals that spread throughout the colonies between the 1720s and 1740s.

Hanukkah (p. 203): Jewish festival celebrating the military success of Judas Maccabeus and his army over Antiochus and the rededication of the Jerusalem temple by Judas Maccabeus. The word *Hanukkah* means "dedication." The festival is also called the "Feast of Lights."

Hellenists (p. 260): Greek-speaking Jews.

high priest (p. 317): During the later period of the Hebrew Scriptures, essentially the "first among equals" of the priests at the temple in Jerusalem, who came to hold much authority with the people.

holy of holies (p. 75): Resting place of the ark of the covenant within the tabernacle.

house church (p. 310): Home where the members of the early Christian community met for worship and fellowship.

infancy narrative (p. 227): The story of a birth, especially Jesus' birth at the beginning of Matthew's gospel.

intercalation (p. 221): The placing of one narrative in the midst of another, so that the center narrative sheds light on the one that frames it.

Israel (p. 56): The new name given to Jacob as a sign of the renewal of God's covenant with the descendants of Abraham.

Israelites (p. 64): Descendants of Jacob.

jubilee year (p. 77): Under Jewish law, as established in Leviticus, slaves were offered their freedom once in every fifty years. In medieval Christian tradition, a time of pilgrimage to Rome every fifty years for the remission of sins.

judges (p. 83): Rulers of the Israelites during the period between the death of Joshua and the kingship of Saul.

justice (p. 147): The habit of fairness and honesty; one of the four cardinal virtues.

Ketuvim (p. 18): The third and final section of the Hebrew Scriptures. From the Hebrew word for "writings."

lament: *See* elegy.

land of milk and honey (p. 66): The "good and broad land" God promised Moses and his people in Exodus.

levirate marriage (p. 167): Under this tradition, when a married man died without children, his closest unmarried male relative (usually a brother if he had one) was obliged to marry the widow and father a child. That child would be, legally and religiously, the heir of the dead man.

liturgy (p. 23): Structured public worship.

lust (p. 147): One of the seven deadly sins; mindless sexual appetite or illicit sexual behavior.

magi (p. 228): Latin word for the three "wise men" who came to the infant Jesus. (Singular: *magus.*)

manna (p. 73): Food from heaven provided to the Israelites during their forty years of migration in the desert.

maranatha (p. 354): Aramaic liturgical acclamation: "The Lord is coming."

menorah (p. 203): A candlestick with eight branches, traditionally used in the celebration of Hannukah.

mercy (p. 125): Compassion or forbearance shown to someone under one's power; an act of divine favor.

midrash (p. 194): An interpretation or exposition of the meaning of a biblical text.

Millennium (p. 350): In John's vision in the Book of Revelation, the thousand years during which holiness is to prevail and Jesus is to reign on earth.

minor prophets (p. 124): Also known as "the twelve"; most were active before or during the Babylonian exile of the Jews.

monotheist (p. 53): Worshipper of one god.

Mosaic Law (p. 72): The laws of the Sinai covenant between God and the Israelites.

Mount Sinai (p. 73): Site of Moses' encounter with God and receipt of God's commandments.

mystery religion (p. 299): A cult devoted to secret knowledge and rites.

natural law (pp. 75, 282): The basic moral truths that people of goodwill can recognize through reason and conscience; the idea of knowing God's will through creation.

nature miracle (p. 220): A wondrous event involving the forces of nature.

Nazirite (p. 85): One set aside and bound by certain restrictions. An example is Samson, whose mother dedicated him to God's service before his birth.

Nevi'im (p. 18): Second section of the Hebrew Scriptures. From the Hebrew word meaning "prophets."

nihilism (p. 152): Denial of moral and religious meaning; rejection of established values and beliefs.

ordained (p. 260): Formally admitted to ministry.

original sin (pp. 38, 197): In Christian theology, the condition of sin that marks all humans as a result of Adam and Eve's disobedience to God.

pagan (p. 117): One who follows a polytheistic religion.

parable (p. 97): A very short story that conveys a moral or spiritual point.

parallelism (p. 139): Structural technique of corresponding phrases or passages used in Hebrew literature; evident in English translations of the psalms.

Passion (of Jesus) (p. 244): The events from Jesus' arrest until his body's death, including his scourging, crowning with thorns, carrying the cross, and crucifixion.

Passover (p. 68): Yearly Jewish festival to commemorate the Israelites' liberation from slavery in Egypt.

pericopes (p. 219): Short passages grouped to form a book, as in the gospels.

plagues (p. 49): Diseases and other natural misfortunes.

pluralism (p. 372): People of many faiths, races, and ethnic and cultural groups, all seeking to live together in one nation and under one government.

polemic (p. 194): Strong, formal, and persistent argument.

pride (p. 147): One of the seven deadly sins; an exaggerated sense of one's own worth.

priest (p. 317): A person who mediates between God and the people.

prophet (p. 66): Defined in Exodus 7:1 as a spokesperson for God.

prophet of doom (p. 117): In modern caricature, shaggy-bearded individual in ragged robes, ranting from a soapbox or wearing a sandwich-board sign that reads, "The end is near!" These caricatures for the most part are based on the figure of Jeremiah, the original biblical prophet of doom.

proverb (p. 144): A wise saying by which to understand and guide one's life.

prudence (p. 147): Applied wisdom; one of the four cardinal virtues.

psalm (p. 98): A sacred poem or song.

psalter (p. 137): Another term for the Book of Psalms.

Qur'an (p. 53): The scripture of Islam.

Rosh Hashanah (p. 76): The Jewish New Year festival.

Sabbath (p. 31): The weekly day of rest and prayer.

salvation (p. 282): Deliverance from the power and effects of sin.

Samaritan (p. 186): A native or inhabitant of Samaria, a territory north of Judea.

scribe (p. 183): In addition to making copies of the Torah when needed, it was the task of the Jewish scribe to interpret the law and uphold the tradition.

sect (p. 262): A religious subgroup, often one dissenting from the main group.

Septuagint (p. 200): A Greek translation of Hebrew Scriptures made 200 years after the Babylonian exile.

seraph (p. 114): A six-winged angel in attendance on God, as seen by Isaiah in his vision.

Shavuot (p. 76): The Jewish Feast of Weeks.

Sheol (p. 151): The abyss into which passed the spirits of the dead, according to ancient Jewish belief.

signs (p. 242): Acts of Jesus performed to bring about belief.

sloth (p. 147): One of the seven deadly sins; spiritual and intellectual laziness.

substitutionary atonement (p. 276): The concept that Jesus died to save others.

Sukkoth (p. 76): A Jewish harvest festival also known as the Feast of Booths.

tabernacle (p. 75): Sacred tent or structure organized according to a hierarchy of holiness; the innermost, most sacred place within the tabernacle, the holy of holies, held the ark of the covenant.

Tanakh (p. 19): Refers to the whole of the Hebrew Scriptures; a Hebrew acronym made up of the initial sounds of the words *Torah, Nevi'im,* and *Ketuvim.*

Targum (p. 154): An Aramaic-language translation and commentary on the Torah compiled in the early Middle Ages.

temperance (p. 147): The habit of moderation and balance; one of the four cardinal virutes.

Ten Commandments (p. 74): The core expression of Mosaic law, brought down by Moses from Mount Sinai on stone tablets written upon by the finger of God.

ten plagues of Egypt (p. 67): Misfortunes visited on Pharaoh's people by God to persuade him to free the Israelites.

Tetragrammaton (p. 20): The four letters (YHWH) that make up the personal name of God; vocalized by Christian translators as *Yahweh.*

theodicy (p. 156): A technical term for the struggle of good and evil that literally means "the defense of God."

tithe (p. 318): A tenth of one's property or possessions, given as a contribution.

Torah (p. 18): The first five books of the Hebrew Scriptures. From the Hebrew word for "teaching."

Tower of Babel (p. 42): Tower built in an attempt to reach heaven; God punished the builders' pride by confusing their language, and they were scattered over the face of the earth.

Trinity (p. 232): Christian doctrine of God as one being who is father, son, and Holy Spirit.

typology (p. 226): A technical term to describe how things in Christian Scriptures are predicted or symbolized by people or events in the Hebrew Scriptures.

virgin birth (p. 228): The Christian doctrine that Mary was a virgin when Jesus was conceived in her.

virtues (p. 83): Characteristics of moral excellence.

Yom Kippur (p. 76): The Jewish day of atonement.

credits

CHAPTER 1: Page 9: © Bob Krist/CORBIS. Page 10: © Bettmann/CORBIS. Page 11: Library of Congress Prints and Photographs Division, Washington, DC 20540 USA. Page 12: Unknown. Page 13: © Hulton-Deutsch Collection/CORBIS. *The Martydome and Burning of Master William Tindall (c. 1494–1536) in Flanders, by Filford Castle,* from *Acts and Monuments* by John Foxe (1516–1587), 1563 (woodcut) (b&w photo), English School (16th century); Private Collection; Bridgeman Art Library. Page 14: *The Trial of John Wycliff (1330–1384) in 1378* (engraving), English School (19th century); Private Collection, Ken Welsh; Bridgeman Art Library. *Martin Luther (1483–1546)* (oil on panel), Cranach, Lucas the Elder (1472–1553), Kurpfalzisches Museum, Heidelberg, Germany, Lauros/Giraudon; Bridgeman Art Library. Page 17: © Bettman/Corbis.

CHAPTER 2: Page 18: Tomb of Pope Julius II (1453–1513) detail of Moses, 1513–1516 (marble), Buonarroti, Michelangelo (1475–1564), San Pietro in Vincoli, Rome, Italy, Alinari; Bridgeman Art Library. Page 19: Ms 137/1687 fol.109r *Solomon Enthroned* (vellum), French School (14th century), Musée Condé, Chantilly, France, Giraudon; Bridgeman Art Library. Page 20: Page from a Hebrew Bible depicting fish with the heads of humans and wildcats, 1299 (vellum), Asarfati, Joseph (fl. 1299), Instituto da Biblioteca Nacional, Lisbon, Portugal, Giraudon; Bridgeman Art Library. Page 22: *Talmudists,* 1927 (oil on canvas), Messer, Abraham H. A. (1886–1931, National Museum in Cracow, Poland; Bridgeman Art Library. *Aaron with the Scroll of the Law* (oil on canvas), Solomon, Abraham, (1824–1862) (attr.), Southampton City Art Gallery, Hampshire, UK; Bridgeman Art Library. Page 24: *David Victorious over Goliath, c.* 1600 (oil on canvas), Caravaggio, Michelangelo Merisi da (1571–1610). Prado, Madrid, Spain; Bridgeman Art Library. Page 25: © Bettmann/CORBIS. Page 28: © Stock Image/SuperStock.

CHAPTER 3: Page 29: *The Ancient of Days,* Blake, William (1757–1827), British Museum, London, UK; Bridgeman Art Library. Page 30: © SuperStock, Inc./SuperStock. Page 31: *The Hand of God, or The Creation,* 1902 (marble), Rodin, Auguste (1840–1917), Musée Rodin, Paris, France, Philippe Galard; Bridgeman Art Library.

CHAPTER 4

Page 36: *Adam and Eve* (oil on panel), Cranach, Lucas the Elder (1472–1553), Private Collection, Peter Willi; Bridgeman Art Library. Page 37: *Adam and Eve Banished from Paradise, c.* 1427 (fresco) (post restoration), Masaccio, Tommaso (1401–1428), Brancacci Chapel, Santa Maria del Carmine, Florence, Italy; Bridgeman Art Library. Page 39: *Cain Slaying Abel, c.* 1608–1609 (panel), Rubens, Peter Paul (1577–1640), Samuel Courtauld Trust, Courtauld Institute of Art Gallery; Bridgeman Art Library. Page 40: *Animals Entering the Ark,* Bassano, Jacopo (Jacopo da Ponte) (1510–1592), Prado, Madrid, Spain; Bridgeman Art

Library. Page 41: © Nik Wheeler/CORBIS. Page 43: *Tower of Babel,* 1563 (oil on panel), Brueghel, Pieter the Elder (c. 1515–1569), Kunsthistorisches Museum, Vienna, Austria; Bridgeman Art Library. Page 44: *John Milton (1608–1674)* (engraving), English School (19th century); Private Collection, Ken Welsh; Bridgeman Art Library. Page 45: *Satan and Beelzebub,* from the first book of *Paradise Lost* by John Milton (1608–1674) engraved by Charles Laplante (d. 1903) c. 1868 (engraving), Doré, Gustave (1832–1883) (after), Private Collection; Bridgeman Art Library. Mihály von Munkácsy. *Blind Milton Dictating "Paradise Lost" to His Daughters* (oil on canvas), 1877; Collections of The New York Public Library, Astor, Lenox and Tilden Foundations.

CHAPTER 5: Page 48: Jacopo Bassano (d. 1592), *The Departure of Abraham* (oil on canvas), 85.1 × 117.3, © The National Gallery, London. Page 49: Erich Lessing/Art Resource, NY. Page 51: From the collection of The Israel Bible Museum and The Dennis and Phillip Ratner Museum. Please visit www.israelbiblemuseum.com. The woodcut is from *Das Alte Testament deutsch,* M. Luther. Wittenberg, 1524. From the Rare Book and Special Collections Division, Rosenwald Collection, Library of Congress, Washington, D.C. Page 52: *ABRAHAM AND ISAAC,* copyright 1976 by John August Swanson, Serigraph 12" × 35", www.JohnAugustSwanson.com. Los Angeles artist John August Swanson is noted for his finely detailed, brilliantly colored paintings and original prints. His works are found in the Smithsonian Institution's National Museum of American History, London's Tate Gallery, the Vatican Museum's Collection of Modern Religious Art, and the Bibliothèque Nationale, Paris. Page 53: © Dean Conger/CORBIS.

CHAPTER 6: Page 54: *Isaac Blessing Jacob,* Ribera, Jusepe de (lo Spagnoletto) (c. 1590–1652), Prado, Madrid, Spain; Bridgeman Art Library. Page 55: Réunion des Musées Nationaux/Art Resource, NY. Page 56: *The Vision after the Sermon (Jacob Wrestling with the Angel),* 1888 (oil on canvas), Gauguin, Paul (1848–1903), National Gallery of Scotland, Edinburgh, Scotland; Bridgeman Art Library. Bacchiacca (1495–1557), *Joseph Receives His Bothers on Their Second Visit to Egypt* (oil on wood), 36.2 × 142.2; © The National Gallery, London. Page 57: *Joseph's Coat,* 1630 (oil on canvas), Velasco or Velasquez, Giuseppe (b. 1540), Monasterio de El Escorial, El Escorial, Spain, Giraudon; Bridgeman Art Library. Page 60: *The Sacrifice of Isaac,* 1603 (oil on canvas), Caravaggio, Michelangelo Merisi da (1571–1610), Galleria degli Uffizi, Florence, Italy, Alinari; Bridgeman Art Library. Portrait of Soren Kierkegaard (1813–1855), 1922 (engraving), German School (20th century); Private Collection; Bridgeman Art Library. Page 61: George Segal, 1924–2000, *Abraham and Isaac: In Memory of May 4, 1970, Kent State University,* bronze; Princeton University

Art Museum. The John B. Putnam, Jr., Memorial Collection, Princeton University. Partial gift of the Mildred Andrew Fund. © Jeffery Eva. Photo of Martin Buber © Hulton-Deutsch Collection/CORBIS.

CHAPTER 7: Page 64: Erich Lessing/Art Resource, NY. Page 65: Erich Lessing/Art Resource, NY. Page 68: F.16.I *The Fifth Plague of Egypt,* from the "Liber Studiorum," engraved by Charles Turner, 1808 (etching), Turner, Joseph Mallord William (1775–1851) (after)/Fitzwilliam Museum, University of Cambridge, UK; Bridgeman Art Library. Page 69: *The Departure of the Israelites,* 1829 (oil on canvas), Roberts, David (1796–1864) © Birmingham Museums and Art Gallery; Bridgeman Art Library. Page 70: *The Delivery of Israel Out of Egypt* (oil on canvas), Colman, Samuel (1780–1845); © Birmingham Museums and Art Gallery; Bridgeman Art Library. Haggadah by Ben Shahn, courtesy of George Krevsky Gallery, 77 Geary St., SF, CA 94108; 415-397-9748. Page 71: *Miriam,* designed by Burne-Jones, executed by Morris Marshall Faulkner and Co., chancel south window, St. Michael & All Angels Church, Waterford, Hertfordshire, UK; Bridgeman Art Library.

CHAPTER 8: Page 72: *Gathering of the Manna* (oil on panel), Master of the Gathering of the Manna (fl. 1460–1475), Musée de la Chartreuse, Douai, France, Giraudon; Bridgeman Art Library. Page 73: Charles Rogers, for permission. Page 74: *The Ten Commandments* (oil on panel), Cranach, Lucas the Elder (1472–1553), Lutherhalle, Wittenberg, Germany; Bridgeman Art Library. Page 75: *Ark of the Covenant,* Field, Erastus Salisbury (1807–1900), National Gallery of Art, Washington DC, USA; Bridgeman Art Library. Page 76: *The Adoration of the Golden Calf,* before 1634 (oil on canvas), Poussin, Nicolas (1594–1665), National Gallery, London, UK; Bridgeman Art Library. Page 77: *Portrait of Moise.* Micrography, late nineteenth century. From the collections of the Hebraic Section, Library of Congress, Washington, D.C. Page 79: *Moses Smashing the Tablets of the Law,* 1659 (oil on canvas), Rembrandt Harmensz. van Rijn (1606–1669), Gemaldegalerie, Berlin, Germany; Bridgeman Art Library.

CHAPTER 9: Page 80: *Daniel Boone Escorting Settlers through the Cumberland Gap,* Bingham, George Caleb (1811–1879), Washington University, St. Louis, USA; Bridgeman Art Library. Page 81: *Zikaron Birushalayim (Remembrance of Jerusalem),* Constantinople, 1743. From the collections of the Hebraic Section, Library of Congress, Washington, D.C. Page 83: *The Death of Sisera* (oil on canvas), Palma Il Giovane (Jacopo Negretti) (1548–1628); Musée d'Art Thomas Henry, Cherbourg, France, Giraudon; Bridgeman Art Library. Page 84: Edgar Degas, French (1834–1917), *The Daughter of Jephtha* (oil on canvas, stretcher: 77 × 117 1/2 in.; Smith College Museum of Art, Northampton, Massachusetts; Purchased with the Drayton Hillyer Fund. Page 86: *Samson*

and Delilah, c.1500 (glue size on linen), Mantegna, Andrea (1431–1506); National Gallery, London, UK;Bridgeman Art Library. Photo of opera performance © Ira Nowinski/CORBIS. Page 88: *The Underground Railroad Aids with a Runaway Slave,* Davies, Arthur Bowen (1862–1928); Private Collection; Bridgeman Art Library. Page 89: © Bettmann/CORBIS.

CHAPTER 10: Page 92: "I Samuel 10 Saul's Coronation and Samuel Anoints Saul" (printed book), Private Collection; Bridgeman Art Library. Page 93: Erich Lessing/Art Resource, NY. Page 94: "I Samuel 31, The Suicide and Beheading of Saul"(printed book), Private Collection; Bridgeman Art Library. Page 95: Smithsonian American Art Museum, Washington, DC/Art Resource, NY. Page 96: *Saul's Daughter Michal Watching David Dance before the Ark,* from fresco cycle depicting the Story of David from the 'Salone dell'Udienza' (Audience Hall) 1553–1554 (fresco), Salviati Cecchino, Francesco de Rossi (1510–1563); Palazzo Ricci-Sacchetti, Rome. Page 97: *Bathsheba Bathing,* 1654 (oil on canvas), Rembrandt Harmensz. van Rijn (1606–1669); Louvre, Paris, France, Giraudon; Bridgeman Art Library. Page 98: Unknown Artist, *Scenes from the Life of Absalom,* Tempera colors and gold leaf on parchment, Leaf (trimmed on all sides): 32.5 × 29 cm (12 13/16 × 11 7/16 in.), The J. Paul Getty Museum. Page 99: Medieval map of Jerusalem, Henricus Bunting (1545–1606) *Map of the World as a Cloverleaf, with Jerusalem as Its Centre...*from his book, *Itinerarium Sacrae Scripture.* Helmstadt, 1585. Rare Book/Special Collections Reading Room, Library of Congress.

CHAPTER 11: Page 100: Scala/Art Resource, NY. Page 101: Apron of a Master, 18th century (painted leather), French School; Musée du Grand Orient de France , Paris, France, Archives Charmet; Bridgeman Art Library. Page 101: *The Temple of Jerusalem,* illustration from a Haggadah, early 20th century (colour litho), Hungarian School (20th Century); Private Collection, Archives Charmet; Bridgeman Art Library. Page 102: *Solomon Meeting the Queen of Sheba,* Ethiopian School (20th century); Private Collection; Bridgeman Art Library. Page 103: Scala/Art Resource, NY. Page 104: *Elijah and the Ravens,* Copyright by Dr. He Qi (www.heqiarts.com) Prints available. Page 105: © Burstein Collection/CORBIS. Page 106: *The Death of Jezebel* (oil on canvas), Coli, G. (1643–1681) & Gherardi, F. (1643–1704) (circle of); Private Collection, Bonhams, London, UK; Bridgeman Art Library. Page 107: Jehu (c. 842–815 BC), King of Israel, paying homage to Shalmaneser III (858–824 BC), King of Assyria, detail from the Black Obelisk, from Nimrud, Iraq, c. 825 BC (stone), Assyrian (9th century BC); British Museum, London, UK, Ancient Art and Architecture © Page 109: Alex Gotfryd/CORBIS.

CHAPTER 12: Page 112: *Roundel of the Prophet Isaiah,* 15th century; Victoria & Albert Museum, London, UK; Bridgeman

Art Library. Page 114: UN/DPI Photo. Page 115: *The Peaceable Kingdom,* c. 1833 (oil on canvas), Hicks, Edward (1780–1849); © Worcester Art Museum, Massachusetts, USA; Bridgeman Art Library. Page 117: *The Prophet Jeremiah,* 1443–1445 (oil on panel), Master of the Aix Annunciation (fl. 1442-1445); Musées Royaux des Beaux-Arts de Belgique, Brussels, Belgium, Giraudon; Bridgeman Art Library. Page 118: *The Western Wall* (oil on canvas), Eyton, Anthony (b. 1923); Private Collection; Bridgeman Art Library. Page 121: "Jeremiah, Isaiah and Ezekiel," from *The Books of Prophets,* 1995 (mixed media on panel), Rapoport, Alek (Contemporary Artist); Private Collection; Bridgeman Art Library. Page 122: *Vision of Ezekiel,* c. 1518 (oil on panel), Raphael (Raffaello Sanzio of Urbino) (1483–1520); Palazzo Pitti, Florence, Italy; Bridgeman Art Library. *The Vision of the Valley of Dry Bones,* engraved by Charles Laplante (d. 1903) c. 1868 (engraving), Doré, Gustave (1832–1883) (after); Private Collection; Bridgeman Art Library.

CHAPTER 13: Page 124: *The Prophet Joel,* from the Sistine Ceiling (prerestoration), Buonarroti, Michelangelo (1475–1564); Vatican Museums and Galleries, Vatican City, Italy; Bridgeman Art Library. Page 126: *Jonah and the Whale,* c. 1305 (fresco), Giotto di Bondone (c. 1266–1337); Scrovegni (Arena) Chapel, Padua, Italy; Bridgeman Art Library. Page 129: © Tony Arruza/CORBIS. Page 130: *Passover Feast in Russia.* 1949. Oil on cardboard. 43 × 56 cm. Inv. 1632. Location :Judaica Coll. Max Berger, Vienna, Austria. Photo Credit: Erich Lessing/Art Resource, NY. Page 132: © Hulton-Deutsch Collection/CORBIS. Page 133: Photo of Elie Wiesel © Sophie Bassouls/CORBIS SYGMA. Photo of American Friends Service Committee workers from AFSC Archives.

CHAPTER 14: Page 136: Scala/Art Resource, NY. Page 137: bottom, © Steve Raymer/CORBIS. top right, Library of Congress Prints and Photographs Division, Washington, DC 20540 USA. top left, © Michael Nicholson/CORBIS. Page 138: Ms 26 f.34 r. Psalm 68, David drowning, c.1380 (vellum), English School (14th century); Collection of the Earl of Leicester, Holkham Hall, Norfolk; Bridgeman Art Library. Page 139: *By the Waters of Babylon,* 1882–1883, Morgan, Evelyn De (1855–1919), The De Morgan Centre, London; Bridgeman Art Library. Page 141: *Psalm 23,* by Andre Berger with The Museum of Psalms. Visit www.MuseumOfPsalms.com. Page 142: *John Bunyan* (1628–1688) (engraving), English School (19th century); Private Collection, Ken Welsh; Bridgeman Art Library.

CHAPTER 15: Page 144: Ms Lat. Q.v.I.126 f.36v; *The Wisdom of Solomon,* from the "Book of Hours of Louis d'Orleans," 1490 (vellum), Colombe, Jean (c. 1430–c. 1493); National Library, St. Petersburg, Russia; Bridgeman Art Library. Page 146: *Prudence,* c. 1470 (tempera on panel), Pollaiolo, Piero del (1443–1496), Galleria degli Uffizi, Florence, Italy; Bridgeman Art Library. *Justice,* from the walls of the sacristy (fresco), Veronese, (Paolo Caliari) (1528–1588), Duomo, Castelfranco, Veneto, Italy; Bridgeman Art Library. *Temperantia,* 1872 (w/c on paper), Burne-Jones, Sir Edward (1833–1898), Christie's Images, London, UK; Bridgeman Art Library. *Fortitude* (panel from the Six Virtues commissioned for the chamber for the Merchant's Guild Hall) 1470 (oil on panel), Botticelli, Sandro (1444/5–1510), Galleria degli Uffizi, Florence, Italy; Bridgeman Art Library. Page 147: *Tabletop of the Seven Deadly Sins and the Four Last Things* (oil on panel), Bosch, Hieronymus (c. 1450–1516); Prado, Madrid, Spain, Giraudon; Bridgeman Art Library. Page 148: *Portrait of Benjamin Franklin* (1706–1790), 1789 (oil on canvas), Peale, Charles Willson (1741–1827); © Atwater Kent Museum of Philadelphia, Courtesy of Historical Society of Pennsylvania Collection; Bridgeman Art Library. Page 149: Giraudon/Art Resource, NY.

CHAPTER 16: Page 150: *All You Need to Know,* 2000 (oil on board), Bootman, Colin (Contemporary Artist); Private Collection; Bridgeman Art Library. Page 152: *Vanitas Vanitatum et Omnia Vanitas,* 1689 (oil on canvas), Collier, Evert (c. 1640–c. 1702); Private Collection, Johnny Van Haeften Ltd., London; Bridgeman Art Library. *Still Life with Skull,* 1895–1900 (oil on canvas), Cezanne, Paul (1839–1906); © The Barnes Foundation, Merion, Pennsylvania, USA; Bridgeman Art Library, *Allegory of Vanity* (oil on canvas), Bigot, Trophime (c. 1595–p. 1650); Palazzo Barberini, Rome, Italy; Bridgeman Art Library. Page 154: *Song of Solomon,* Copyright by Dr. He Qi (www.heqiarts.com); Prints available. Pair of wedding rings illustrated by Eliot Azzam.

CHAPTER 17: Page 156: © Robert Essel NYC/CORBIS. Page 157: The Pierpont Morgan Library/Art Resource, NY. Page 158: Erich Lessing/Art Resource, NY. Page 159: Ms 65/1284 f.82r Job (vellum), Colombe, Jean (c. 1430–c. 1493); Musée Conde, Chantilly, France; Bridgeman Art Library. Page 160: "Then the Lord Answered Job out of the Whirlwind," published 1825 (engraving), Blake, William (1757–1827); British Museum, London, UK; Bridgeman Art Library. Page 161: "Job and His Daughters" (pl. 20) from the Book of Job, c. 1793 (hand-tinted line engraving), Blake, William (1757–1827); © Fitzwilliam Museum, University of Cambridge, UK; Bridgeman Art Library. Page 162: © Bettmann/CORBIS.

CHAPTER 18: Page 164: *Naomi Entreating Ruth and Orpah to Return to the Land of Moab,* from a series of 12 known as "The Large Colour Prints," 1795, Blake, William (1757–1827); Victoria & Albert Museum, London, UK; Bridgeman Art Library. *Ruth Returning with Naomi,* 1997 (w/c on paper), Palmer, Simon (b. 1956); Private Collection; Bridgeman Art Library. Page 165: *The Gleaners,* 1857 (oil on canvas), Millet, Jean-François (1814–1875); Musée d'Orsay, Paris, France, Giraudon; Bridgeman Art Library. Page 166: *Summer,* or *Ruth and Boaz,* 1660–1664 (oil on canvas), Poussin, Nicolas (1594–1665); Louvre, Paris, France, Giraudon; Bridgeman Art Library: Page 168: "Esther," costume for *Esther* by Jean Racine, from Volume I of *Research on the Costumes and Theatre of All Nations,* engraved by Pierre Michel Alix (1762–1817) 1802 (coloured engraving), Chery, Philippe (1759–1838) (after); Private Collection, The Stapleton Collection French, out of copyright. Page 169: *Esther Chosen by King Ahasuerus,* c. 1475–1480 (tempera on panel), Lippi, Filippino (c. 1457–1504); Musée Conde, Chantilly, France; Bridgeman Art Library. Page 170: *Ahasuerus (Xerxes), Haman and Esther,* 1660, Rembrandt Harmensz. van Rijn (1606–1669); Pushkin Museum, Moscow, Russia; Bridgeman Art Library. Page 171: "The Jewish Feast of Purim, or Lots" in 1721, engraved by W. Forrest, from *World Religion,* published by A. Fullarton & Co. (engraving), Picart (19th century) (after); Private Collection; Bridgeman Art Library. Megillah (Scroll of Esther) in a silver case, Vienna, c. 1715, Jewish Museum, London; Bridgeman Art Library. Page 172: *The Story of Ruth and Boaz,* 1894 (oil on canvas), Topham, Frank (1838–1924); Rochdale Art Gallery, Lancashire, UK; Bridgeman Art Library. *The Story of Esther,* 1994 (oil on canvas), Holzhandler, Dora (Contemporary Artist); Private Collection; Bridgeman Art Library. Page 173: Photo taken by Mark Tanner. © CORBIS. Caricature from the archives of the Seneca Falls Historical Society.

CHAPTER 19: Page 174: "The Hanging Gardens of Babylon," from a series of the "Seven Wonders of the World" published in *Munchener Bilderbogen,* 1886 (colour litho), Knab, Ferdinand (1834–1902); Private Collection, Archives Charmet; Bridgeman Art Library. Page 177: *Shadrach, Meshach and Abednego* (oil on panel), German School (15th century); © The Barnes Foundation, Merion, Pennsylvania, USA; Bridgeman Art Library. Page 178: *The Hand-Writing upon the Wall,* published by Hannah Humphrey in 1803 (hand-coloured etching), Gillray, James (1757–1815); Courtesy of the Warden and Scholars of New College, Oxford; Bridgeman Art Library. Page 179: Rembrandt (1606–1669), *Belshazzar's Feast,* Oil on Canvas, 167.6 × 209.2 © The National Gallery, London. Page 180: *The Prophet Daniel,* in the Chigi Chapel, 1655–1661 (marble), Bernini, Giovanni Lorenzo (1598–1680); Santa Maria del Popolo, Rome, Italy; Bridgeman Art Library. *Daniel in the Lion's Den,* 1872 (oil on canvas), Riviere, Briton (1840–1920); © Walker Art Gallery, Liverpool, Merseyside, UK, National Museums Liverpool; Bridgeman Art Library. Page 181: "St. Michael Weighing the Souls," from *The Last Judgement,* c.1445–1450 (oil on panel), Weyden, Rogier van der (1399–1464); Hotel Dieu, Beaune, France; Bridgeman Art Library.

CHAPTER 20: Page 182: Miniature Torah Scroll, probably English, c. 1765 (vellum), Jewish Museum, London; Bridgeman Art Library. Page 185: "Ezra 6:16 The Temple of Jerusalem Is Dedicated by Darius" (printed book), Private Collection; Bridgeman Art Library. Page 186: © Scott Gog/CORBIS. Page 189: Courtesy of Professor Naseeb Shaheen.

CHAPTER 21: Page 192: © Richard T. Nowitz/CORBIS. Page 193: *Madonna and Child Enthroned* (altarpiece), Giotto di Bondone (c. 1266–1337), San Giorgio alla Costa, Florence, Italy; Bridgeman Art Library. Page 195: *George Frederick Handel* (1685–1759), Hudson, Thomas (1701–79); Private Collection; Bridgeman Art Library. Photo of conductor © LWA-Dann Tardif/CORBIS. Page 197: *St. Augustine in His Cell,* c. 1480 (fresco), Botticelli, Sandro (1444/5–1510), Ognissanti, Florence, Italy; Bridgeman Art Library. Page 198: Courtesy of South Caroliniana Library, University of South Carolina.

CHAPTER 22: Page 200: *St. Jerome Writing,* c. 1604 (oil on canvas), Caravaggio, Michelangelo Merisi da (1571–1610); Galleria Borghese, Rome, Italy; Bridgeman Art Library. Page 202: *The Triumph of Judas Maccabeus,* 1635 (oil on canvas), Rubens, Peter Paul (1577–1640); Musée des Beaux-Arts, Nantes, France, Giraudon; Bridgeman Art Library. Page 203: *Lighting the Chanukah Lamp,* 1996 (oil on canvas), Holzhandler, Dora (Contemporary Artist); Private Collection; Bridgeman Art Library. Page 205: *The Madonna of the Fish (The Madonna with the Archangel Gabriel and St. Jerome),* c. 1513 (oil on canvas), Raphael (Raffaello Sanzio of Urbino) (1483–1520), Prado, Madrid, Spain, Giraudon; Bridgeman Art Library. *Judith and Holofernes,* 1599 (oil on canvas), Caravaggio, Michelangelo Merisi da (1571–1610); Palazzo Barberini, Rome, Italy; Bridgeman Art Library. Page 207: Scala/Art Resource, NY.

CHAPTER 23: Page 208: © Bettmann/CORBIS. Page 209: *Mount Athos and the Monastery of Stavroniketes,* 1857 (oil on canvas), Lear, Edward (1812–88). © Yale Center for British Art, Paul Mellon Collection, USA; Bridgeman Art Library. Photo of manuscript by Erich Lessing/Art Resource, NY. Page 212: MS 58 fol.27v Introductory page to the Gospel of St. Matthew depicting winged symbols of the Four Evangelists framed in panels, Gospel book, Irish (vellum); The Board of Trinity College, Dublin, Ireland; Bridgeman Art Library. Page 213: Ms. 69 fol.138v *The Lamb of God Surrounded by the Symbols of the Evangelists* (vellum), French School (9th century); Bibliotheque Municipale, Valenciennes, France; Bridgeman Art Library. Page 215: Sistine Chapel: *The Last Judgment,* 1538–1541 (fresco) (pre-restoration), Buonarroti, Michelangelo (1475–1564); Vatican Museums and Galleries, Vatican City, Italy; Bridgeman Art Library.

CHAPTER 24: Page 218: Cott Nero DIV f.93v St. Mark's portrait page; British Library, London, UK; Bridgeman Art Library. Page 219: Erich Lessing/Art Resource, NY. Page 221: "The Swine Driven into the Sea," illustration for *The Life of Christ,* c. 1886–1894 (w/c & gouache on paperboard), Tissot, James Jacques Joseph (1836–1902); © Brooklyn Museum of Art, New York, USA; Bridgeman Art Library. Page 222: *The Last Supper,* 1495–1497 (fresco) (post-restoration), Vinci, Leonardo da (1452–1519); Santa Maria della Grazie, Milan, Italy; Bridgeman Art Library. Page 223: TIME Magazine © 1971 Time Inc., Reprinted by permission. *Yellow Christ,* 1889 (oil on canvas), Gauguin, Paul (1848–1903); Albright Knox Art Gallery, Buffalo, New York, USA; Bridgeman Art Library. Page 224: © Bettmann/CORBIS. Page 225: © Bettman/CORBIS.

CHAPTER 25: Page 226: *Tree of Jesse,* French, 12th century, Chartres Cathedral, Chartres, France; Bridgeman Art Library. Page 228: *Adoration of the Magi,* 14th century (tempera on panel), Bartolo di Fredi, (1330–1410); Pinacoteca Nazionale, Siena, Italy; Bridgeman Art Library. *The Sermon on the Mount,* 1442 (fresco), Angelico, Fra (Guido di Pietro) (c. 1387–1455); Museo di San Marco dell'Angelico, Florence, Italy; Bridgeman Art Library. Page 229: © Richard T. Nowitz/CORBIS. Page 230: *St. Matthew and the Angel,* 1655–1660 (oil on canvas), Rembrandt Harmensz. van Rijn (1606–1669); Louvre, Paris, France, Peter Willi; Bridgeman Art Library. Page 233: *Portrait of Dr. David Livingstone* (1813–1873) (oil on canvas), English School (19th century); Private Collection; Bridgeman Art Library.

CHAPTER 26: Page 234: *St. Luke Painting the Virgin* (oil on panel), Weyden, Rogier van der (1399–1464); Alte Pinakothek, Munich, Germany, Interfoto; Bridgeman Art Library. Page 235: Tony Freeman\PhotoEdit, Inc. Page 236: *The Annunciation,* c. 1430–1432 (tempera and gold on panel), Angelico, Fra (Guido di Pietro) (c. 1387–1455); Prado, Madrid, Spain, Giraudon; Bridgeman Art Library. Page 237: *Johann Sebastian Bach* (1685–1750) c. 1715 (oil on canvas), Reutsch, Johann Ernst (fl. early 18th century); Stadtische Museum, Erfurt, Germany; Bridgeman Art Library. *Adoration of the Shepherds* (oil on canvas), Tour, Georges de la (1593–1652); Louvre, Paris, France, Giraudon; Bridgeman Art Library. Page 239: *Christ in the House of Martha and Mary,* c. 1654–1656, Vermeer, Jan (1632–1675); National Gallery of Scotland, Edinburgh, Scotland; Bridgeman Art Library. Page 240: *The Resurrection of Christ,* Titian (Tiziano Vecellio) (c. 1488–1576); Palazzo Ducale, Urbino, Italy; Bridgeman Art Library. *The Supper at Emmaus,* 1648 (oil on panel), Rembrandt Harmensz. van Rijn (1606–1669); Louvre, Paris, France, Giraudon; Bridgeman Art Library.

CHAPTER 27: Page 242: © Stapleton Collection/CORBIS. Page 243: *The Marriage Feast at Cana,* c.1562 (oil on canvas), Veronese (Paolo Caliari) (1528–1588); Louvre, Paris, France, Peter Willi; Bridgeman Art Library. Page 244: *Woman of Samaria,* 1940 (oil on canvas), Pippin, Horace (1888–1946); © The Barnes Foundation, Merion, Pennsylvania, USA; Bridgeman Art Library. Page 246. Dinodia Page 248: Erich Lessing/Art Resource, NY. Page 251: *Return of the Prodigal Son,* c. 1668–1669 (oil on canvas), Rembrandt Harmensz. van Rijn (1606–1669); Hermitage, St. Petersburg, Russia; Bridgeman Art Library.

CHAPTER 28: Page 254: Top: © Stapleton Collection/CORBIS. Bottom: © Burstein Collection/CORBIS. Page 255: *The Pentecost,* c. 1604–1614 (oil on canvas), Greco, El (Domenico Theotocopuli) (1541–1614); Prado, Madrid, Spain, Giraudon; Bridgeman Art Library. Page 257: *St. Peter Healing the Lame Man,* detail from the south transept portal, 16th century (wood), Pot, Jean le (d.1563); Beauvais Cathedral, Beauvais, France; Bridgeman Art Library. Page 258: Victoria & Albert Museum, London/Art Resource, NY. Page 259: *St. Peter Healing with His Shadow,* c. 1427 (fresco), Masaccio, Tommaso (1401–1428); Brancacci Chapel, Santa Maria del Carmine, Florence, Italy; Bridgeman Art Library. Page 260: *St. Lawrence and St. Stephen,* 1580 (oil on canvas), Sanchez Coello, Alonso (1531–1589); Monasterio de El Escorial, El Escorial, Spain, Paul Maeyaert; Bridgeman Art Library.

CHAPTER 29: Page 262: *The Dispute with Simon Mago and the Crucifixion of St. Peter,* c. 1480 (fresco), Lippi, Filippino (c. 1457–1504); Brancacci Chapel, Santa Maria del Carmine, Florence, Italy, Alinari; Bridgeman Art Library. Page 263: Nigerian crucifix, Private Collection; Bridgeman Art Library. Page 264:*The Conversion of St. Paul,* 1601 (oil on canvas), Caravaggio, Michelangelo Merisi da (1571–1610); Santa Maria del Popolo, Rome, Italy; Bridgeman Art Library. Page 265: *The Vision of St. Peter,* 1913, Gere,

Margaret (1878–1965); Private Collection, The Fine Art Society, London, UK; Bridgeman Art Library. Page 266: *The Guardian* (acrylic on canvas), Crook, P. J. (b. 1945); Private Collection; Bridgeman Art Library.

CHAPTER 30: Page 269: Photo of Mission San Miguel © Richard Cummins/CORBIS. Photo of Mission San Juan Bautista © Michael Freeman/ CORBIS. Page 272: *St. Paul Preaching at the Areopagus,* from a series depicting the Acts of the Apostles, woven at the Beauvais Workshop under the direction of Philippe Behagle (1641–1705) 1695–98 (wool tapestry), Raphael (Raffaello Sanzio of Urbino) (1483–1520) (after). Page 273: Scala/Art Resource, NY.

CHAPTER 31: Page 281: Giraudon/Art Resource, NY. Page 283: © CORBIS. Page 284: *The Holy Trinity,* Russian icon, Novgorod School, 15th century (tempera on canvas), Museum of Art, Novgorod, Russia; Bridgeman Art Library. Page 285: *The Olive Grove,* c. 1910 (oil on canvas), Sargent, John Singer (1856–1925); © Indianapolis Museum of Art, USA, Gift of Hirschl and Adler Galleries, New York; Bridgeman Art Library. Page 286: *Nathaniel Hawthorne* (1804–1864) 1840 (oil on canvas), Osgood, Charles (1809–1890); (r) Peabody Essex Museum, Salem, Massachusetts, USA; Bridgeman Art Library.

CHAPTER 32: Page 290: *Eucharistic Banquet,* 3rd century (fresco), Catacombs of San Calixto, Rome, Italy, Index; Bridgeman Art Library. Page 293: *The Expulsion of Hagar* (oil on panel), Rubens, Peter Paul (1577–1640); Private Collection; Bridgeman Art Library. Page 295: "The Centurion," illustration for *The Life of Christ,* c. 1886–1894 (w/c & gouache on paperboard), Tissot, James Jacques Joseph (1836–1902); © Brooklyn Museum of Art, New York, USA; Bridgeman Art Library.

CHAPTER 33: Page 296: Scala/Art Resource, NY. Page 297: © Peter M. Wilson/CORBIS. Page 298: © Bettmann/CORBIS. Page 299: *Christ Pantocrator,* 6th century (encaustic on panel), Monastery of Saint Catherine, Mount Sinai, Egypt, Ancient Art and Architecture Collection Ltd.; Bridgeman Art Library. Page 301: © Bettmann/ CORBIS. Page 302: © Chris Heller/CORBIS.

CHAPTER 34: Page 304: *The Infant Timothy Unfolding the Scriptures,* c. 1853 (oil on canvas), Sant, James (1820–1916); Bury Art Gallery and Museum, Lancashire, UK; Bridgeman Art Library. Page 307: *Andrew Carnegie* (1835–1919) after a portrait by Walter William Ouless (1848–1933), 1925 (oil on canvas), Ouless, Catherine (1879–p. 1937); Scottish National Portrait Gallery, Edinburgh, Scotland; Bridgeman Art Library. Page 308: *The Early Days of Timothy,* Le Jeune, Henry (1820–1904); Private Collection, Bonhams, London, UK; Bridgeman Art Library. Page 309: *Portrait of William Wilberforce* (1759–1833) 1828 (oil on canvas), Lawrence, Sir Thomas (1769–1830), National Portrait Gallery, London, UK ; Bridgeman Art Library. Page 310: © Bettmann/CORBIS. Page 312: © Scala/Art Resource, NY. Page 313: © Roger Wood/CORBIS.

CHAPTER 35: Page 316: Lancet window from the north wall (stained glass), French School (13th century); Chartres

Cathedral, Chartres, France, Giraudon; Bridgeman Art Library. Page 318: "Abraham and Melchizedek," from *Altarpiece of the Last Supper,* 1464–1468 (oil on panel), Bouts, Dirck (c.1415–1475); St. Peter's, Louvain, Belgium, Giraudon; Bridgeman Art Library. Page 319: © Hulton-Deutsch Collection/CORBIS. Page 321: *Noah Webster* (1758–1843), engraved by Frederick W. Halpin (1805–1880) (engraving), Flagg, Jared Bradley (1820–1899) (after); Private Collection, The Stapleton Collection; Bridgeman Art Library. Page 322: *Esau Selling His Birthright to Jacob,* 1630 (oil on canvas), Corneille, Michel (1602–1664); Musée des Beaux-Arts, Orleans, France, Giraudon; Bridgeman Art Library. Photo of Mount Zion © Shai Ginott/CORBIS.

CHAPTER 36: Page 324: *Rahab and the Emissaries of Joshua* (oil on canvas), Italian School (17th century); Musée des Beaux-Arts, Nimes, France, Giraudon; Bridgeman Art Library. Page 326: © Hulton Archive/Getty Images. Page 327: *Crucifixion of St. Peter,* 1546–1550 (fresco), Buonarroti, Michelangelo (1475–1564); Cappella Paolina, Vatican, Vatican City; Bridgeman Art Library. Page 328: *The Descent into Limbo,* 1442 (fresco), Angelico, Fra (Guido di Pietro) (c. 1387–1455); Museo di San Marco dell'Angelico, Florence, Italy; Bridgeman Art Library. Page 329: "The Fall of the Rebel Angels," from Book I of *Paradise Lost* by John Milton (1608–1674), c. 1868 (engraving), Doré, Gustave (1832–1883) (after); Private Collection; Bridgeman Art Library. Page 330: Bildarchiv Preussischer Kulturbesitz/Art Resource, NY. Page 332: *Martin Luther* (1483–1546), 1526 (oil on panel), Cranach, Lucas the Elder (1472–1553); Private Collection; Bridgeman Art Library. *Portrait of John Calvin* (1509–64) (oil on canvas), Titian (Tiziano Vecellio) (c. 1488–1576); The Reformed Church of France, Paris, France, Lauros; Giraudon; Bridgeman Art Library. Page 333: Portrait of Henry VIII, Scala/Art Resource, NY. Photo of Amish buggy © Mary Ann McDonald/CORBIS.

CHAPTER 37: Page 336: Aureus (obverse) of Domitian (AD 81–96) wearing a laurel wreath. Inscription: DOMITANVS AVGVSTVS (gold), Roman (1st century AD); Private Collection; Bridgeman Art Library. Page 339: © Chris Heller/CORBIS. Page 341:Bottom: © Roger Wood/CORBIS. Top: © Michael Nicholson/CORBIS. Page 342: © Chr. Kaiser/Gütersloher Verlagshaus GmbH, Gütersloh. Page 343: *The Light of the World,* c. 1851–1853, Hunt, William Holman (1827–1910); Keble College, Oxford, UK; Bridgeman Art Library.

CHAPTER 38: Page 344: "Christ Enthroned with the Apocalyptic Beasts and the Twenty-Four Elders," no.4 from *The Apocalypse of Angers,* 1373–1387 (tapestry), Bataille, Nicolas (fl. 1363–1400); Musée des Tapisseries, Angers, France, Lauros; Giraudon; Bridgeman Art Library. Page 346: "The Four Horsemen of the Apocalypse, Death, Famine, Pestilence and War," from *The Apocalypse* or *The Revelations of St. John the Divine,* pub. 1498 (woodcut), Durer, Albrecht (1471–1528); Private Collection; Bridgeman Art Library. John WorldPeace, *Four Horsemen of the Apocalypse;* November 1, 2002; oil on canvas: www.johnworldpeacegalleries.com.

Daniel O. Stolpe, American, b.1939, *The Four Horsemen of the Apocalypse,* Hand-pulled lithograph, 1995, Edition 30. Prints available at www.nativeimagesgallery.com. Page 347: *St. Michael,* one half of a diptych, c. 1505 (oil on panel), Raphael (Raffaello Sanzio of Urbino) (1483–1520); Louvre, Paris, France, Giraudon; Bridgeman Art Library. Page 349: *The Revelation of St. John the Divine* or *The Apocalypse* (b/w engraving), Durer, Albrecht (1471–1528); Private Collection; Bridgeman Art Library. Page 350: *The Angel Michael Binding Satan ("He Cast Him into the Bottomless Pit, and Shut Him Up")* c. 1800 (w/c, ink & graphite on paper), Blake, William (1757–1827); © Fogg Art Museum, Harvard University Art Museums, USA, Gift of W. A. White; Bridgeman Art Library. Frontispiece to *Eighty Sermons Preached by That Learned and Reverend Divine, John Donne,* pub. 1640 (engraving) (b&w photo), Merian, Mattaus the Younger (1621–1687); Private Collection; Bridgeman Art Library.

CHAPTER 39: Page 352: Erich Lessing/Art Resource, NY. Page 353: "The New Jerusalem," number 80 from *The Apocalypse of Angers,* 1373–1387 (tapestry), Bataille, Nicolas (fl. 1363–1400); Musee des Tapisseries, Angers, France, Lauros; Giraudon; Bridgeman Art Library. Page 354: *The Tree of Life and the Last Supper,* 1360 (fresco), Gaddi, Taddeo (c. 1300–1366); Opera di Santa Croce, Florence, Italy; Bridgeman Art Library. Page 355: Top: *John Bunyan* (1628–1688) engraved by W. McFarlane (engraving), English School (19th century); Private Collection, Ken Welsh; Bridgeman Art Library.Bottom left: © Bettmann/CORBIS. Bottom right: Conde Nast Archives/CORBIS. Page 356: *Jesus Christ as Pantocrator,* Scala/Art Resource, NY. Portrait of Charlotte Brontë © Bettmann/CORBIS. Page 357: *Dante Reading from the "Divine Comedy"* (tempera on panel), Domenico di Michelino, (1417–1491); Duomo, Florence, Italy; Bridgeman Art Library. Photo of tympanum at Moissac © Vanni Archive/CORBIS. Page 359: © Kong Stephanie/CORBIS SYGMA. Page 360: Statue of Dante Alighieri (1265–1321) (photo); Piazza dei Signori, Verona, Veneto, Italy; Bridgeman Art Library. Page 361: © Playbill Magazine, New York.

CHAPTER 40: Page 364: *Homer Singing with His Lyre,* early 19th century (oil on canvas), Boisselier, Felix (1776–1811) (attr. to); Private Collection, Archives Charmet; Bridgeman Art Library. Page 365:Top: Philippe Wojazer © Reuters/CORBIS. Bottom: © TIM SHAFFER/Reuters/ Corbis. Page 366: Erich Lessing/Art Resource, NY. Page 367: Frontispiece to *The Holy Bible,* pub. by Robert Barker, 1611 (engraving) (b&w photo), Boel, Cornelis (c. 1576–1621); Private Collection; Bridgeman Art Library. Page 368: *John Wycliffe Reading His Translation of the Bible to John of Gaunt,* 1847-1848, Brown, Ford Madox (1821–1893); © Bradford Art Galleries and Museums, West Yorkshire, UK; Bridgeman Art Library. Page 369: © Steffan Hacker/Habitat for Humanity Int'l. Page 370: *But Revealed to the Babes* © 1991, by R. V. Moseley. Contact for artwork or information: mosart@bellsouth.net, 770.426.5152. © Swim Ink2, LLC/CORBIS

Note: Page numbers in *italics* refer to illustrations.

Aaron, brother of Moses, *22,* 66–67, 71–77, 112–113
Abednego (Asariah), 176, 177–178
Abel, *see* Cain and Abel
Abigail, wife of David, 96
Abimelech, son of Gideon, 82
abolition of slavery, 11, 309, 310
Abraham (Abram), 48–53, 54, 60–61, 77; in letter of James, 325; in letters of Paul, 284, 293, 318, 320; in Matthew's gospel, 227
Absalom, son of David, *25,* 98
Absalom, Absalom! (Faulkner), 24, *25*
Ackermann, Carl, 188, 189
Adam and Eve, 31–38, 40, 44–45, 306, 340, 347
Addison, Joseph, 367
Adonai (a name for God), 20
Adonijah, son of David, 100
African Americans
    and Christianity, 64, 67, 73, 77, 88–89, 198–199, 310
    and slavery, 11, 34, 42, 64–66, 77, 88–89
Agabus the prophet, 266
Agee, James, 204
Ahab, king of Israel, 104–105
Ahasuerus (Xerxes), king of Persia, 168–172
Aikman, David, 373
Aitken, Jane, 15
Aitken, Robert, 15
Alexander the Great, 201, 224
Alexius I, emperor of Byzantium, 339
Allah, 53
Alter, Robert, 24, 29, 116, 140
allusions, biblical, 24–25
American Friends Service Committee, 133
American Standard Version (of Bible), 15
Amish, 258, 333
Ammonites, 84
Amnon, son of David, 25, 98
Amos the prophet, 129–130, 132
Anabaptists, 333
Ananias, a disciple in Damascus, 264
Ananias and Sapphira, 258
Angelico, Fra, *228, 236, 328*
angels of God
    in Hebrew Scriptures, 50, 51, 55–56, 65–66, 83, 180–181, 205
    in New Testament, 227, 232, 236–238, 267, 347–348, 350

Anglican Church, *see* Church of England
annunciation, 236
Anthony, founder of Christian monasticism, 258
Anthony, Susan B., *173,* 294
Antioch, city of, 266, 268, 269–270, 271
Antiochus Epiphanes, 201–202, 203
anti-Semitism, 196, 212; *see also* Holocaust; Nazi persecution of Jews
Apocalypse Now (film), 358, *359*
apocalyptic writings in the Bible, 215, 338
Apocrypha, 15, 21, 200–207
archetypes, 41
Areopagus (Athens), 272
Aristotle, 109
ark (Noah's), 40–41
ark of the covenant, 75, 93, 100, 102, 107
Armageddon, 349
Artaxerxes, king of Persia, 184, 186, 187
Artemis (Greek goddess), 273
Asarfati, Joseph, *20*
Asmodeus the demon, 205
Assyrians, 107, 126, 128, 205
Athanasius, bishop of Alexandria, *208,* 209
Athenagoras, Orthodox patriarch, 297
Athens, city of, 272
Athos, Mount, *209*
atonement, 276, 283
Augustine, bishop of Hippo, 197–198, 258, 312–313
Augustus, emperor of Rome, 237

Baal, Phoenician god, 105
Babel, Tower of, 42–43
Babylon, 174–180, 182–183, 185, 349, 353
Babylonian exile (of the Jews), 18, 107; and the Apocrypha, 203, 206; and the prophets, 119, 120–123, 131, 175, 182–184
Babylonians, 102, 107, 108
Bacchiacca, Francesco, *56*
Bach, Johann Sebastian, 137, 237, 333, 358
Bacon, Sir Francis, 34
Balaam, a heathen sorcerer, 329
Balfour Declaration, 108
baptism, 232, 255–256, 263, 328
Barabbas the criminal, 224
Barak, military commander, 83
Barnabas, colleague of Paul, 266, 268

Baruch, secretary to Jeremiah, 203
Basil the Great, 258
Bassano, Jacopo, *40, 48*
Bataille, Nicolas, *344, 353,* 357
Bathsheba, wife of David, 97–100, 227
"Battle Hymn of the Republic," 348
beatitudes, the, 229
Beatus of Liebana, 357
Beethoven, Ludwig van, 29, 290
Behemoth, 160
Belshazzar the Chaldean, 178–179
Benedict of Nursia, 258
Benedictional of St. Aethelwold, 254
Benedictus, the, 236
Berger, Moshe Tzvi, *141*
Bernini, Giovanni, *101, 180*
Beroea, town of, 272
Berrigan, Philip, 123
Bethlehem, town of, 165, 237
Bible in Shakespeare, The (Ackermann), 188
Bible translations into English, 13–16
Biblical References in Shakespeare's Plays (Shaheen), 189
Bigot, Trophime, *152*
Bildad the Shuhite, 158
binding of Isaac, the, 52, 54, 60, 61
Bingham, George Caleb, *80*
"Birthmark, The" (Hawthorne), 286
bishops in the early Church, 305
Bishop's Bible, 15
Blake, William, 29, 44, *157, 160, 161, 164,* 357, 358
Boaz, cousin of Naomi, 165–168
Boisselier, Feliz, *364*
Bonhoeffer, Dietrich, 342
Book of Kells, 212
Bootman, Colin, *150*
Bosch, Hieronymus, *147, 330, 361*
Botticelli, Sandro, *146, 197*
Bouts, Dirck, *318*
Bradbury, Ray, 358
Braverman, Hillel, 77
Brecht, Berthold, 361
Bride of the Lamb, 352–353
Brontë, Charlotte, 356
Brothers Karamazov, The (Dostoevski), 35
Brown, Ford Maddox, *368*
Brown, John, 88
Browning, Elizabeth Barrett, 66
Bruegel, Pieter the Elder, *43*
Buber, Martin, 61
Buechner, Frederick, 205